WITHDRAWN FROM
THE LIBRARY
UNIVERSITY OF
WINCHESTER

D1429115

The Port of New York

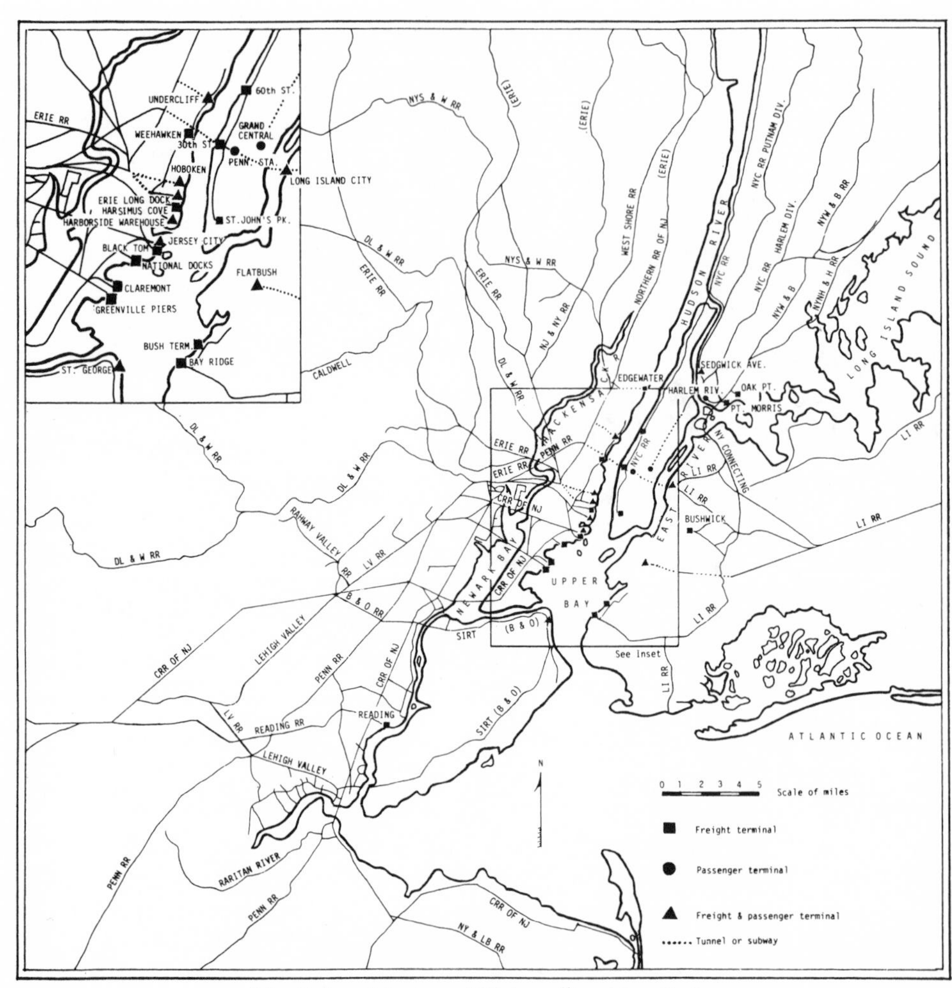

The Railroad System of Metropolitan New York

Carl W. Condit

The Port of New York

A History of the Rail and Terminal System from the Grand Central Electrification to the Present

The University of Chicago Press

Chicago and London

The University of Chicago Press, Chicago 60637
The University of Chicago Press, Ltd., London

Printed in the United States of America

85 84 83 82 81 5 4 3 2 1

Permission to quote is gratefully acknowledged:
From "The Roaring Traffic's Boom."
Lewis Mumford; © 1955
Reprinted by permission, The New Yorker Magazine, Inc.

From "The Towers of Light."
Suzannah Lessard; © 1978
Reprinted by permission, The New Yorker Magazine, Inc.

Library of Congress Cataloging in Publication Data

Condit, Carl W
The port of New York.
Bibliography: v. 1, p.
Includes indexes.
CONTENTS: [1] A history of the rail terminal system from the beginnings to Pennsylvania Station — [2] A history of the rail and terminal system from the Grand Central electrification to the present.
1. Railroads—New York (N.Y.)—History.
2. Railroads terminals—New York (N.Y.)—History.
3. New York (N.Y.)—History. I. Title.
HE2781.N7C66 385′.09747′1 79-16850

ISBN 0-226-11460-0 (v. 1) AACRI
ISBN 0-226-11461-9 (v. 2)

Carl W. Condit is professor of history, urban affairs, and art history at Northwestern University. He is an acknowledged authority on urban architecture and has published many books and articles on the subject.

Contents

Illustrations

Preface

The second of the two volumes in which I have sought to record the history of New York's terminal system at least affords the reader an extreme contrast of tone between its beginning and its end. The early years of the twentieth century formed perhaps the greatest creative period in the evolution of the modern city and modern urban technology, and no achievement better demonstrated this fact than the electrification of Grand Central Station, followed by the construction and successful operation of the new terminal and by the creation of a new kind of urban precinct over the trackage. It was an age of confidence and buoyant expectations, an age sure that it possessed the means for solving all urban problems through a new partnership between the municipality and the supporting economy. A half century after the opening of Grand Central this once unassailable confidence was largely gone. The automobile brought the city far more problems than advantages, not because it is an intrinsically evil thing, but because in the United States it became a psychological crutch which demanded that everything be swept aside to make way for its unlimited mobility. The consequence was that the expected mobility turned into progressive strangulation, and the great circulatory network of New York deteriorated to the point that it could no longer function appropriately in the city's vascular system. The traditional values, beliefs, and political and economic institutions that underlay the confidence of 1900 disappeared, to be replaced by a kind of uneasy agnosticism that had discarded the old answers but shrank from the steps necessary to finding the new. As a result, our history cannot even end with a rousing cataclysm, like the sack of Rome by the Ostrogoths—nuclear power may see to that—but only with more of the same gropings, sometimes promising, more often mere purchases of time. My conclusions are thus pessimistic, and I see no reason for sketching a possible brave new world of the future, which would only take on the character of a sophomoric utopia.

The completion of the task ran up a few more debts, accumulated through the kindness of those who were always ready to respond to my demands on their time. I am grateful to various members of the Tri-State Regional Planning Commission for statistical data, to the architect Robert Geddes for arranging my tour of the Central Railroad of New Jersey station in Jersey City during the renovation process, to Sharon Irish and Debra Mancoff for taking care of the nagging odds and ends that are always left over in the process of completing a long bibliography, and to the staff of the Transportation Center Library at Northwestern University, particularly the director, Mary Roy, who was called on to find the answer to still another question on the very day I wrote the last sentence of this work. My wife, Isabel, has continued to read every word of it with critical intelligence and a patience I long ago lost. All who labor in the vineyard know the value of this kind of painstaking editorial advice.

1

The Grand Central Electrification

The Immediate Background to the Grand Central Plan

Unlike the building and the electrification of Pennsylvania Station, which were preceded by a long period of discussion, proposal, and counterproposal, the decision to electrify through-train and suburban operations at the existing Grand Central Station, and then to replace the station facilities and yards by an entirely new terminal, was launched upon the railroad world with little preliminary planning or announcement. Moreover, the idea for this project, astonishing in its magnitude and its daring, appears to have sprung at least in a modest tentative form from the mind of one man. The imaginative author of the original proposal was William John Wilgus, who has so far received less attention than he deserves from those who celebrate and record the works of the creative figures in American history. Born in Buffalo, New York, his formal education confined to little more than the district high school, he began his professional career as a rodman and then advanced through a succession of positions on the engineering staffs of various midwestern railroads. In 1893 he joined the engineering department of the Rome, Watertown and Ogdensburg Railroad, a controlled affiliate of the New York Central and Hudson River that later comprised much of the larger company's Rochester and Saint Lawrence divisions. Wilgus must have made an immediate impression on his superior officers, who were little concerned in those days with the question whether or not a man held a university degree. By 1899 he was chief engineer of construction and maintenance of way for the Central, and in 1903 he was elevated to the position of vice-president in charge of realizing his own mental creations, the electrification and the building of what was to become the world's largest railroad terminal. Wilgus went on to a long and distinguished career, and we will have occasion to consider his work repeatedly, but his later accomplishments could only seem anticlimactic after the Grand Central project.

The idea for drastic revisions in the operating techniques at the station coincided almost exactly with the preparation of plans for the reconstruction and enlargement of the 1871 depot. In the spring of 1899 Wilgus met Frank J. Sprague, who was still the commanding figure in the pioneer age of rail electrification. During the conversations between the engineer and the inventor, Sprague proposed the electrification of the Yonkers Branch of the Central's Putnam Division (former New York and Northern Railroad), apparently on an experimental basis. This appears to have been the first suggestion for the electrical operation of trains on the New York Central lines lying in the New York metropolitan area, and it obviously fell on sympathetic ears. In June of that year Wilgus drew up a plan which, in the form that it eventually reached in 1901, was a hybrid of steam and electrical operations. The Park Avenue tunnel of the New York and Harlem Railroad was to be widened in the block between 56th and 57th streets from four to eight tracks, from which point they were to extend southward to 49th Street. At this latitude an additional four tracks were to diverge on either side of the main approach, descend via tunnels through a full clearance level below the station yards, and form a continuous semicircular loop under the part of the head house standing in the block bounded by 43d and 44th streets. Throughout the length of the curving portion of the loop the four tracks were to be reduced to two, each one lying along one side of a 1,200-foot platform built to conform with the curvature of the tracks. The tunnel and loop tracks were to be reserved for through and suburban trains, the cars and locomotives of which did not need to be parked in the storage and engine terminal yards. The great innovative feature was that the through trains in the loop tunnels would be hauled by electric locomotives, while the suburban trains would be composed of self-propelled multiple-unit equipment. In the 1901 formulation of the plan, an underground pedestrian passageway was to unite the loop platform with the new Interborough subway that was then under construction. Meanwhile, the general idea of the electrical movement of trains, whatever the form of traction and motive power, was considerably advanced on 22 November 1900, when a train of electrically powered multiple-unit cars made a trial run on the Second Avenue elevated line from 67th to 97th Street. Regular operation was inaugurated on 30 December of the following year over the Second Avenue tracks between South Ferry and 129th Street. The new day for elevated rapid transit had at last dawned in New York.

Two dominant characteristics of the New York Central service acted to place irresistible pressure on the officers of the railroad company to eliminate steam motive power on the Grand Central approach and in the station yards, each factor reinforcing the other in a way that made some kind of change inescapable. One was the sheer density of rail traffic in midtown Manhattan, all of it funneled into the four-track stem that constituted the terminal accessway. The other, of course, was the Park Avenue tunnel, in which smoke, dust, noise, and heat had reached a level by 1900 that was intolerable to passengers and trainmen alike. Finally, there was the outright danger of operating at excessive densities with inadequate, poorly visible signaling, and the risks were soon to be violently demonstrated. The tunnel was the object of vehement popular attack, and there was extensive discussion in the newspapers, in the engineering press, and among the officers and operating personnel of the railroads on the question of eliminating steam locomotives from its foul confines.

3 The Immediate Background to the Grand Central Plan

A steady stream of proposals came and went throughout the century year for the use of motive power driven by compressed air to haul trains over the approach tracks. But there were many valid objections: without technological antecedence, there were no data on the weight, size, and power for the individual machine; a number of refractory questions arose concerning the type and location of motors needed to operate pumps and compressors; there was the problem of where and how to make the change from one type of power to the other under heavy traffic loads, and where to park the idle engines. In order to place this seemingly fruitless discussion on an empirical basis, the railroad company participated in a series of tests of a compressed-air locomotive conducted at Rome, New York, in the winter of 1900/1901. The results were hardly impressive: starting with a total of 3,000 pounds of air pressure contained in the reservoir, sufficient to provide an initial working pressure comparable to the ruling boiler pressures of existing steam power, the locomotive hauled one Pullman car 11 miles, at which point the pressure had fallen so low that it was barely enough to keep the train in motion.[1] The correspondent of the *Railroad Gazette* thought the technique showed some promise, but the motive power officers whose engines kept the Empire State Express running on time were understandably skeptical.

By the following summer the situation in the tunnel reached ominous proportions. During the particularly hot and humid weather of July, 1901, the need to keep windows and ventilators closed for the passage through the tunnel raised temperatures and the concentrations of noxious gases to the level where strong men as well as ladies were overcome. The passengers and the newspapers demanded action. The district attorney for New York County responded to popular outcry by convening a grand jury with a view to bringing an action for criminal negligence against the railroad company. The question was complex, and the issues were such as to require consideration by state commissions and the city's Board of Health as well as the administrative and engineering staffs of the railroad. The jury's recommendation, nevertheless, was clear and unambiguous. The jurors urged:

> That the motive power in the tunnel be changed to avoid the use of coal.
>
> That the brick walls separating the center from the side tunnels be removed, and that steel girders be put in their places.
>
> That sheds be erected to cover cars standing in the yards to keep the temperature at a more endurable degree in the cars.
>
> That the Board of Health do something to compel the changes.[2]

The company's engineers knew Wilgus's loop plan of 1899 and 1901, but they took no action on it or any other proposal while they explored all the alternative forms of motive power, including fireless or direct-steaming locomotives and those operated by superheated water as well as electric and compressed-air types. It was clear, however, that electricity had gained the commanding position, and some variation on an electrified underground system appeared likely. After reviewing all the possibilities, the editors of the *Railroad Gazette* were sure of the conclusion. "It follows that at some point the suburban tracks will probably be dropped under the yard, and a loop will be made around which the suburban trains will be run without switching," most likely by means of multiple-unit operation.[3]

The officers of the railroad company took the decisive step at the very moment when the *Railroad Gazette* proclaimed that they could hardly avoid a commitment. In August, 1901, they engaged the electrical engineer and transportation planner Bion J. Arnold to investigate the feasibility of the electrical operation of trains between Grand Central Station and Mott Haven. The investigation and the ensuing report provide another demonstration of the fact that by the end of the nineteenth century advanced technology had become exactly comparable to experimental and theoretical science expanded to a scale that far transcended the laboratory and its associated conceptual world. Borrowing a dynamometer car jointly owned by the Illinois Central Railroad and the University of Illinois, Arnold and his staff were able to make direct measurements of the drawbar pull or exerted tractive force of every locomotive engaged in hauling trains over the test run from Grand Central Station to 138th Street. Knowing the weight of the train and its average speed, he could readily calculate the horsepower (foot-pounds of work per unit of time) and hence the equivalent wattage expended (with the factor of one horsepower to 746 watts) in moving every train over the established run, and by summing the data for all trains over a 24-hour period, he and his associates could then arrive at the average daily power consumption and the total consumption for the year. In the same way, the investigators could obtain the sum of the ton-miles for all train and locomotive operation over the test distance, including loaded and empty passenger-train runs, and the movements of all switch engines, work trains, and engines running light. The particular end result distilled from all these measurements and calculations was the average unit consumption of power, namely, 63 watt-hours per ton-mile.[4]

Arnold not only demonstrated the feasibility and economy of electrification, but provided precise data on power consumption. He then went on to outline the appropriate technological details. He recommended direct-current motors over alternating current because of readier starting, faster acceleration under load, and the fact that manufacture in comparatively large quantities offered the standardization of the various motor sizes, including subsidiary equipment, and hence the easy replacement of parts. For distribution he proposed the third rail, to be located in the standard position close to ground level along open track and in the overhead position at concentrations of switches and crossing points (features derived from the well-tested precedents of the Gare d'Orsay). The determination of the optimum forms of generating, transmission, and distribution equipment involved so many variables, including relative unit costs of different arrangements, that the investigators offered twelve separate plans, from which Arnold recommended the twelfth, the essential characteristics of which are in use to this day. The chief elements of this plan were a power station located on the Harlem River to generate alternating current at a potential of 11,000 volts for transmission, a substation near the south end of the electrified zone equipped with rotary converters and transformers to convert the alternating to direct current and to reduce the potential to 660 volts for the distribution system. The unit operating cost under plan number 12 was discouragingly close to that for steam locomotives—$0.2363 per locomotive mile for the former, against $0.2418 for the latter. The reason for only a slight reduction in favor of electricity was that whereas the actual operating and maintenance costs for electric locomotives were only two-thirds the total of those for conventional power, the unit fixed charge was seven times greater, reflecting the staggering capital investment involved in electrifying even a short segment of a high-density multitrack rail line.[5] Arnold's concluding assessment, presented to the railroad company in the spring of 1902 and first made public in a paper read before the convention of the American Institute of Electrical Engineers on 19 June of that year, was as much a model of cautious sobriety as it was of careful scientific analysis.

> From these figures it appears that while there would be a slight annual saving in operating expenses in favor of electricity, it is not sufficient to warrant its adoption on the grounds of economy of operation alone, although its adoption can be justified on other grounds.
>
> The figures could be made more favorable to electricity were an optimum view of many of its advantages taken, and the probability is that practical operation will show a somewhat greater gain than here indicated, but it has been deemed best by the writer to maintain a conservative view throughout the entire investigation.[6]

Arnold's report to the railroad was supplemented by a series of tests conducted in the winter and early spring of 1902 at Schenectady, New York, under the joint sponsorship of General Electric and the railroad company and carried out under the direction of Arnold and W. B. Potter of the manufacturer's engineering staff. The aim was to analyze the comparative performances of a standard New York Central and Hudson River steam locomotive designed for suburban service and a pair of electric motor cars specifically manufactured by General Electric for experimental purposes. The test train consisted of five coaches of the type regularly assigned by the railroad to suburban service and the dynamometer car on loan from its Illinois owners. The locomotive and the paired motor cars were nearly identical in their weight and capacity, however radically different in their mode of operation.[7] In acceleration tests the electric power outperformed the steam for every trailing weight, from one to six cars, and in each of the designated periods of time (10, 20, and 30 seconds) within which the one-mile test track was covered. The comparison of energy consumption led to even more impressive results: for every weight of train and number of passengers, ranging from 64 for one car to 384 for six, the electric locomotive consumed less energy, measured in watt-hours per passenger, than the steam, the minimum difference being a reduction of 32.3 percent in the case of the six-car train, and the maximum 76 percent in the case of the single car.[8] A comparative measurement of the coal consumed in the steam locomotive against the quantity burned in the power plant to generate the electricity necessary for the equivalent weight and speed of train, favored the electric motive power by a factor of 3.3:7.8, or to put it another way, the steam locomotive consumed 2.36 times more coal per watt-hour than its electric counterpart. The chief conclusion, embodied in a paper presented by Arnold and Potter at the same meeting of the Institute of Electrical Engineers (19 June 1902), offered the railroad very convincing arguments: energy consumption at any speed or for any trailing weight was substantially lower for the electric power, and the higher acceleration rate indicated that the electric locomotive would consume less energy in covering the same distance in an equal interval of time, or consume an equal quantity of energy while covering that distance in a shorter interval of time.

The railroad company would probably have been prepared in the summer of 1902 to adopt an electrification program on the basis of the Arnold-Potter investigations, but a notorious catastrophe of the previous winter had removed the whole issue from the realm of dispassionate scientific inquiry. At 8:20 on the morning of 8 January 1902, a New York and Harlem train from White Plains collided with the rear car of a New Haven train from South Norwalk, the latter having stopped for an adverse signal set to protect a preceding train while it cleared the station throat and entered its assigned track. As in the case of nearly all rear-end collisions, the locomotive telescoped the wooden coach through a sufficient length to kill 15 people outright and cause injury to 41 others, among whom two subsequently died of their injuries. All trains running through the tunnel were governed at the time by a manual-block signaling system, the signal lights of which were described as equivalent to the ruling standard and not inferior in visibility to those used in any other tunnel. The chief problems in any historical inquiry into the causes of the accident are, first, to determine precisely the extent to which steam operation contributed to the disaster, and, second, to decide whether the company had been morally obligated to use electric power before it could have occurred. Unfortunately, the discoverable facts strongly support the view that the use of steam engines in tunnels under conditions of high traffic densities virtually guaranteed that a collision would, soon or late, occur. In the first place, four trains passed the immediate vicinity of the accident within a period of a few minutes, three southbound and one northbound, the last accelerating and hence filling the tunnel with smoke and condensing steam. Among the immediate fatalities, four were the consequence of asphyxiation and scalding by the steam escaping from the damaged locomotive. The testimony of enginemen and firemen during the subsequent investigation indicated that on many occasions enginemen were relying on a kind of intuition of possible hazards ahead of them, or "feeling their way" in the expectation of obstructions or adverse signals. The immediate cause of the accident was the apparently well-established fact that the New York and Harlem train passed both an approach and a stop signal with an inadequate reduction in speed. Evidence was presented that the engineman, John M. Wisker, was trying to make up time, but more to the point was the testimony of the flagman and rear-end brakeman on the New Haven train to the effect that visibility was seriously impaired by the smoke in the tunnel.

Years of passengers' indignation reached a climax of outrage at a public meeting held on 11 January, with the consequence that the district attorney convened a grand jury, secured an indictment of engineman Wisker on a charge of manslaughter, and criticized the railroad company's officers for the dangerously irresponsible management of local operations. The editor of *Railroad Gazette* defended the company, arguing that the convictions were unjust and the public outcry against the tunnel little more than prejudice. The State Board of Railroad Commissioners, on the other hand, took a considerably more radical view of the matter. In a report issued on 8 February 1902 the members of the board accused the railroad management of being negligent, derelict, and unprogressive in their training of enginemen and in their failure to expand and in other ways to improve the terminal and its approach tracks to keep pace with the steadily growing traffic. They recommended detailed improvements in tunnel signaling, the construction of a loop for suburban trains, and a more rigorous control of speed in the tunnel, which they originally fixed at 18 miles per hour but were willing to raise to 24 miles per hour following the installation of the new signals. Far more drastic than these changes, however, was the first requirement set down in the board's special order on 27 January and reaffirmed in the later report. The order expressly called for an end to operation with steam locomotives after a date to be fixed by the board and authorized in the necessary legislation to be passed by the General Assembly at Albany. The other provisions of the order were designed to increase the safety of passengers while the fundamental changes were being made—reduction in train speed to 18 miles per hour, an end to oil illumination in cars, the employment for operations within the terminal and the tunnel approach of only those enginemen who had made at least 25 trips through the tunnel, a prohibition against the use of bituminous coal in locomotives, and the installation of more brightly illuminated signal lamps (spelled out in detail in the report of 8 February). The implementation of these requirements through the spring and summer of 1902 included the first use of cab signals on the New York rail lines, which were installed in 12 locomotives initially on an experimental basis.[9]

The officers and engineers of the New York Central and Hudson River Railroad, official bodies of the state and municipal governments, and the general public were by early 1902 vociferous, if not sometimes downright hysterical, in their demands for the elimination of steam locomotives from the Park Avenue tunnel, and although most of the parties concerned favored electrical operation, the verdict was far from unanimous. The most authoritative voice raised in opposition to electricity, surprisingly enough, was that of George Westinghouse, who argued that there were dangers involved in the use of the new form of motive power because the heavy current required for the Park Avenue program would inevitably result in fires arising from short circuiting. He cited several accidents that had led to such results to confirm his argument.

> It is yet to be demonstrated that the electric art today is so far advanced as to successfully handle the traffic through the tunnel by electricity. . . . By the time the tracks are ready to receive electric trains the method of handling and using the current will be so developed in detail as to make it reasonably successful. But there is no place in the world today where anything approximating the New York Central tunnel traffic is handled by electricity. Many great railroads have made serious studies of this subject and have stopped to wait until experience could be carried further. . . . The prodigious traffic in and out of Grand Central Station cannot be made a matter of experiment. . . . And we are not unmindful of the Orléans terminus in Paris [Gare d'Orsay] when we say this. The volume of traffic there is too small to affect this statement.[10]

S. S. Neff, the general superintendent of the Boston Elevated Railway, concurred in this opinion. He argued that the inexperience of manufacturing employees and railroad operating personnel made it unlikely that they could devise protective techniques by means of which the causes of short circuits could be detected or their consequences controlled. He recommended the adoption, at least for the time, of an automatic block system, semaphore signals with clearly visible electric lamps, and an automatic stop activated by means of a mechanical trip. He also urged, in a burst of uncommon enlightenment, that for electrical operations the railroad hire the most intelligent young men, train them thoroughly, and pay them salaries above the ruling levels.

Few understood the state of the electrical arts better than George Westinghouse, but the Arnold report, backed by the reputation of its author, the demands of the situation, and the experience gained from European installations, had convinced the Central's directors that there was no alternative to electrification. They began the long and staggeringly expensive process of transformation shortly after accepting the conclusions of Arnold and Potter. The railroad company presented a petition to the president of the Borough of Manhattan on 30 August 1902 for the authority to widen Park Avenue, to close ten intersecting streets, to secure such other properties as might be required, and to make such changes as were necessary to enlarge the terminal yard and its approaches and to install the fixed electrical equipment. A preliminary announcement of the railroad's plan was made in July, and the first official presentation came in September, 1902. The estimated cost of the program was $10,000,000 for the electrical work and $4,000,000 for the expansion of the station trackage (the total would be equivalent to about $355,000,000 at the 1980 building-cost level). In order to organize and to administer the implementation of this plan, which was entirely unprecedented in scale and complexity, the directors of the raiload followed the suggestion of William J. Wilgus and appointed an Electric Traction Commission on 17 December 1902. The membership included some of the leading talents available in railroad electrical technology—Bion J. Arnold, Frank Julian Sprague, George C. Gibbs, Edwin B. Katté, secretary to the commission and later to be chief engineer of electric traction for the New York Central and Hudson River Railroad, and Arthur M. Waitt, shortly succeeded by John F. Deems, the railroad's superintendent of motive power and rolling stock. The commission was to act as a collective consultant on all engineering problems, to draw up a general schedule of construction, and to serve as advisers in the administration of the task.

With the important decisions made and the machinery set in motion, the railroad company sought the necessary authorization from the legislature at Albany. The first two bills to embody the recommendations of the Board of Railroad Commissioners were vetoed by Governor Benjamin Odell, the first because under it the city would have lost control to the state over the properties required by the company for the generation and transmission of electric power, and the second because it needlessly restricted the company's right to acquire the properties necessary to the realization of its program. The third revision was passed by the Assembly on 7 May 1903. The essential provisions of the act and its immediate implications were summarized by E. H. McHenry, a vice-president of the New Haven, whose company was one of the parties to the electrification plan.

> The act of the Legislature of May 7, 1903, of the state of New York, providing for the future regulation of the terminals and approaches thereto of the New York & Harlem Railroad in the city of New York, authorized the New York Central & Hudson River Railroad Company and the New York, New Haven & Hartford Railroad Company, "to run their trains by electricity, or by compressed air, or by any motive power other than steam, which does not involve combustion in the motors themselves," through the tunnel and over the tracks more specifically described. The act required that the change of motive power be made on or before July 1, 1908, and provided a penalty of $500 per day on or after that date for failure to comply with its terms. As there was no available form of motive power other than electricity which met the conditions of the act, it accordingly became necessary for the New York Central and the New Haven companies to provide the equipment for electrically operating all trains between the Grand Central Station at Forty-Second Street and the prescribed sub-limits within the limits of the city of New York.[11]

Before authorizing legislation had been passed, however, Wilgus revised his original loop plan beyond all recognition and proposed that the entire existing complex be swept away in favor of a new terminal of vastly greater size (see chapter 3). Since it was impossible to complete this structure by the 1908 deadline, the Grand Central electrification had to be confined for the time to the station yard and approaches as they existed in 1901.

Locomotive Designs and Tests

The Arnold plan, which determined the extent and the general form of the electrification, implied that the northern limit of the system would be Mott Haven in The Bronx, but the Electric Traction Commission in mid-1903 recommended that these limits be extended to Croton on the Hudson River and hence on the New York Central's line, and to White Plains on the New York and Harlem. A number of economic and political-demographic factors underlay this revision. The first was a matter of preparing for a future contingency, namely, that the municipal authorities of New York might require the electrical operation of all suburban trains serving Yonkers and Mount Vernon, the two stations immediately outside the city limits, as well as all stations within those limits. Since the majority of trains originated and terminated at points beyond these two communities, however, the practical decision would have been to electrify all mileage within the limits of suburban commutation service, which were Peekskill on the Central and North White Plains on the Harlem. The former was quickly eliminated in place of Harmon, immediately contiguous to Croton, because the river terrace at Peekskill is much too narrow to provide a site for the engine terminals and repair facilities that had to be built at the transfer point between the two forms of power. Legal and technical necessities were reinforced by metropolitan demography: the area north of The Bronx (Westchester County), along with the eastern shore served by the New Haven, was admirably suited to upper-income suburban development, its two great virtues being the attractive wooded and shoreline topography and the absence of a ferry transfer in and out of Manhattan. The officers believed that even if commutation traffic failed to earn a profit or even to pay for itself, good suburban service would enhance the company's reputation and thus yield dividends in the form of increased freight and through-passenger business, both of which were highly profitable. And finally, the railroad company was determined to prevent the establishment of a competitive interurban-car network in the Westchester area by providing a superior service of its own, and in this respect it enjoyed a most gratifying success.

The implementation of the expanded program was carried out in stages over a period of nearly ten years, of which the first two phases, completed at about the same time, covered only the segments extending from Grand Central Station to High Bridge on the New York Central line and from Mott Haven Junction at 138th Street to Wakefield on the Harlem. With the installation of fixed equipment in progress, the engineers concentrated their attention on the design of a suitable locomotive. The process by which the design concepts were translated into a practical working machine is perhaps the supreme example in technological history of technique carried to the level of a highly complex, multidimensional scientific enterprise. In the technological revolution that produced electrified mass transportation, the creation of the New York Central's pioneer class of electric locomotives constituted one of the most decisive steps. The first stage of design was the preparation of specifications for the operational characteristics to be expected in regular service. The locomotive was to be one of a pool used to protect the schedules of a minimum of 300 trains per day. It was required to make two successive round trips at any season of the year between Grand Central Station and Harmon, the distance of 34 miles to be covered in an overall time of one hour with a train of 550 tons in tow and one stop en route, and the layover time between trips not to exceed twenty minutes. The engineers further specified that the locomotive must be able to run between the two terminal points in a time of 44 minutes without stops (the existing schedule of the Empire State Express) and to maintain such runs continuously throught the day, with no more than a one-hour layover in that period of time. The machine was called upon to adhere to any regular schedule then in the timetable while hauling a maximum load of 14 Pullman cars and to make a smooth start followed by a uniform, rapid acceleration. In actual practice, however, this load (about 1,000 tons) required such high current consumption as to make it advisable to operate the locomotives in pairs. No regularly scheduled train and few extra trains in the early years of the century ever included 14 Pullman cars in their consist. The numerous curves in the line, especially along the Harlem River, the densely built surroundings at the New York end, and the heavy traffic density throughout its length precluded operations at high speeds, so that certain conclusions of the Marienfelde-Zossen tests in Germany were not applicable to the New York Central's requirements. Everyone except the engineers of the Westinghouse company and the New Haven Railroad agreed with Arnold on the merits of direct-current motors. They were chosen primarily because of their familiarity, their quick, accurate, and uniform response to the levels of tractive force required to start, accelerate, and maintain the speed of trains, and their close correspondence among load, power consumption, field strength, and the accompanying armature torque.

The New York Central and Hudson River awarded contracts for 35 locomotives to the General Electric and the American Locomotive companies in the fall of 1903; the first unit was completed in October, 1904, and made its initial trial run on 12 November of the same year (figs. 1, 2). Through the years of 1905–6 it completed a series of test runs that eventually totaled more than 50,000 miles to provide the basis for an exhaustive program of controlled performance analysis that undoubtedly placed the locomotive in a unique historical position. The primary creators of this paragon of the electrical and mechanical arts were Edwin B. Katté, chief engineer of electric traction for the New York Central and Hudson River Railroad, and Asa F. Batchelder, theorist and engineering designer with the General Electric Company. Their handiwork was initially given the number 6000 and, after two earlier alternatives, placed in a class designated as S-1. The trial run of 12 November drew such a gallery of notables among the spectators that it must have seemed like the opening

Fig. 1. New York Central and Hudson River Railroad. The first electric locomotive, 1904.

Fig. 2. New York Central and Hudson River Railroad. The first electric locomotive. Side elevation showing the bipolar motors in longitudinal section.

1

2

game of a Yankees-Dodgers World Series. In addition to the five members of the Electric Traction Commission, the railroad company was also represented by other officers, among them George H. Daniels, the flamboyant general passenger agent who had created such travel sensations as the Empire State Express and the Twentieth Century Limited. The manufacturing industry sent W. B. Potter and Elihu Thompson of General Electric, and George Westinghouse of the Westinghouse Electric and Manufacturing Company. Members of the administrative and engineering staffs of a dozen other railroads included Samuel Higgins, general manager of the New Haven, whose company had just embarked on an even more revolutionary electrification program, and Samuel Rea, vice-president of the Pennsylvania Railroad, which was well launched on the construction of its own New York terminal. It was in every respect an auspicious occasion, and if designers and manufacturers were a little premature in congratulating themselves, they were shortly to be given abundant evidence of how well they had done their work.

Locomotive Number 6000 belonged to the type later designated 1-D-1, which indicates that it was carried on one unpowered pilot-truck axle, four driving-wheel axles, and a single trailing-truck axle. Since the engines were designed to be operated with equal facility in either direction, as the center-cab arrangement indicates, the terms pilot and trailing truck are applicable only to steam locomotives and are arbitrary conventions in the case of electric power. The total weight of the machine was 189,000 pounds, of which 138,000 pounds were carried by the eight driving wheels. The four motors, one on each driving axle, were rated at 550 horsepower each, or a total of 2,200 for the locomotive. The current delivered to the armatures was controlled by a variation on the multiple-unit system invented by Sprague and manufactured by General Electric, a technique that allowed the ready operation by one motorman of two or more machines coupled together. Two were ordinarily used to maintain scheduled speeds with the heaviest trains (875 tons maximum weight), but a single unit was sufficient to haul 450 tons at the maximum allowable speed of 65 miles per hour, although there are few places on the railroad's Electric Division where this speed can be safely attained. The Class S locomotives were not designed for high-speed heavy-duty service, but rather for efficiency, durability, simplicity, and reliability, virtues they possessed to a superlative degree.[12]

For the driving mechanism of the 660-volt direct-current motors, the engineers went back to the beginnings of electric traction in adopting the gearless form, in which the armature is pressure-fitted directly to the axle, thus making the driving-wheel axle in effect a solid core of the armature. The resulting advantages of simplicity and strength gained through minimizing the number of wearing surfaces and parts moving relative to one another are offset by the fact that shocks arising from the passage over frogs and uneven track cannot be absorbed by springs or other devices but must be transmitted directly to the relatively delicate armature.[13] Another element contributing to the general simplicity of the machine was the bipolar motor field, that is, one in which the electromagnetic flux within which the armature rotates lies between two large, slightly concave pole faces (fig. 2). Bipolarity was adopted as a necessary concomitant of the fixed or gearless drive: since the vertical movement of the axle in the passage over uneven track would be transmitted directly to the armature, it was inadvisable to locate pole faces above and below the rotating element. The most remarkable feature of the locomotive, and one for which it may again have been unique, was that the flux extended continuously through all eight poles and their associated armatures, returning through the cast-steel side frames of the driving wheels but avoiding the iron cores of the armatures. The poles and coils of the field were thus constructed as integral parts of the locomotive underframe. The rigid, continuous arrangement of the field poles was still another feature designed to realize the aims of maximum ruggedness and simplicity. The final innovation in this thoroughly novel work was the spring-controlled underrunning contact shoes, four on each side of the locomotive, the form and working of which we will examine in a succeeding passage of this chapter.

The prolonged testing of Number 6000 began in December, 1904, and ended in mid-June, 1906. An account of the entire program may be divided into five categories, all of which were carried out on either a segment of the New York Central and Hudson River main line between Schenectady and Hoffmans, New York, or on a specially built 5.5-mile test track adjacent to this line. These tests were conducted jointly by the railroad and the General Electric Company and were supervised by the men who had played the chief roles in the creation of the work that was now asked to show its mettle—W. J. Wilgus and Edwin Katté of the railroad company, and Asa Batchelder and W. B. Potter of the manufacturer. The first series, undertaken in the winter and early spring of 1904–5, were concerned with the behavior of the essential working and controlling elements of the machine under running conditions, and they were carried out with trains weighing 400, 435, and 550 tons (fig. 3). The primary aims were the determination of electrical resistances in the controller necessary to obtain a smooth acceleration curve, the temperature rise of motor and controller components, friction and external mechanical resistance, maximum speeds with various loads, wheel slippage, acceleration, traction, and commutation perfor-

Fig. 3. New York Central and Hudson River Railroad. The first electric locomotive on a test run, 1905.

3

mance, and a host of lesser characteristics arising from what the engineering staffs called accidental conditions, or placed under a catch-all heading designated "special tests."[14]

The second series aimed to reveal what all those concerned were anxious to establish in comparison with theoretical predictions, namely, the relative economy and performance of steam and electrical operation. The motive power against which Number 6000 was measured was the newly built Pacific-type locomotive Number 2797, Class K, and the contest was set in motion on 29 April 1905. The tests were concerned chiefly with the rate of acceleration up to 50 miles per hour and were carried out with trains of six and eight cars, the two of each length being nearly identical in weight. The electric locomotive clearly outperformed its steam counterpart by factors close to 1.6:1, but what was most impressive was the uniform and rapid acceleration of the former, running light, up to 85 miles per hour. The short length of the test track discouraged any further excitements of this kind.[15] The special tests, constituting the third series and restricted entirely to the electric locomotive, were conducted on 7 September 1905 with trains of six and eleven cars, including the borrowed dynamometer car from Illinois. The chief purpose in this series was the determination of the exact relations among the variables of maximum speed, rate of acceleration, voltage levels, current withdrawal, and tractive force. The highest speed attained with the eleven-car train was 62 miles per hour, reached in a little more than six minutes, and with the six-car train, 71 miles per hour (time unspecified).

Another question that generated inconclusive controversies during the early years of electric traction was the optimum form of the distribution system. The weight of practical consideration favored the overhead wire, but the necessary supporting structure made it far more expensive than the third rail. The Electric Traction Commission adopted Arnold's recommendation of the grade-level rail from the beginning of their deliberations on technical as well as economic grounds, so that the investigation of alternatives focused entirely on the forms of the contact shoe and the electric rail. The engineers devoted the same thought to the design of these small but essential details as they lavished on the rest of the locomotive, and the results offered the only satisfactory solutions to the problem of picking up current from a third-rail distribution system. The current-carrying rail, I-section in form, is covered at both the sides and the top with wood sheathing, leaving only the bottom surface exposed (an insulating plastic material was later substituted for the wood). The "shoe" is thus an underrunning plate held in tight contact with the rail by means of springs designed to exert an upward pull of 40 pounds. In areas with high concentrations of switches and crossings, the rail is shifted to the overhead position, and contact is effected by means of a miniature pantograph raised and lowered by an air-operated piston working in a cylinder mounted on the cab roof. The advantages of the underrunning shoe over the Long Island's top-contact variety were numerous enough to offset the slightly higher cost—protection of the rail from snow and ice, nearly complete protection of workers and trespassers from contact with the charged metal, reduced strain in the insulators supporting the rail on the ties because the shoe pressure acts against the force of gravity, reduced corrosion because of the superior protection of the metal, and greater accessibility for cleaning because of increased clearance between the rail and the ties. In the tests that led to the adoption of the particular forms of rail and shoe (the fourth series in the program), five variations on the protective covering were investigated, and questions about the action of the shoe in heavy snow were satisfactorily answered when the snowy Mohawk Valley obligingly produced a 13-inch fall on 9 February 1906. The shoe performed very well, which proved to be more than one could say about the Long Island Rail Road under similar conditions.

The fifth phase, which marked the completion of the full testing program, was the most impressive part of this immense laboratory exercise. The locomotive was run for a total of more than 45,000 miles on the special test track at Schenectady in what the engineers modestly described as a service test. This feat was accomplished by operating the locomotive continually for 112 eight-hour days at an average speed of 50 miles per hour, sufficient to cover an average distance of 403 miles per day. The machine completed this grueling test run on 12 June 1906 in sound condition except for the inevitable wear of running surfaces. The conditions of the run were more exacting than those likely to be encountered in normal service: trains were heavier, speeds higher, rates of acceleration and deceleration were greater, with a consequently more severe wear on braking equipment. No detail was overlooked in this relentless determination to find out how everything worked. The daily shuttling on the test track, for example, included runs made through the turnouts to and from the passing track in order to observe the wear on frogs and switch points and on the wheels passing over them. The ultimate conclusion was exactly what the railroad officers hoped to discover: the unit maintenance cost for motors, wheels, trucks, brake shoes, controllers, and related circuitry ranged from about one-sixth to one-eighth of the comparable costs for steam locomotives. The respective figures were $0.0126 per mile for the electric power, and $0.08 to $0.10 per mile for the steam. The choice of the gearless motor was confirmed by the discovery that the maximum motor efficiency of 93 percent was 4 percent higher than the best that had been achieved with the geared forms.

Further analysis of the behavior of electric locomotives unfortuntely came in the wake of another disaster, the first and the only one to occur after the inauguration of the new service. On 16 February 1907 the New York and Harlem's White Plains and Brewster Express was derailed on a 3-degree curve at 205th Street in The Bronx. (The degree of curvature in railroad curves is measured by the angle through which the track turns for a length of arc of 100 feet.) The wooden cars were badly damaged, and as a consequence 20 passengers were killed and 150 were injured. The track was in excellent condition, and the curve was properly superelevated for an equilibrium speed of 46.5 miles per hour (the overturning speed would have been considerably higher). The cause was quickly discovered: a sufficient number of outside spikes holding the outer rail to the ties were sheared by the tangential momentum of the locomotive, to cause the rail in question to spread outward under the driving wheels. The coroner's jury threw the net of blame widely enough to include the members of the Electric Traction Commission as well as various officers and employees of the railroad company. Arnold and Sprague personally wrote to the assistant district attorney for New York County on 4 March 1907, pointing out that the commission could in no way be regarded as culpable. They were probably right in their view; nevertheless, the preliminary results of the Pennsylvania Railroad's tests of locomotives with and without guiding trucks and of the Central's own special tests aimed precisely at these phenomena should have alerted the engineers to the possibility of trouble arising from the low center of gravity in electric locomotives equipped with axle-mounted motors. The investigation of the accident conducted by the New York Central engineering staff revealed that the shearing force exerted on rail spikes is greater for electric power than for steam at all speeds up to 80 miles per hour, and the shearing force at 60 miles per hour (the probable speed of the Harlem train) on a 3-degree curve exceeds the shear strength of a steel spike adjusted for a reasonable safety factor.[16] The grand jury indicted the railroad company and two officers on the ground of inadequate training of motormen as well as incomplete understanding of the action of electric motive power. It was a calamitous way to learn a lesson, but all electric locomotives were henceforth equipped, or re-equipped, with four-wheel guide trucks.

Electrical System and Operations

The installation of fixed electrical equipment for the New York Central and Hudson River Railroad was initiated as soon as the materials began to flow from the General Electric Company and other manufacturers in 1904. Although the first operations were restricted to the original New York Central line in Manhattan and along the Harlem River in The Bronx, the plan from the beginning looked toward North White Plains and Peekskill as the terminals. In the case of the latter, as we have seen, the electrified line was shortened to a joint station serving Harmon and Croton.[17] The original generating plants, located at Port Morris on the Harlem River and at Yonkers on the Hudson and constructed in 1905–6, produced alternating current at a potential of 11,000 volts. Each of the two installations was designed for an ultimate capacity of 30,000 kilowatts. The locations were dictated by several factors: they were close to the load centers of the projected electrical system; they lay on rail lines and waterways, so that coal could be delivered either by barge or freight car; and the presence of the two streams offered an unlimited quantity of circulating and cooling water, its salinity, of course, preventing its use as boiler feed water. The architectural design of the generating stations was the work of Reed and Stem of Saint Paul, who were co-architects of the new terminal at 42d Street and several way stations of the railroad (see chap. 3), while the engineering details were designed by the General Electric and the New York Central engineering staffs. All power was generated at Port Morris until 1907, when the Yonkers station was placed on the line.[18] The three-phase 25-cycle alternating current was transmitted by underground and overhead lines to eight substations, where it was converted by the standard rotary converters and reduced in potential by transformers to a direct current at 660 volts. The choice of the third-rail distribution system arose from technological as much as economic considerations. It was familiar and regarded as reliable because of the thorough testing in the B. and O. tunnels in Baltimore and at the Gare d'Orsay in Paris. It was more practical in both installation and use than the overhead catenary because of the restricted clearance envelope of the Park Avenue tunnel and the terminal, neither of which was designed with an overhead distribution in mind. Finally, although the engineering factors clearly supported the third-rail choice, the consideration of alternatives was rendered meaningless when the municipality passed an ordinance prohibiting the use of overhead trolley wires under high voltage within the city limits. It was for this reason also that the transmission lines had to be placed in underground conduits throughout Manhattan and The Bronx.[19] Preparation for the operation of trains was rounded out with the establishment of provisional repair and maintenance facilities at High Bridge, Wakefield, and North White Plains (figs. 4, 5).

With everything in working order, the New York Central and Hudson River Railroad ushered in the new day on 30 September 1906, when the company operated the first train into Grand Central Station by means of electric power (fig. 4). The scene brought together in melodramatic juxtaposition the new locomotive that powerfully foreshadowed a new century and the 35-year old curtain wall at the rear end of the train shed, which by this time had come to seem antique, if not downright bizarre. Architectural fashions had changed almost as drastically as the technology, and Victorian intricacy hardly seemed appropriate to American Renaissance elegance and the gentle hum of electric motors. Since electrification in 1906 extended only to High Bridge on the Harlem River, the new motive power was limited to this seven-mile segment. The initial run was made by a special train consisting of an office car, four coaches, and three Pullman cars, drawn by locomotive Number 3406, with William J. Wilgus himself at the controls. The guests in the office car included the engineering and administrative notables of the railroad and the chief manufacturer—the members of the New York Central's Electric Traction Commission (Arnold, Deems, Katté, and Sprague); Alfred H. Smith, general manager of the railroad company, later to be its president and the assistant director-general of the United States Railroad Administration (see chap. 4); George A. Harwood, chief engineer of the electric zone improvements; five members of the General Electric engineering staff, among whom Asa Batchelder was the most distinguished; and officers of various other railroad companies. It was another memorable occasion in the long evolution of man's technical skills, and if William Wilgus's comment was a little too consciously aimed at the ages, his words, nevertheless, came close to the unvarnished truth. "The electrification of the passenger traffic of two of the most important steam railroads in the world, for distances of from 25 to 35 miles, radiating from a terminus in the greatest city in the Western hemisphere, may well be termed the marking of the commencement of a new epoch in the history of transportation."[20]

The trial run of 30 September, however much it was an event to be celebrated, was only another step in the New York Central's five-year preparation for regularly scheduled electrified service on a scale commensurate with the traffic of Grand Central Station. Since the electrification of suburban operations was the primary aim of the project, the next step after the locomotive tests had to be the design, manufacture, and testing of multiple-unit cars. The discussion of alternatives was little more than a formality before the obvious superiority of Sprague's invention for all operating requirements. Moreover, the technique offered the possibility of unifying the entire suburban rail and urban rapid transit systems on a metropolitan basis, as the planning for the Interborough subway had already suggested to the officers of the Long Island Rail Road. The editors of the *Railroad Gazette* were first to fill out this vision in some detail, about a year before the manufacture of the suburban equipment was initiated.

Fig. 4. New York Central and Hudson River Railroad. Top: the first electric train, shown leaving High Bridge, 30 September 1906. Bottom: the first electric train, shown leaving Grand Central Station on the same date.

4

Fig. 5. New York Central and Hudson River Railroad. The first phase of the electrification of Grand Central Station, 1903–6. Top: track and third rail on the Harlem Division. Bottom: track, lower-quadrant signals, and third rail on the N. Y. C. and H. R. line (later Electric Division).

> The multiple-unit system of train control will give the desired flexibility which makes for economy of operation. If corporate differences can be overcome it will be possible for local cars to take up passengers throughout suburban towns and villages and then join an express line and pass at high speed to the urban points of distribution. At these points the train may again be split up into separate units and pass to the various parts of the city over the existing underground or elevated roads. Even if corporate differences prevent the full developmentof this scheme, it will be possible to divert much of the traffic to the several local roads running north and south through Manhattan Island, instead of concentrating it at one point—the Grand Central Station.[21]

Unfortunately, this brave and perfectly feasible scheme was never realized, and after a brief flirtation with the idea of unifying the West Side and Park Avenue lines by means of a subway in 53d Street, the company restricted its suburban service to the existing Central, Harlem, and Putnam Division main lines.

The initial lot of multiple-unit rolling stock, consisting of 125 motor cars for passengers, 6 for baggage, mail, and express, and 55 trailers, were manufactured in 1905–6 and first placed in service on the Grand Central–High Bridge run on 11 December 1906. The electrical equipment was produced by the General Electric Company, and the trucks by the American Locomotive Company, while the car bodies with their fixed interior equipment were divided between the American Car and Foundry Company and the Saint Louis Car Company. They were the first suburban coaches of all-steel construction and standard railroad weight, which was 102,600 pounds for the individual unit. They were the first cars of their kind to be provided with electric heating as well as lighting and tractive power. Each motor unit was driven by two direct-current motors rated at 200 horsepower, both fixed to a single truck and engaging the axles through geared drives, clearly indicating that the long controversy on driving techniques remained unresolved. The multiple-unit control was the kind invented by Sprague, in which the resistance in the master controller for the motor circuits of all the cars is progressively reduced, thereby correspondingly increasing the current flowing to the motors and hence the armature torque. Many details of control and motor circuitry, dead man's control, and other automatic elements, however, were devised by the General Electric engineers working in collaboration with Edwin Katté, the railroad company's chief engineer of electric traction. The air-brake system, manufactured by the Westinghouse Traction Brake Company, was specifically designed for high-density suburban service: the quick recharging of the brake cylinder, the high emergency pressure, and the ready and accurate response of braking equipment to the motorman's control valve together provided the flexibility of operation and the rapid deceleration essential to the safe movement of trains running under close headway, on schedules mostly calling for numerous closely spaced stops. The railroad's usual practice in suburban service was to operate two motor units to one trailer for optimum speed and control. Since the weight of the standard suburban coach in steam-powered service was a little less than three-quarters of that of the electric motor car, the advantage in train weight alone lay with the traditional forms. This difference, however, was offset by the 275,600-pound weight of the steam locomotives customarily assigned to suburban trains. Test runs conducted in January, 1908, with a 365-ton train making a 12.5-mile run with three stops at an average speed of 31.4 miles per hour, revealed the very creditable power consumption of 35 watt-hours per ton-mile. Katté and his collaborators thus found still further reason for congratulating themselves.

Electric motive power and rolling stock numbering more than 200 units, on the successful working of which 260 regularly scheduled daily trains and 50,000 weekday passengers depended, required maintenance and repair facilities of a size comparable to the major installations built for the servicing and shopping of steam locomotives. The company constructed its primary repair shops, with their associated yards and storage space, directly beside the station at Harmon in 1907–8, adding details over the succeeding four years as the temporary installations at High Bridge and Wakefield were progressively phased out. Since Harmon became the interchange point between steam and electric power, the facilities had to include the engine house, coaling equipment, and water supply that marked every engine terminal in the land.[22] The extensive complex was designed and constructed by company forces working under the immediate supervision of C. H. Quereau, the superintendent of electrical equipment, and L. H. Byam and Carl Schwartz, respectively the engineers of railroad construction crews and power stations. Behind and above them, of course, were the men who had been administering the whole vast program, with the exception of Wilgus, who had turned to a private consulting practice in 1908. Supplementing the Harmon complex was a similar though much smaller installation at North White Plains, which included an engine house, maintenance and storage facilities, shop, and power plant, all in full operation by 1910.

The New York Central's original program of electrification was rounded out with the design and operation of still another novel form of electric locomotive. The first unit was manufactured by the General Electric–American Locomotive consortium in 1912, put through test runs on the Harlem Division in 1913, and followed by the production of 36 units which were placed in service at intervals over the years 1914–26. A locomotive distinguished primarily by a highly articulated wheel base, it was carried on four independent four-wheel trucks (designated a B-B-B-B arrangement, indicating that all wheels were driving wheels) and driven by gearless motors fixed to all eight axles (figs. 6, 7). The aims underlying the design of this unprecedented form were to secure greater power than that available in the original model, to gain a more equitable distribution of weight combined with a smaller axle load, to improve running through switches and turnouts by drastically reducing the length of the rigid driving-wheel frame, and to increase the efficiency of operation by transforming the guide-wheel trucks into motorized units. The available horsepower in the newer locomotives was somewhat lower than that of their predecessors, since the individual motor was rated at 175 horsepower, or a total of 1,400 horsepower for the entire unit. But the total motor torque was sufficient to haul a 1,000-ton train at 60 miles per hour and to deliver a starting tractive force of 65,150 pounds, which was double the comparable figure for the 1904 machine.[23] The appearance of the new locomotive on the rails coincided with the completion of the Grand Central–Harmon–White Plains electrification program, which was marked by the operation of through passenger trains to Harmon on 20 June 1913, nearly ten years after construction had begun on the new terminal and four months after its opening. The average number of scheduled trains operated over the newly electrified lines was about 260 per day, of which the major proportion were carried by the Harlem Division.[24] The economy and reliability of electric service were the objects of the same careful inquiry that preceded the decision to adopt it. Investigations conducted under the direction of Edwin Katté revealed that the average maintenance expenses for the locomotives over the three years of 1910 through 1912 were little more than three cents per locomotive mile, and for the multiple-unit equipment less than two cents per car mile. The calculation of time lost because of engine failures measured against miles run yielded even more impressive conclusions. During the year 1912 the electric locomotives were operated nearly 8,700 miles for each minute of train time lost as the result of the failure of electrical equipment, and the multiple-unit cars close to 11,000 miles for one minute lost. The mileage per minute lost consequent on mechanical failure was over 10,000 for the locomotives and close to 12,500 for the multiple-unit cars. Over the four years of 1912 through 1915 the mileage per engine failure of any kind, irrespective of time lost, clearly favored the electrical equipment: the average distance operated per year for each mechanical failure was 41,372 miles, against nearly 89,000 miles for each electrical failure.[25] Many of the men who played the key roles in the physical realization of the New York Central's program lived on through expanding traffic, war, boom, and Depression, but they never had cause to question the excellence of their handiwork. The railroad company later abandoned

Fig. 6. New York Central and Hudson River Railroad. An electric locomotive of 1912.

Fig. 7. New York Central Railroad. The Lake Shore Limited at Riverdale. The train is drawn by an electric locomotive of the class manufactured in 1912. The photograph, made in 1931, shows the upper-quadrant semaphores that superseded the lower-quadrant variety installed with the Grand Central electrification.

6

7

its generating system in favor of purchasing power from the Consolidated Edison Company; the aging electric locomotives eventually gave way to diesel-electric forms equipped with contact shoes for direct electrical operation, and the multiple-unit cars were for the most part progressively replaced by newer rolling stock. In all other respects, the installation remains to the present day as it was when the first operations were undertaken. There were alternative techniques, of course, as the New Haven was already convincingly demonstrating, but the Central's system stands as the leading exemplification of technology created for enduring human use, not passing kinesthetic sensations.

2

The New Haven Electrification

The Electrical System

When the officers of the New York Central and Hudson River Railroad decided to electrify the company's metropolitan lines, they followed the well-founded advice of the engineers in adopting the familiar and thoroughly tried system of direct-current distribution through the grade-level third rail. The New Haven, for better than half a century a tenant on the New York and Harlem's Bronx and Manhattan properties, was originally prepared to follow in the same path, since it could draw on abundant first-hand experience with direct-current techniques through the branch-line electrifications it had pioneered in 1895. The immediate and compelling need to adopt the new form of operation within the New York suburban zone obviously arose from the legislation of 7 May 1903, which in effect gave the road no alternative; at the same time, however, the character and growth of the New Haven's passenger traffic would unquestionably have dictated the same choice within a very few years. In the first decade of the new century the number of passengers carried on the entire system increased 59.1 percent, while the commutation traffic at Grand Central Station nearly doubled. If the systemwide increase was below the spectacular 73.9 percent of the New York Central over the same years, the New Haven trains, nevertheless, transported on a ten-year average about 80 percent more passengers than did the larger road.[1] Moreover, the rate of increase of commutation traffic was itself rising, the total volume more than doubling in the decade of 1910–20. This immense flood of business, far outdistancing that of the nearest competitors (the Central and the Pennsylvania), was as important financially to the railroad as its heavy freight traffic. For years throughout the nineteenth century its income from the operation of passenger trains exceeded that derived from freight, and in 1904, when the New Haven began systematic planning for electrical operations, passenger-train revenues equalled nearly half the total obtained from all sources.[2]

The New Haven's electrification program, as it was drawn up in preliminary form during the summer and fall of 1904, involved two interrelated parts. The primary phase was the introduction of electrified operations on the main line between the junction with the New York and Harlem at Woodlawn in The Bronx, 12 miles from Grand Central Station, and Stamford, Connecticut, 21.5 miles to the east. The second part was the expansion, improvement, and partial electrification of the Harlem River Branch. Curiously enough, it was the latter that was first brought to public attention, when C. S. Mellen, the president of the company, announced in

August, 1904, that the Harlem branch was to be expanded in capacity and electrified, but the completion of this project did not come until five years after the inauguration of electrical operations on the main line.[3] There appears to have been no reliable public announcement of this event until September, 1905, and then it came in the form of a paper read before a meeting of professional societies. This interval of little more than a year witnessed what was very likely the liveliest debate on high-level technological questions in the history of the art. The long controversy over the relative merits of direct and alternating current for traction motors burst forth with renewed vigor, stimulated afresh by the New York Central's program, and the final consequence was that the New Haven's officers almost overnight took what was to prove the boldest and most radical step in the early years of railroad electrification. The company's adoption of a total alternating-current system, extending from the generating plant to the locomotive motors, was innovative and prophetic to the highest degree and thus constituted a major event in the history of world technology. The complex background of ideas and inventions that led to this decision was compressed into no more than a year, and it involved the foremost minds of the profession.

When the New Haven's engineers began to formulate preliminary electrical plans in the fall of 1904, it seemed a foregone conclusion that they would be compelled to adopt third-rail, direct-current distribution in order to conform with the New York Central's practice. Since the New Haven operated by trackage rights over the line of the Central's subsidiary New York and Harlem, the adoption of direct-current seemed inevitable. This argument was strengthened by another factor, namely, the tentative decision to operate multiple-unit cars on the Harlem River Branch similar to those adopted by the Interborough Rapid Transit for the new subway and possibly to establish through service over the two lines via the station at 129th Street. Moreover, as we have seen, the New Haven was thoroughly familiar with direct-current techniques through the development of electrically operated branch lines that had begun in 1895. At this moment, however, an ironic combination of unfortunate circumstances and innovative engineering propelled the company's officers in an entirely different direction. The exposed third rails along the branches in Connecticut had been the cause of numerous accidents, of which some produced fatal consequences, and these mishaps soon brought the railroad into the courts. Popular animosity toward the new techniques was reinforced by jurisprudence, and the outcome was a decree handled down by the Superior Court of Connecticut on 13 June 1906 requiring the New Haven to abandon electrical operations throughout the state and return to the familiar and presumably less dangerous steam locomotive.

This costly step the road's officers were understandably reluctant to take. Meanwhile, beginning at least two years before the court decision, the engineers of the Westinghouse Electric and Manufacturing Company, who had pioneered in the development of alternating-current motors, had been disseminating heretical doctrines. The ruling opinion, however, clearly favored direct current, and by 1905 it was backed by the authority of Frank Sprague, the manufacturing investments and financial power of the General Electric Company, and the experience of the New York Central and Hudson River Railroad. The heart of the established view, derived from the Central's exhaustive test program, was summarized by one of the *Street Railway Journal*'s indefatigable correspondents.

> Should the New York Central Railroad Company have adopted the single-phase motor, in its present stage of development, it would have required a geared motor, with attendant losses of from 3 per cent to 5 per cent, in addition to the greater losses of the single-phase motor itself as compared with the gearless d.c. motor. In place of 93 per cent maximum efficiency, the a.c. locomotive would probably have had a maximum of 87 per cent to 88 per cent, or from 5 per cent to 6 per cent greater loss in the d.c. type of locomotive adopted. The extra losses obtaining in the a.c. locomotive would have largely offset the losses of the rotary converters required with the d.c. system so far as energy consumption is concerned. The cost of maintaining an electric locomotive of the d.c. gearless type must also be considerably less than one of the a.c. type with its attendant gearing, more complicated and expensive winding and small air gap.[4]

Nevertheless, the New Haven's engineers and officers were convinced by mid-1905 that a single-phase alternating-current system was not only feasible, but that it offered conspicuous advantages. The decision to adopt the unfamiliar form was probably made and urged by William S. Murray, the company's chief electrical engineer. The primary factors underlying this decision were both negative and positive—the troubles with branch-line third rails, the unwillingness of the railroad to sacrifice the investment as well as the operating and competitive advantages of electricity, and the superiority of high-voltage, alternating-current transmission and distribution where comparatively long distances were involved. The announcement of the revised plans, however, immediately precipitated a conflict with the New York Central, whose engineers saw no possibility of installing alternating-current on the Harlem line and the Grand Central approaches. The only technique that seemed to be available if both systems were to be retained would have been to introduce either a transfer point between direct- and alternating-current locomotives at Woodlawn, an expensive and time-consuming operation, or alternating-current trolley lines over the Central's tracks. This impasse was broken when the engineers of the Westinghouse company developed an alternating-current motor that would operate equally well with direct current.[5] The Hector and Achilles in this battle of the systems both exhibited their prowess before the New Haven's officers in the summer of 1904 and asked them to judge their respective merits. The General Electric Company submitted a proposal for direct-current distribution similar to that of the New York Central, while the Westinghouse company offered an entirely novel plan based exclusively on the use of alternating current. At the time there were very few installations in the United States that could offer reliable guidance on the design and working of such a system, and the service offered by the railroads did not remotely approach the enormous tide of diversified traffic that flowed over the New Haven's four-track main line (very likely 400 trains per day at the peak). The Indianapolis and Cincinnati Traction Company operated ten interurban cars per day between Indianapolis and Rushville, Indiana, by means of a single-phase alternating-current system, having established the service in 1904. The Spokane and Inland Railway introduced the operation of both freight and passenger service by the same method in the following year and thus became the first standard railroad in the United States to employ the new technique for the movement of freight as well as passenger trains. An even more radical form of electrification had reached the planning stage in the same year: the officers of the Erie Railroad decided to electrify the road's Rochester Branch, employing a 60,000-volt three-phase transmission system and an 11,000-volt single-phase distribution trolley line, with the power to be generated by one of the hydroelectric plants at Niagara Falls (constructed 1906–7).

These modest installations served to back the claims of the Westinghouse engineers, and to the great advancement of the electrical arts, the New Haven's decision makers listened to their advice and chose alternating current. The essential elements were novel not only in character but also in scope: power was to be generated as single-phase alternating current at a potential of 11,000 volts, distributed directly to the locomotives by means of an overhead catenary system at the same voltage, and stepped down by locomotive transformers to an operating potential of 560 volts. At the same time, the locomotives had to be equipped with contact shoes for use on the New York Central's third rail, and with such devices as were necessary to render the motors operable on direct current. The power plant was to be located at Cos Cob, Connecticut, and equipped originally with four steam-powered turbine-generator units each rated at 3,000 kilowatts. The process of installing the elaborate overhead trolley and transmission lines, building the power plant, and testing the prototype of the new locomotives began in September, 1905, and was completed to New Rochelle, New York, a distance of 16.6 miles from Grand Central Terminal, in July, 1907. The new service was extended to Stamford, Connecticut, the original limit and an additional 16.9 miles from the terminal, in July, 1908. The first lot of 35 locomotives, manufactured by the Baldwin-Westinghouse team, was delivered in 1906–7, and the pilot model was subjected to extensive testing during the first three months of 1906. The motive power was the B-B type, indicating that the individual machine was carried on driving wheels only, which were divided between two four-wheel trucks. The weight of 100 tons made the complete unit the heaviest electric locomotive manufactured to that date, and the specifications called for the capacity to haul a 250-ton train at a maximum speed of 60 miles per hour. The design and installation of the New Haven's fixed equipment were carried out under the direction of Calvert Townley, a consulting electrical engineer, and William S. Murray, the railroad's chief electrical engineer (fig. 8).

The successful completion of the New Haven's program ought to have laid the controversy to rest, one would have supposed, but this proved to be far from the case. The manufacturers of direct-current equipment, led by the polemical Sprague, strenuously opposed the railroad's plan, and they were answered with equal warmth by the savants of the Westinghouse team. The first description of the New Haven program, including responses to much of the criticism, was presented by the Westinghouse engineer Charles F. Scott in a paper read before a joint meeting of the American Street Railway Association and the American Railway Mechanical and Electrical Association, convened at Philadelphia in mid-September, 1905. Scott argued that alternating-current motors behaved as satisfactorily as the direct-current varieties with respect to torque (the equivalent of tractive force), acceleration, and commutation, and then went on to describe the clear advantages of the unified, all-embracing alternating-current system with the overhead trolley wire. Reduced to their essentials, his arguments could be summarized under four categories: the high transmission voltages made it possible to transmit current over a greater distance at a lower power loss; feeder lines and connecting equipment were no longer necessary; rotary converters could be eliminated, and the equipment of the few remaining substations reduced to the fully automatic transformers, with the consequent elimination of substation operators; and the total number of substations could be reduced as a further consequence of abandoning the converters. On the question whether there would be a sufficient steady contact between the pantograph bow and the trolley wire, Scott argued that such contact was at least as reliable as that between the shoe and the third rail and far superior to that of the traditional and trouble-plagued trolley wheel. And finally, to the predictable outrage of the direct-current propo-

Fig. 8. New York, New Haven and Hartford Railroad. A train running over the first electrified trackage, 1906–7.

Fig. 9. New York, New Haven and Hartford Railroad. A freight train on the Harlem River Branch, 1913.

8

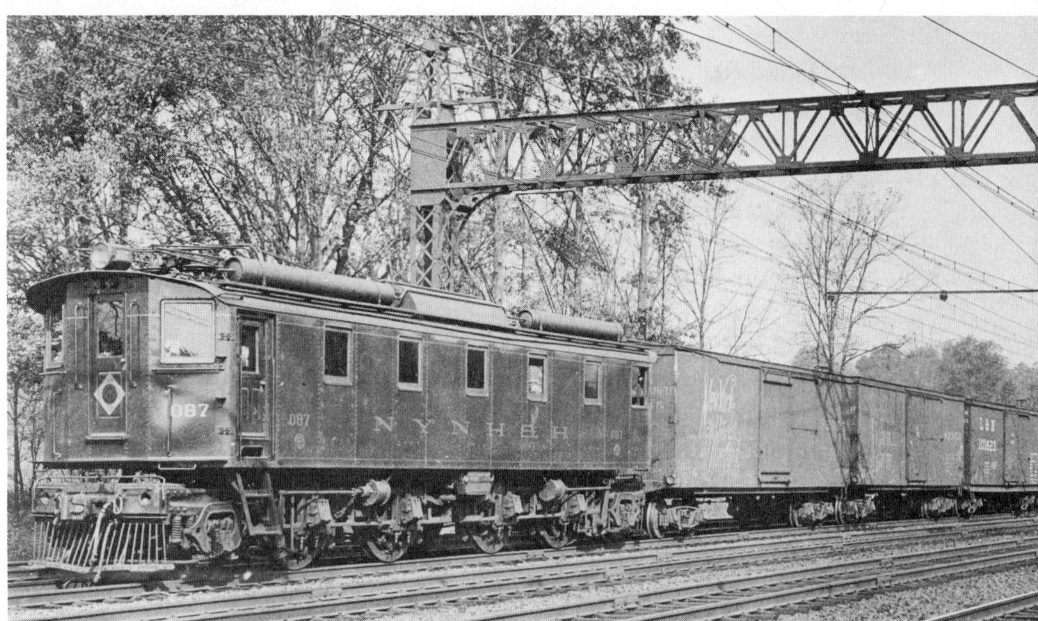

9

nents, he claimed that the voltage and hence the motor control were more accurate and efficient with alternating current than with direct. Following the Philadelphia meeting, his words were published in the prestigious *Street Railway Journal*, where the entire profession could read them.

All this failed to satisfy either Sprague, who was the chief voice of the New York Central's Electric Traction Commission, or the conservative editors of the *Railroad Gazette*, who represented his viewpoint. The latter criticized the New Haven's officers not only for adopting an untried technique, but specifically for not deciding in favor of the standard usage and thus failing to conform to the New York Central's practice. These attacks brought to the fore the most authoritative voices of the Westinghouse company. George Westinghouse answered the charges in the *Gazette*, arguing that the single-phase overhead alternating-current system was at least equal to the direct-current techniques in most respects and superior to it in two, namely, the absence of electrolytic action on metal pipes and conduits close to the third rail and the greater efficiency of alternating-current motors at high speeds. He then went on to develop this theme in a letter to W. H. Newman, the president of the New York Central and Hudson River, in which he urged the company to adopt the New Haven's system on the grounds of the extensive testing and successful operation of the technique in Europe, the superior efficiency of motors, the absence of the numerous problems and dangers in third-rail distribution, and—most surprising, since all the previous allegations had stood to the contrary—the lower cost of installing the fixed equipment. He even went on to claim that the Central could convert the power plants and substations then under construction (late 1905) to alternating current at little expense.[6] Benjamin Lamme, the leading authority and chief engineer of the Westinghouse team, in a cautious, scientifically reasoned letter to E. M. Herr, a vice-president of Westinghouse, offered a considerable body of evidence derived from tests conducted by himself to support the conclusion that alternating-current locomotives were well-tested machines and at least as reliable, efficient, and subject to exact positive controls as their direct-current counterparts. Such pronouncements made some impression on the more objective engineers of the General Electric Company, but Lamme's further assertion that the New York Central's Number 6000 was an untested novelty understandably aroused a measure of animosity. Considering the total operations of the two systems, Lamme concluded that on final balance the overall efficiency and economy of the alternating-current installation were greater than those of the direct-current form because the inherent character of the former allows substations and power plants to be reduced in number and to operate more closely to a constant load than was the case with the latter.[7]

What appears to have been the second-last word on the subject for the time being, at any rate, came from E. H. McHenry, a vice-president of the New Haven, who at least waited until the main-line installation was nearly complete though not yet in service. Further comparative investigations of the two systems, based in part on the first-hand experience of the New Haven, the Westinghouse, and the Baldwin Locomotive companies with full-scale railroad motive power and operations, led to conclusions substantially favorable to the single-phase technique.

> While both methods under consideration included high-tension transmission by alternating current, it was believed that the combination method requiring transforming devices and continuous current motors was less well adapted to the conditions than its simpler single-phase competitor for many reasons. The electrical efficiency of the combination system between power house bus-bars and engine shoes is 75 per cent only, as compared with 95 per cent for the single-phase system, [and] the flexibility of former is impaired by the limited radius of the secondary low-tension distribution, requiring sub-stations at frequent intervals, and still further by the limitations imposed by the use of a third or conductor rail. The position and height of this rail in its proper relation to the track rail must be rigidly maintained, and the practical margin of permissible variation is measured in fractions of an inch. Moreover, its continuity is broken at switches and crossings by frequent transference [sic] of the conductor rail to the opposite side of the track or to an overhead position. In contrast, the single-phase system requires no substations or secondary circuits; the continuity of the overhead conductor is complete, and its position and height may vary within vertical and horizontal limits of 8 ft. and 4 ft. respectively, without losing contact with the collecting shoes on the pantograph frames.[8]

Translated into economic terms, the technical advantages of the alternating-current system clearly implied a reduction in both continuing costs and initial capital investment. The simpler and hence more durable electrical equipment and the superior efficiency meant lower operating and maintenance expenses, while the reduced number of substations, combined with the absence of conversion and fixed high-capacity transforming equipment, promised a lower capital investment and hence reduced fixed charges.[9]

While all these words were multiplying, the engineers and construction crews of the New Haven Railroad were rounding out their plans and organizing the battalions that were to implement them. The crucial decisions with respect to the main line having been settled, the company turned its attention to the improvement of the

Harlem River Branch. This vital appendage, operated under a 99-year lease as the Harlem River and Port Chester Railroad, originally extended from a junction with the main line at New Rochelle to a point close to the 129th Street station of the Third Avenue elevated line, but on the completion of the New York Connecting Railroad, the boundary between the two properties lay at 133d Street and Willis Avenue. C. S. Mellen, the president of the New Haven, announced as early as August, 1904, the company's plans for drastic improvements to the branch: it was to be widened to six tracks; all grade crossings were to be eliminated; four tracks were to be converted to electrical operation, with fixed equipment identical to that eventually planned for the main line; and an electrified suburban service was to be introduced by means of multiple-unit cars similar to those of the Interborough subway. The total cost of all this high technology on a short branch line was estimated at $7,000,000, of which nearly three million was assignable to the electrification alone (the total would be about $170,000,000 at the 1980 building cost level).

Two potent factors underlay the decision to spend additional sums on top of the heavy financial burdens incurred by the New York–Stamford electrification. In the first place, the Harlem branch was planned as the link between the north end of the New York Connecting Railroad and the New Haven main line, which meant that it was an essential element in the chain that united the railroads south and west of New York with the New England carriers. Although the completion of Pennsylvania Station and the Connecting line was expected to bring a flood of through freight and passenger traffic that the branch had never previously borne, the number of additional trains hardly justified a right of way of six tracks. The second factor arose from another of those farsighted assessments of traffic potential in what we might call the demography of metropolitan rail and rapid transit systems. The overwhelming bulk of the New Haven's suburban business was derived from the main-line communities lying between Mount Vernon and Greenwich, Connecticut, with the consequence that a very high proportion of the suburban trains, together with all through trains, was funneled through the bottleneck at Woodlawn Junction. One of the aims in the drastic upgrading of the Harlem River Branch, and the chief reason for its enlargement to six tracks, was to generate new commutation traffic in the sparsely settled, largely undeveloped area in the eastern part of The Bronx, which lay outside the high-growth corridors with their chains of long-established suburban nuclei. Again, it was the unification of the various modes of metropolitan transit and the interdependency between these modes and metropolitan growth that gave the New Haven's plans their urbanistic importance, as the perspicacious editors of the *Railroad Gazette* well understood.

> The extent to which suburban territory is dependent for its development upon a thoroughly harmonized transportation service is nowhere better shown than in the country which the New Haven road now proposes to open up by the improvement of its Harlem branch between the Harlem River at Port Morris and New Rochelle. The suburban territory along the Harlem road [New York and Harlem] . . . has been highly developed for a great many years, like the suburban territory across the Hudson river and that along the main line of the New York Central as far as Yonkers and beyond, but the towns reached by the inadequate service of the old Harlem branch of the New Haven road have scarcely developed at all, although situated within a radius of ten miles from New York. The service was inconvenient, involving a change of cars at the Harlem river and the use of the elevated line from that point into the city, and hence resulted in the curious anomaly of an undeveloped district in the midst of a thickly populated suburban territory. The present plans contemplate not only a frequent service over a first class roadbed, but also a through connection with the subway, and it may readily be imagined that the towns along the shore between New Rochelle and Port Morris will develop a very profitable traffic. The building of the subway really furnished the key to the situation, so far as the passenger traffic is concerned; for, during all these years while the overflow population from New York has been seeking homes within a short distance of the city, the electric lines as well as the steam road have been effectually prevented by their lack of through connections from giving this particular district a service that would make it an important suburban community.[10]

The Harlem River Branch, the chief function of which had been to provide a connection to the Port Morris ferries, was soon destined to accommodate a great volume of diversified traffic—suburban, through passenger, and through and local freight—but the slow progress on the construction of the New York Connecting Railroad allowed the New Haven to delay the implementation of these plans until 1908, after the Stamford extension was completed and opened to service.

The catenary system of the main-line installation remains unique in form and extent, and there was little precedent for it in the standard railroad practice of the United States. The trolley wire is suspended in the horizontal position from two parallel catenary or hanger cables so located that the three elements form an equilateral triangle in vertical section, with the conductor at the lower apex (fig. 8).[11] The great majority of gantry frames that carry this assemblage of cables are a light construction composed of girders in the form of Warren trusses and trussed or open-web box columns, and they are ordinarily spaced at 300 feet over main-line track. The gantries erected for the initial installation between Woodlawn and Stamford (1906–8) were of conventional column-and-beam form, but those adopted for the later extensions were treated as rigid frames, which is indicated by the riveted-plate boxlike connection between the horizontal and vertical elements and by the downward-tapering legs. The newer type was adopted for the Harlem River Branch, for which the original program of electrification was completed in July, 1912, and for the extension to New Haven (fig. 9). At two-mile intervals the lightly framed gantries give way to the more heavily constructed anchor bridges, which serve two essential functions. First, as the name indicates, they are designed to provide stability against the unequal tension in the hanger cables arising from unbalanced horizontal forces along the line (usually caused by wind loads or progressive icing). The resistance of the anchor form is derived not only from its greater weight, but equally from the A-frame bents that support the parallel trussed and thoroughly braced girders. The second function is the support of the automatic circuit breakers that make possible the electrical isolation of track sections, the shunt transformers necessary to the operation of the circuit breakers, and the lightning arresters, along with the customary walkways and handrails. The entire distribution system was designed so that each track may be electrically isolated from all the others. The block signals—another device peculiar to the New Haven—are placed on short posts suspended below the gantry and carry short upper-quadrant semaphores extending toward the left of the post rather than the right, as is the custom on all other American railroads. On curves the trolley wire and its hangers had to be constrained to follow the curving alignment of the track by means of pull-over wires that subject the catenary assemblage to forces having a horizontal component directed outward along radial lines. In open or lightly settled areas the transmission lines are carried on posts projecting above the legs of the gantries, but in urban areas they had to be buried in underground conduits. All current-carrying wires are supported by porcelain insulators of the skirt type fixed to cast-iron yokes. The only unusual problem in the stringing of transmission circuits arose from the presence of the drawbridge at Cos Cob, where the wires had to be elevated on steel towers to 110 feet 6 inches above grade in order to provide adequate clearance over the waterway and the raised bridge.

This immense and complex circuitry, eventually to become commonplace as the new electrical technology spread over every region of the land, was as impressive in itself as it was novel in the early years of the century. After all the controversy the New Haven deserved applause, and it came at last from the authoritative *Street Railway Journal*.

> The recent installation of the electric service on the New York, New Haven & Hartford Railroad adequately completes the reorganization of the terminal work in New York. It has been a long pull, this breaking down the walls of conservatism,

> and ridding the metropolis of smoking engines, but the time is now come and a review of some of the methods that have led to the result is in order. . . . No electric traction system has ever been put in under more strenuous conditions than this, since the terminal requirements of direct-current operation demanded not only motors of very remarkable properties, but a complete duplicate collection and control system. . . . The railroad is to be congratulated upon having done thoroughly well the task undertaken, and upon giving the first great demonstration of high-voltage railroading upon this side of the Atlantic.[12]

The Long Island, the New York Central, and the Pennsylvania railroads, on the one hand, were content to restrict their electrical zones to the New York metropolitan area, although it must be said that the Central went comparatively far afield in its invasion of Westchester County. The New Haven, on the other hand, struck out in new directions. Withn the year following the opening of main-line service to Stamford, the company undertook to implement the Harlem River program, which was completed in July, 1912. In this enterprise the railroad company left no stone unturned to produce the best in right of way, track, structures, motive power, and rolling stock. The broad six-track line free of grade crossings, the deep ballast, the light and open framework of the gantries, the long horizontal lines of wires and tracks in diminishing perspective—all combined to provide a distinctive impression of elegant railroad technology (fig. 9). The stations were constructed to conform with this generous spirit: designed by Cass Gilbert in a variety of styles, yet unified in plan and overall profile, they were delightful representations of what the correspondent for *Architectural Record* called "the suburban and sylvan picturesque."[13] While the improvement of the Harlem River Branch was progressing, the company was involved in even more spectacular undertakings. The first multiple-unit cars were delivered in 1909, to begin the abandonment of the antique and dangerous wood-sheathed rolling stock. The longest forward step came at almost the same time: the electrification was extended eastward from Stamford to New Haven, with the inauguration of service coming in June, 1914. In the following year the New Haven strung its electric lines still further to the east, when it converted the Cedar Hill, Connecticut, freight yard to the new power. The ultimate goal was Boston (with the state legislature of Massachusetts as the most enthusiastic proponent of the plan), but this proved unattainable as the road's financial troubles began to multiply. These extensions of four-track catenary required the addition of four more turbine-generators to the existing group at the Cos Cob power house. Through a decade of highly innovative engineering and construction, the New Haven became the first railroad in the United States to offer intermetropolitan and interstate electrical operation of freight, passenger, and switching service. All of the novel locomotives that came at intervals over the years are now gone, but the fixed equipment is still in place and in full working order, except for the generating station at Cos Cob.

Locomotives and Operations

The New Haven's pilot locomotive was delivered to the road by the Baldwin-Westinghouse consortium in the early weeks of 1906 and subjected to test runs totaling 2,000 miles through the months of February and March of the same year. A sober-looking box-cab model, it was carried on two four-wheeled trucks (the B-B arrangement) driven by motors on all four axles (fig. 10). The individual motor was rated at 250 horsepower, providing a total of 1,000 horsepower for the unit, and it was designed to operate at 450 volts on alternating current, or at 550 to 600 volts on the New York Central's direct current. For the driving mechanism the New Haven's engineers rejected both the Pennsylvania and the New York Central choices and decided in favor of the quill drive, the most complex and expensive of all, yet the one that was ultimately destined to supersede all the rest in standard rail practice (fig. 11). In the New Haven machines the armature was neither geared nor fixed directly to the driving-wheel axle, but was instead pressure-fitted to a cylindrical sleeve known as a quill, which transmitted the armature torque to the driving wheel by means of a plate bearing projecting pins, the device called a spider in the argot of the craft.[14] There was sufficient clearance between the sleeve and the axle to prevent damage to the armature arising from any vertical play caused by passage over uneven track. To guarantee the integrity of the armature, however, this characteristic of the quill drive had to be supplemented by an elaborate suspension system in the motor-driving wheel assemblage. A helical spring wound between the armature and the wheel absorbed transverse movements (that is, movements parallel to the axle) and hence the lateral thrust of the rotating element. A circular spring immediately inside the plane of the spider and driving wheel damped the movement of the armature in the vertical direction, at right angles to the driving-wheel axle. These various devices were designed not only to eliminate shocks to the armature, but also to contribute to the maintenance of an unvarying armature torque. The current for operating the motors was drawn from the overhead conductor by means of a pantograph (another novelty in the United States at the turn of the century), and from the New York Central's third rail through an underrunning shoe. The control of the armature speed was effected by means of transformer taps, which allowed the motorman to vary the

42

Fig. 10. New York, New Haven and Hartford Railroad. The first electric locomotive, 1906–7, shown in longitudinal section.

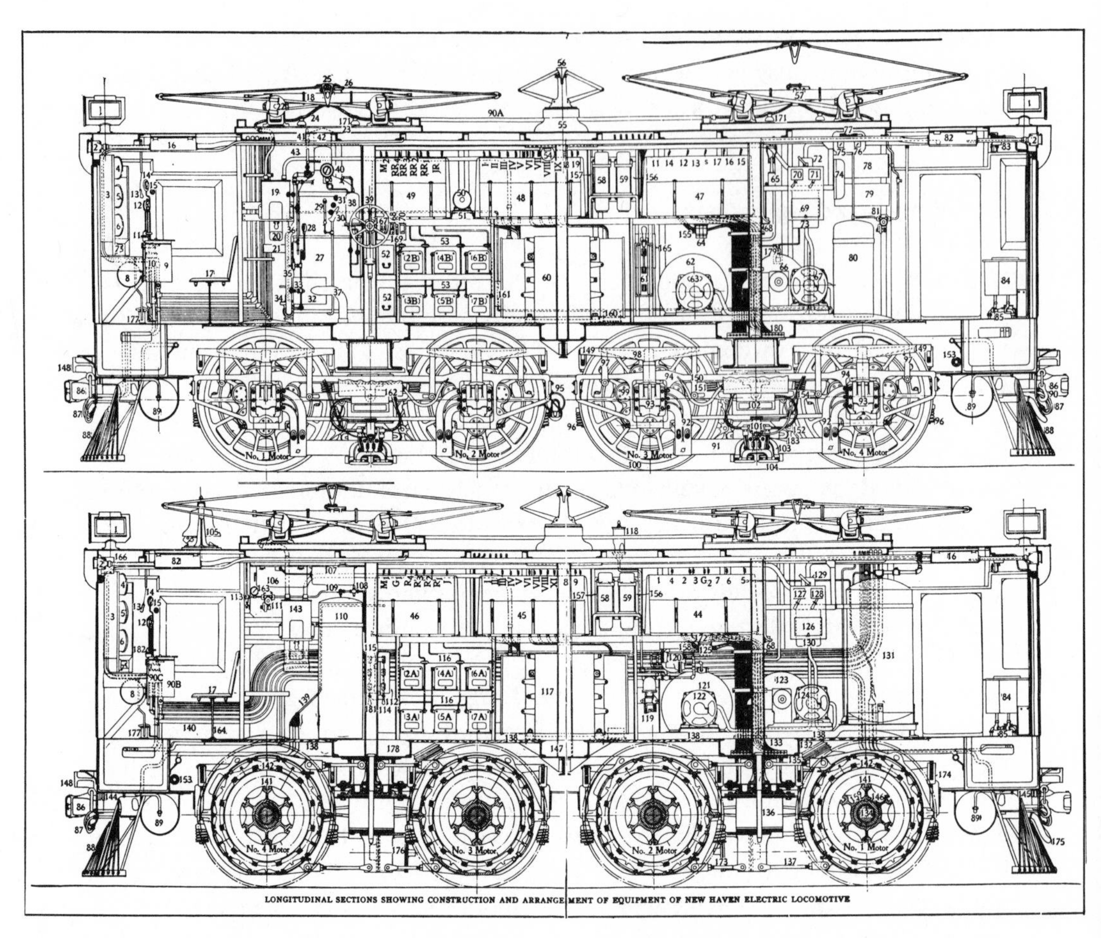

Fig. 11. New York, New Haven and Hartford Railroad. The driving-wheel assembly of the locomotive of 1906–7: *a.* the spider, quill, and armature shown as separate elements; *b.* the three elements assembled; *c.* the motor and driving-wheel assembly; *d.* the motor and driving-wheel assembly with motor housing.

11

resistance in the motor circuit and thus to increase or decrease the voltage and the flow of current to the field coils and the armature.

The specifications for the first group of New Haven locomotives called for the capacity to haul a 250-ton train in through service at 60 miles per hour, and a 200-ton train in local service, with stops spaced at an average interval of two miles, at a maximum speed of 45 miles per hour. The test train weighed 289 tons, and the locomotive was able to accelerate it from zero to 45 miles per hour in two minutes, yielding an acceleration rate of 0.375 miles per hour per second. The manufacturers, however, claimed that their admirable product was capable of a maximum speed of 88 miles per hour (trailing weight unspecified), and in a test run of 1907 the pilot model, running light, reached a speed of 100 miles per hour. If this was indeed the case, it was the first electric locomotive manufactured in the United States to reach this velocity.[15] The current consumption rose very steeply to about 1,475 amperes in 0.2 of a second, then more slowly and irregularly to a maximum of 1,600 amperes in 25 seconds (figures scaled from curves). The original six machines, delivered in 1907, revealed precisely the same operating defects that manifested themselves in the Pennsylvania and New York Central tests of 1904–7. The absence of guiding trucks resulted in unstable movements and excessive lateral thrust at the rail on curves and turnouts, and the New Haven's solution was exactly the same as that adopted by the other roads, namely, the addition of guiding trucks, which were applied to the 35 units manufactured in 1908 and to all subsequent road locomotives (the wheel arrangement was thus altered to 1-B-B-1). These excellent works of a scientific craftsmanship represented a highly rational design. They were, indeed, compact, perfectly controlled, rolling substations: the homely box cab housed in tight arrangement not only the controlling devices, switches, circuit breakers, train-heating boiler, and cooling devices, but also heavy-duty transformers to reduce the high trolley-wire potential of 11,000 volts to the operating range of 450 to 600 volts. All motors and transformers were air cooled by means of automatically controlled blowers. Everything stood in the necessary functioning relation to everything else, and not an inch of space was wasted.[16]

The foremost talent among those responsible for the design of the New Haven's pilot model was Benjamin G. Lamme, chief engineer of the Westinghouse team, and he was the first to describe and defend the company's handiwork on a public stage. His forum was a meeting of the New York Railroad Club held in early March, 1906. He began by explaining why the railroad and the manufacturer, having decided on alternating current for distribution as well as transmission, chose the single-phase rather than the polyphase variant, although there were several promising examples of the latter in Europe. Polyphase distribution, he thought, could be quickly rejected, in spite of the European experience, for a single overriding reason. If the operating current is transmitted entirely through the trolley wires, the common three-phase system requires three overhead conductors, or a minimum of two if one of the running rails is used to distribute current (the latter technique was adopted by the Great Northern Railway for the original Cascade Tunnel electrification, completed in 1909). But the double or triple conductors were not only expensive to install, but as one can readily imagine, a perfect nightmare of overhead wires at terminals, yards, and major junctions, a tangle that guaranteed troubles, with their attendant high repair and maintenance expenses. Moreover, Lamme argued, the constant-speed induction motors of polyphase distribution require costly structural features and are generally characterized by an inefficient control of variations in locomotive speed. The positive virtues of single-phase alternating current for distribution, motors, and motor control were patent and numerous, and Lamme outlined them in clear and convincing terms.

> 1st. Alternating current is used on account of its facilities of transformation [and transmission at high voltages].
> 2nd. One trolley wire only is used, by adopting single-phase alternating current.
> 3rd. With alternating current and one trolley wire only, any desirable voltage can be used on the trolley line.
> 4th. By using alternating current an efficient means for varying the voltage to the motors is obtained. With single-phase there is only one supply circuit to be handled, and the variable voltage apparatus can be given the simplest and most efficient form.
> 5th. A type of motor was developed which can have its speed varied by varying the voltage supplied to it, and which uses power practically in proportion to the load, when operated in connection with the above variable voltage supply circuit.
> 6th. The motor is preferably wound for low voltage and the same transformer which is used for stepping down from the trolley voltage to the motor voltage can also be used for obtaining the desired voltage variation, for varying the speed, and the power in proportion to the speed.
> 7. The motor is inherently of a variable-speed type, and can automatically adjust its speed to that of other motors driving the same load, with but very small unbalancing of the loads on the individual motors.
> 8. The type of motor developed is one which can be used on direct current also.[17]

One may be sure that nothing could have kept Sprague and Wilgus at home on the evening Lamme read his paper, and they were probably the first to rise during the question period. The consequence was that the battle of the systems broke out with renewed vigor. Wilgus's objections turned mainly on the expense and difficulty of installing an overhead distribution system, especially one involving two hanger cables. Moreover, he argued, the high-voltage conductor carries with it a host of dangers—fatal contact with trainmen standing on the roofs of cars, the threat to public safety at overpasses, short circuits, and the possibilities of electrocution arising from contact between derailed equipment and fallen wires, or wires in position in places of impaired clearance, collapse of catenary supports in the event of a derailment, and the close proximity of the high-voltage wire to moving equipment.[18] Sprague's arguments at the meeting itself were disappointing because they were concerned almost entirely with the high initial cost and the likelihood that direct current could also be transmitted at high voltages (no one, however, appeared to be interested in exploring this possibility). In the following month, with time to organize his boundless thoughts on the subject, he wrote a letter to the editor of the *Street Railway Journal* which is a formidable exercise in thorough, recondite, and highly technical analysis. His essential point was that the alternating-current motor is inherently inferior to its direct-current counterpart chiefly because of an excessive consumption of power for a given tractive force and an excessive overheating of motors. His conclusions were stated without qualification, virtually as received dogma.

> It is . . . quite evident that the New Haven locomotive, despite an excess of fully 20 per cent [in weight] on the drivers, does not approach the Central's in tractive possibilities, and will, in yard movements in the d.c. zone, require at least double the line current for equal tractive effort. . . . Moreover, it seems clear that, leaving aside comparison between motors each built solely for d.c. or a.c. operation, which cannot but be to the ultimate disadvantage of the latter, the attempt to make the same machine acquit itself with equal satisfaction on either circuit cannot but meet with disappointment.[19]

The editors of the journal in question had already taken their turn, and they had delivered a relatively simple comment carrying large implications.

> The anticipations of a radical departure from previous heavy traction work, raised through the adoption by the [New Haven] company of the single-phase system, are certainly realized in the plans which are now announced in detail. It certainly seems startling to think of operating a four-track line, now 22 miles long and with a probable future length of 61 miles [to New Haven], without the help of sub-stations or feeders. We are so accustomed to a sub-station with its accompaniment, up to within recently, of an attendant or attendants, and to an elaborate

> system of high-tension and low-tension feeders, that a railway system hardly seems complete without them. but the plan adopted by the New Haven company is electric railroading reduced to its simplest terms.[20]

While argumentation flourished, the officers of the New Haven's motive-power department began their preparations for the first electrical operations of trunk-line freight trains in the United States. The immediate culmination of these plans was a series of four .experimental locomotives manufactured by the Baldwin-Westinghouse team and designed to provide empirical-pragmatic tests of the ruling theories relating to electric traction. All four were designed to operate under either alternating or direct current, and they were approximately similar in weight and power, but beyond these features they possessed a number of novel differences. The first two, carried on two driving-wheel trucks and one guide wheel on each side at the ends (the 1-B-B-1 wheel arrangement), were equipped with four motors each rated at 315 horsepower. The driving mechanism must have been the most complicated ever developed: gears fixed to the motor armature transmitted the torque to a quill which in turn rotated the driving wheels by means of helically coiled springs set between the spokes of the wheels. The individual machine delivered a maximum tractive force of 47,000 pounds and was designed to be used in either freight or passenger service. The next two locomotives embodied radical departures from the New Haven's practice. They were much like the Pennsylvania Railroad's Class DD-1 power in several fundamental respects: the wheel arrangement was the same as that in the first two New Haven models, but the locomotive was divided into two permanently coupled units each of which was driven by a single 630-horsepower motor mounted above and between the two driving axles; the armature torque was transmitted to the driving wheels by means of a connecting rod, jackshaft, and side rod. The New Haven adopted the gear-and-quill drive and the 1-B-B-1 wheel arrangement for the 36 locomotives manufactured in 1912–13 by the Baldwin and Westinghouse companies. They were relatively light machines, having a total weight of 110 tons, but the four motors were together rated at 1,600 horsepower and delivered a maximum tractive force of 40,000 pounds. To meet the demands of switching service the railroad had already placed 16 electric switching locomotives in service in 1911–12. The operation of freight and passenger trains from New York to New Haven which were dependent on a large fleet of locomotives and multiple-unit cars compelled the company to build centralized inspection, repair, and maintenance facilities. These were completed in 1916 at Van Nest, in the eastern Bronx, near the southern terminal of the Harlem River Branch. The benefits to the railroad, to shippers and passengers and to the many communities it served, were so great and so apparent as to make the steam locomotive, with its noise and dirt and inefficiency, seem downright primitive by comparison.[21]

What we might regard as the final professional and official assessment of all the programs of railroad electrification in New York City was provided by William S. Murray in a paper presented before a meeting convened on 20 January 1915 under the joint sponsorship of the Franklin Institute and the Philadelphia chapter of the American Institute of Electrical Engineers.

> Electrification points to three principal places where economy of operation can be secured, and in the order of their importance they may be mentioned as follows: Saving in fuel; saving in motive-power maintenance and repairs; and saving in train-miles.
>
> Assets created by electrification, which may be controlling factors, as, for example, the reclamation of city terminal property, after the removal of gas and smoke by elimination of steam locomotives, are of most important consideration. In cases, however, that do not involve large city terminal electrification, the general credits and debits resulting from electrification work may be said to about offset each other, and thus the value of the returns can be based upon the three items just mentioned. . . .
>
> Experience with the movement of billions of ton miles in freight, passenger and switching service by electricity has justified the early predictions that one pound of coal burned under the boilers of a central electric power station and converted into electrical energy and transmitted into an electric engine will develop twice the drawbar pull at the same speed as a similar pound of coal burned in the firebox of a steam locomotive; and, second, that the maintenance and repairs on electric locomotives of the straight alternating-current type are on the order of one-half of those required for steam locomotives of equal weight on drivers. It is thus seen that the problem of electrification merely revolves around the question of the density of traffic in which the economies aforesaid can be practiced, and, therefore, the denser the traffic the greater the requisite motive power for its movement, and hence the greater the saving to be effected. . . . While the savings to be effected under certain conditions of electrification may be considerable, on the other hand, the construction investment necessary to these savings may be very great. . . . Only a healthy condition of finance throughout the country will warrant the consideration of electrification, and . . . partial electrification, such as that applying to yards only and not main line, while it might prove of advantage to a public, might at the same time prove to be a serious and unfair burden for the railroad to carry.[22]

The New Haven's program in particular appeared as the culmination of an extraordinarily rapid progress—without parallel in the previous history of technology—

concentrated in the two decades of 1888–1907, and the editors of the *Street Railway Journal* were prepared to celebrate the fact at the moment the latest entry into the new technical world turned its first electrically powered wheel.

> It seems a far cry from the Richmond road of 1888, with its two 7½-hp motors per car hung on the underframing, to the powerful electric locomotives which are now hauling trains of twelve or more heavy Pullman sleepers out of the Grand Central Station in New York—to the high-speed motor trains which are carrying more passengers between Camden and Atlantic City and on the Long Island Railroad than were ever transported by their steam predecessors—to the single-phase leviathans of the New Haven and Pennsylvania railroads, and to the latest developments in electric traction locomotives in England and on the continent of Europe. The past nineteen years, which have been crowded with developments in other branches of engineering, have constituted practically the entire history of the modern electric road. Starting almost as a toy at an exposition it soon developed into the street railway as we know it now, then into the suburban extension of the city system, then by almost insensible gradations into the interurban road. . . . From this point the advance to heavy electric traction was a rapid one.[23]

The Westchester Railroad

The last entry into the immediate family of New York railroads began with the best of intentions and the highest expectations, only to die in its adolescence with scarcely one of them realized. The history of preliminary planning and speculation that formed the background to the establishment of the New York, Westchester and Boston Railroad extended over a longer period of time than the history of the road's operations. A company apparently known from its inception as the New York and Portchester Railroad was incorporated on 20 March 1872 to build a line from Port Morris in The Bronx to the New York–Connecticut state line. The early date suggests that the promoters may have seen, or at least guessed at, the traffic potential of the eastern shore before the officers of the New Haven had properly gauged it. That was as far as the matter went until the consolidation of the outlying boroughs into an expanded New York City on 1 January 1898, an event that suggested to the promoters of the Port Chester line the need for expanded rail service in the eastern metropolitan area. The chief among them, William C. Gottshall, secured a renewal of the original charter on 23 April 1901 to construct a four-track electrified railroad from 132d Street, on the Harlem River in The Bronx, northward and eastward to

Port Chester. The intended line would lie parallel and almost contiguous to the Harlem branch and the main line of the New Haven, and would thus serve the same suburban communities, primarily Pelham, New Rochelle, Larchmont, Mamaroneck, and Rye, as well as the terminal points. With the four tracks segregated by character of traffic, two for local service and two for express, it was expected that the line could comfortably accommodate 200 trains per day, which would have been a conservative estimate. In the three years following the granting of the charter various legal and financial maneuvers led to the incorporation of the New York City and Westchester County Railroad and the New York, Westchester and Boston Railroad, and then to the transfer of the former company's franchises to the latter road. The New York and Portchester was consolidated with the enlarged Westchester line in 1909, but three years previous to this date the New Haven had acquired control of the company through the purchase of a majority of the stock. These financial negotiations were carried out at the highest level: the agents for the railroad in the acquisition program were none other than William Rockefeller and J. P. Morgan.

The region traversed by the lines of the New Haven and the Westchester railroads, though marked by long-established communities, was largely undeveloped at the turn of the century, and the population of the entire tributary area in 1905 was only 110,000 inhabitants. The planning of the road and the first phase of construction appeared to promise another beneficial symbiosis of good suburban rail service and vigorous suburban growth. A network of local street railways and interurban lines offered the possibility of a well-developed hierarchical pattern of transportation, and the Westchester's officers, backed by the financial power of the New Haven, were anxious to take full advantage of the opportunities. These were accurately described by the correspondent of *Engineering Record*.

> [The road] passes through localities desirable for residences, many of which are not yet built up, but are already experiencing great appreciation of values in consequence of the facilities promised by the railway. [The first] division connects New Rochelle, Mount Vernon, and smaller towns, and serves a district containing many extensive estates. For a considerable distance it lies between the existing steam railroad and the shore, where the population has extended most rapidly, and it is approached by a number of short local trolley lines which will act as feeders. It is, therefore, believed that this division will immediately secure a large local and suburban traffic, much of it included with that of the Interborough Rapid Transit lines.[24]

With some reason to believe that the road would generate a heavy traffic through the suburban development that would follow its opening, the construction of the Westchester line was pushed vigorously after its revival at Mount Vernon in 1909. The main track, extending from 180th Street and Morris Park Avenue to New Rochelle, was completed on 29 May 1912, and a branch to White Plains was opened on 5 July of the same year. The extension to Port Chester, however, was delayed until 1929, coming only after the intervening suburbs had undergone the rapid building up that followed the First World War. The Connecticut state line was thus barely touched, and a Boston terminal remained an ever receding dream.

The building of the Westchester line was accomplished in accordance with standards that not only would have aroused the envy of trunk-line railroads, but that also suggested an unlimited access to funds. The grading for the 100-foot right of way and the construction of bridges began in the fall of 1904. Nothing but the best was acceptable to the generous spirit of the Westchester's and the New Haven's officers. Except for a single 500-foot station approach, the ruling grade was held to 0.6 percent, which involved among other operations the removal of 1,632,000 cubic yards of tough Fordham gneiss. Local and express stations were spaced at intervals of one mile. The entire line was built without grade crossings, which required the construction of 128 concrete-arch and steel plate-girder bridges in a distance of 30 miles, for an average of 4.3 structures per mile (the total included 12 bridges over streams). Maintaining the railroad grade above or below the numerous parkways and boulevards in the eastern metropolitan area compelled the company to erect long viaducts over Columbus Avenue and the New Haven tracks in Mount Vernon and over the Hutchinson River Parkway in The Bronx, and to dig a 4,000-foot tunnel under the Bronx and Pelham Parkways. The electrical equipment was similar to that of the New Haven: the overhead catenary system was suspended from steel-frame gantries; both transmission and distribution lines carried single-phase 25-cycle alternating current at a potential of 11,000 volts, which was reduced to 250 volts for the motors of the multiple-unit cars. The control of train movements was effected by an automatic electric-block system, with signal indications given by upper-quadrant semaphores. Only the Pennsylvania's New York extension, among roads in the metropolitan area, could boast at this early date of using the newly developed upper-quadrant signaling, although the New Haven was not far behind. The grading of the Westchester right of way and the emplacement of a number of bridges were substantially completed by the end of 1905, but the laying of track, the construction of stations, and the installation of signaling, distribution, and transmission circuits appears to have been delayed until 1909. A high level of talent lay behind this exhibition of quality railroading: William Barclay Parsons and Lewis B. Stillwell were engaged as consulting engineers to the company's own engineering staff.[25]

The officers of the Westchester, with the New Haven supplying an ultimate total of $50,000,000 in capital, spared no pains to make the railroad a model of flexible, high-speed, efficient suburban transit. Low grades, easy curves, the absence of grade crossings, and automatic block signals invited the best in rolling stock. The multiple-unit cars, designed by Lewis Stillwell, were characterized by heavy all-steel construction having a total weight of 60 tons per car, and the individual unit was driven by four Westinghouse motors each rated at 175 horsepower and built for a maximum speed of 60 miles per hour. The company inaugurated a modest freight service in the latter half of 1912, but there was obviously little connection traffic, so that the few industries in these dormitory suburbs were adequately served by a single locomotive.[26] It is doubtful whether a traffic that amounted to little more than a switching service ever earned the road a profit. The excellent rolling stock and the useful if miniature freight service were matched by the handsome stations that were designed in a simplified Spanish Renaissance style. They were of monolithic reinforced concrete construction, and wherever possible the station building and its associated overpass were treated as a single unified structure. The prize example was the Fifth Avenue Station at Pelham, where the functioning enclosure was integrated with a huge semicircular barrel vault that supported the railroad viaduct over the street. The author of these elegant and structurally advanced works was the architectural firm of Alfred Fellheimer and Allen Stem, which was founded in 1911 following the death of Stem's earlier partner, Charles Reed. All three were associated with Warren and Wetmore in the design of Grand Central Terminal. It marked the beginning of a 25-year series of triumphs for Fellheimer, who quickly became the nation's leading architect of railroad stations.[27]

The opening of the Westchester lines and the completion of the Harlem branch improvements, both occurring almost simultaneously in 1912, and the year-by-year extensions of the two eastern rapid transit lines serving The Bronx, together stimulated a residential development of such magnitude as to transcend anything the *Engineering Record*'s editors, or anyone else, could have imagined. Nor was it all what Henry James had in mind when he talked "of the spreading woods and waters amid which the future [of New York] . . . appears still half to lurk," and of "that mainland region of the Bronx, vast above all in possibilities of Park."[28] By the time of the First World War an enormous tide of newcomers and New Yorkers was sweeping over the Harlem River to fill up what eventually became one of the greatest and most diversified bodies of middle-class dwellings ever built: they appeared in every possible form, from old detached houses that survived from the earlier agrarian years to row houses, walk-up apartments, and elevator apartments ranging from seemingly endless blocks of modest six-story buildings to skyscraper towers. When the Westchester railroad inaugurated service in the auspicious year of 1912, the future seemed full of rich promise, and everything was done to guarantee the realization thereof. Within a generation, however, disaster struck, and the company became the first of the New York family to suffer total abandonment (see chap. 5). In the first full year of operations the Westchester carried nearly 3,000,000 passengers, a number that rose to a little more than 14,000,000 in the peak year of 1928, but this was far below the capacity of a multiple-unit service conducted on a four-track main line.[29]

What prompted the New Haven management to pour money to the sum of $50,000,000 into this precarious enterprise, which was a direct competitor over every foot of its main stem? The decision rested in part on a sound assessment of the larger road's traffic and revenues, as they existed at the turn of the century and in their potentialities for the future. The New Haven enjoyed a density of both freight and passenger traffic unique among trunk-line carriers, and the freight tonnage expanded 77 percent and the passenger volume 105 percent during the first two decades of the century. Moreover, the railroad carried on its main line a balanced movement of freight that guaranteed a high revenue density in either direction. Bulk commodities and heavy shipments—coal, grain, fibers, perishables, building materials, and steel components—were dispatched eastward through the Port of New York to the manufacturing centers of lower New England, while high-tariff merchandise freight—hand and machine tools, electric equipment, clocks, watches, precision instruments, shoes, and shoe machinery—traveled westward. By the time the electrification program was complete, the New Haven was operating more than two hundred passenger trains per day and possibly as many freight movements over the main line east of New Rochelle. Commutation traffic within New York state was beginning to look like a nuisance, whereas the prospects for through freight and passenger traffic were flooded with the sunshine of steadily rising revenues. It seemed reasonable around 1905 to suppose that if the company invested heavily in an alternative main line reserved for local service, both suburban and through traffic would earn their appropriate returns. As we shall see in later chapters, this supposition proved to be disastrously without foundation. Some of the difficulties were unforeseeable; but the New Haven's officers were also prone to buying up marginal competitors in the expectation that the additional traffic would swell the income account, and in the case of the Westchester, they built one. The full exploitation of the creative electrical technology we have reviewed in this chapter was frustrated by questionable managerial decisions as well as by economic developments on a national scale.

3

The New Grand Central Terminal

Preliminary Plans and Constructions

The decision to introduce electrical operation into Grand Central Station was marked, as we saw in the first chapter of this volume, by a certain ambiguity, since the demands of an ever mounting high-density passenger traffic were powerfully reinforced by legislative acts. No such extraneous and, to the railroad's officers, undesirable influences, however, urged the directors to build an entirely new terminal in midtown Manhattan on a scale and in a form that give it a unique status to this day. It was clear scarcely after the turn of the century that no amount of enlarging, rearranging, and embellishing of Grand Central Station would offer any more than a brief palliative for meeting overwhelming needs. If the task of accommodating Grand Central's traffic was to be undertaken at all, it seemed inescapable that the owners would have to begin all over again. The chief proponent of this unsettling doctrine was William Wilgus, who must have been remarkably eloquent in persuading his employers to spend vast sums on monumental enterprises. But much of his persuasiveness lay in the unvarnished facts—rapidly climbing traffic volume as challenge and the financial resources to do the job right as potential response. The number of passengers using the station increased steeply and at an accelerating rate during the first twenty years of the century: the traffic grew by somewhat less than half in the first decade, but it nearly doubled in the second, so that by 1920 the total had expanded by more than two and two-thirds times. The great majority of these passengers fell into the local and commutation categories, but what taxed to the utmost the capacity of the coach yard as well as the station was the railroad's heavy and equally fast-growing sleeping and parlor car traffic. Before the end of the century's first decade the New York Central and Hudson River was operating 77 Pullman-car runs per day in each direction, requiring a minimum of about 160 cars to protect these numerous schedules. To add still further to the tight squeeze in the terminal complex, the New Haven offered 19 daily sleeping and parlor car runs, which called for a total of 192 cars on an average day.[1] And to make everything as difficult as possible for travelers and operating personnel, the New York Central handled nearly 50 percent of all mail received at and dispatched from New York City. Keeping pace with this mounting tide compelled the railroad to double the total number of scheduled and extra trains, from 330 per weekday in 1900 to 680 in 1920.[2] Even a conservative projection of future traffic indicated that the Grand Central of 1901 could not possibly cope with the crowds and the trains necessary to carry them.

Moreover, the intensive commercial building in midtown Manhattan, the diversifying and mounting pressures on land use, and the attendant rise in prices and property taxes, made it equally clear, at least to the farsighted, that some kind of double-level arrangement was a matter of financial, operating, and urbanistic necessity.

The resources of the New York Central and Hudson River Railroad and its many affiliates to the east and west did not quite match those of the Pennsylvania, nor were they ever to reach that level, but they were not far behind. Like the Philadelphians who ruled the Pennsylvania, the Vanderbilts in New York had early recognized the importance of gaining control of connecting lines extending north, east, and west of the Central's major terminals. At the turn of the century the parent company directly operated nearly 3,800 miles of line, of which somewhat less than half were made up of leased properties.[3] It was the control through stock ownership of an immense tributary empire to the west, however, that guaranteed the prosperity and the economic importance of the New York Central. In the case of the Pennsylvania and the Erie, the steady enlargement of control over western roads had begun in the decade of the 1860s, and Cornelius Vanderbilt needed no very remarkable powers of business acumen to recognize that he had to do likewise. He had scarcely consummated the merger of the New York Central and the Hudson River railroads in 1869 when he began his western campaign. During the thirty years from that date to the end of the century, he and his successors secured control through the acquisition of stock of a rail domain that rivaled the Pennsylvania's and far outdistanced that of the Erie. By 1900 the Central had extended its sphere of influence by means of western affiliates to Cleveland, Detroit, Chicago, Saint Louis, Cincinnati, and Pittsburgh. Another thirty years were to pass before these properties were merged into a unified system, but meanwhile the interline traffic to and from the eastern seaboard flowed through the Central's gateways, and their dividends flowed into the treasury to bring a nonoperating income of around $5,000,000 per annum in the early years of the century.[4]

The Central itself, its mileage little more than half that of its western fiefs together, transported nearly 37,600,000 tons of freight in 1900, and a little more than 47,000,000 tons in 1910, for a gain of over 25 percent. Passenger traffic, as we have already noted, rose at an astonishing rate: the total increase of nearly 74 percent in the first decade, close to 28,000,000 passengers in 1900 to more than 48,000,000 in 1910, was wholly unforeseen. To move this material and human cargo required more than 1,300 locomotives, nearly 1,500 passenger-train cars, and over 58,000 freight cars. The extent of the company's marine operations in New York Harbor may be gauged from the fact that the movement of tonnage and passengers over the water required 186 pieces of floating equipment.[5] The vast complex of financial, administrative, clerical, and operating activities that characterized the daily conduct of the New York Central and its leased properties brought so much money to the bank that the officers were easily persuaded to entertain the grandest of monumental schemes. For the year ended 30 June 1900 the company's total revenues reached a level close to $55,000,000, of which 34 percent was derived from the operation of passenger trains. With expenses little more than $34,000,000 and a nonoperating income of nearly $5,000,000, the road ended the fiscal year with a disposable gross income equal to almost half the total revenues. After the payment of interest charges, rentals, taxes, and a dividend of 4.75 percent, a sum of $3,000,000 was left to be transferred to the profit account. Three years later all these figures rose by gratifying amounts, but it must be admitted that thereafter the operating expenses showed a disturbing tendency from time to time to rise more rapidly than revenues. For the fiscal year ended 30 June 1903 gross revenues climbed to well over $77,000,000, a level 42 percent above the figure for 1900, and the proportion of revenues derived from passenger trains rose to 36 percent of the total. A nonoperating income of $5,250,000 left the company with a gross income of nearly $29,500,000, more than enough to keep the holders of stocks and bonds happy and to pay the charges on the capital investment that Wilgus's new Grand Central Terminal might require.[6]

Traffic mounting year by year at an ever accelerating rate, the cheerful sound of coin flowing into the till, imperial schemes for creating a new gateway into New York and out to the nation, bold plans for electrical operations, the engineering talents to carry out this multitude of designs—all these called for a grand gesture which would at once express the heart of the railroad enterprise, astound the multitudes with a great civic monument, and bring still more money into the passenger accounts. The choice of how best to realize these various aims fell initially to the New York Central's waggish, free-spending, and exceedingly imaginative general passenger agent, George Henry Daniels, who proposed in the early weeks of 1902 that the road establish an all-Pullman luxury flyer on the New York–Chicago run in cooperation with the Lake Shore and Michigan Southern Railroad. In a stroke of genius at the highest reaches of public-relations esprit, Daniels proposed that the train be called the Twentieth Century Limited, and its inaugural runs, east and west, came on 15–16 June 1902. The opening schedule fixed the time at 20 hours for the 964 miles that then separated Grand Central in New York from La Salle Street Station in Chicago, requiring an unprecedented average speed of 48.2 miles per hour. The first train left New York with four Pullman cars and picked up a dining car at Albany, the five wood-sheathed cars comfortably handled by Atlantic-type (4-4-2) locomotives. Well-built track on a water-level route, first-class motive power, and skilled engine-men with unlimited nerve made the Century a model of punctuality and comfort, but it was reserved to the Lake Shore to demonstrate the possibilities of high-speed running in the new style. On one occasion within the first month of its operation, 12 July 1902, the westbound train (Number 25) left Brocton, New York, 2 hours, 28 minutes late and arrived in Chicago only 28 minutes behind schedule. Reducing the normal running time by two hours meant that the 481-mile distance had to be covered in a few minutes more than 8 hours, for an average speed of 60 miles per hour. Repeated performances of this kind emboldened the officers of the two railroads to cut the overall schedule between the terminal cities to 18 hours, which went into effect on 18 June 1905. Five days before that date the Lake Shore had established the speed mania as a way of life when it operated a special train on a test run between Chicago and Buffalo in 7 hours, 27 minutes to post an overall average speed of 70.5 miles per hour.[7] But the shorter schedule proved unwise: the difficulty of maintaining track to appropriate standards, especially in the winter, compelled the two railroads to return to the old schedule on 24 November 1912. The 20-hour run of both the Century and the Broadway was retained for nearly twenty years, until April, 1932, when both trains were returned to the fast time of 18 hours.

George Daniels's love for fast, expensive trains as the true expression of the age was matched by his unmitigated scorn for the newly emerging automobile, which struck him as an abomination in the sight of the Lord, just as the locomotives on Manhattan streets had seemed to the pious of seventy years past. The Bible-quoting Daniels had no difficulty in finding sacred texts to support his view, and in a talk before the meeting of the General Passenger Agents Association in 1903 he expounded the correct doctrine. In the course of this inspirational address he quoted an obscure passage from the prophet Nahum, whose imagery is one of the more confused and incoherent varieties in the prophetic tradition. "The chariots shall rage in the streets; they shall jostle one against another in the broad ways; they shall seem like torches; they shall run like the lightnings." Biblical scholars may have been puzzled by passages such as this, but George Daniels readily grasped the inner meaning, according to the editor of the *Railroad Gazette*.

> Brother Daniels held himself firmly in check and did not use the prophet's imagery to advertise the Empire State Express when he dispensed with the gospel in his Murray Hill address to the General Passenger Agents' Association. . . . Mr. Daniels says that the prophet evidently referred to automobiles. . . . Indeed, this

inspiring Scripture arouses a hope that the devilish chariots, which race up and down Fifth Avenue, rivaling the Twentieth Century Limited in speed, will yet jostle each other off the earth and give the meek pedestrian a chance to live.[8]

Daniels, of course, was a professional attention-getter, and his citations of Scripture were probably not intended to be taken seriously. Yet the lofty plans that characterized this age of rugged individualism combined with newborn Progressivism and dreams of the City Beautiful often came clothed in a kind of religious fervor. The strictly financial concerns of a hard-boiled capitalism underlay the conduct of the New York Central's affairs, but its officers, like those of the Pennsylvania, were determined to give New York the best in station grandeur. What finally took shape was the only work of American building art that could rival the Pennsylvania's achievement ten blocks to the south. The process of drawing up preliminary plans for the new Grand Central Terminal must have been as confusing to the participants and other interested contemporaries as it remains to the historian who tries to discern some order in the bewildering succession of designs. The planning of all great public works is usually a long, tedious, and frustrating process, but Grand Central may very well have outdone all the rest in this respect. For nearly ten years proposals were put forth, drawn up in varying detail, revised, rejected, and replaced by still others, while architects were engaged, given conflicting instructions, and suddenly compelled to associate with other architects who had not previously been parties to the agreement. The first general plans were worked out in some detail in the century year, but the working drawings for the finished structure were not finally completed until 1909. It was not always a model of professional ethics, and the inability of the company's officers to make up their minds undoubtedly contributed to the long construction period, more than two years longer than the time required to complete the Pennsylvania's New York extension.

As we noted in the first chapter of this volume, the original idea for a double-level, electrically operated terminal emerged from the mind of William J. Wilgus as early as 1899. It was enlarged, spelled out at least in general terms, adopted by the directors of the New York Central and Hudson River Railroad during the following year, and first publicly reported in the issue of *Railway Age* for 11 January 1901. There were four primary features that distinguished it from any of its predecessors: suburban trains were to be accommodated in a subgrade terminal; suburban service at the start was to be electrified; trains were to be turned on an underground loop track; and there was to be a direct connection with the future I. R. T. subway line under Fourth Avenue and 42d Street. This plan was much enlarged and revised in 1901, and a public account was provided by the railroad press in January, 1902 (described in detail in chap. 1). The underground suburban trackage and the loop were retained, and the four-track tunnel approach was to be widened to eight tracks at the line of 56th Street. About six months after this plan was announced, various officials of the New York Central, their names never made public to the best of my knowledge, proposed an inexpensive alternative that would have materially increased the frustrations of already harried commuters and would have done nothing to improve the existing Grand Central Station. The chief element in this indefensible scheme was a new terminal to be constructed at Mott Haven and used by all the suburban trains of the New Haven Railroad as well as those of the Central's Hudson, Putnam, and Harlem divisions. A system of loop tracks in the station would allow the numerous trains to turn and head out over their respective routes as soon as they had loaded or discharged passengers. The commuters destined for or coming from Manhattan were exptected to transfer to or from the existing elevated line or the proposed subway. It was estimated that 80 percent of the traffic at Grand Central Station would be transferred to the new Mott Haven facility and thus eliminate the "nuisance" of the smoke-filled tunnel. Another argument in favor of the plan—indeed, the only thing that can be said for it—was that it would have ended the isolation of the Putnam Division, but the physical connection between the main line and the seemingly unwanted little appendage was never effected.

Fortunately the Mott Haven scheme quickly died, and it was the Wilgus plan which, in one form or another, persisted through the vicissitudes of the succeeding two years. The plan that was then jointly formulated by the New York Central and the New Haven, however, embodied few novelties, since it appeared to be a rather cautious compromise between the Wilgus proposal for depressed trackage and the retention of as many of the existing facilities as could usefully be preserved. The chief innovation, and the one that looked toward a new urban world, was the proposal to replace the 1901 head house with a skyscraper 16 to 20 stories high which was to contain a hotel, a department store, and a theater, as well as the usual terminal facilities (the store and the theater were regarded as tentative). The main features relating to the operation of trains were a six-track approach extending from 56th Street to the terminal throat at 49th, the depression of all station tracks to a level 10 feet, 6 inches below street grade, the expansion of the station yard to 20 tracks, with the concomitant enlargement of the train shed, and the concentration of vehicular traffic at 45th Street (the north end of the station building) rather than at overloaded 42d Street. A number of internal changes were to be included in the general expansion. Changes in the local street pattern included the elevation of 46th, 47th, and 48th streets on bridges spanning the station tracks and—most valuable of all from the standpoint of local traffic circulation—the continuation of Park Avenue past or around the terminal area by means of an elevated driveway. In addition to the 20 tracks within the station proper, the plan called for 16 storage tracks on the west side of the station yard and 23 on the east side, for a total of 59 tracks in an unbroken single-level file. The joint plan was submitted to the municipal authorities in the late fall of 1902 and was unanimously approved by the Board of Estimate and Apportionment on 22 December of that year. The only controversy that arose between the railroad and the municipality was the question of compensation to the city for the private use and the blocking of various streets (the only direct or physical use of street areas appears to have been the proposal to erect overhead signals on viaducts). The company successfully argued that it should pay less for street usage than the Pennsylvania on the somewhat ironic ground that the latter gained a new terminal for its own operations, whereas the two Grand Central companies were spending great sums of money entirely for the convenience of the public, which would be realized chiefly through partial electrification.[9]

This program had a certain makeshift quality about it, and its cost to the proper functioning and development of the city was so great that one must question why the Board of Estimate approved it. The removal of additional areas up to eleven blocks of prime midtown land from diversified urban uses represented a sacrifice that no increase in municipal revenues derived from fees and taxes could balance.[10] Wilgus must have been the first to recognize the unsatisfactory features, and in the early months of 1903 he made the radical decision to remove and rebuild the entire terminal complex below 56th Street, except for the four tracks of the original tunnel approach. What he proposed was a new head house, a double-level track-platform area embracing 57 tracks, a 10-track inner approach, air-rights construction over the entire area outside the station building and its appurtenant structures, and electrical operation. He submitted the plan to the New York Central's president, William H. Newman, in March, 1903, with an estimated cost of $43,000,000, an investment which he persuaded Newman to accept by arguing that the air-rights rentals would yield a return of 3 percent, or $1,290,000, per annum.[11] Municipal approval for these enormous revisions and their translation into physical reality came in stages over the next few months. A competition for the architectural design of the new terminal building had been announced on 15 January 1903, the designs to be submitted by 1 March of that year, although the city's final approval was yet to be secured. The authorities at City Hall moved with surprising dispatch: on 19 May 1903 they granted subsurface rights to the New York Central and Hudson River Railroad over most of the area bounded by Madison and Lexington avenues between 42d and 47th streets;

on 3 June the railroad submitted the final plan to the Board of Estimate and Apportionment and secured unanimous approval on the 19th. The physical initiation of construction came on 18 July, when company forces began the rearrangement of tracks at 47th Street, but the demolition of existing buildings on the site had begun the previous month. In August the contract for the excavation of the terminal area and the laying down of new tracks was awarded to the O'Rourke Engineering and Construction Company of New York. The rearrangement of trackage was a temporary expedient that allowed the railroad to offer the sorely tried passenger a little shelter by converting the original Grand Central Palace on Lexington Avenue into an interim station. By the end of the year the company had acquired all the land it did not already own between 42d and 50th streets.

Working plans, however, were still in the process of chaotic preparation, and final municipal approval of the whole program was contingent at least on their completion to the point where precise areas of land coverage could be determined. Another year was to pass before the plans were submitted to the appropriate bureaus and the official public announcement could be made. Both occurred on 23 December 1904, when Ira A. Place, the company's general counsel, placed the necessary documents before the Board of Estimate. The proclamation of the event, very likely accompanied by a claim of divine blessing, fell to George Daniels, who saw the possibilities for publicity on an Olympian scale. The announced program was clearly staggering—the demolition of all existing railroad structures and most of the remaining buildings distributed over the 19-block area extending from 42d to 57th Street in the Madison-Lexington corridor; the construction of a head house, baggage facilities, and a post office within a blunt L-shaped area defined by Vanderbilt Avenue, 42d Street, Depew Place, 43d Street, Lexington Avenue, and 45th Street; the excavation for and the laying out of two track levels, the total of 43 tracks divided between an upper or through-train level and a much smaller lower or suburban level.[12] The first reactions of the railroad and architectural press came in the joyful week between Christmas and New Year's Day. The editor of the *Street Railway Journal* stated the fundamental fact. "The whole station is planned on a scale so elaborate and generous as regards facilities as to eclipse anything heretofore planned for terminal facilities in any other cities." His counterpart on the staff of *American Architect and Building News* readily saw the architectural implications. "This structure is so very un-American, with its big arches, its pylons and blank well spaces, so very European . . . , and so much like a Beaux-Arts *projet* that it has rather caught the popular fancy."[13] The design of 1904, however, was later much altered and much improved in its engineering and operating character.

But other events were simultaneously taking place on the outer reaches of the New York Central's metropolitan trackage, events that briefly interrupt the early scenes of the main drama. While the railroad company and the architects were making, remaking, and revising plans for the new terminal, the Central undertook two smaller projects involving relocations and other improvements of lines in The Bronx, which may be regarded as that part of the Grand Central program having to do with the requirement to eliminate all grade crossings within the city limits. The first, carried out in 1903–5 and known as the Marble Hill Cut-off, followed the straightening of the Harlem River and Spuyten Duyvil Creek that provided a new channel for the waterways across the base of the Kingsbridge oxbow in the Harlem. Since the railroad line lay along the old course of the stream, the straightening made it possible to establish a new four-track alignment along the north bank of the river free of the sharp curves in the former horseshoe segment. The construction involved less than a mile of track, but the right of way had to be carved and tunneled through a complex mass of dense rock consisting of Manhattan schist, Inwood limestone, the beds of which are here tilted into a vertical position, and Fordham gneiss (the so-called limestone is actually a marble, as the designation Marble Hill more accurately indicates). The cut-off included a 648-foot concrete-lined tunnel through the spur of gneiss at old Spuyten Duyvil Road, which was thought to be the first single-bore tunnel designed for a four-track line. The accommodation of this broad right of way required a clear interior width of 51 feet, a little below the later standard clearance of 56 feet for a four-track line. The tunnel was later replaced by an open cut ("daylighted" in the railroad argot), which is still a conspicuous engineering-geological feature along the upper Harlem, at the point where it curves into Spuyten Duyvil Creek. The cut-off reduced the length of line by only three-quarters of a mile, but it eliminated 97 degrees of curvature and eight grade crossings. The second of these ancillary projects was the complete reconstruction of the New York and Harlem Railroad's Port Morris Branch, a little one-and-a-quarter-mile spur extending from Melrose on the Harlem Division to Port Morris. In 1904–5 the single-track line was expanded to two tracks and depressed below grade level by means of a succession of cuts and a 600-foot tunnel, again carved and blasted through the dense metamorphic rock of the Manhattan Prong.[14]

About a year after the completion of the two projects in The Bronx the officers of the New York Central proposed the construction of a crosstown connecting line which seems never to have passed beyond the stage of a preliminary report, although it would have brought a permanent and valuable improvement to the circulation system of Manhattan. On 15 November 1906 the railroad company's chief engineer,

George S. Rice, submitted a report to the Board of Rapid Transit Commissioners recommending the construction of a double-track subway under 53d Street to connect the West Side freight line (the original line of the Hudson River Railroad) at Twelfth Avenue with the Grand Central approach under Park Avenue. The plan called for the operation of passenger trains over the West Side line above 53d Street and in the crosstown subway directly to and from the terminal. Two benefits were expected to flow from this admittedly very expensive program. The first would have been to expedite the flow of the Central's suburban traffic by placing a portion of it on the new route, and the second, long-term consequence would have been the provision of suburban service and the resulting improvements in public transit and land use on the West Side. The absence of such service is a puzzling feature of transit planning in New York. It was probably thought that the old Ninth Avenue elevated and the Eighth Avenue subway that replaced it took care of the area's needs, but in truth they did not. The lack of public transportation through the western corridor on a north-south axis has been one factor in the continuing failure to develop the West Side below 72d Street and west of Eighth Avenue into the intensive and diversified land-use patterns elsewhere on the island. The one question that might be raised about the Rice plan has to do with the location of a major railroad junction at the throat of a terminal with two track levels. The details were never spelled out, to my knowledge, but it suggests an interlocking towerman's nightmare.

The railroad's officers and engineers could once again give their undivided attention to the heart of their New York program. One might suppose that the appointment of architects and the preparation of working drawings would have clearly defined the boundary between preliminary and final planning, but nothing was further from the truth in the case of Grand Central. A bewildering succession of overlapping revisions increased confusion, which escalated into overt conflict, and a melancholy drama highly questionable in its ethical and legal character eventually brought the conflict into the courts. It was far from an edifying spectacle, but morality and good architecture finally triumphed. The process of design may be said to have begun with the announcement by the railroad's officers of a tightly closed competition to which only four architectural firms were invited to submit entries. The invitations, as we have seen, were sent to the architects on 15 January 1903, and the entries were required to be submitted by 1 March of that year. Two members of this select group were large offices of international prominence, D. H. Burnham and Company of Chicago, and McKim, Mead and White of New York; the third, Samuel Huckel, Jr., of Philadelphia, was fairly well known in the East and had previously served the railroad in the reconstruction of Grand Central at the turn of the century;

the fourth, Charles Reed and Allen Stem of Saint Paul, hardly enjoyed the same reputation, but they had been involved in close personal as well as professional relations with the railroad company in recent years. After being graduated from the Massachusetts Institute of Technology, Reed moved to Saint Paul, where he opened an office with Allen Stem in 1884; his sister May became the wife of William Wilgus in 1892, a year before the latter entered the engineering department of the New York Central's northern affiliate, the Rome, Watertown and Ogdensburg Railroad. Associated with the Saint Paul firm from the early years of the Grand Central project was Alfred Fellheimer, who was to establish himself in a later partnership with Stewart Wagner as the leading architect of railroad stations in the last years of large-scale rail construction. Reed and Stem did not enjoy their association with the New York Central simply because Wilgus was a member of the family, but there can be no question that the close personal tie guaranteed his familiarity with their work, which was good enough to command his respect. They were engaged by the railroad company in 1901 to design way stations, and three were completed by 1903, among which the Union Station at Troy was the largest and most impressive.

Among the designs submitted for the Grand Central competition the great bravura piece, clearly outshining all the rest for sheer audacity, came from the office of McKim, Mead and White, where the specific authorship fell to Stanford White (figs. 12, 13). The project was the one work of this magisterial firm that might justly be described as sensational in the mode of world's fairs as well as the style of first-class urban architecture. The 14-story head house was to constitute the base for a 60-story tower (the height calculated from grade level) which would have been 5 stories and at least 100 feet taller than the future Woolworth Building (1911–13) and by far the tallest building in the world at the time. The top of this skyscraper was to be marked as a kind of gigantic beacon by means of a 300-foot jet of steam illuminated at night in a rather lurid fashion by red floodlights. The particular form of the tower was derived, like White's Madison Square Garden of 1890, from the Giralda Tower of Seville Cathedral.[15] Less sensational but standing on the same level as civic art was the plan to design the head house so that Park Avenue and the transverse streets could be continued along their respective lines without break by allowing them to penetrate the building mass. It was a sophisticated plan throughout, like all the highly urbanistic commercial and public work to emerge from the McKim office, and it is a major loss to the building arts that the talented and imaginative White never enjoyed an opportunity to put his hand to a skyscraper project.

It was perhaps a foregone conclusion that the railroad company would adopt the proposal of Reed and Stem, since Wilgus himself had contributed certain essential

Fig. 12. Grand Central Terminal. The competition entry submitted by McKim, Mead and White, 1903. The original drawing, showing the main elevation on 42d Street.

Fig. 13. Grand Central Terminal. The competition entry submitted by McKim, Mead and White. A drawing showing the rear elevation of the station building and the track area.

12

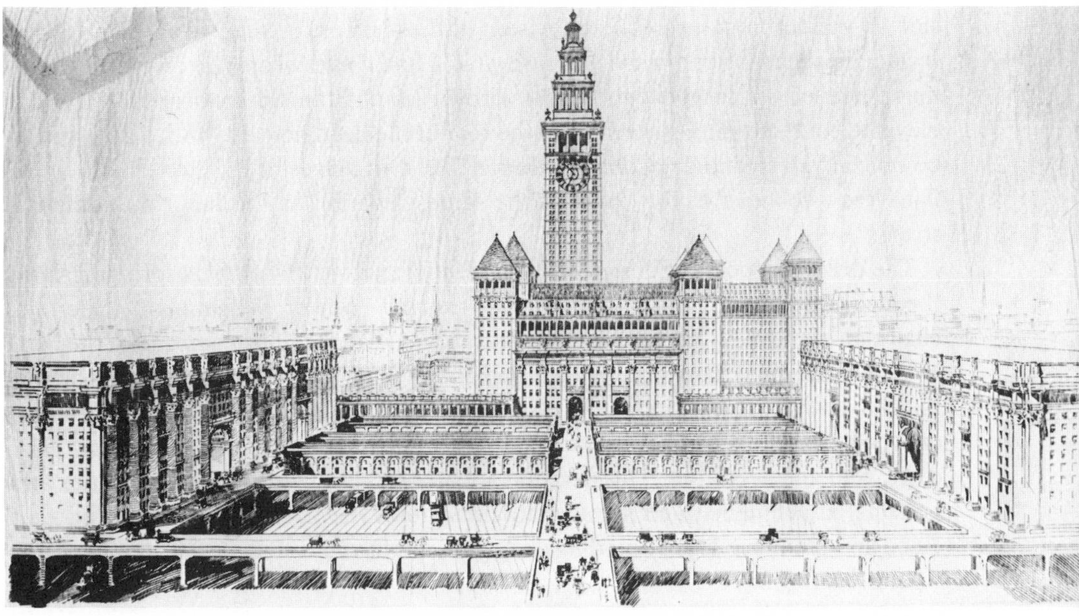

13

ideas to the competition entry. The officers of the railroad company signed a contract with the architects in mid-spring, 1903, immediately submitted a request to the municipality for authority to undertake construction according to the accepted plans, and were granted the construction permit by the Board of Estimate and Apportionment on 19 June 1903. The revisions made during the following year had to be resubmitted for approval, and a second authorization was granted on 23 December 1904. Both the original plan and the revision were resubmitted to the Board of Estimate as the joint work of William Wilgus and the architects, and it included not only the station building with the usual mail and express terminals, but also office buildings, a 22-story hotel above the rear of the head house, flanking hotels, a post office, and possibly an opera house. The distinguishing features were the presence of internal ramps rather than stairways and the continuation of Park Avenue by means of its division into two roadways flanking the main station group. Demolition under the permit of 19 June 1903 began on very nearly the same date, but all the structures on the site were not finally removed until July, 1910. Long before that date, however, the architectural planning of Grand Central Terminal passed into a state of thoroughgoing confusion, which soon gave way to acrimonious controversy and litigation. What was apparently the first proposal by Reed and Stem consisted essentially of a head house with a T-shaped plan, the stem facing 42d Street, the building extending over about one-third of the track-platform area, and the flanking buildings disposed along the corridor between the tracks and the west side of Vanderbilt Avenue. The revision of these plans, involving radical changes, included an extraordinary civic feature which, had it ever been built, would have let much needed space and light into midtown Manhattan. Reed proposed a great elevated court extending north from the rear of the head house to 48th Street and to be officially designated a Court of Honor. The two halves of Park Avenue were to flank the two sides of the court at the same elevation as the inner monumental space.[16]

The orderly process of design then suddenly gave way to conflicts springing from the high-handed acts of the Central's chief executive officer. William K. Vanderbilt, chairman of the New York Central Corporation, the controlling company of the New York Central and Hudson River Railroad and its numerous affiliates, decided before the end of 1903 that the design of Grand Central Terminal should be the product of a collaborative effort by the contracted architects and the prestigious New York firm of Warren and Wetmore. This decision apparently sprang from family loyalties and personal attachments, and it was made in spite of the fact that Wilgus's choice of Reed and Stem was legally binding and could not have been made without the prior approval of the New York Central board and its chairman. Whitney Warren was a cousin of William Vanderbilt, a close personal friend as well as a relative, and a highly educated man with whom the railroad executive shared a lively interest in the visual and building arts. The architect, who was born in New York in 1864 and held a diploma from the Ecole des Beaux-Arts in Paris, formed a partnership with Charles D. Wetmore in 1896. They quickly rose to the front rank for their designs of railroad stations and hotels, of which two were erected over the air-rights spaces above Grand Central Terminal.[17] Warren was a Beaux-Arts sophisticate who undoubtedly brought the highest levels of taste, learning, and talent to his profession, but the intrusion of his office into the design of the terminal was an act of questionable ethical character and doubtful legal validity which brought a great deal of trouble and eventually a costly lawsuit to all concerned. William Vanderbilt asked Reed and Stem to form a temporary partnership with the New York firm; the Saint Paul architects understandably objected, but they were no match for the wealthy and powerful chairman of the board, who got his way until the courts finally redressed the balance. The two offices formed the new partnership on 8 February 1904 under the title of the Associated Architects of Grand Central Terminal. Warren immediately set out to undo much of Reed and Stem's work by eliminating all the features that gave it a unique distinction: he moved the Court of Honor, placed an immovable barrier before the orderly circulation of traffic in the vicinity of the terminal by dropping the elevated circuit of Park Avenue, replaced the ramps by stairways, and removed the 22-story hotel, the presence of which offended Vanderbilt's sense of monumental grandeur. The high and nervous silhouette of the Reed and Stem design for the head house was eliminated in favor of a low enclosure in which the lofty arched openings of the main street elevations and the vaults rising above the roof form the dominant motifs (fig. 14).

All the parties concerned with the design of the terminal save Reed and Stem were presumably satisfied with the alterations of 1904, and the plans of Warren and Wetmore were worked out in detail during the next four years. This process would probably have been carried out readily enough if it had not been for the sudden resignation of William Wilgus in 1907, following still another dispute with the board, and his replacement by George W. Kittredge as chief engineer of the terminal project and George A. Harwood as chief engineer of the electrical installation. This change, however, proved to be only a temporary obstacle. The beginning of the undoing of Vanderbilt's autocratic plans came from an unexpected quarter, but injustice, unfortunately, continued to triumph for several more years. According to the agreement covering the New Haven's trackage rights, the officers of the New

Fig. 14. Grand Central Terminal. The original design for the station building by Reed and Stem, and Warren and Wetmore, 1904.

Fig. 15. Grand Central Terminal. The original design sketch by Whitney Warren, 1910, showing the main elevation of the station building as constructed.

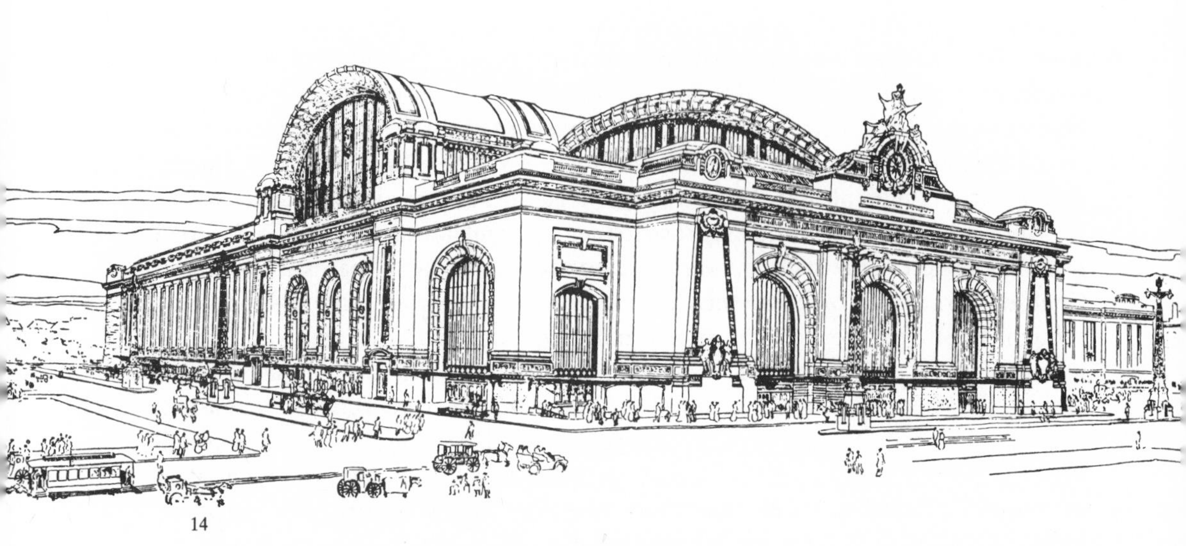

14

15

England railroad had to be consulted on all plans for altering the New York station. What was expected to be a routine consultation in 1909 proved to be a shock to the Central's officers: the New Haven refused to accept the changes introduced by Warren and Wetmore and demanded that those of Reed and Stem be reinstated as the basis of construction. The office staffs of both architectural firms were thus compelled to return to the drawing boards, but on this occasion a genuine union of talents seems to have developed, and by 1910 the plans that were to be realized in the finished work had taken shape, as Whitney Warren's hurried little sketch suggests (fig. 15). While all this making and unmaking of plans was going on, engineering designs remained largely fixed, so that demolition proceeded steadily up to 1908, when the train shed of 1871 and much of the reconstructed head house fell before the wreckers. But the misfortunes of the honest men from Saint Paul had only begun, in this astonishingly accurate preview of Fitzgerald's *The Great Gatsby*, and the easterners were to exhibit still greater depths of depravity. Charles Reed died suddenly on 12 November 1911, and on the occasion of his funeral at Scarsdale on 15 November Wetmore talked to William H. Newman, the former president of the New York Central, on how the designing program was to be continued. Who took the more cynical view cannot now be determined, but whatever the case, Wetmore wrote the officers of the railroad on the following day, without consulting Allen Stem, that since the previous contract was now terminated, the company would be well advised to draw up a new instrument appointing Warren and Wetmore as the sole architects of Grand Central Terminal. The pliable directors willingly complied, ordered their attorneys to draft the suggested document, and the parties thereto quietly signed it on 19 December 1911, again without consulting Stem. Construction on the building group had started early in the previous year, and when the completed work was opened to the public on 2 February 1913, Warren and Wetmore were given sole architectural credit for the achievement.

That was enough for Stem in this shabby melodrama. In the following year he brought suit against his tormentors, and while the mills of the courts ground slowly, justice was eventually done. The specific injury for which Stem sought redress was the failure of the railroad company and its architect to pay the share due the office of Reed and Stem from the balance of the fee deposited to the account of the Associated Architects on 8 July 1913 (the unpaid balance was $203,233.24). The suit was heard in the New York Supreme Court for New York City; on 17 July 1916 Judge Francis B. Delahanty decided in favor of the plaintiff and ordered the payment to Stem and to Reed's estate of their share of the original fee plus 2 percent interest accrued over the years 1913–16. The total came to about $219,000, or more than

$3,000,000 translated from the 1916 to the 1980 building-cost level. Judge Delahanty not only recognized the clear violation of the law, but brought out many useful facts through court testimony on the range of the several architects' responsibilities. In addition to the terminal itself, the Associated Architects were commissioned to design a great number of structures ranging from temporary facilities for the use of passengers during the construction process to large office and hotel buildings.

> The organization which the Associated Architects had built up [the judge concluded in his summary] was a partnership asset of which they would deprive the plaintiff and the Reed estate if they were not compelled to account for the profits which they had been able to make through its use. . . . The conclusion is irresistible that the cancellation of the old contract and the making of the new were brought about by the actions and attitude of Warren and Wetmore and . . . they violated their legal obligation as surviving partners and should be required to account accordingly.[18]

The ruling was appealed; the suit was heard again in the Appellate Division of the New York Supreme Court in January, 1919, and the presiding judge, John Proctor Clarke, upheld the Delahanty decision. He awarded Allen Stem and the Reed estate "their share" (presumably half) of the architects' fee, fixed at 3 percent of the construction cost of the Grand Central Terminal only, omitting the cost of the Biltmore Hotel from his calculations on the ground that the original architects were not involved in the supervision of construction (they appear to have acted as consultants rather than collaborators). The railroad company, possessing unlimited legal and financial resources, appealed the decision once more. The third round went to the New York Court of Appeals, Judge John W. Hogan presiding, in January, 1920. The judge ruled in favor of the plaintiffs and handed down what proved to be the final decision on 22 January 1922: he ordered payment to Stem and William J. Reed as executor of the Charles Reed estate a fee equal to 2 percent of the cost of the Grand Central Terminal building plus 1.5 percent of the cost of the Biltmore, for a final settlement of very nearly $500,000. Reed had been dead more than ten years, the terminal was approaching its ninth birthday, and Stem had long ago returned to Saint Paul, where he died in 1931. Warren and Wetmore prospered, for the good reason that they were talented architects with enviable connections; Warren died in New York on 24 January 1943 and Wetmore on 9 May 1941. It is a sorry record with which they tarnished the image of Grand Central, but their handiwork stands in the front rank of world architecture.

Architectural and Engineering Design

Throughout these years of planning, revising, double-dealing, and suing, the sober business of preparing detailed architectural and engineering drawings, with their associated specifications, was going steadily forward, in spite of the repeated changes introduced over the years of 1903–10. Although the external form of the head house, vehicular drives, and courts was to be drastically altered between the original and final concepts, the interior spaces and the track-platform system, the extent of which fixed the outer limits of the construction area, remained fairly constant after the preliminary consultations between Wilgus and the architects. Three distinguishing features of the functional planning of 1903–4 were immediately striking—the great size of the entire complex, a track area of unparalleled extent, and the double-level track layout. The spacious enclosures, the two levels, and a number of tracks more than double that planned for Pennsylvania Station (a total that was to be increased more than 50 percent in the final plan), all pointed to a work of such magnitude as to dwarf the largest American and European terminals in existence at the time. It is doubtful whether the size could ever have been justified on the basis of rail traffic alone, but we can readily discover why the company's engineers thought that it was. Foremost among the deciding factors, as we noticed at the beginning of this chapter, were the absolute volume of the traffic and the accelerating rate of its expansion. The number of passengers more than doubled in the twenty years from 1890 to 1910, then nearly doubled again in the succeeding decade. The problem of coping with this tide within the station enclosure and of handling the increasing number of trains on the terminal tracks strongly encouraged the company to plan on a generous scale; the determination to avoid once and forevermore the multiplying delays, confusions, expenses, mishaps, and exasperating frustrations of the existing station compelled them to think in grandiose terms. There was another factor the consequences of which were becoming apparent in terminal operations at the turn of the century. Grand Central had to be a stub-end facility, which offers maximum convenience to the passenger, but which is, in comparison with a through station like Pennsylvania, a nuisance to operate because empty- and light-engine movements must be made on the same station and approach tracks as those used by loaded trains. Most railroad officers, possessed of penny-pinching minds, would ordinarily have allowed operating personnel to limp along with whatever they had. Monumental grandeur, nevertheless, was congenial to the New York Central directorate, as the later stations at Buffalo, Cleveland, and Cincinnati indicate, and it is to their lasting credit that they were willing to pay for the best.

The truth of the matter is, however, that no one at the turn of the century appears to have conducted a systematic inquiry into the relation of terminal capacity and size to traffic volume. While it was recognized that through stations could be efficiently operated with fewer tracks than those required for the stub-end variety, reliable evidence as to precisely how many tracks were needed for a given number of trains did not exist. The major terminals completed over the thirty years prior to the opening of the Grand Central varied in the number of platform tracks from 8 to 67 and in traffic density, measured in number of trains per track per day, from 7.2 to 35.9. What was the optimum figure to minimize delays and expenses and to maximize the rates of entry and departure? Given the lessons derived from terminal operations in the early years of the century, it seems clear that the great extent of the Grand Central track area, either the original 43 tracks planned in 1903 or the 67 laid down in 1910–13, considerably exceeded the traffic requirements. The chief handicap in conducting operations at the terminal was its walled and tunneled four-track approach, which may have suggested to its engineering designers that its restricted capacity could be offset by expanding the terminal trackage. Whatever the case, the original plan was to settle on 22 tracks for the upper or through-train level, 9 for the lower or suburban, 2 tracks for a suburban loop, and a total of 12 for handling baggage, mail, and express. This total fell far short of the number of platform tracks eventually built, and the station, as a consequence, has been radically underused throughout its history.[19]

In the restricted plan of 1903 the entire terminal complex of structures and tracks covered an irregular T-shaped area comprising most of 19 blocks bounded at the extremes by 42d and 57th streets, and Madison and Lexington avenues. The head house itself, with its associated mail and express terminals, occupied the area defined by Vanderbilt Avenue, 42d Street, Depew Place, 43d Street, Lexington Avenue, and 45th Street. It was to be set back generously on both the facade along 42d Street and the long side elevation with a subsidiary entrance and exit along Vanderbilt Avenue. The main and west side elevations were marked by three immense arched openings that were the most prominent features of the buildings and were retained in the main elevation throughout the vicissitudes of succeeding years (figs. 14, 15). Both the main and side entrances opened into a lobby lying at street level and surrounded by ticket offices on the periphery of the space. Baggage-handling and checking facilities for incoming passengers were located on the east side of this lobby. Passengers were to proceed from the lobby to a gallery or mezzanine floor located on the periphery of the grand concourse, to which passengers descended by four broad stairways (Warren and Wetmore's improvement on the original circulatory system). The immense concourse was the climactic interior feature and was thought to be the largest interior space ever planned for a conventional building, as opposed to exhibition halls, train sheds, markets, and the like. The usual service facilities were disposed around the periphery of this space. The concourse and the two track levels were depressed below street grade at the successively lower elevations dictated by structural and clearance requirements. A number of special entrance and exit ways, in the form of stairways and passageways, were planned to connect through-train and suburban levels with Madison and Vanderbilt avenues and the future stations of the Lexington Avenue and Times Square subways. Additional baggage rooms were located on Depew Place, 45th Street, and Vanderbilt Avenue, with their special entrances and especially generous street frontages. Around the concourse and on the north side of the head house, space was provided for company offices. The whole complex was said to be planned for a possible doubling of capacity in the future with minimal revision of interior planning and exterior decor, but how this was to be accomplished was never specified.[20]

The editors of the *Railroad Gazette* praised the new plan, which they credited to Reed and Stem, associated with Warren and Wetmore, as vigorously as they had condemned its predecessors.

> In preparing the plans for the new station everything has been sacrificed to the comfort and convenience of the traveling public. The distinguishing features of the arrangement of the yards, platforms and head house may be summarized as follows: Ample facilities for getting to and away from the station. Cab stand situated in most convenient place for arriving passengers. Outgoing baggage room convenient to the ticket offices and incoming baggage room convenient to the exits. Separation of incoming and outgoing passengers, thus avoiding confusion. Ample waiting rooms and accessories and a grand concourse large enough to accommodate the largest holiday or excursion crowds. Separation of suburban and through passengers but with arrangements for easily getting from one part of the station to the other. Waiting vestibule for those desiring to meet incoming passengers. Ample baggage handling facilities.[21]

And the editors might have added, a station track layout and inner approach tracks which together formed a paragon of rational planning for the expeditious movement of trains.

The changes introduced with the genuinely collaborative plan of 1909–10 were primarily the replacement of the stairways by ramps carefully designed for a maximum slope of 10 percent, the elimination of the separate entrance lobby and the consequent relocation of the ticket offices to the concourse, a considerable increase

Fig. 16. Grand Central Terminal. Plan of the main or street level.

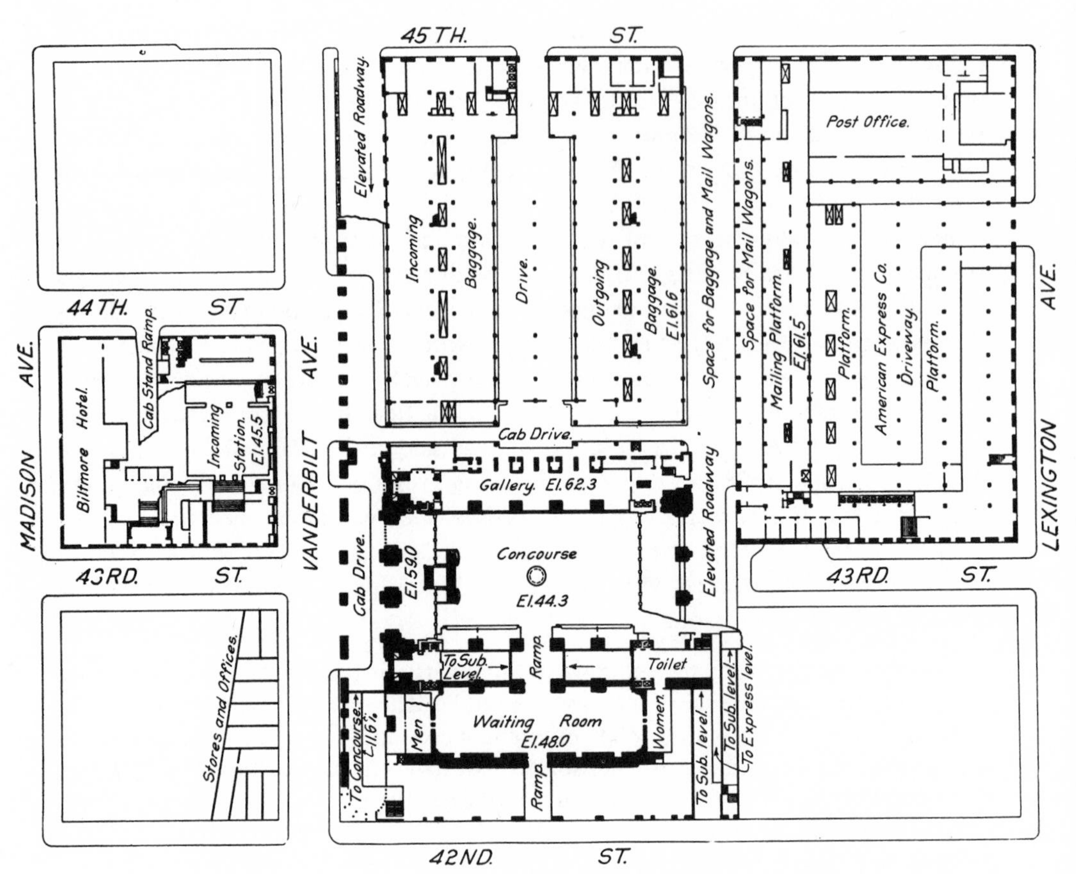

Fig. 17. Grand Central Terminal. Plan at the express (through-train) floor level.

Fig. 18. Grand Central Terminal. Plan at the suburban floor level.

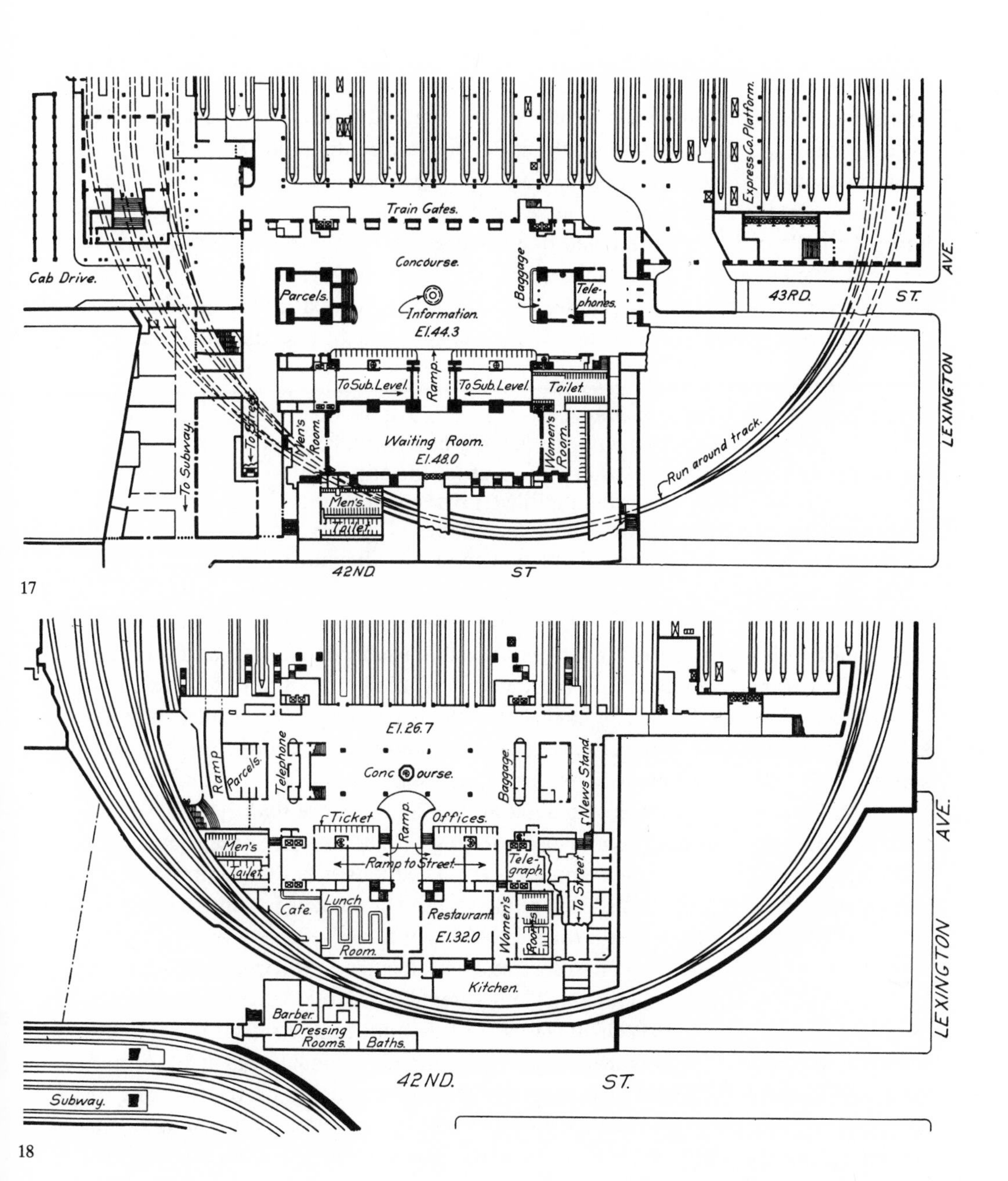

17

18

in the number of both through-train and suburban tracks, the first step toward future air-rights development in the form of an office building to rise 23 stories above the third-floor level, or 26 stories above the street, and the continuation of Park Avenue as an elevated drive divided on either side of the head house group (figs. 16–18, 22). The ramps and the depressed concourse were particularly important elements in an internal circulatory system designed to accommodate immense numbers of people (up to a maximum of half a million per day), and their value continued to be recognized by planners and architects more than fifty years after the terminal was completed. The urban planner Frank Williams expressed the essential point particularly well.

> The floor of the Grand Concourse was placed 16 feet below grade for three major reasons: to prevent friction with the activity at street level; to bring it on a level with the underground pedestrian concourse [to the east], and to serve the gravitational principle upon which the multilevel movement system is based. The idea was that people instinctively follow the course of gravity, so the most natural movement pattern is a system of one-way ramps flowing down from street level.[22]

Among the lesser changes were numerous revisions in the size, proportions, and distribution of interior spaces, the introduction of a suburban as well as a through-train waiting room, and an expansion in the capacity of the restaurant (the celebrated Grand Central Oyster Bar). The baggage rooms were located on the east and west sides of the head house at the street-grade level, and they extend the entire north-south length of the quadrangle. The out-to-out dimensions of the building are 301 feet × 722 feet, 6 inches, enclosing a net area of a little more than 200,000 square feet, including the central court and its driveways, but the total floor area devoted to station purposes is over a million square feet.[23] The number of through-train tracks serving platforms is 42, of which 32 are regularly used by passengers, and the number of suburban tracks on the lower level is 25, of which 12 are reserved for passengers. There is a multitude of storage and service tracks located in the trapezoidal spaces between the ladder tracks and the track limits along the Lexington Avenue wall (figs. 19–21). The four-track approach line in the Park Avenue tunnel widens to ten tracks between 56th and 57th streets, which spread out in the terminal throat at 52d Street, while the leads to the lower level begin their descent roughly on the line of 55th Street. The total track area, comprehended within the interlocking limits of the terminal proper, is a little more than three million square feet, or 71.6 acres, nearly three times the floor area of the station building. The out-to-out width of the track-platform system is 810 feet, again nearly three times the width of the head house (this is clearly shown by the transverse section in fig. 21).[24] This gigantic walled temenos, much of it in near-darkness but all of it in perfect working order, possesses an awesome, infernal character that stands in profound contrast to the high-style splendors and costly materials of the head house.

The supporting structure of all buildings, viaducts, and upper-level track floor is an intricate steel frame of columns, girders, beams, ribs, and trusses which comprises nearly all the forms of steel construction regularly used in the early years of the century. The external curtain walls of the building are finished in Stony Creek granite at the base and Bedford limestone above that level (figs. 22, 23). The interior spaces, though later disfigured by the obscenities of the billboard hucksters, stand clothed in a princely raiment of Bottocino marble and Caen limestone so warm and delicate in texture as to transcend the cold inertness of calcium carbonate. The long-delayed cleaning of 1977–78 made this texture visible once again, where it is not covered by signs. The ellipsoidal domes above the bays of the Oyster Bar are finished on the underside by Guastavino tile vaulting nicely accented by rows of little incandescent bulbs fixed to the boundary ribs. The sculpture that adorns the facade—Cornelius Vanderbilt facing into the traffic of the elevated Park Avenue, Mercury and assorted allegorical figures around the clock at the parapet—was for the most part the creation of the French sculptor Jules-Alexis Coutan. The majestic figure of the Commodore, however, had been moved from the old Hudson River Railroad freight station at Saint John's Park. The most impressive and most celebrated work of decorative art is the belt of zodiacal and equatorial constellations depicted in gold-leaf and electric illumination on the blue plaster ceiling of the concourse vault. The artist responsible for this unique piece of interior decor was Paul Helleu, who received the commission because he had once painted an acceptable portrait of Consuelo Vanderbilt, the daughter of Alva Smith and William Kissam Vanderbilt and later the Duchess of Marlborough. The problem of projecting a 360-degree zone of the celestial sphere on a cylindrical surface can theoretically be solved in projective geometry, but the distortions would be so extreme as to render the result baffling, if not meaningless. As a consequence, Helleu restricted his stellar circuit to that lying approximately between the vernal and the autumnal equinox, but depicting even half of the zodiacal belt compelled distortions in the angular relations of stars and between the equator and ecliptic. The solution would have been perfectly satisfactory, since the representation is art rather than science, but in the execution of the program the artist and his craftsmen committed an unfortunate error. They located the stars and the ecliptic as though the artist stood outside the celestial sphere instead of inside—in other words, in working from above the ceiling they neglected

Fig. 19. Grand Central Terminal. Top: plan of the upper-level track system, for express or through trains. Bottom: plan of the lower-level track system, for suburban trains.

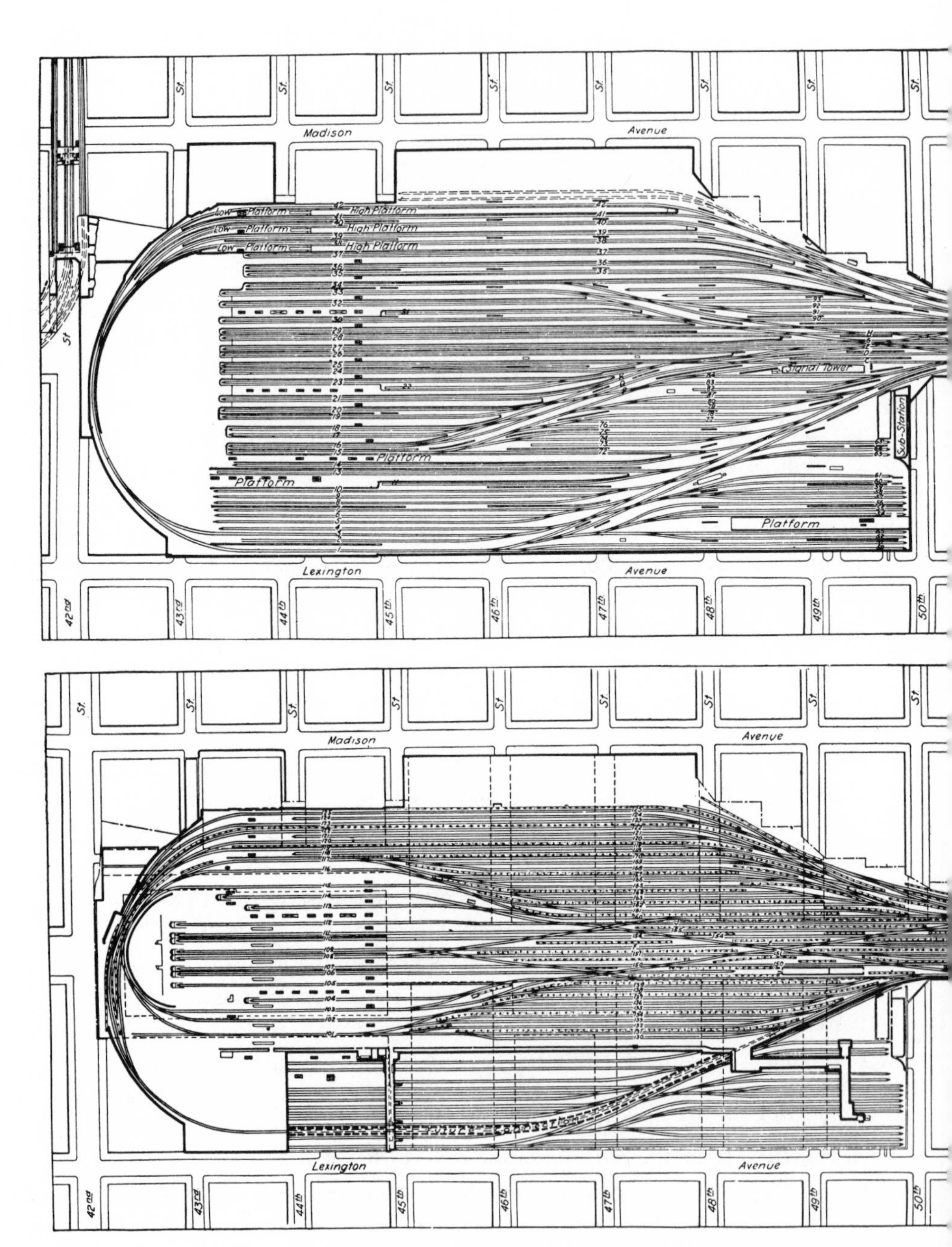

19

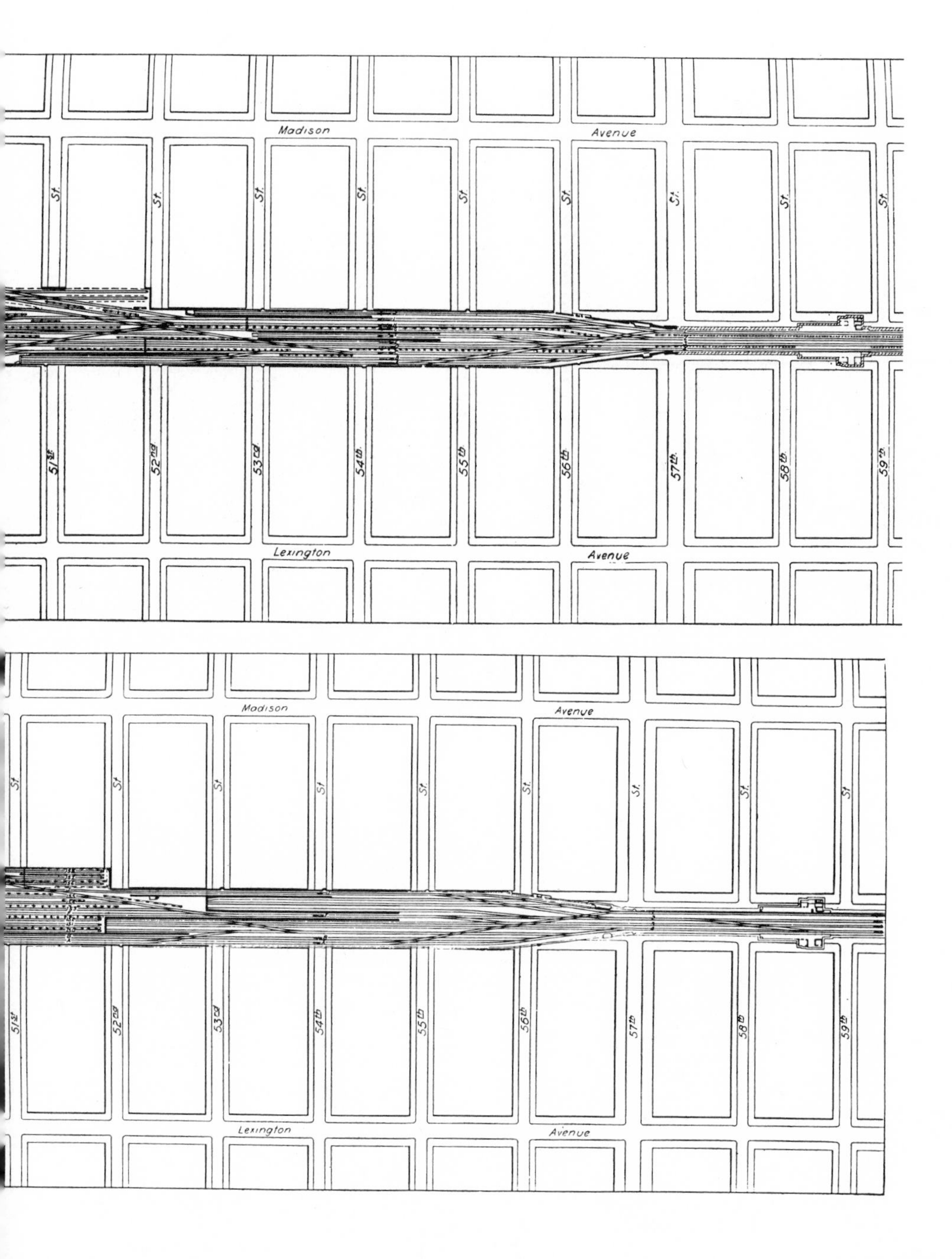
Madison Avenue
Lexington Avenue
51st St.
52nd St.
53rd St.
54th St.
55th St.
56th St.
57th St.
58th St.
59th St.
Madison Avenue
Lexington Avenue
51st St.
52nd St.
53rd St.
54th St.
55th St.
56th St.
57th St.
58th St.
59th St.

Fig. 20. Grand Central Terminal. Cutaway drawing showing the concourse and track levels.

20

Fig. 21. Grand Central Terminal. Longitudinal and transverse sections of the head house and track levels.

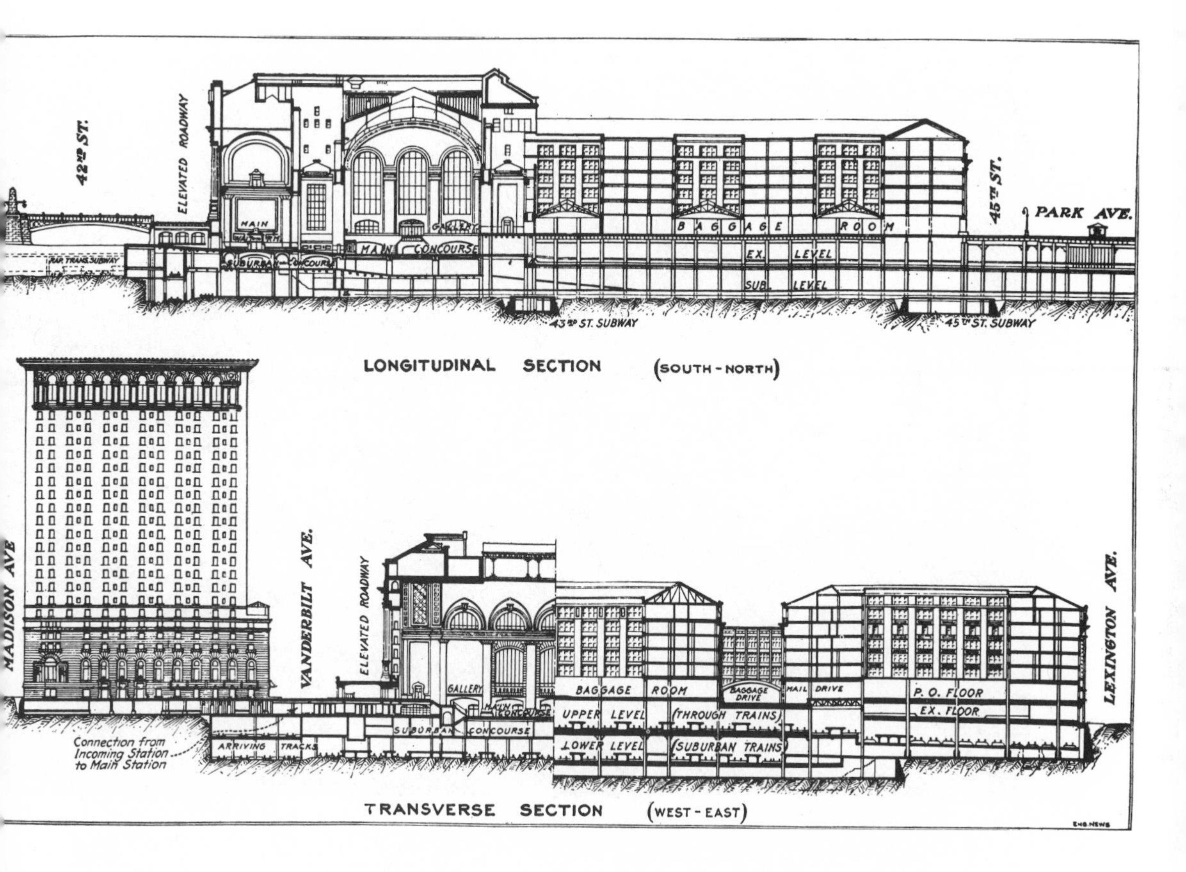

Fig. 22. Grand Central Terminal. The completed building as it appeared around 1930. The Commodore Hotel stands on the right, and the New York Central Office Building in the background.

Fig. 23. Grand Central Terminal. Park Avenue north of 45th Street, 1914, showing the open areas above the terminal tracks.

22

23

to arrange objects as though they were below—and in consequence east and west are reversed. But the ceiling over the concourse of Grand Central is part of the established iconography of the nation, like the Statue of Liberty or Washington Monument, and the error fixed in plaster is one of the amusing features of the whole symbolic expression.

The structural system of the terminal is the most intricate of all comparable buildings by virtue of the multiplicity of its separate elements, the air-rights construction, and the double-level track system that stands in extreme disparity to the dimensions and the plan of the head house. In addition to the straightforward problems of supporting loads (dead, traffic, and wind), the various engineering designers of the station complex had to design a steel frame to cope with special exigencies imposed by the planning, formal design, construction, and operation of the terminal.[25] In the head house the framing was designed to provide support for the exterior walls with their immense arched openings, for the flat and vaulted ceilings of the waiting rooms and concourse, and for the appropriate distribution of columns, girders, and beams in the office areas above the peripheral public spaces. Much of the steelwork is standard column-and-girder framing on the conventional 21-foot bay span. Gable roofs and the great concourse vault are carried by or hung from a variety of trusses divided between the Pratt and Warren web systems. Certain formal details required special structural supports: the recessed wall at the fourth floor, set back 2 feet for the decorative panels above the lower cornice, necessitated offset columns at the fifth floor; the heavy stone cornice had to rest on steel cantilever girders 4 feet in length.[26] All columns for the head house and for existing or future air-rights construction, of which the first are the present Grand Central Palace (1905–8), and the company's office building at 466 Lexington Avenue (1908–9), are sustained by solid rock (Manhattan schist) that was excavated down to shallow depressions and leveled off with concrete. The minimum bearing capacity of the rock is 72,000 pounds per square foot, none too generous for column loads in areas of long-span girders and trusses as high as 2,200,000 pounds. Bracing designed to resist wind loads affecting only the head house was confined to office space above the fourth-floor cornice, since the New York code then held that the effects of wind may be regarded as negligible below a level of 166 feet, 6 inches. The chief moment-resisting devices at these upper floors are conventional knee braces and horizontal distributing bracing in the eighth-floor frame. The projected 26-story office building, however, posed the problem of bracing a skyscraper, and more elaborate expedients were adopted. All lengths of columns lying within the envelope of the head house were grouped into bents or towers of four columns per group, forming a rectangle measuring 7 × 9 feet in plan and joined by diagonal bracing in the form of the Warren truss. These bents, hidden within the immense pierlike enclosures bordering the long sides of the concourse, support the vault and roof trusses over the concourse floor.

Throughout the track area, by contrast, all loads, dimensions, and framing patterns were exaggerated and distorted in ways that required unprecedented structural solutions. Bay spans vary from 22 to 44 feet, the maximum fixed by the necessity of spanning two tracks and the intervening platform. Clearance limits, the need to minimize the obstructions presented by columns, deviations from straight-line framing dictated by the presence of turnouts and ladder tracks, a double-level track system, which made the upper level in effect a peculiarly shaped bridge, street viaducts above the trackage, loading factors determined by locomotive weights, air-rights buildings, the damping of vibrations caused by moving trains—individually as well as collectively these exigencies set problems of a magnitude and complexity for which there were no antecedents. The tracks and elevated platforms of the lower or suburban level offered the least difficulty. The ties for running tracks and third rails and the footings for the platform walls everywhere lie in a concrete floor that rests directly on the leveled bedrock, except where it is supported by beams over the baggage-trucking subway, the low point of which is 51 feet below the grade level along the subway axis. The upper or through-train level, however, taxed the resources of the engineering designers to the utmost. The entire hornet's nest of detailed problems arose from three paramount determinants—differences in track layout and area between the two levels, offset columns, and extremely high dead and live loads. The floor frame and supports consist of columns, predominantly of H-section but including the heavier built-up box forms, built-up plate girders spanning transversely between the columns, longitudinal floor beams framed into the girders, and a solid concrete floor poured as a series of parallel vaults equal in depth to the girders at their springing lines and spanning from beam to beam (figs. 24, 26, 27). The sectional dimensions of columns and girders were calculated on the basis of the following factors: a dead load of 650 pounds per square foot and a live load determined primarily from the weight on the driving wheels of a standard freight locomotive of the time; a maximum allowable stress in tension of 19,000 pounds per square inch.[27] The floor beams are a uniform 36 inches in depth, but the total load imposed by the track floor construction, trains, and offset columns required primary girders of such depth as one would ordinarily encounter in railroad bridges, which the upper track floor in fact is. Most long-span girders are slightly more than 7 feet in depth, but the heaviest of all, calculated to carry two offset columns, exceeds 10 feet in depth. Few of the bending moments to which the girders were assumed to be subjected would have been less than 3,000,000 foot-pounds, and one would have exceeded 7,000,000 foot-pounds.[28] Nearly all of this massive steelwork is hidden in the concrete flooring, the maximum depth of which is 9 feet, 6 inches. Since the overhead office building originally planned was never constructed, the girders were never subjected to these high moments, but their sections had to be calculated on the assumption that they would be called upon to bear such loads. Above the track floor the viaduct frames offered a comparatively simple exercise in plate-girder bridge construction except between 56th and 57th streets, where numerous switches and diverging tracks precluded the use of intermediate columns, so that the Park Avenue roadway and sidewalks are carried on two parallel Warren trusses with a span of 150 feet (fig. 25). It was an easy last problem for the engineers who had created the rest of this unique exhibition of structural virtuosity.

Construction and Operation

The first step in the realization of the Grand Central program, following the acquisition of extensive areas of land in the corridors bounded by the property lines (at the extremes, Lexington Avenue to the east and Madison to the west), was the destruction of the existing urban fabric to clear the land. This preliminary step required the demolition of about two hundred buildings forming a well-rooted residential and commercial mixture of detached houses, small flat buildings, shops, churches, and one hospital. The process began in June, 1903, and had advanced sufficiently by August so that work crews could begin the coordinated activities of excavation, the removal, shifting, and reconnection of gas, water, and sewer lines, including the laying of a new interceptor sewer under Park Avenue below 54th Street, the removal or realignment of transverse bridges, and the construction of a temporary interlocking tower.[29] The total volume of excavation, which covered nearly all of the blocks bounded by 42d and 50th streets south and north, and Lexington and Madison avenues east and west, in addition to the corridors at the sides of Park Avenue from 50th to 57th Street, was 2,800,000 cubic yards, divided between 1,600,000 cubic yards of rock and 1,200,000 cubic yards of earth (figs. 26–28). The removal of the dense schist required the detonation of about one million pounds of dynamite. The work was carried out in stages which advanced progressively though irregularly from north to south. The first two steps were the widening in succession of both sides of the Park Avenue tunnel from 57th to 50th Street and the concomitant shoring of

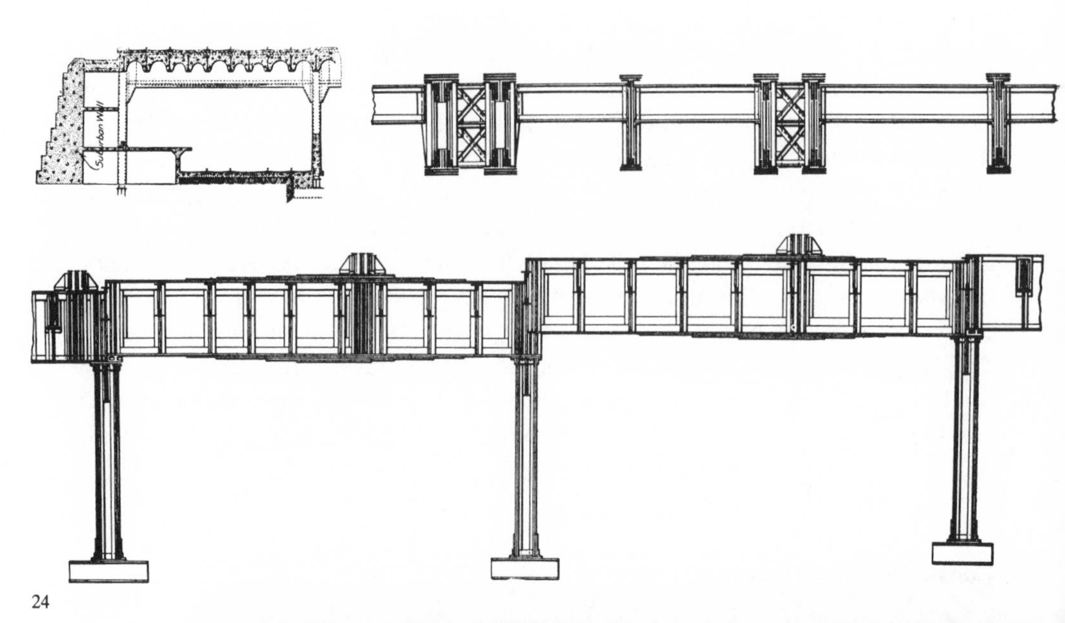

24

Fig. 24. Grand Central Terminal. Detail of the express-track floor frame showing typical transverse bays.

25

Fig. 25. Grand Central Terminal. Detail of the street-viaduct framing, exposed during construction of the Union Carbide Building, 1958.

Fig. 26. Grand Central Terminal. The track area during construction, 1910.

Fig. 27. Grand Central Terminal. The track area during construction, 1911.

26

27

Fig. 28. Grand Central Terminal. The track area during construction, 1911, with the future Waldorf-Astoria Hotel shown in dotted outline.

28

contiguous building walls to accommodate the expansion of the inner approach from four to ten tracks. The existing tracks were left in the original walled cut, while the additional three on each side were covered with a concrete slab on steel girders and trusses. The laying out of a temporary yard at Lexington Avenue and 51st Street for construction operations was a necessary preliminary step to gouging out the huge rectangular crater that was to contain the terminal tracks. This work was accomplished in stages that advanced southward to 42d Street, first along the east half of the terminal yard in order to leave shrinking fragments of the existing structures as temporary station facilities, then southward along the west half of the yard. As excavation progressed, the concrete flooring and retaining walls were poured, and the lower-level tracks were laid down, again from east to west, the completed tracks being pressed into service while the excavation moved westward. With the opening walled, floored, and tracked, so to speak, the steelwork for the upper track floor was erected, the concrete poured, and still more tracks laid down.[30] Continuing at very nearly the same time was the installation of water and drainage lines and the incredibly intricate electrical circuitry necessary for the operation of signals, interlocking towers, and trains, and for the illumination and ventilation of buildings. Erecting steel for the street viaducts was nearly completed before the construction of the head house began; simultaneously with this climactic phase came the building of the first air-rights structures, of which the most notable are the Grand Central Palace (1905–8), 466 Lexington Avenue (1908–9), and the Biltmore Hotel (1911–13). Midway in the long process, which excited awe and wonder among the citizens as much as it harassed those who had to come and go through the area, the once celebrated train shed and station building went down (1908). The replacement opened its doors on 2 February 1913.

The excavation of earth and rock was a laborious and agonizingly slow process still extensively dependent on the endurance and strength of individual workers. The earth was excavated by hand and loaded by bucket hoists and steam shovels into the spoil trains. All rock was loosened and broken by dynamite blasts, loaded by steam shovel into the dump cars, and transported up the river to form riprap shore protection for the railroad's Hudson Division, where the tracks in many places are precariously close to the water. Only one disaster marred the immense enterprise. On 19 December 1910 a work train moving into a yard track near the partly completed power plant on 50th Street, skidded on slippery track, overran the bumping post, and severed a gas line. The resulting explosion took ten lives and caused injury to another hundred workers, and pretty well demolished what structures still survived in the vicinity. Steel erection, by contrast, proved a safer but far more formidable task that had to be organized on quasi-military lines. All steel members were received, sorted, and stored at the company's yard in Port Morris, whence they were called for in manageable lots three to four days in advance of use. The steel was conveyed to the site in 12-car trains of gondola cars that were operated over the suburban tracks during late night hours. The material came in every shape and size, ranging from small struts each weighing 25 pounds that could be emplaced by hand to two-story column lengths weighing 88,000 pounds. The lower members were erected by locomotive cranes, then by stiff-leg power-operated derricks when the level of work rose beyond the reach of the cranes. The whole process of erecting steel was carried out in repetitive longitudinal strips, like the excavation and the pouring of concrete that had preceded it. Finishing work, particularly in the head house, required special skills, many of which belonged to ancient handicraft techniques rather than the new power-operated varieties. When the job was sufficiently done in the early weeks of 1913 to admit the public—though with many odds and ends still remaining—the final cost of land and construction came to about $80,000,000, nearly double the estimate of $43,000,000 made in 1903. The replacement value of the terminal at the building-cost level of 1980 is at least $1.6 billion.

The day-to-day operation of this impressive and costly monument quickly grew to be as intricate as its design and construction, yet here, too, every detail was foreseen. Just as a railroad terminal consists of two distinct parts, the head house and the track area, so the daily working of the whole complex is divided into two separate aspects of what we might call station technology. A necessary adjunct to the functioning of both parts is the generating station that supplies hot water, steam, and electric power to the terminal structures and the railroad cars. Since the power plant that generated the current for the operation of trains was located on the Harlem River at Port Morris, the terminal installation was primarily a heating plant and a substation constructed slightly to the east of the head house axis between 49th and 50th streets. Its electrical functions were the generation of alternating current for consumption in the station and the conversion of the 11,000-volt, 25-cycle alternating current received from Port Morris to the 660-volt direct current used by the locomotives. Since the signal, clock, and lighting circuits, however, operate on alternating current, the locally generated power was reduced in voltage but not converted. The mechanical and electrical utilities of the head house exist to render these large public spaces and the smaller private enclosures safe, comfortable, and reasonably salubrious to their occupants. Since little natural light penetrates the concourse and the many interior passages, electrical illumination plays a greater role than in the more common skylighted structures, and the erection of skyscrapers on the south side of 42d Street on either side of Park Avenue has increased this dependency over the years. Heating the main building and the numerous subsidiaries is accomplished entirely by means of hot water delivered by two mains from the generating plant on 50th Street. The forced-draft ventilation of the head house interior is provided by the electrically operated fans that had by then become commonplace in this rapidly expanding technology. Storage tanks, 300 hose connections, and 125 alarm boxes offer a fire protection that the station personnel have never had to call upon. Even the water made available for direct human consumption was altered in keeping with the new progressive spirit: a special supply purified by ozonation was provided for drinking fountains, lavatories, and kitchens. Baggage is handled by battery-powered trucks operated between trains, cab stand, and baggage rooms, the passage under the tracks made possible by electrically operated elevators and a subway under the suburban tracks. Drainage of this huge subterranean area, which once had to cope with direct rainfall and storm run-off as well as the internal discharge of the buildings, is provided by electrically operated pumps that move the effluent to the main crosstown interceptor for the 42d Street corridor.

The sheer extent of internal trackage, the great number of tracks divided between two levels, the ten-track inner approach, and the inclined lead tracks to the lower level, all of which far exceeded their counterparts at Pennsylvania Station and which together made Grand Central the largest terminal in the world, also guaranteed that its successful operation would require the largest signaling and interlocking systems ever installed. The various factors underlying the decision to build a track layout of unparalleled size followed not only from the volume and diversity of traffic, which in truth never reached the levels obtaining at Pennsylvania Station, but more from the peculiar difficulties of operating a stub-end terminal with an inadequate outer approach (above 57th Street) and a coach yard miles removed from the terminal trackage. There were additional considerations, however, that were not susceptible of a quasi-scientific analysis. The sheer inability of the old station to cope with the traffic in spite of all the extensions and rearrangements of thirty years, and expectations of continued future growth, which seemed justified in the early years of the century, urged the officers and engineers of the railroad company to do the job right once and for all. Having laid out tracks in such number, the builders then faced the task of controlling train movements in and out of the station berths and through the intricate system of throat tracks. The traditional solution of the single, centrally focused interlocking tower was obviously out of the question; in its place there had to be a unified multitower installation governing precisely defined areas equally precisely interconnected. The solution originally adopted by the signal engineers for

Grand Central was to introduce five interlocking towers distributed over the area comprising the inner approach and the terminal trackage from a point roughly midway between 43d and 44th streets to 57th Street.[31] The equipment and operation of these towers were based on the assumption that the upper and lower loop tracks would form part of the track system in existence at the opening of the terminal, but these tracks were not finally completed as planned until 1917, in the case of the upper loop, and 1927, in the case of the lower.

Under this elaborately subdivided organization Tower U, located on the line of 57th Street, acted as the valve that controlled the flow of train movements over the inner approach toward both levels of the terminal and from the inner to the outer approach for movements away from the terminal. Beyond the throat inward, or southward toward 42d Street, movements to and from the station and storage tracks on the upper level west of track 16 came under the jurisdiction of Tower A, placed directly beneath Park Avenue at 50th Street, while all traffic on the lower level except for that moving through the loop fell under the control of Tower B, at the same location but at still another stage below the street grade. Tower C, under 48th Street on the east side of the upper level, controlled movements to and from the storage tracks east of track 16, and Tower F, near the east end of the lower loop tracks, controlled all movements in both directions on both upper and lower loop tracks.[32] The normal operating procedure for inbound traffic began when any given train passed the tower at Mott Haven. The towerman immediately notified his counterpart at Tower U by telephone (later radio), and the latter, with the assistance of his levermen, set up the route through the terminal throat, ordinarily a matter of executing familiar and well-rehearsed movements since the trains customarily ran over predetermined routes fixed long in advance by the train dispatcher. The towerman at U then notified one or another of his fellows in A, B, C, or F, who selected the final routing into the appropriate platform or loop track. The sequence of events was essentially reversed for outbound trains. On the four-track approach, above 57th Street, and throughout the length of the Electric Division trains were operated according to the right-hand principle. The nicely adjusted parts of this system worked like a finely made watch, but it was marked by two defects. The balanced right-hand operation on the four-track approach meant that only two tracks were available for movements in any direction, regardless of the density of the traffic, whereas the most efficient usage of tracks dictated that at least three and sometimes four tracks be available for inbound trains during the morning rush hour and for outbound in the evening. Moreover, the distance between 138th and 57th streets was too great, and between 57th and 50th streets too short, to avoid delays arising from the excessive spacing of trains on the longer stretch and too little headway on the shorter. In little more than a decade after the opening of Grand Central, it was recognized that improvements were essential, and the necessary changes began to be introduced in 1929.

Since the view of tracks and trains is severely restricted in these underground avenues that appear to extend into the darkness without limit, illuminated track diagrams showing the position and movement of all trains were part of the necessary equipment in the interlocking towers. Signal indications in the terminal area up to 57th Street are given by motorized dwarf signals each carrying a semaphore blade and lights, but within the close clearances of the tunnel, indications are given by color-light signals attached to the walls. The electro-pneumatic switch signals are a special variety having a profile low enough to lie flush with the top of the running rail in order not to require another break in the third rail, which is interrupted in many places by switches and crossings. Improvements in dispatching and signaling techniques over the years, many embodied in the extensive revision of 1929–30 (chap. 6), have resulted in changes in the operation of towers, but the essentials of this extraordinary system, the interlocking and switch machines, signals, circuitry, batteries, and all the rest still survive in active use much as they were when installed over the years prior to 1913. Coincident with the construction of the terminal and its electrification, the New York Central and Hudson River Railroad placed in service an automatic electric block signal system over the electrified lines to Harmon and White Plains. It represented the largest contract of its kind up to that time, and the General Railway Signal Company of Buffalo was the contractor that received this plum. No sooner was the new system in place, however, than the company began to replace the lower-quadrant semaphores with the superior upper-quadrant varieties (figs. 5, 7). These, in turn, eventually fell before the simpler and more efficient color-light signals.[33]

The presence of loop tracks on even a single level would have placed the Grand Central in a unique category; the double-level system carried out consistently through all details of track, signaling, interlocking, and train movements guarantee that it will very likely never be duplicated. The size of the station track area stands well beyond any foreseeable need in the heyday of rail ascendancy (the station could probably accommodate at least 1,500 trains per day if they could be squeezed into the outer approach tracks), but this reserve capacity makes possible a flexibility of train operation that allows for the emergency movement of 200 trains and the accommodation of 70,000 passengers in a single hour. During the peak traffic of later years the number of passengers seldom reached a quarter of a million in a day and only once exceeded the figure. Reliable pronouncements on the volume of traffic at the passenger terminals of metropolitan New York are difficult to discover, if they exist at all, but the data assembled by the Regional Plan Association of New York probably come closest to accuracy. In the first full calendar year following its opening in February, 1913, Grand Central accommodated 22,615,018 passengers, for a range of about 71,000–75,000 per week-day. The number of daily trains shown in the public timetables was 384, which meant a likely total of 470, requiring at least 620 train movements. More important than the average flow of passengers were the rate of growth and the maximum volume. During the ten years of 1903 through 1912 the number of passengers using the terminal increased at an average rate of 7.1 percent per annum. The high point came in the eight days of 30 August through 6 September 1912, which included the Labor Day holiday, when the huge terminal that was still under construction somewhat uncomfortably accommodated an average of 604 trains, 3,909 cars, and 118,000 passengers per day. During the peak hour of 8:30 to 9:30 A.M. the average movement was 52 scheduled trains. Although these are impressive totals, they fall short of the records of later years, when the number of daily passengers rose to more than double the totals for 1912. The peak-hour volume at Grand Central was a consequence of the fact that the heavy suburban flow in the morning rush hours coincided with the high tide of incoming sleeping-car passengers.

The crux of the problem at the terminal was moving empty trains out of the station as expeditiously as possible—in short, clearing the space for the successive waves of paying customers. The loop tracks offered the most workable solution. On the upper level the four westernmost tracks converge into a single loop track, laid out on a semicircle with spiral ends, that expands into three tracks connecting with the storage and throat tracks at the east side of the station. On the lower level eight of the platform tracks converge on two loop tracks arranged according to the same interconnecting geometry (figs. 17–19). By means of this internal connection between east and west sides, or between inbound and outbound tracks, incoming trains can be unloaded, then moved directly into the loop and turned either into the storage tracks within the body of the terminal, or to departure tracks for return to the coach yard at Mott Haven. Trains parked on inner station tracks had to be backed through the throat to a ladder track in order to be moved to and turned on one of the loops. Even this cumbersome operation, however, was preferable to reverse movements of trains, especially long trains of sleeping cars, on the heavily used four-track approach line above 57th Street. The combination of the two loop tracks, the great number of station tracks disposed on two levels, and the separation of through and suburban trains gave the station a reserve capacity which it has never been called upon to use.

The closest the volume of traffic rose to the theoretical maximum of 70,000 passengers in an hour came at times during and immediately after the Second World War, when peak hours sometimes saw the passage of 100 trains and 40,000 passengers.[34]

The full urbanistic role of Grand Central Terminal—the place, function, life, and meaning of this civic monument in the circulation and architectural ambience of New York—far transcends internal rail traffic and the lively commerce of the numerous shops and restaurants that make it the greatest microcity in America. With respect to urban movement the terminal is one of the primary nodes in the whole New York pattern of interrelated circulatory systems, not only by virtue of the traffic within the body of the station complex, but also through the interaction of that complex with the surrounding arteries. The many entrances, exits, internal passages, and ramps, and the principle of gravitational flow for pedestrians serve not only to tie all the parts of the terminal together into a working unity, like a living organism, but equally to interconnect the complex with the arterial pattern around it. At the time the station was opened three modes of mass transit formed a multilevel system at the intersection of Park Avenue and 42d Street, namely, the streetcar line on 42d Street, the stub-end branch of the Manhattan Elevated Railway's line above the same street, and the recently completed subway of the Interborough Rapid Transit, which curved from Fourth Avenue into 42d Street immediately in front of the station and continued westward to Broadway at Times Square. When the Lexington Avenue subway was completed, this east-west segment of the I. R. T. was converted to a dead-end shuttle and the north-south main tracks were than turned eastward to reach the Lexington Avenue tunnel.

Before these revisions were completed, however, extraordinary schemes were proposed that would have converted the Grand Central node into the greatest multilevel transit nexus ever conceived. The Hudson and Manhattan Railroad planned a subway to extend northward and westward from its terminal at 33d Street under Sixth Avenue, Bryant Park, and 42d Street to the new station, the extension to be known as the McAdoo Tunnels. The subway tracks were to lie a full clearance depth below the I. R. T. line, which occupies the first level below street grade. In order to provide a similar service to the east the directors of the abortive New York and Long Island Railroad proposed a rapid transit service between Long Island City and Grand Central to be provided by operating trains in the empty Steinway Tunnel, which had been opened in 1907 for a streetcar line that was never built and which was to pass under Fourth Avenue at a depth sufficient to place it entirely below the McAdoo Tunnels. The officers of the New York Central and Hudson River were cooperative enough to plan a continuous subgrade concourse to extend from the level of the suburban platforms at their inner ends southward to the I. R. T. subway station under 42d Street and eastward to Lexington Avenue. By this means the railroad company would have directly tied the intercity rail service to the local subway arteries. The final result of all this subterranean activity would have been a unique seven-level transportation ganglion, consisting from top to bottom of the elevated line, the surface car line, the upper and lower track floors in the terminal, and the I. R. T., McAdoo, and Steinway tunnels.[35] These fantastic schemes were, of course, never realized in full, but what was accomplished in the building of the terminal and the existing arteries marks the boldest step so far taken toward the creation of a multidimensional transit web.

The chief strands in this vast network as it exists constitute a continuous underground rail and subway system that is laid out on parallel and intersecting axes which in turn are tied to the street above and to the vertical transportation provided by the elevators in the high-rise buildings. It is a staggering urban phenomenon, and not even the Circle Line of the London Underground, which unites the city's 16 railroad terminals in a complete circuit, can show anything remotely comparable to it. The architectural editor Douglas Haskell described the essence of it most eloquently.

> The brilliant break through of the the Grand Central Terminal project came of the fact that there, during the first decade of our century, New York brought together her two major achievements—concentrated building and swift urban transportation—into a single, interrelated, planned operation. The event was majestically fantastic. It stood at the pinnacle of creative effort. Here was compounded the great movement of urban "futurism". . . .[36]

Through the years during which Grand Central Terminal was conceived, planned, erected, and its operating procedures worked out, a multitude of office buildings and hotels was being constructed over the terminal air rights in the immediate vicinity of the head house, on neighboring streets, and in downtown Manhattan. The best of these—and there were many at the highest levels of art—demonstrated to all who could comprehend the full meaning of the city's iconography that, with respect to commercial and public building, New York was becoming the architectural mentor and pacesetter to the world. The principles of the Ecole des Beaux-Arts were being transmuted into something wholly unexpected, and they were being returned to the land of their origin in novel forms. It was now Europe's turn to learn from America, and New York was the place to begin. By the time the terminal was completed, other buildings were rising over its tracks to give some hint of the splendors to come, but these had been repeatedly foreshadowed by earlier architectural works, some of which had been placed under construction before the turn of the century. Closest to the Grand Central in character and location were the elegant hotels that were rising around the 42d Street-Park-Lexington focus. The first to point out the new path was the Manhattan, on the north side of 42d Street west of Vanderbilt Avenue (1894–1901), the pioneer steel-framed hotel in the city and the creaton of Henry J. Hardenbergh, the foremost designer of hotels at the time. The pace of constructon quickened under the stimulus of the Grand Central program. Shortly after the Manhattan was completed, the Belmont began to rise on the southwest corner of Park Avenue and 42d Street, to be opened in May, 1906. While the terminal plans were still being revised, one of its two firms of associated architects, Warren and Wetmore, received commission for the Vanderbilt Hotel, erected on Park (Fourth) Avenue between 33d and 34th streets in 1909–11. The exhibition building known as Grand Central Palace, on Lexington Avenue between 46th and 47th Street and hence within the air-rights precinct, took form during the same years, with the same architects in charge of the design. The Palace required special solutions, but the basic plan of the high-rise midtown hotel was approaching a standard form in which narrow, slablike blocks rise above a continuous base two to six stories in height, while exterior curtain walls and interior surfaces were embellished with varieties of detail transmuted from Renaissance and Neoclassic antecedents (Robert Adam was a major influence, for example, in the case of the Vanderbilt).

Downtown, on the periphery of City Hall Park, two New York classics were taking form in a commanding display of the new architectural imagination. The earlier of the two, the Municipal Office Building, was the product of a competition, like the Customs House on the Bowling Green. Twelve offices submitted entries in April, 1908, and McKim, Mead and White were awarded the prize in the following year.[37] Construction of the enormous volume, widely spread in a U-shaped plan formed by short advancing wings at the ends of the main mass, was completed in 1913, but all interior details were not finally in place until 1916. A host of classical details were expertly adapted to the functional requirements of the high office building that had at the same time to give strong symbolic expression to the concept of civic authority. The second of the two downtown showpieces is the Woolworth Building, erected at 230 Broadway in 1911–13 from the plans of Cass Gilbert, who had given some hints of the masterwork to come in the West Street Building of 1906–7. The Woolworth, in its height of 55 stories, its structural engineering, and its formal design, brought the skyscraper to its climax, and it is questionable whether it has ever been surpassed.[38] The powerful vertical movement, the upward-rising hierarchy of volumes, and the aerial delicacy, all perfectly appropriate to the overall form, make the Woolworth, like Grand Central, however far removed in architectural character, perhaps the most imaginative transmutation of Beaux-Arts principles in existence. The Franco-American architect Jean Paul Carlhian recognized the essential quality of the skyscraper and by implication of the railroad station as well.

> The building rises . . . from an understated base . . . to the richest of crowns, befitting a Gothic cathedral (and in fact inspired by the Tour de Beurre of the cathedral of Rouen). . . . American is the use of materials, the free-from-precedent handling of the details, the irreverent borrowing from a Gothic masterpiece, and a no-fuss massing. The Woolworth Building seems to say that mere functionalism is inadequate for expressing the role of business in the life of the city, and so it adds more portentous architectural elements imported from afar to proclaim its civic function, and to clad its essentially simple form.[39]

Up on 42d Street the architects and the builders were equally busy filling the immensely inviting, though rather forbidding, void over the tracks of the double-level terminal. By the time it was opened to service in February, 1913, seven buildings of varying size and quality had either been completed or were rising over the lower air-rights areas between Madison and Lexington avenues (figs. 23, 28). Among them the largest and most impressive is the Biltmore Hotel, erected in 1911–13 in the block bounded by Madison and Vanderbilt avenues and 43d and 44th streets. The same association of Warren and Wetmore with Reed and Stem acted as designers, but they engaged D. H. Burnham and Graham, Burnham and Company of Chicago as consultants, as though there were not talent enough between the two offices of terminal designers. The Biltmore, standing to a height of 26 stories, is divided into two wings forming a U-shaped plan so deeply indented as to give the wings the appearance of twin towers. The architects adapted elegantly restrained Italian Renaissance forms to this steel-framed structure, and in order not to overshadow the terminal head house standing beyond the narrow width of Vanderbilt Avenue, they set back the wings 21 feet at the sixth-floor level to minimize their visual presence and to maintain the proper height relation to the station building. The climactic interior features are the glass-roofed garden terrace on the sixth floor, and the banqueting hall on the 22d, where the Caen limestone of the Grand Central interior forms a softly colored and textured wall veneer to set off the green marble sheathing of the columns. The Biltmore was originally tied to the terminal in two ways: a stairway and an elevator directly joined the lobby to the concourse (at its west end, near the gate for track 42), while the very lifeblood of the hotel, electric power and hot water, were provided by the railroad's generating plant on Lexington Avenue at 50th Street.[40]

The Biltmore Hotel remains a conspicuous prize in the subcity of which the terminal is the focus, but in truth the whole of Manhattan below 42d Street was experiencing a civic and commercial efflorescence that compelled world attention by the time of the First World War. The most powerful and evocative of architectural images continued to be concentrated in the downtown area, although their counterparts were beginning to multiply in the Grand Central neighborhood. Yet the endless avenues that connected them—Fourth, Fifth, Sixth, Broadway, and Seventh in particular—could show long, sometimes continuous segments of great architectural vigor revealed in commercial, public, residential, and industrial buildings. Thus the urban paths could in places be as compelling in their own kind of architectural imagery as were the great nodal areas. Fourth Avenue provided the ideal perspective for the terminal seen at once as climax and closing feature, and it was again the well-trained urban vision of Douglas Haskell that produced the liveliest appreciation.

> If you approached the "downtown" side, the south, you had a mile-long vista up Park Avenue to a Beaux-Arts version of a *people's palace*; the vista was far the longest in New York; the three large arched windows explicitly promised one Big Room, as in a Roman Bath. On arrival by vehicle this was not, however, a road block to the Avenue then; raised on a ramp you found yourself circling the monument, on each side of which stood a tall hotel like an emperor's guard. For the monumental station is lower on purpose; it *needs* space above to stand out. Then on the opposite, northern side of the terminal . . . . You were on a broad boulevard, centre-stripped with a broad planted pedestrian meander, punctuated with benches. . . . America's first "parkway" was at hand. . . . Noble structures lined the boulevard on both sides, most of them Beaux-Arts apartments, by various architects but controlled in style, and brought to a quietly even cornice height. Interspersed were hotels and business blocks, and here and there a superior church or club house; St. Bartholomew's by Bertram Goodhue, and McKim, Mead and White's Racquet Club. Many apartment interior spaces had elaborte flower courts, they were almost a garden city urbanized.
>
> This was the "Grand Central City" precinct and "Gold Coast," pacing the character of Park Avenue as far as you could see it; the *first designed precinct* in New York, no matter how completely some creators of Rockefeller Center, more than a decade later, have forgot. . . . In the long view from the north, too, the terminal was the vista closer; but was held, there, to more domestic scale than was the opposite 42d Street side.
>
> [It was] a people's monument, celebrating their city, a park way boulevard with a pedestrian mall centre-lining a residential precinct harmoniously controlled and with garden-city features at the center of metropolis.[41]

The building of recent years has brought nothing but deformity to this masterpiece of total design, like the results of some crippling sickness. The abuses of later years taxed the capacity of the interior arteries to the limit, but as long as the fundamental principles were maintained, even the most ill-conceived additions to the air-rights family could be contained. The Regional Plan Association of New York best recognized its continuing urban role.

> The Grand Central Terminal Complex . . . is the conceptual archetype of integrated multi-level development, mixed activities and direct mass transportation access. It has yet to be surpassed either in its original or its present form, although its success is beginning to over-run it as many of its elements have become overcrowded with people and signs in recent years.
>
> The flow of train passengers of unprecedented volume was carefully designed so that people could move with ease, and often in an atmosphere of grace and grandeur. The basic elements of the Access Tree principle can be seen in the high-capacity sub-surface transportation lines, the vast mixing chamber of the great concourse where pedestrians can move in random directions and to the escalator or elevator banks of the Pan Am Building or underground passage connections to nearby buildings. All that is missing is more conscious architectural organization of the buildings above, as in the early Rockefeller Center. In addition to the attention paid to the multi-level pedestrian paths, the Grand Central concept incorporated a very wide range of activities both in and around the terminal, including the initiation for this purpose of the use of sixty acres of air-rights. . . . The original plan anticipated today's office buildings, hotels, restaurants, banks, shops and multitudinous services. Twenty-one buildings are tied directly to the main concourse today.[42]

The concept of "Grand Central City" has proved to be permanently valid for the modern commercial metropolis.

4

The Freight Terminal System

The Yard and Terminal Pattern after 1900

Perhaps the most remarkable characteristic of the Port of New York in the years of rail ascendancy was not its size, but the fact that it worked. Nearly every element in the complex system was determined by natural processes posing enormous planning and constructional problems, and the inevitable political and economic conflicts further militated against this achievement. Yet human artifice contrived to keep it functioning through the years, even in its crippled state during the cumulative disasters of 1916–18, and to maintain its operations at a constantly expanding level that brought the city an enviable prosperity. As we noted throughout the first volume of this work, the very features that gave the port its prominence in world commerce acted to frustrate the movement of freight into, out of, through, and around it. With the exception of the New York Central Railroad's West Side line, the continental rail system of the United States terminated at the New Jersey piers, whereas the outposts of the vital regional system of New England were Port Morris and Poughkeepsie. The Brooklyn steamship docks were isolated from the East and North River railheads, while the working heart of the city lay between them. The shipment of freight required patterns of movement over water that grew in number and intricacy until the overburdened waterways took on the character of Manhattan squares during the rush hours. The maintenance and constant expansion of this vast enterprise guaranteed many thousands of jobs, the existence of which was a crucial element in the city's flourishing economy. And there is no question that it flourished: in the first thirty years of the century the population more than doubled, while the total value of manufacturing, shipping, wholesale and retail trade expanded well over three times. The railroads, carrying two-thirds of all the tonnage shipped into and through the port, were as important a factor in contributing to this prosperity as they were sharers in its benefits.

Reliable data on the tonnage moving by rail within the port area appears to be nonexistent for the early years of the century, but if the expansion of harbor traffic corresponded roughly to the increases experienced by the railroads of the New York family taken as a whole, we may conclude that the port enjoyed a continuous and rapid rise in all categories of traffic up to the years following the First World War. Between 1900 and 1920 the tonnage carried by the roads of the New York group substantially more than doubled, while the number of passengers rose nearly three times. Equally important is the fact that the rail companies serving the port increased their share of the total rail traffic in the United States over the same two decades nearly 30 percent in the case of freight tonnage and about one quarter in the case of passengers.[1] For the individual railroad companies meaningful comparisons over the years are difficult to make because the mergers of subsidiaries with parent companies suddenly and enormously expanded the traffic and revenues listed in the annual reports. Among roads that remained fairly stable in mileage, the Central of New Jersey and the Lackawanna were typical of the prosperous group, their freight tonnage rising respectively 125 and 130 percent between 1900 and 1920. But the increasingly troubled New Haven saw its freight traffic expand only 75 percent in the same period. The number of passengers in all cases more than doubled, except for the Long Island, on which the volume multiplied nearly six times in twenty years. The mergers of western affiliates into the corporate bodies of the Pennsylvania and the New York Central and Hudson River railroads nullified the possibility of comparisons on a uniform basis. The evidence for the years prior to 1910, however, suggests unlimited horizons: the Pennsylvania's heavy investment in freight-handling facilities at the Port of New York would seem justified in view of an average increase for the system of 2,000,000 tons per annum, and the smaller New York Central could hardly complain about a steady increment of 1,000,000 tons. The great program of merging controlled and leased lines that began in 1914 improved the efficiency and economy of operations, and, at least in the case of the two largest roads, it strengthened their positions with respect to net operating and total income.[2]

The fundamental problem in handling cargo at New York was to bring the railroads and the marine shipping lines into an appropriate union marked by the most nearly complete physical contact that was possible in this complex physiographic setting (figs. 29–31). The importance of this marriage for the national economy was obvious from the beginning of rail ascendancy, but the accomplishment of such an end in a rational, systematic, and properly organized way apparently defied solution. The facilities essential to the operation of railhead marine terminals were built up piecemeal over the years following the Civil War; many were in place at the turn of the century, and most of the remaining were added by 1920. At the end of the First World War the Port of New York embraced 50 miles of working waterfront, with berthing space for 450 to 500 ocean vessels, the number depending on their size. Of all the docking facilities, 90 percent were distributed along the shore lines of Manhattan, Brooklyn, and Staten Island, and 10 percent along the Jersey shore. The consequence was that the unified terminals, serving both rail trunk lines and marine shipping, all of them located in New Jersey, provided space for only 31 ships, or 6–7 percent of the total. In other words, a high proportion of the steamship piers for handling cargo were in the New York boroughs, whereas the railroads terminted in

New Jersey. The irony bordered on the incredible: the foremost harbor in the world, its metropolitan area embracing one-tenth of the national population, its export-import tonnage equal to 40 percent of the national total, was not "designed" for direct rail-water transshipment. About 90 percent of the freight moving to and from foreign ports was handled at the New Jersey piers, but so few of these were equipped with docking facilities that the railroad companies had to depend on an enormous fleet of highly specialized vessels to transfer cargo between freight cars and ships. This peculiar state of affairs guaranteed that the port would be the greatest lighterage harbor in the world, for it was only by such complex means that the monster could be made to work. The railroad switching or terminal district for metropolitan New York, as it existed at the conclusion of the First World War, comprised a total land and water area of 300 square miles, divided almost equally between New York and New Jersey, and a grand total of 196 freight terminals, stations, yards, and interchange tracks between one railroad line and another. The chief focal points in this tangled web, the anchors of the system, so to speak, were the huge classification yards strung out in an irregular line on the meadows west of Bergen Hill. By 1920 their combined capacity had reached 50,000 cars, and by the end of the decade about 60,000 cars. The normal traffic of the system—interchange, local, and rail-water—in 1919 was 25,000 cars moving in and out of the entire freight-handling network per day, with a maximum on peak days of 65,000 cars. In the same year the passenger-carrying roads conveyed 522,000 daily passengers into and out of the metropolitan terminals, a volume that had been considerably augmented in 1917–18 by the passage of 1,321,000 troops through the port area.[3]

The techniques of rail operations in the port were substantially fixed at the turn of the century, as were all too many of the associated structures, and they were maintained with almost religious fidelity until the advent of containerized shipments around 1960 (figs. 32, 33). Through or line-haul freight arrived at or departed from the classification yards on the periphery of the terminal district. Following classification according to destination, the incoming freight was moved from the yards to the harbor terminals, freight houses, industrial spurs, or interchange points in local runs (variously known over the years as yard cuts, drills, pullers, switchers, or transfers) powered by the ubiquitous and homely little switch engines. The transfer runs consisted of three kinds of freight separated and identified according to destination: domestic freight terminating in the harbor area (usually at freight houses, team tracks, or industrial spurs); connection or overhead freight conveyed through the terminal area from one railroad to another and destined for a terminating point outside the district; export freight destined for unloading and reloading into ships.

Fig. 29. Map showing the passenger-carrying lines and the passenger terminals of the New York metropolitan area as they existed from 1913 to about 1960.

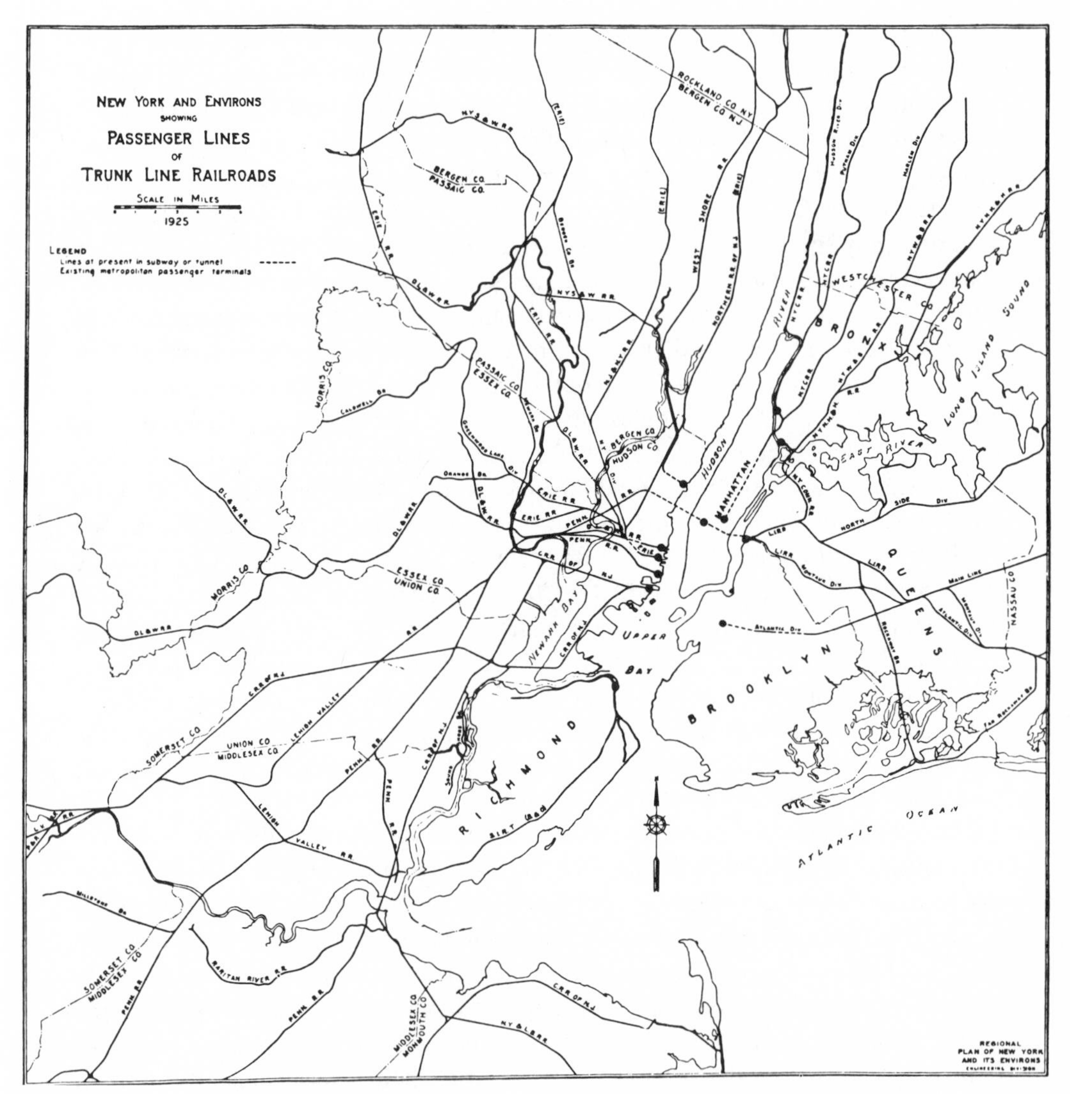

29

Fig. 30. Map showing the freight-carrying main lines and the principal freight terminals of the New York metropolitan area as they existed from the time of World War I to about 1960.

Fig. 31. Map of New York Harbor showing the rail-marine facilities and terminal equipment as they existed from the time of World War I to about 1960.

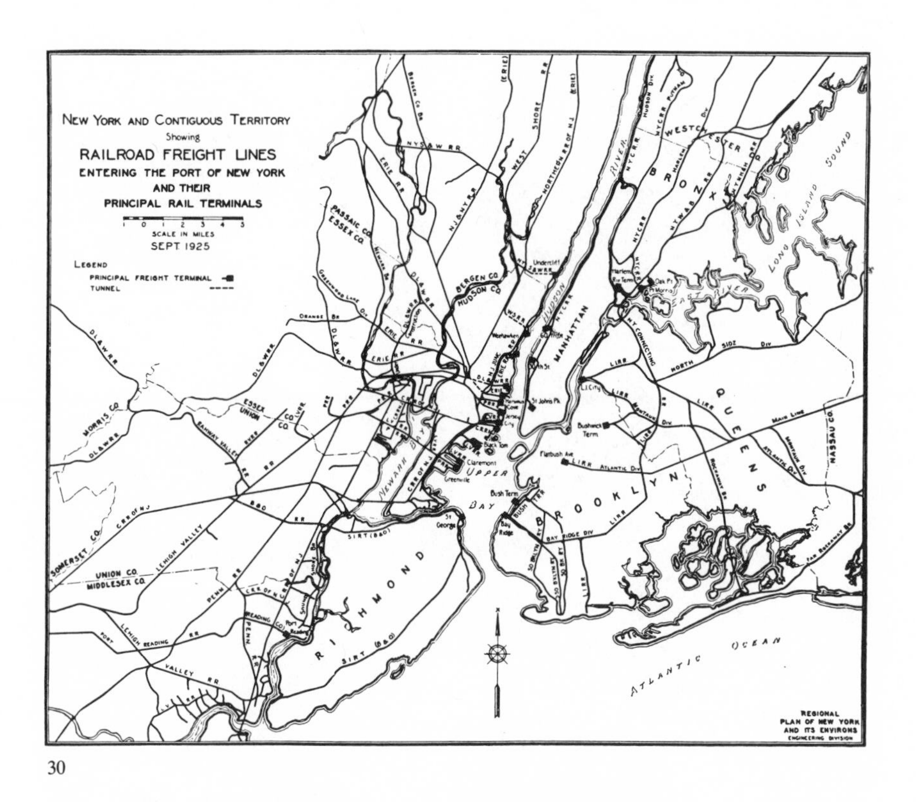

30

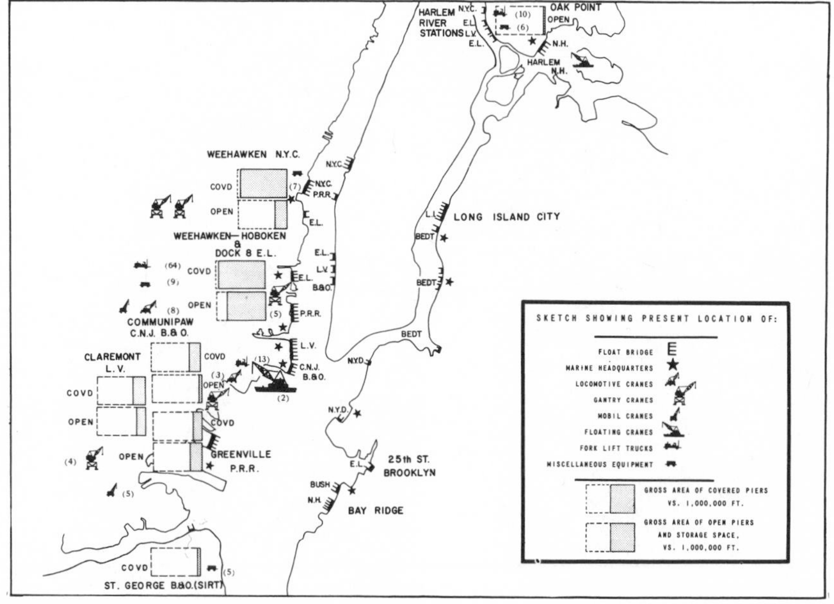

31

Fig. 32. Map of New York Harbor showing car-float routes for interchange freight, 1960–61.

Fig. 33. Map of New York Harbor showing car-float routes for freight to be loaded or unloaded at freight stations on piers or on the land, 1960–61.

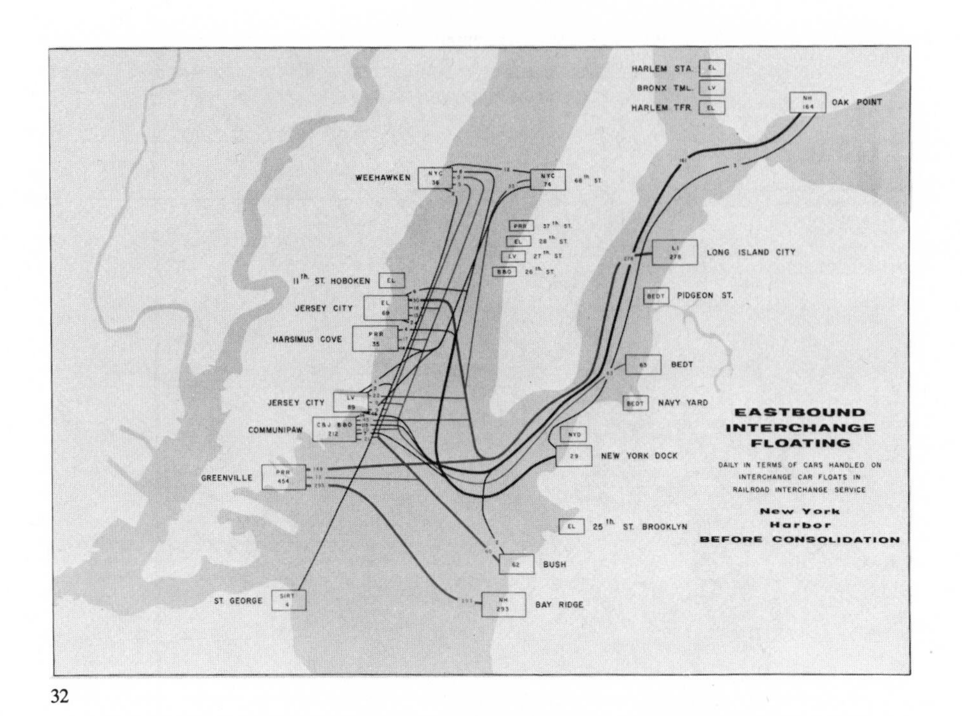

32

33

For freight originating in the district the sequence of movements would be reversed, the final step being the dispatching of an assembled train out of the classification yard. The tedious, cumbersome, expensive, but visually exciting part of this intricate process, of which little survives today, is the marine transfer across the harbor and through its waterways, which is effected either by carfloat or lighter. The carfloats, designed to carry entire cars with lading intact on the tracks of large decked barges, are loaded or unloaded at float bridges adjustable to the tidal level and are propelled over the water by tugs. The simpler of the two kinds of such movements is the interchange float transfer, in which the float is essentially a car ferry conveying cuts of cars from one terminal to another, where they are drawn off by the switch engine to the appropriate destination. The alternative is the operation of the station float transfer, which involves a floating freight station complete with platforms and platform canopies, designed to be made fast to a special pier supporting a freight house for the loading and unloading of the cargo carried inside the water-borne cars. At the high point of transfer operations, the New York roads owned 73 interchange floats and 160 station floats. The technique for moving what is called break-bulk cargo—that is, less-than-carload freight comprising miscellaneous general cargo—between freight cars and ships is lighterage, derived from the name of the type of vessel involved.[4] The car-to-ship transfer is necessitated by the fact that we have dwelt on at some length, namely, that in the Port of New York the great majority of steamship piers are widely separated from the railheads. As a consequence, half the ocean-born commerce of the harbor was once moved from point to point by lighter, which represented by far the highest proportion of such harbor transportation in the world. The squat little lighters, almost square in plan, were a picturesque feature of the kaleidoscopic river scene that fascinated the photographers and painters (among whom Reginald Marsh was easily the foremost); it must be said, however, that they constituted something of an expensive nuisance, which grew out of the perverse objection to rational transportation planning in the port area. At the same time, of course, the labor-intensive operations associated with shipments and the maintenance of marine equipment guaranteed jobs in abundance, and the vast complex of activities was an important factor in preserving the extraordinarily diversified, multidimensional economy of the city.

The railroad officers understood the value of lighterage very well, and they offered the service without an additional charge beyond the point-to-point freight tariff. To carry out this intricate pattern of rail and marine operations on a constantly expanding scale required the introduction of new terminal and transfer lines into the New York family. The first of the miniature newcomers was the Bush Terminal Railroad, which was incorporated on 10 February 1902 as a subsidiary of the Bush Terminal Company of Brooklyn. The property is little more than a concentrated and elongated file of spurs, sidings, and yard tracks serving warehouses, manufacturing plants, and piers of the terminal company, and various additional piers lying between 39th and 57th streets in Brooklyn. The New York Dock Railway, incorporated on 12 April 1910, provides switching service for the piers of the Brooklyn Port Authority, which lie in unbroken rank southward from Brooklyn Bridge to Atlantic Terminal at the foot of King Street, and service for the float bridges along the segment of the Brooklyn shore used for the interchange of traffic with the B. and O., C. N. J., Lackawanna, Erie, Lehigh Valley, New York Central, New Haven, and Pennsylvania railroads. The Brooklyn Eastern District Terminal Railroad came next, its date of incorporation 4 November 1915, and it performed similar functions at the piers between 3d and 12th streets and at the United States Naval Shipyard in Brooklyn. The Eastern District line connects with the Long Island Rail Road at the Pigeon Street Terminal in Long Island City and by carfloat with six of the New Jersey trunk lines (B. and O., C. N. J., Lackawanna, Erie, Lehigh, and Pennsylvania). On the New Jersey side of the harbor area the Bay Shore Connecting Railroad, a joint creation of the Central of New Jersey and the Lehigh Valley, was incorporated on 29 September 1904 to connect the lines of its owners in the Newark Meadows. The little Jay Street Connecting Railroad, which appears to have been a creation of either the Brooklyn or the New York port authority, serves the East River piers between Brooklyn Bridge and the Naval Shipyard and rounds out this subfamily of small but vital links in the huge rail system of the port. There was a continual expansion of harbor facilities up to 1930, at which time the various railroad, shipping, dock, and terminal companies operated more than 4,000 pieces of marine equipment and maintained yards and stations with a capacity of almost 70,000 cars. Following the peak, except for the brief resurgence of the war, depression, changes in modes of transportation, and the migration of industry to the South and Southwest, coming very nearly in succession, turned growth into a long decline.[5]

Only two ports in the world, Hamburg and Rotterdam, rivaled but did not surpass New York in tonnage handled, but none remotely approached it in the multiplicity and complexity of its coordinated rail and marine operations. An analysis of the port traffic made in 1914 by the New York and New Jersey Port and Harbor Commission revealed that the total volume of freight conveyed through, into, and out of the harbor by all modes of transportation reached nearly 133,000,000 tons for the year, of which 66.2 percent was carried by rail and the balance of 33.8 percent by vessels. The importance of this commerce to the city and to the nation may be gauged from two massive facts: more than one-fifth of the entire foreign commerce of the United

States passed through the port, and somewhat more than 40,000,000 tons of the total, or 30.3 percent, were consumed in the port area, for an average consumption of 5.6 tons per capita.[6] Considered strictly from a quantitative standpoint, these totals are indeed impressive, yet the entire operation was inefficient and disorganized to the point of chaos. Moreover, the port was vulnerable to natural and human events of a destructive character, and the disasters of the First World War threw this weakness into high relief. Perhaps the first defect was the nearly absolute dependence on a combination of rail and water transport, two kinds of chains for the movement of goods, each of which could break down in its own way and thus nullify the utility of the other. There was only one all-rail route through the port area for the movement of freight: the central link was the New Jersey Junction Railroad, a subsidiary of the New York Central that connected the Pennsylvania and the Central of New Jersey railroads at National Junction in Jersey City with the West Shore at Weehawken. The New York Connecting Railroad closed part of the gap that separated the New England from the western roads, but the water passage between Greenville Piers and Bay Ridge was never circumvented until the decline of through traffic that followed the Second World War. The vulnerability of water transport arose from the limitations of waterfront space and from the sheer age of the docks and their associated structures. Of the 20 piers owned by the city of New York and leased to the railroads, for example, 16 were constructed before the turn of the century, between 1881 and 1898; two of the remaining four were added in response to the pressures of the First World War, and the two of most recent date were built in 1926 and 1940. Nearly all of the yards and harbor facilities constructed or laid out by the railroads were in place when the war began in Europe. The only major works added by the rail companies during the war or in the decade following it were the big coal-handling pier built by the Reading Company at Port Reading on Arthur Kill (1917–18) and the Oak Island Yard of the Lehigh Valley (1927), lying between the Lehigh freight line and the junction of the Pennsylvania Railroad's main line with the Greenville Branch.[7] Cars, locomotives, ocean vessels, harbor craft, and their respective repair facilities all depended absolutely on the working presence of each other, but their potentialities were squandered on the multitude of overlapping and conflicting movements that grew out of the crazy pattern of docks and terminals. The defects and possible remedies were apparent, at least to the editors of the leading railroad journal, even before the guns were fired in August, 1914.

> New York has done less to develop its port along modern lines than any other important shipping center in the world and is far behind naturally inferior ports as regards adequate terminal facilities and cheap and quick means of transportation. The present congestion of traffic and the recognized impossibility of relieving it by

> the old methods have induced the city and manufacturers to start a strong movement to bring about the necessary improvements. The difficulty is greatly aggravated by the separation of the port into four parts, viz., the New Jersey section, the Manhattan and Bronx section, the Long Island section, and the Staten Island section. Freight communication between these four parts is now only possible by car floats and lighters, and it will not be until they are connected by freight tunnels that the disadvantages of this separation will be entirely overcome.[8]

No one would deny that the troubles which plagued the port during the war years grew in good part out of events far beyond the control of those who operated it, but at the same time there is evidence that the growth of tonnage even in a peacetime economy, had it continued, would have pushed the whole terminal fabric to the point of breakdown. The congestion of 1916–18, which threatened the life of the city, might have become endemic. During the five years of 1915 through 1919 exports through the port doubled, yet no change was made in the physical character of port facilities other than the lengthening and partial reconstruction of the North River piers in the Chelsea district. The piers lying between Chelsea and The Battery, which had been built prior to 1885, were restricted in width to a range of 60 to 95 feet and enclosed slips so narrow as to be usable only by obsolete vessels that were rapidly disappearing. If larger ships had been introduced, there would have been no space remaining for lighters. Insufficient areas of water and antique equipment resulted in such delays or such cumbersome operations that the loading and unloading of vessels required twice as much time in 1919 as these activities consumed in 1914. Delays had a cumulative or circular effect: immobilized rolling stock increased the length of time of transshipment, while the growing length of time spent in moving cargo in and out of vessels resulted in further immobilization of cars. And with delays came an increase in costs, eventually reaching the point in 1919 where the cost of handling a carload of freight between a primary classification yard in New Jersey and a consignee in New York was equal to the cost of hauling it in a train from Pittsburgh or Buffalo to the yard in question. The irony of all this was that railroad and port officers, as well as shippers, recognized that increasing reliance would have to be placed on the motor truck for the local movement of cargo, and as a consequence all concerned looked forward to the completion of the Clifford M. Holland vehicular tunnel, which was planned in 1919 but not opened until 13 November 1927. The railroads did not foresee that the useful adjunct in the terminal area would quickly become a mortal competitor in the transportation of general freight. A copious stream of plans for the improvement of the port poured out for twenty years, but not even the ghastly lessons of the war years brought the necessary implementations.

The Port during the First World War

The events of 1915–18, ranging from the decisions of military commanders meeting in secret enclaves to the vast but little understood movements of air currents in the upper atmosphere, offer the classic example of how a universe of acts and processes may suddenly converge on a world city in multiple interacting layers touching every aspect of life. If New York had been an ordinary place, most of these events would have left no extraordinary consequences; but since it belongs to the limited category of cities that affect and are affected by world affairs, the cumulative results reached awesome proportions. The great overriding fact, of course, was the initiation of world war in August, 1914. Remote from the battlefields in distance and seemingly in any possible relatedness was the physical and financial state of the railroad industry in the United States. This crazy quilt of fragments, embracing everything from powerful corporations in the vanguard of rail technology to mismanaged threads of uneven track staggering into bankruptcy, was so diversified in its financial and working character as to defy general description.

The establishment of the Interstate Commerce Commission in 1887, the passage of the Hepburn Act in 1906, and the proliferation of state commissions over the years placed the railroads under a complex pattern of draconian regulations. In the view of railroad officers, the industry as a whole was treated unrealistically, if not punitively, by numerous regulatory commissions, which, they claimed, prevented the companies from earning an adequate return on their investment in the face of steadily rising costs. From 1900 to 1915, for example, the general price level rose 35.1 percent, railroad wages increased 50 percent, and railroad taxes climbed 200 percent, but in the same period freight tariffs increased only 5 percent, an increment granted at one stroke by the Interstate Commerce Commission in 1913. The passage of the Adamson Act on 29 August 1916 reduced the working day from 10 to 8 hours, adding to the railroads' expenses in effect by raising wages 20 percent. To add injury to these perceived injustices, a short-lived recession in 1915 caused a substantial loss of freight traffic, which amounted to 100,000,000 tons between 1910 and 1915, as opposed to an increase of 31 percent in the previous five-year period.[9] The consequence of this unhappy state of affairs was that many of the roads lacked the financial means to expand their fixed and rolling equipment sufficiently to meet the crucial burdens of the war. By comparing total construction and purchases over parallel three-year periods, 1905–7 and 1915–17, the earlier having been chosen as immediately preceding full federal regulation, the railroad spokesmen showed that in the later period construction of new line fell 80 percent below that of the earlier, freight car orders declined 56 percent, and locomotive orders 53 percent.[10] Furthermore, the officers argued that the failure of the Congress to suspend the Sherman Anti-Trust Law and various antipooling laws (a suspension eventually recommended by the Interstate Commerce Commission) prevented them from coordinating service in ways that would allow unified operations in the face of wartime exigencies.

But a more impartial view reveals a more favorable situation than that described by railroad officers, at least for the larger and more prosperous roads. There had been a steady year-by-year increase in freight-car capacity and locomotive tractive force, improvements in automatic signaling, increases in the efficiency of operations on the line, in the yards, and at terminals—so that the trunk-line companies, with reserves to fall back on, produced 16 percent more ton-miles in May, 1917, for example, than in the comparable month of 1916, and they did so with negligible increases in the number of cars and locomotives. As a consequence, in the full tide of wartime traffic during the following year many records began to fall.[11] The railroads of the New York family posted varying financial results for 1915, but except for the chronically troubled Erie, the operating ratios stood within a few points of the 69 percent for the group as a whole, high, to be sure, but not dangerously so. The seven western trunk lines (B. and O., C. N. J., Lackawanna, Erie, Lehigh Valley, New York Central, and Pennsylvania) carried a little more than 414,000,000 tons of freight in 1915 and very nearly 535,000,000 tons in 1918, for an increase of 29.1 percent, but they managed to do so against staggering difficulties from which they were finally extricated only by federal control.

At first the troubles arose directly from the conduct of the war, which in turn followed from deliberate military policy that was to trap the presumably neutral United States in an untenable position. Since the nation was supplying material to the Allies, the German government in 1915 adopted the policy of unrestricted submarine warfare, which led to immediate and devastating results, the most appalling being the sinking of the *Lusitania* on 7 May of the same year. A repetition of such events, with the inevitable loss of American lives, led the American government to complain to the German ambassador. Germany agreed to halt sinkings without prior warning, but the need to survive what was becoming a war of attrition led the German High Command again to adopt unrestricted submarine activity aimed at sinking all merchant vessels, armed or otherwise. There were minor changes in this policy from time to time, but the essential consequence was that the so-called U-boats began operating off America's eastern coast in the spring of 1916, and from then until the end of the war no Atlantic shipping lane was safe. The United States entered the war on 6 April 1917, but at least six months before that date the sky had begun to fall on American railroads. The chief result of the submarine campaign for rail transportation was that the destruction and crippling of ships serving eastern ports cost so much cargo space that it was impossible to unload cars as rapidly as they entered the harbor areas. This difficulty was compounded by the loss of rail and port manpower to the draft and to the mushrooming war-related industries. The failure to unload cars not only increased port congestion, but it also aggravated the endemic railroad car shortage to the point of paralysis. The deficit in cars and the congestion at the ports, the two acting in a double cause-and-effect relationship, reached threatening proportions in the fall of 1916; yet for a few months following a summertime interlude in full-scale submarine depredations and the adoption of certain emergency measures by the railroads, the companies appeared to be gaining the upper hand. The shortage of 114,908 cars on 1 November 1916 fell by nearly half, to 59,892 cars,on 1 January 1917, only to pass 100,000 cars again by February. The first consequence for long-suffering humanity was a drastic shortage of coal in Ohio, Pennsylvania, New York, and New England. From that time matters grew progressively worse until they reached the level of disaster. By the fall of 1917 the deficit in rolling stock rose to 158,000 cars, and by November 180,000 loaded and immobilized cars were trapped at the eastern ports, about a third of them in the New York yards alone.

The German navy enjoyed the unintended though effective cooperation of shippers and railroad operating personnel in the United States. There were domestic factors that seriously aggravated the existing state of affairs, minor vicious circles, so to speak, that rotated within the larger cycle of wartime destruction and its widening consequences. Some part of the shortage of rolling stock grew out of the overloaded warehouses, which compelled shippers to use cars for storage purposes. Further reductions in the car supply followed from the wasteful practice of partial loading of cars, sometimes adopted out of carelessness or errors in billing, at other times because of the mistaken belief that this would expedite shipments. Beginning in February, 1917, the American Railway Association and various railroad officers repeatedly urged the holding of cars at points of origin until they were fully loaded, but whether such appeals had any effect was impossible to determine, since the practice continued through the year. Finally, the quick-money artists, who operate everywhere at all times, but who flourish particularly in time of war, found ways to make windfall profits by secretly holding grain and perishables in cars, elevators, and warehouses against the inevitable and accelerating increase in prices. The more every kind of shortage was intensified, the more rapidly the prices rose. Investigations conducted by various newspapers, most notably the *Baltimore Sun*, discovered the speculators' favorite trick: goods were repeatedly consigned to different destinations without the unloading of cars, since the shippers or the consignees knew that they could maximize their profits by paying the freight and demurrage charges over a period of days or even weeks rather than unloading the car and selling the contents immediately on receipt thereof. The cheerfully informal commodities markets of the United States greatly facilitated this cynical artistry.

Underlying and extending far beyond these aggravating elements, however, was the fundamental problem of rail operations that has defied solution down through the years. Progressive technology in the form of increasingly powerful locomotives, the steady expansion of freight-car capacity, and the spread of automatic block signaling and electropneumatic interlocking was constantly frustrated by the inordinate amounts of time that cars spent immobilized in yards, terminals, team tracks, and industrial spurs. The full extent of this problem was apparently never documented until the Interstate Commerce Commission carried on a systematic investigation and compiled the relevant data in the fiscal year of 1 July 1913–30 June 1914. The situation described in the very sobering conclusions grew steadily worse through the wartime years. A freight car on an average journey, the Commission's investigators discovered, traveled 260.19 miles loaded and 124.14 miles empty; the time consumed in this journey was divided into three periods, namely, 1.6 days in transit, that is, moving in trains, four days for loading and unloading, and 12.12 days in yards, or 68 percent of the total time of 17.72 days. The distance traveled by an average car per day was a direct function of the length of haul and the concentration of terminals for a given road mileage: on the transcontinental Northern Pacific Railroad, for example, this fictional car covered 73.5 miles per day; on the Pennsylvania, 24.19 miles; on the New Haven, 14.2 miles. The point was obvious: the instrument by means of which the railroad earned its income and on which the nation depended for its goods and commodities spent more than two-thirds of its time standing idle on secondary tracks. It proved to be the secret weapon of the motor truck as well as the German military machine. The problems thrown into clear relief by the Commission's investigation called for long-term developments (for example, an increase in the number of cars, yard tracks, and mileage of automatic controlling devices; the rearrangement of yard and main tracks for improved efficiency of movement; appropriate demurrage charges to enforce the rules for the prompt unloading of cars), but the increasingly desperate car shortage called for immediate and drastic remedies.

The railroad companies, acting collectively through the American Railway Association, took steps in the direction of unified service in cooperation with the federal government. On 16 February 1917 they established an organization to direct the movement of troops as the nation moved unmistakably toward the mobilization of men and resources. The chief function of this group, acting under the chairmanship of Fairfax Harrison, president of the Southern Railway, was to work out a program of large-scale troop movements in cooperation with the Council of National Defense, which had been created in the previous year by Newton D. Baker, the secretary of war. The second action was broader and more decisive. Immediately following the declaration of war on 6 April, the roads established a Railroad War Board, composed of another group of leading executives—Howard Elliott, chairman of the New Haven; Fairfax Harrison; Hale Holden, president of the Chicago, Burlington and Quincy; Julius Kruttschnitt, chairman of the Southern Pacific; and Samuel Rea, president of the Pennsylvania. The aim was to consolidate operations and work as a unified rail industry in cooperation with the federal government. Both groups were abolished, however, when the government was finally compelled to act. With freight-car miles falling steadily, with 180,000 cars to be unloaded at the eastern ports, and the likelihood of severe winter weather, national control was an urgent necessity. On 26 December 1917 President Woodrow Wilson announced the establishment, effective as of noon, 28 December, of the United States Railroad Administration to acquire the properties and to operate the railroads of the United States. He appointed William G. McAdoo, his secretary of the treasury, as the director general of the organization, and Alfred H. Smith, the president of the New York Central Railroad, as the assistant director general. McAdoo immediately formed an advisory committee composed of five executive officers of major railroad companies—namely, Edward Chambers, vice-president of the Atchison, Topeka and Santa Fe; Walker D. Hines, chairman of the executive committee of the same company; Hale Holden; Henry Walters, chairman of the Atlantic Coast Line; and John S. Williams, former president of the Seaboard Air Line.

The United States Railroad Administration was granted vastly greater authority than any private body could command. Although operations were to be conducted by the existing railroad organizations and their staffs, such operations, together with all capital expenditures, were to be carried out strictly in accordance with the program drawn up by McAdoo and his advisors. It was, in effect, government ownership of the railroads, and the aim of the new dispensation was clearly set forth by the director general.

> The operation of the railroads as a thoroughly unified system is of fundamental importance to the success of the war. Without it we cannot get the effective use of our resources. . . . Victory will depend on our speed and our efficiency. We can get neither . . . unless the railroads are equal to the demands of the situation.[12]

The reaction of the railroad officers to this new order, surprisingly enough, was at first enthusiastic, but the time was to come when the favorable view would change to its opposite. There were expressions of relief on the part of the majority of executives because the responsibility for the direction of the roads was lifted from their shoulders, while leaving them free to operate the lines in cooperation with the federal government rather than under the restrictions imposed by regulatory commissions. The financial markets posted substantial increases in the prices of railroad securities, and McAdoo received "hundreds" of congratulatory telegrams from bankers, owners of railroad stocks and bonds, and railroad executives. There were expected negative reactions, most of them arising from the belief that the government thought the railroads had failed and was taking the first step toward socialism. The opinion among railroad officers held that McAdoo was in a position to establish a utopian state of affairs, as the editor of *Railway Age* suggested.

> The Director General of Railroads is free from all those trammels which government has imposed upon the managers of the railways. He can route traffic any way he pleases. He does not have to take orders from state legislatures as to how many men he shall employ in a train crew. He can reduce service as much as he thinks desirable. He can reduce as much as he likes the time given shippers to unload their freight and he can raise freight and passenger rates as high as he pleases. He can control the use of freight preference orders by government representatives. If, unlike most of the regulating authorities, he acts wisely and fairly he can get the loyal support of the railway officers.[13]

The time would come when the officers were to complain bitterly about the United States Railroad Administration, chiefly because of an 80 percent increase in the average wage of railroad workers (from $1,004 in 1917 to $1,820 in 1920), but on final balance the railroads enjoyed great benefits flowing from government operation. The paralysis of the eastern ports was ended, 1,930 locomotives were added to the existing stock, and 100,000 new freight cars appeared on the rails; motive power, rolling stock, and many operating techniques were standardized, with resulting economies for the trunk-line roads and the manufacturers.

The only weapons that the railroads and the government possessed at the close of 1917 were embargoes and priorities. The first had been used since early 1916, chiefly by the eastern lines, to stop the shipment of various classes of freight for varying periods of time into the overloaded eastern yards. The embargoes were imposed primarily at the huge gateway centers, particularly Chicago, Saint Louis, and Pittsburgh, of which the last suffered from the most extreme congestion among all the major centers other than the ports themselves. The use of priorities, or what came to be called preference freight, was inaugurated in the late weeks of 1917 and widely extended by the Railroad Administration. The government established the office of priority director and appointed Judge R. S. Lovett to the chief administrative position. In December, 1917, he issued a sweeping order that gave food, fuel, and military supplies priority over all other freight. The United States War Department then introduced an extensive system of zonal embargoes designed chiefly for moving unloaded boxcars westward for the return shipment of grain. The General Operating Committee of Eastern Railroads, which held its first meeting in Pittsburgh on 28 November 1917, developed a multidimensional program in the following month aimed primarily at the conservation of fuel, the increase in tonnage per train, the improvement of schedules, and an embargo on nonessential freight.[14] The progressive cancellation of temporarily expendable passenger service began at the same time, although the editors of *Railway Age Gazette* had urged it as early as May, 1917.

William McAdoo moved with extraordinarily effective energy in implementing such plans as had already been formulated and creating a great many more. The first four acts of the director general had an immediate and beneficial effect on the Port of New York, where the devastating winter of 1917/18 was pushing the terminal area to the point of total immobility. At the peak of congestion in the early weeks of 1918, there were 65,000 cars in the terminal yards at one time, a total which, as we have seen, was almost exactly equal to the combined capacity of the yards. McAdoo's initial step was to give the capable Alfred Smith complete control over all rail operations in what is called by the Interstate Commerce Commission the Official Classification Territory, where the greatest volume of freight and passenger traffic and the most congested ports were concentrated.[15] All orders to railroad officers originating from Smith's office in New York were issued under the authority of the director general. The second act showed how far Smith's power extended, for it was clearly set forth in the general instructions he dispatched to the respective headquarters of the eastern railroads on 31 December 1917.

> By order of the Director General of Railroads, Judge [R. S.] Lovett concurring as to priority modifications, please direct every attention to clearing your line of any congestion that exists, wiring me of any condition which is beyond individual control, with suggestions as to most available method of relief.

> You are authorized to disregard priority orders to the extent necessary to clear up a serious congestion, keeping in mind vital necessity for moving food and fuel.
>
> Wire me particularly where coal is congested without prospect of immediate movement, so that matter of diversion to open line, or markets, can be arranged with the Fuel Administrator.
>
> Embargo any consignee who does not release freight promptly on arrival.
>
> So far as practicable, annul passenger trains which interfere with giving necessary freight service.
>
> Keep in touch with your connections and afford help to each other in any way possible to further movement, change routing, short haul freight, and make any mutual arrangements that will facilitate the delivery of traffic.
>
> Call on all employees to lend their efforts in this matter of service to the Government and the people.
>
> Endeavor to start trains promptly from terminals and load to permit of prompt movement over divisions.
>
> Advise by wire daily to New York number of cars of freight you have to move above capacity, location of congestion in the order of extent, with prospects of gaining or losing on the situation in the following 24 hours.
>
> If you have capacity to handle more business on any part of your line, advise between what points and how much, and what you can best handle and dispose of.
>
> If you are holding freight for connections, give number of cars, loads, or empties, and divide loads into coal, food, Government freight, and other.[16]

The third step in this sequence of acts was aimed directly at breaking the New York impasse. In early January, Smith dispatched a telegram to Mayor John P. Mitchel (shortly to be succeeded by John F. Hylan) requesting the release of all city employees who could be spared from their normal duties to unload cars at the city's congested terminals and team tracks. The fourth was a long overdue plan formulated by the officers of the New York roads for the unified operation of the rail-water terminals of the harbor. The problem had reached a crisis: by mid-January, in addition to government priority freight, 30,000 cars of food and military supplies destined for the British, French, and Italian governments were being held by western roads for shipment to eastern ports.

At this juncture the most formidable enemy on the domestic scene mounted a campaign that for one month at least seemed irresistible. All the troubles arising from the successes of German submarines and the breakdown of railroad service were transformed into an unremitting plague by the deadly winter of 1917/18. If God was on the side of the Allies, as the clergymen regularly proclaimed, He proved a hard problem for the theologians when the heavens began to blast the works of man after the Christmas and New Year holidays. The prolonged snowfalls and sub-zero temperatures that began in December were bad enough, and they pushed more than one road to near-paralysis. The blizzards of January, however, seemed to be aimed directly at the Middle Atlantic ports and their lifelines, for they struck with special fury at the railroads across New York, Pennsylvania, and the Virginias. There was no break for seven weeks over a front from Boston to Cape Charles, and when temperatures finally rose, they brought floods to the Ohio River and the waterways of eastern Kentucky. The Pennsylvania Railroad, possessed of the greatest resources and staggering under the heaviest traffic, had to abandon repair and building operations at its sprawling Juniata Shops in Altoona simply to cope with snow. In the month of 20 December–21 January the company repeatedly called out all shop employees to man the shovels: by investing 92,250 man-hours in this activity they managed temporarily to clear main tracks and yards in the immediate area, but 19 locomotives, 45 passenger cars, and 58 freight cars stood unrepaired, and 39 new cars on order went unbuilt. At Bellwood, Pennsylvania, shopmen cleared snow for a total of 11,000 man-hours, with similar ambiguous results. There was worse to come. The blizzards that buried the middle belts of New York, Pennsylvania, and West Virginia on 26–28 January immobilized 7,930 cars on the Pennsylvania Railroad alone. The Pocahontas roads, many of their shopmen lost to the draft, borrowed 1,100 miners from the West Virginia shafts to remove snow from yard tracks. The Pennsylvania was compelled to adopt herculean measures: all through passenger trains westbound out of Philadelphia were annulled on the afternoon of 28 January; a force of 25,000 men taken from every operating department throughout the state was called on to shovel snow, and they managed to open the entire main line by nightfall of the 29th, only to see the huge backlog of unrepaired cars (2,357 on the Pittsburgh Division alone) cripple the railroad as effectively as the snow. Equipment failures and human exhaustion rounded out the siege of troubles: stalled trains, frozen air hoses, broken journals and hot boxes, broken rails, frozen signals and snapped signal wire, frozen water columns and water scoops, beaten veterans of shops and track gangs forced to give up the job because of intolerable cold, young and old alike falling before a raging influenza epidemic—together they seemed as devastating in their effects as war itself. The trunk lines might have been bowed to the ground under their burdens, but they were not broken. The giant Pennsylvania Railroad, for example, simply defied nature, like Prometheus before Zeus, and succeeded in operating 2,773 trains consisting of 110,457 cars over its mutilated main line through the Alleghenies during this frightful month. An average movement of 90 freight trains per day, with an additional 30 to 50 passenger trains, the number varying with temporary cancellations, had to be regarded as an impressive volume of traffic for any season of the year. The editors of *Railway Age* paid the operating staffs a well-deserved tribute.

> These results, in the face of unprecedented difficulties, were only accomplished by the self-sacrifice, loyalty and devotion to duty of many thousands of officers and employees who cheerfully endured unaccustomed and arduous work and repeatedly faced hardship, danger and real suffering, in the struggle to keep the lines open so that the public and the government might be served.[17]

The crippling of the Pennsylvania and the Erie was enough to place New York in a state of siege, especially with respect to fresh fruit and vegetables, but the congestion that afflicted the B. and O. and the anthracite carriers resulted in a shortage of coal that pushed the city and New England to the point of desperation. In order to clear tracks and conserve fuel so that they might move fuel for domestic uses, the big passenger carriers of the New York family began to cancel passenger schedules in June, 1917, and by the fateful January of 1918 some 600 trains had been removed from service. The New Haven led the way with the annulment of 199 trains; the Pennsylvania dropped a total of 138, including the Broadway Limited, while the New York Central removed a maximum of 100 trains, mostly from the lines through middle and upper New York. The Central of New Jersey, the Lackawanna, and the Erie followed with the cancellation of varying numbers of suburban trains. Among the minor details in this program of curtailment were two aimed at assuring those who were accustomed to luxury accommodations that they were doing their part: the New York Central dropped observation cars from all trains carrying them, and the Pennsylvania withdrew wintertime sleeping cars from the trains operated between New York, Florida, and the Gulf Coast. The coal shortage, nevertheless, steadily approached the crisis stage, and the presidents of the New York roads called a conference in early January, 1918, to draw up measures for coping with the situation. The usual practice was to convey the coal by lighters to the waterfront terminals of Brooklyn, or by barge to the coal pockets of Manhattan, where the tedious labor of loading into street vehicles took place. The plan the executives adopted, however, called for the movement of train loads of coal by carfloat directly to the waterfront team tracks in Manhattan, where a small army of City Hall recruits shoveled the fuel out of hopper cars or from the street grade into wagons and trucks for delivery to the coal yards of Manhattan and The Bronx.

But in order to make even this modest effort effective the Railroad Administration had to adopt far more stringent measures than those embodied in its first directives. On 23 January 1918, A. H. Smith ordered an embargo of general freight on all lines of the B. and O., Pennsylvania, and Reading railroads in order to make way for the movement of food, fuel, military supplies, and high-priority or preference shipments for the government. Even more drastic for the region affected was his order of 26 January, which called for the suspension of all rail operations in middle and upper New York state until main lines could be cleared at least sufficiently to carry food, fuel, and priority freight.[18] To place embargoes on main-track shipments for even a day, Smith understood perfectly well, meant that alternative routes had quickly to be opened. As a consequence, his unprecedented order of 29 January spelled out in voluminous detail how freight moving from or through the Chicago and Saint Louis gateways to New York Harbor was to be classified, where it was to be concentrated, how trains were to be made up, over what routes they were to be dispatched, and what information pertaining to these operations was to be daily transmitted by wire to Smith's office in New York. Moreover, the competitive positions of the individual roads, the network of reciprocal agreements that had been built up over the years among the railroads and between them and the shippers, the relations of affiliated lines to parent companies, these were set aside where necessary in favor of a strictly pragmatic approach. Smith's order thus possesses a historical importance transcending its temporary *ad hoc* character: for the first time the railroads, at least in the Eastern or Official Territory, were called upon to act as interrelated units of a national system. For the handling of freight at the Port of New York, the assistant director presented a plan of unified operations that should have been adopted long before the war. Because of a shortage of harbor equipment, especially lighters and tugs, arising from insufficient manpower in the shipyards to repair them, he required that ships destined for Great Britain, Belgium, France, and Italy were to be sailed directly to those railhead piers on the New Jersey and Staten Island shores that could accommodate ocean-going vessels. Since there were few piers that were equipped to transfer loads directly between car and ship, other port traffic had either to be diverted or be held until space was available. The continuing foul weather of January delayed the implementation of the Smith plan until mid-February, when higher temperatures at last turned the trick. At the beginning of the month the number of delayed cars was being reduced at the rate of 5,000 per day, and this rate was to rise to 8,000 in March. By the week of 7–14 February coal was moving into New York Harbor at the customary rate prior to the American entry into the war; by mid-month all freight traffic on the eastern railroads was moving well above the normal peacetime rate, and the unloading of cars was expedited sufficiently to maintain the harbor yards in a state no worse than the congestion of other years. So war and blizzards taught the railroads what they could always have done if they had not shared in the national phobia about comprehensive planning.[19]

Plans for Unification and the Port Authority

The delays and the congestion that characterized the Port of New York, and the resulting inefficiency and expense of shipping freight through the huge terminal area, were burdens that had come to be recognized before the turn of the century. The railroads, the steamship companies, the city, and the terminal companies built what they all thought was needed, but the intricate pattern of overlapping movements that eventually emerged, involving through and local trains, switching runs, ocean vessels, tugs, barges, carfloats, lighters, wagons, and later trucks, simply could not be made to work in a systematic way by means of the traditional individualist and competitive approach. The presence of refractory problems on the one hand and of imaginative engineers and planners on the other, together with the progressive spirit that informed municipal enterprise at the turn of the century, stimulated planning zeal, and proposals for unifying and otherwise improving the port soon began to multiply. The first step in this process was the establishment on 9 December 1903 of the New York City Improvement Commission, which issued a preliminary report on 1 January 1905 and a final version exactly two years later.[20] The commission was concerned with the entire urban fabric, and its suggestions for port improvements were limited to the physical renewal of docks and associated structures and the building of circumferential arteries that would serve partly to unite harbor facilities. The results of these proposals for harbor installations appear to have been negligible.

In little more than a year after the commission issued its final report, the indefatigable William J. Wilgus offered the most completely novel plan for the unification of freight yards, piers, freight houses, team tracks, warehouses, and factories throughout the metropolitan area. The program revealed above all Wilgus's unshakable devotion to underground electrified operations as the key to efficient urban circulation. The central feature of his plan was in effect a belt and transfer railway having the form of an extensive system of freight-carrying tunnels equipped with rails, electrical distribution and transmission, and suitable controls. The concept, Wilgus readily admitted, was not original with him: it was derived from the narrow-gauge freight-carrying tunnels built in Chicago in 1901–9 by the Illinois Telephone and Telegraph Company and the Illinois Tunnel Company. Wilgus's system was far greater in length than its Chicago predecessor, and the method of transporting cargo may be regarded as the original form of containerized freight-handling in which shipments are conveyed directly between shipper and train or train and consignee without detainment in yards or stations (later to be called pick-up-and-delivery service). In short, he anticipated two essential characteristics of modern intermodal transportation. Its historical value deserves that it be presented in detail in his own words.

> The method . . . [employs] a standard-gauge small car of say ten tons capacity, with demountable body, adapted to the handling of every kind of freight, except very bulky or long articles, electrically operated by the multiple unit system in long trains headed by a single man between transfer yards at the outskirts and various destinations within the Region, and passing beneath navigable waters, and beneath the surface of streets in the congested centers, in small dimensioned tunnels and subways placed as near as possible to the surface.
>
> At suitable locations such trains would be brought together in marshaling yards, operated by gravity [hump yards, in the railroad argot], where the cars for a common destination would be sorted and assembled in trains of the desired make-up.
>
> In each of the more congested centers, access to the larger establishments would be had by means of direct track access, so that their freight would not affect the street surfaces at all, while access to the smaller shipper and householder would be effected by mechanically transferring the laden demountable car bodies, at a multiplicity of inland union freight stations, from the small car subway chassis to motor truck chassis for short-radius distribution on the street surface.
>
> In all, this is a method that lends itself to a single control in the interest of all the railroads and the public; that offers promise of savings in operations much more than sufficient to defray fixed charges on the new investment in small cross-section tunnels and subways; that guarantees freedom from existing hindrances to the speedy, reliable and safe movement of freight and to the quick release of the standard long-haul car; that minimizes or makes unnecessary the use of the surface of city streets for slow moving freight trucks, and to that extent, or even in a larger degree, increases the capacity of the streets for higher speed automobiles; that is adapted to nearly all classes of freight shipments; and that frees the waterfront for its legitimate uses.[21]

Everything that Wilgus claimed for this ambitious program could be readily justified, but it had two serious though not fatal defects. It would have cost a staggering sum of money, at least as much as and possibly several times more than the cost of the Pennsylvania Raliroad's New York Extension, and the investment would have had to come either from a municipal issue of revenue bonds or from a cooperative financial program sponsored by all the New York railroads, which always revealed a marvelous capacity for resisting such unified effort. Further, the fixed underground right of way possessed a troublesome inflexibility in the face of the expanding patterns of demographic as well as industrial development. Yet its merits were such that one can only lament the failure to create some such system of hierarchical and interdependent relations among through railroads, water transfer, freight tunnels, and motor trucks.

Discussions and suggestions like those of William Wilgus greatly stimulated interest in the question of port improvement, and the municipal authorities as well as private bodies began to act. In the summer of 1910 an ad hoc committee appointed by the Board of Aldermen issued a report on the need for and the feasibility of a union freight terminal in Manhattan, but details such as the cost of construction, how it was to be born, and what access was to be provided for the New Jersey roads were not spelled out. A second report again bearing the stamp of municipal authority and appearing in January, 1911, proposed an elevated railroad belt line connecting all the Manhattan piers and their associated freight houses. At mid-year a third report, drawn up by E. P. Goodrich and H. P. Nichols, was submitted to the Board of Estimate and Apportionment. The authors suggested the transformation of many existing facilities into what they called unit terminals characterized by double-deck piers and float bridges, which were to be connected by rail with the second floors of freight houses and warehouses located on the shore side of peripheral streets. The terminals were to be designed for the handling of all kinds of freight and to function as warehouses or as distribution centers for delivery by railroad car and truck. The plan of Goodrich and Nichols, unlike the Wilgus proposal, did not consider the problem of the intracity movement of freight other than to suggest the use of motor trucks. Reports now began to flow in a copious stream, their authors undeterred by the failure of the city and the railroad companies to offer any realizable plan of action. The officers of the New York Central and Hudson River presented a document to the commissioner of docks in September, 1911, recommending a system of interconnected freight terminals and an associated belt line. A committee of the City Club, in the same month, reported on the problem of the West Side terminals and the necessity for expanding and reconstructing them. Nothing new was added in this report, so that perhaps its only value lay in keeping the issue alive. In December of that year the Department of Docks and Ferries took a much longer step when they recommended to the Chamber of Commerce a comprehensive expansion, unification, and interconnection of all freight-handling terminals in the Port of New York.

The department's proposal was drastically enlarged and, for the first time, spelled out with considerable supporting detail in the plan offered by Calvin Tompkins, the newly appointed commissioner of docks, in 1913. Tompkins, as a matter of fact, drew up a program of new construction for the movement of freight comparable in form and magnitude to the Pennsylvania Railroad's extension for the conveyance of passengers. The central feature, as far as Manhattan was concerned, was a system of jointly operated freight terminals and warehouses on the West Side, which were to be connected by suitable relocations and expansions of the New York Central's West Side line. The most impressive and ambitious feature of the Tompkins plan was the proposal to construct railroad freight tunnels under the Hudson River on the line of 42d Street and under The Narrows between Brooklyn and Staten Island. A union classification yard with a capacity of 6,000 cars was to be laid out in the meadows near the New Jersey end of the North River tunnel. Tompkins's program was thoroughly imbued with the spirit of the new Progressivism: the tunnels were to be constructed by public bodies and publicly owned, and the city of New York was to acquire and retain control of West Street, the docks and freight-handling facilities of the West Side, and the proposed West Side viaduct of the New York Central (see the last section of this chapter). This extraordinary and costly scheme was predicated on certain assumptions that were readily granted in 1913—namely, the unrivalled status of New York Harbor and the continued growth of its unrivalled volume of cargo, the supremacy of metropolitan New York as a shipping, railroad, and manufacturing center, and its ready accessibility to the continent. The only explicit opposition came from the officers of the New Jersey railroad companies, who believed that hauling freight directly into Manhattan would increase their expenses without any gain in revenue. If others were silent, it was probably because they saw no likelihood that Tompkins's admirable plan would ever be implemented. Eventually, of course, the Port of New York Authority borrowed its most prominent features in the construction of Lincoln Tunnel and Verrazano-Narrows Bridge.

Two more modest proposals followed during the war. Robert Rosenbluth, an urban planner with the New York Institute for Public Service, in February, 1917, offered at one stroke a solution to wartime freight congestion as well as a step in the direction of a comprehensive improvement of freight terminals. The essential proposal, conceived as an initial phase, was the reconstruction of the four city-owned piers in the East River, so that they could accommodate freight shipments carried by lighter from the existing railheads in New Jersey. Another plan for the unification of scattered freight terminals was advanced in the following year by William R. Wilcox, the chairman of the Harbor Development Commission. The most thoroughgoing solution, however, to the problems of the New York terminals, all of which were magnified by the troubles of the war, was also the one most susceptible of practical realization, since it was the first to be predicated on the necessity for municipal, state, federal, and railroad cooperation. It was put forth in December, 1919, by J. J.

Mantell, the manager of the New York Terminal District, whose position entitled him to a respectful hearing. The clearheaded though admittedly preliminary character of his program deserves restatement.

> Speaking of pier development, New York has practically stood still for several years and with the exception of the development in the Chelsea district, which was more or less on the old order of pier construction, no recent improvements have been made. . . . This situation can be corrected by the development of facilities along the lines of economic handling with the co-operation of the States interested, the Federal Government and the railroads. The solution . . . is the development of two large clearing yards in New Jersey, one to the south and one to the north, to take the place of present individual classification yards. It would be necessary to have two clearing yards as one yard sufficiently large to accommodate the business of the port would be unwieldy in its handling. These yards could be connected by a belt line railroad; floatbridges could be centralized and the water front developed to provide multiple story steamship piers along the New Jersey shore from Greenville to Weehawken, a distance of approximately nine miles, the upper floors to be used for storage and the lower floors equipped with teamways and tracks for the handling of freight direct from cars to steamer. Piers should be developed to suit the needs of individual interests and so constructed as to provide for the handling of weight and measurement cargo at the same pier. Outside open tracks should be provided, where necessary, and piers equipped with overhead cranes and various other mechanical devices. . . . A vehicular tunnel [Holland] has been planned by the States of New York and New Jersey to connect Manhattan Island and Jersey City, with the New York end to be located at Canal Street and the New Jersey end at 12th Street. The traffic which is now trucked via ferry will no doubt be diverted to the tunnel, but the full benefits of the proposed tunnel will not be felt until the railroads have money available for the further development of their Jersey shore properties. . . . Further, the heavy interchange of cars between New Jersey and New England roads should be via tunnel connecting Greenville and Bay Ridge under New York Bay.[22]

The idea of a direct rail connection between New Jersey and Manhattan or Brooklyn, or both, was first publicized in 1869, and similar proposals for tunnels or bridges came at intervals up to the First World War. The proponents of bridges showed remarkable perseverance in spite of the obstacles that stood in the way of practical realization. The architect Alfred C. Bossom in 1920 proposed the construction of a huge double-deck truss bridge, to be called Victory or Memorial Bridge, connecting downtown Manhattan on the line of the Williamsburg span (Canal Street on the West Side) with Weehawken or upper Jersey City. The upper deck was to be used by vehicles, streetcars, and pedestrians, while the lower, carrying ten tracks, was reserved for rail traffic. The height of the deck was fixed to coincide with the top of Bergen Hill, with the consequence that the Manhattan approach or the Manhattan segment of a continuous elevated structure, would have posed insuperable difficulties, of which Bossom appears to have been innocently unaware. As a matter of fact, he cannot have paid attention to any of the problems involved: he made no provision for a station at the Manhattan end, and the alignment he describes would have placed the west end above the Erie Railroad yards along Pavonia Avenue. The celebrated engineer Gustav Lindenthal, undeterred by the lack of interest in his earlier proposal, offered still another plan for a Hudson River crossing in 1921. It was to be a double-deck suspension bridge carrying a total of 34 arteries for every mode of transportation: the upper deck was to be divided into 2 walkways, 16 traffic lanes, 2 streetcar tracks, and 2 bus lanes, and the lower was to support 12 railroad tracks. The transverse deck beams constituted the most interesting structural feature. The individual member was an enormous Vierendeel truss divided into six panels, each of a size sufficient for two rail lines, with an overall depth of about 35 feet. The cost of this behemoth would clearly have been beyond the means of the railroad companies at the time, and neither the states nor the Corps of Engineers seem to have been interested in the project.[23] The grandiose schemes for bridges were perfectly feasible and could have been realized under the aegis of the United States Railroad Administration, supplemented in its action by an appropriate partnership among the railroad companies, the city, and the states of New York and New Jersey.

The federal control of the roads was continued until 1 March 1920, but by that date their officers had become obsessed by two aims, the ending of national control and such revisions in the rate structure as were necessary to put an end to the operating deficits of 1918–20. Rapid and drastic increases in railroad wages, the high costs of operating under the exigencies of war and the ravages of winter storms, the postwar recession of 1919–20, an inflation of prices that pushed the index up from 100 in 1915 to 294 in 1920—these factors submerged the railroads in a sea of red ink, while at the same time the accumulated backlog of unfulfilled needs for new equipment reached a value of $6,000,000,000 at 1920 prices. Insofar as traffic volume was concerned, the railroads of the New York family were booming, but their financial returns were uniformly dismal. From 1915 to 1920 the roads serving the port enjoyed an increase in tonnage of 33.5 percent, and in number of passengers of 60.1 percent. While their share of the national total of freight traffic dropped slightly, from 54.5 to 53.6 percent, the proportion of total passenger traffic rose markedly, from 36.3 to 44.9 percent.[24] For the year 1920 the eleven trunk lines operated at a deficit, posting a collective operating ratio of 102.5 percent at the close of the year. The individual companies either showed a deficit for the year, or emerged with incomes too small to cover interest charges, taxes, and rentals. If dividends were paid, they were drawn from reserve funds. The operating ratios ranged from a minimum of 84.4 percent for the Long Island Rail Road (ironically enough, in view of the financial difficulties that were soon to come) to a staggering 121 percent for the New York, Susquehanna and Western. Even the largest and most prosperous carriers showed losses—more than $3,000,000 for the B. and O., nearly $11,000,000 for the Erie, and more than $42,000,000 for the Pennsylvania.[25] It was clear that if the Mantell plan was to be implemented, the task would have to fall to a public body authorized to issue revenue bonds backed, directly or indirectly, by the taxing powers of the states. One of the great misfortunes for the Port of New York was that when such a body was finally established, it soon lost interest in the primacy of a unified expansion and reconstruction of rail and harbor facilities.

The ancestor of a port authority at New York was the city's Department of Docks, which suffered from the serious limitation of having no jurisdiction over the New Jersey waterfront, where most of the railroads, yards, and terminals were concentrated. Two great and complex factors underlay the need for a single governmental agency owning and operating harbor facilities, like those that had begun to appear in Europe at the turn of the century. The first, which we have reviewed at length, was the failure of the port to cope with the exigencies of the war; the second was an intermittent conflict of many years standing between the city of New York and the state of New Jersey over the ownership of subaqueous land, the taxation of privately owned harbor facilities, navigation rights, and the rates charged for the marine services of the railroads. In 1917 the legislatures of the two states established the New York–New Jersey Harbor Development Commission to find ways of relieving port congestion and to plan the orderly development of the harbor in the future. The chairman of the organization was J. Spencer Smith, the vice-chairmen Eugenius H. Outerbridge, after whom the bridge over Arthur Kill at Perth Amboy was named, and George W. Goethals, the chief engineer of the Panama Canal. The commission issued a report in 1920 which consisted of a comprehensive plan of development predicated on a complete analysis of the shipping and railroad facilities of the port area, and a recommendation for the establishment of a bistate agency to regulate the operations of the port and to construct its own port installations. A compact drawn up by the two state legislatures in April, 1921, established a Port of New York Authority and a Port District of 1,270 square miles over which it was to have jurisdiction.

The specific model for the organization was the Port of London Authority, which had been established in 1909. The municipal administration of New York City expressed an immediate antipathy to the idea of such an agency and sought to weaken its power, and the state legislatures introduced various restrictions as the result of this opposition. The authority was to be headed by six commissioners "constituted as a body corporate and politic, with full power and authority to purchase, construct, lease, and/or operate any terminal or transportation facility within the said District."[26] These sweeping powers were further enlarged by a definition of "terminal and transportation facility" so broad as to include railroads, bridges, tunnels, trucks, any harbor craft, as well as piers, docks, ferries, and float bridges. The authority, however, could not interfere with the municipal construction and ownership of harbor facilities; neither could it acquire property without due process of law and just compensation, nor use the credit of either state for acquisitions, improvements, and operating expenses unless expressly authorized to do so by the appropriate legislature. The authority was further charged with the responsibility of issuing a comprehensive plan of port development and for recommending to Congress and the state legislatures specific improvements in the operation of the port. In short, the new creation was presented with formidable tasks, but it was also granted very broad and loosely defined powers without an exactly corresponding accountability.

The first act of the authority was the preparation of the *Comprehensive Plan* for the improvement of the port, which was completed in 1922, approved by the two state legislatures in the same year, and amended several times, again with legislative approval, during the succeeding ten years. What was described as the "keystone of the arch" in the proposed structure of unified and coordinated terminals was a continuous Middle Belt Line planned to connect all the railroad lines entering the New Jersey waterfront corridor with their counterparts in the boroughs of Richmond, Brooklyn, Queens, and The Bronx, the circuit to have a total length of 61.5 miles, of which 51.5 miles were already in place. To establish a continuous rail circuit uniting the existing lines required at least one crossing of harbor waterways between New Jersey or Staten Island and Brooklyn. The authors of the *Comprehensive Plan* were not disposed to find the easiest solutions: they recommended a double-track tunnel extending under New York Bay from the Greenville Piers of the Pennsylvania Railroad to the Bay Ridge Yard of the Long Island, a distance of nearly five miles. The proposed tunnel proved to be the one feature of the plan that was born into immediate controversy. In May, 1921, when the Port Authority was scarcely a month old, the General Assembly at Albany passed a bill authorizing the city of New York to construct combined railroad and rapid transit tubes under The Narrows between Richmond and Brooklyn and requiring that the municipality initiate the work by 1923. The city thus objected to the longer tunnel on the understandable ground that its location as well as its restriction to freight service left the rapid transit lines of Staten Island in a continuing state of isolation from the rest of the city's transit system. The whole discussion, however, turned out to be an exercise in futility because both schemes were abandoned in 1925.

The rest of the *Comprehensive Plan* fared better, at least in a documentary form. Concentric to the Middle Belt there was to be an Outer Belt Line, 71 miles in length, to lie in a crescent along the western limits of the Port District between Piermont on the north and the west shore of Newark Bay on the south. The chief function of this arc of double- and multiple-track railway was the expeditious transfer of freight from one New Jersey trunk line to another outside the congested switching areas. Supplementing the two belt lines, and indeed forming an inner belt of discontinuous segments, were a number of so-called marginal railroads lying along the shores of the navigable and largely developed waterways and along Jamaica Bay, the navigability of which at the time was open to question. There were to be eight of these transfer and connecting lines, their purpose being to connect docks in series, separated rail lines, and docks with rail lines. The marginal road in Queens and Brooklyn, for example, was designed in part to unite the Brooklyn Eastern District, Jay Street, New York Dock, and Bush Terminal railroads into a continuous line. In places these little shore roads were to be built beyond the limits of existing docks and trackage in order to provide the customary stimulus for new commercial and industrial development, an aim which explains the proposed route along Jamaica Bay. The balance of new railroad construction suggested in the plan comprised a great multitude of improvements, extensions, and realignments of existing trackage in order to connect belt lines with each other, with marginal railroads, with existing terminal and industrial enclaves, and with open land suitable for development. This extensive network of belt and transfer lines could directly serve the metropolitan economy only through readily accessible freight stations. The Port Authority virtually proposed the elimination of most existing facilities in favor of union freight stations for less-than-carload shipments to be located near the major interchange points of the whole port system. Two recent innovations were embodied in the planning of freight stations: all less-than-carload shipments were to be carried by truck to and from rail cars and the structures with their associated drives, platforms, and tracks were to be built so as to allow for overhead air-rights construction.[27]

The *Comprehensive Plan* of 1922, along with its predecessor formulated by the Harbor Development Commission two years earlier, had everything to recommend it, but no part of it was ever realized for two overriding reasons. Although the Port Authority could have issued revenue bonds that were retirable by means of rentals charged for the use of freight stations and other facilities, the commissioners quickly lost interest in the railroads and turned to the construction of transharbor arteries for automotive vehicles, which offered an immediate, abundant, and ever increasing revenue from tunnel and bridge tolls. In addition to the indifference of the authority, the railroad officers exhibited their customary reluctance to sacrifice what they regarded as their private advantages for the good of the commonwealth. The authority twice attempted to exercise some control over railroad activities, but both attempts proved abortive. In 1923 it sought jurisdiction over the design and location of the bridge across Newark Bay that the Central Railroad of New Jersey planned to build as a replacement for the older span (pp. 206–7); the railroad company, however, brought suit against the authority for this interference in the conduct of its affairs, and the Supreme Court decided in favor of the plaintiff in 1924. Four years later the authority sought to compel the Pennsylvania and the New Haven railroads to grant trackage rights to the New York Central for operation over the New York Connecting Railroad, which was regarded as a major segment in the Middle Belt Line proposed in the *Comprehensive Plan*. Once again the Supreme Court found that the rights of the corporation took precedence over the jurisdiction of a public body and denied the authority's request. In the matter of passenger service, the agency offered a convincing account of the defects and possible remedies in the mid-twenties, but that was as far as it was prepared to go (fig. 34).

> While the Port Authority has no mandate to solve the distressing passenger problems of the Metropolitan district, it realizes that these are intimately bound up with its own problems of coordinating the means for transshipment of goods. The late A. H. Smith, president of the New York Central Railroad, prophesied future calamity in New York unless the passenger traffic can be separated from the freight traffic, with added facilities for both. While hundreds of millions of dollars have been spent in urban mass transit during the past decade, no commensurate amounts have been expended on surburban rapid transit, and the commuter has reached the limit of his endurance where the trunk lines leading into New York City are incapable of handling both surburban and through traffic. The passenger service of every railroad in the Port District is taxed to its limit by the requirements of this service. There is barely room during the rush hours for the trains carrying

132 Fig. 34. Map showing the relative volume of passenger traffic of the New York railroads in 1924, measured in number of trains per weekday.

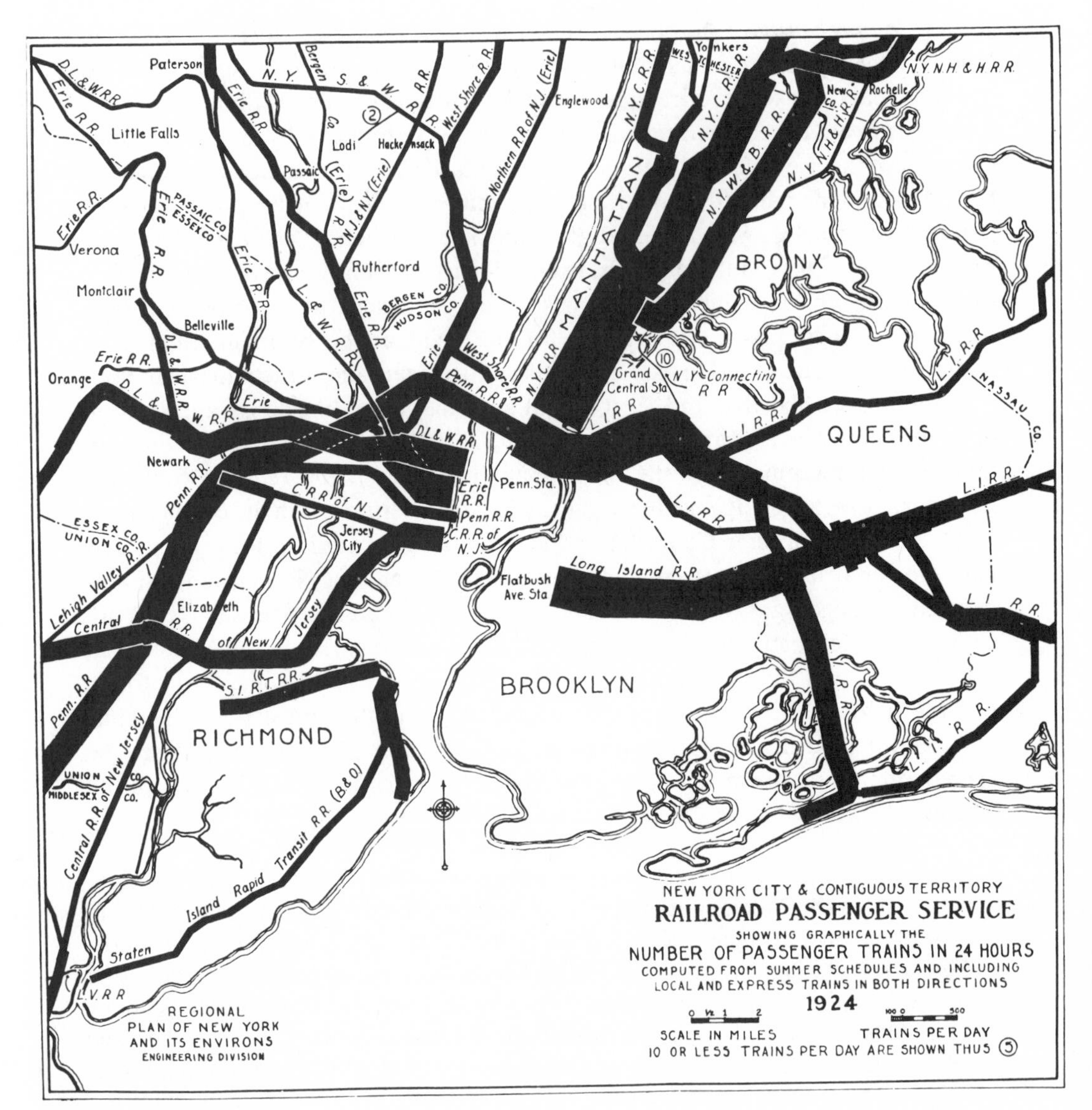

> freight because of the commuter service, while passengers and freight must both necessarily move during these hours. For example, . . . all trains leaving the Weehawken yard of the West Shore Railroad pass over a track crossed by 120 conflicting passenger movements daily.[28]

The sheer volume of traffic was enough to suggest the magnitude of the problem: the number of daily passengers rose from 840,000 to 1,132,000 over the ten years from 1920 through 1929, and the number of daily trains passed 3,000 around 1925. The potentially powerful Port Authority, however, was easily discouraged: two adverse court decisions, the inability to secure the cooperation of the railroads, and the lack of a specific mandate to tackle the problem of passenger facilities confirmed its growing preference for highway over rail transportation. In a strictly quantitative and financial sense this proved to be a spectacular success, and it led to the creation of world-famous engineering works, but the end results for metropolitan New York are open to serious question.[29]

If the authority grew indifferent to improving the rail terminal system, William Wilgus had lost none of his enthusiasm for metropolitan transportation planning on the grand scale. In a paper read before the International City and Regional Planning Conference, held in New York on 20–25 April 1925, he developed his plan of 1908 into the most far-reaching proposal for the expansion, rearrangement, and inter-modal unification of port facilities (fig. 35). His own presentation was such a model of verbal economy that we can do no better than to restate it largely in his own words. He sweeps around the urban periphery and moves in centripetal fashion to the internal working units.

> An outer belt railway and boulevard, so located as to by-pass centers of congestion, serve the purpose of an "open door" to the waterfront, afford access to industrial sites on the outskirts and coordinate the unified railway terminals of the Port.

The chief points on this circuit, taken in clockwise order, are Paterson, the Hudson River near Hastings, Mamaroneck, the East River at Throg's Neck, Valley Stream, Sandy Hook, and Plainfield. Concentric to the outer loop is a middle belt which lies within the boroughs of the city. The separate radial arteries are further united by

> twin inter-connected inner belt railways and boulevards, designed to bring all trunk-line passenger service—both through and commuter—and also the main streams of highway travel, in direct touch with each other and all of the principal centers of the Region.

Fig. 35. Map of New York Harbor showing the system of railroad belt lines proposed by William J. Wilgus in 1925.

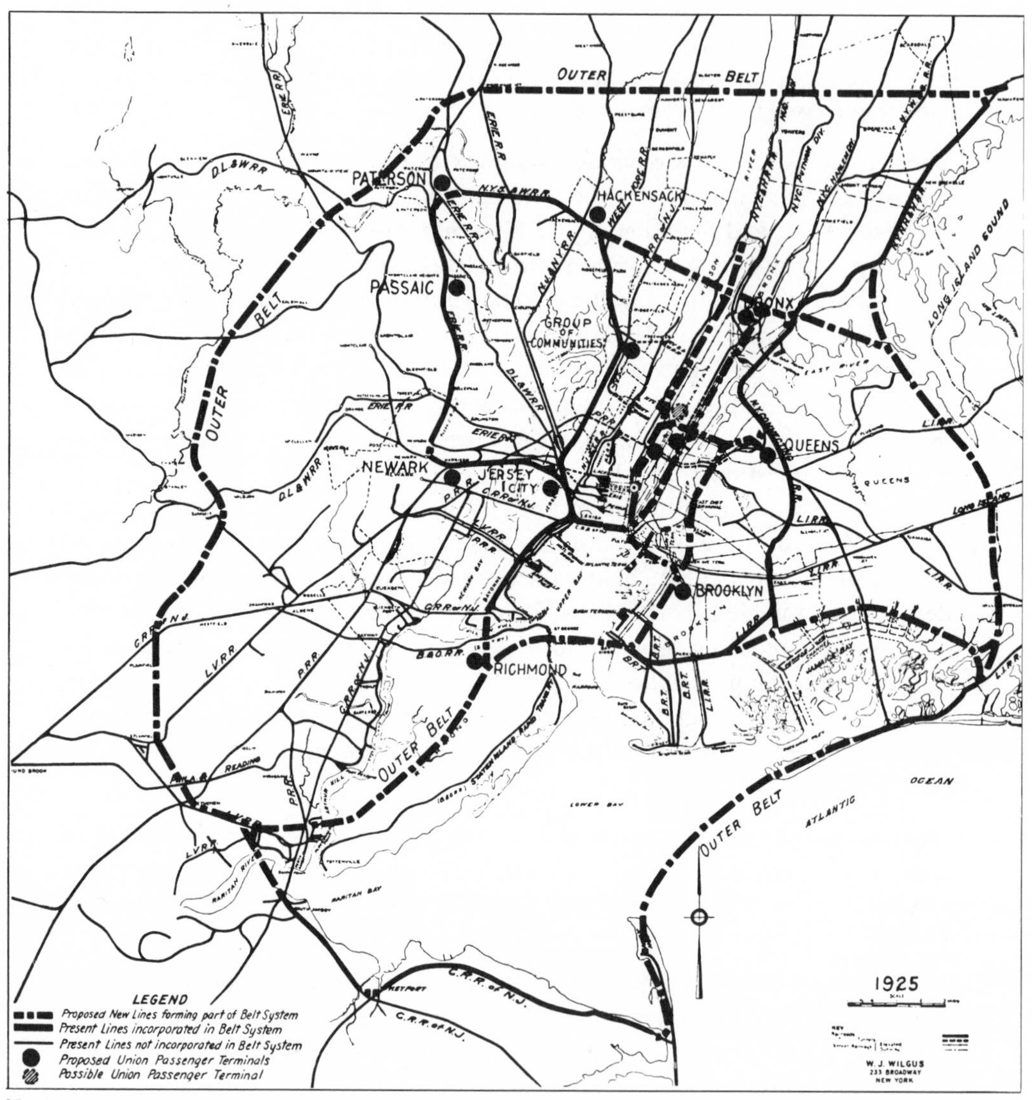

35

> A unified passenger rapid transit system, laid out with a view to promoting decentralization and use as far as possible of existing railroad rights-of-way, and financed on the basis of public ownership and private operation and on equitable distribution of costs among the beneficiaries.

Wilgus proposed a radial and circumferential rapid transit system, with the outer circuit lying contiguous to the outer rail-boulevard belt, and the new radial extensions concentrated particularly in the boroughs of Queens and Richmond, both of which were at the time undernourished with respect to transit. Supplementing the primary network was a number of transmetropolitan lines extending across Bergen, Passaic, Essex, and Hudson counties in New Jersey, Manhattan, The Bronx, and Westchester County in New York, and eastward into Queens.

> An internal freight distribution system under unified control, predicated on the universal "store door" method of collection and delivery, the avoidance of delays, expenses and hazards of water carriage, the minimized use of the surface of city streets, and the quickened release of the railroad car—all through the use of electrically operated trains [specially designed for the distribution of freight].

The prime advantage of the dispatching of freight in tunnels was, and remains, the reduction of automotive traffic and of conflicting forms of traffic on the streets, which were strangling surface circulation in Manhattan as early as the mid-twenties.

> A system of internal waterways connected with all parts of the harbor, protected where necessary from ocean storms, and operated in close harmony with rail and other carriers as regards transshipping facilities and joint rates.

The waterway system that Wilgus proposed consisted primarily of the rectification, deepening, and improved maintenance of the existing channels, mainly those of the Hudson, Harlem, and East rivers, Upper and Lower Bay eastward to Jamaica Bay, and the Staten Island kills. The aim was to open all bays and waterways within the belt circuit to deep-water cargo. The program included the removal of all bridge piers standing in open water from Spuyten Duyvil Creek and from the Harlem, Passaic, and Hackensack rivers. The only new waterway construction that he recommended was the digging of a canal across the Bayonne peninsula to join Upper Bay with Newark Bay and hence its two tributary streams, the Hackensack and Passaic rivers.

> Recreational areas, conveniently served by rail and highway—where feasible by water carriers too—in order that such areas may be easily and cheaply reached by the populace of the Region regardless of state lines.

The recreational possibilities of the Long Island shore line had been well developed for many years at Coney Island, Rockaway, and Long Beach, and all were accessible either by the trains of the Long Island Rail Road, extensions of the Brooklyn transit lines, or, in the case of Coney Island, by steamship from a Manhattan dock as well as rapid transit. Unfortunately, the next great expansion of the metropolitan recreational areas, Jones Beach (opened 1929), was located beyond the reach of the Long Island Rail Road and thus became the first step in Robert Moses's invitation to the invading armies of automobiles. The proposal for harmonious development of commercial and recreational activities was perhaps the most valuable feature of Wilgus's program, and it recalls the equally valuable characteristic of the plan that Daniel Burnham and Edward H. Bennett prepared for Chicago in 1906–9.

> Industrial and port developments broadly laid out on modern lines . . . . and served, without discrimination, by all carriers; channel depths ample for the purpose. . . . [Industrial enclaves and their supporting facilities] should be so located as to escape the danger of discriminatory transportation charges and in the case of port developments should be accessible to all rail and water carriers. Opportunity should be afforded for later expansion. Centers of population should be reasonably near. The surroundings should be pleasing.

The chief proposal for new construction of harbor facilities in Wilgus's prescription was the recommendation that Jamaica Bay be deepened and rectified for use as an ocean port, with the necessary docks,warehouses, loading equipment, and deep-water channels to make such usage possible.[30]

If William Wilgus's admirable plan suggested the utopian, it was nevertheless a valid blueprint for continuing expansion together with a concomitant efficiency and economy of port operations such that men as well as machines might prosper. To the loss of all concerned, however, there were no public bodies on any level that were prepared to do their share in implementing this grand design, and the expansion of all rail and water traffic through the decade of the 1920's was not likely to suggest unlimited horizons. Water-borne tonnage, on the one hand, was increasing at an average rate of about 3 percent per annum, sufficient to swell the total by better than 30,000,000 tons for the decade. The surge in rail traffic during the years up to 1920, on the other hand, was clearly leveling off, even in the halcyon days of the extravagant decade: for the New York roads the volume of freight traffic increased less than 6 percent through 1929, while the total number of suburban and through passengers carried on all lines declined by an ominous 30 percent in the same period. The steep and continuing rise in metropolitan suburban traffic, however, more than offset the system losses, so that the New York and New Jersey terminals saw a 35 percent increase over the ten years ending with 1929.[31] If traffic volume showed no clear trends, gains and losses tending to cancel each other, the financial state of the railroads in the New York family was so far improved by 1925 that the ghastly returns of 1920 were cheerfully forgotten. The operating ratio for the eleven companies had fallen to 76.7 percent, and it exceeded 80 percent only for the two dwarfs, the Ontario and the Susquehanna, both of which lived from time to time in a precarious state. The astonishing fact is that the debacle of 1929 and the subsequent depression left the New York companies in a still better state: there were staggering losses of traffic, but the collective operating ratio in 1935 fell to 74.4 percent. In short, if the coffers of the railroads were not overflowing with money, they were nonetheless well filled, and there was some to spare. The situation was ambiguous enough, however, so that few roads were disposed to undertake major projects.

The most conspicuous exception to the rule of caution in making capital expenditures was the extensive program of reconstructing both freight and passenger facilities launched by the Central Railroad of New Jersey six years before wartime exigencies demonstrated the need for the improvements (for the passenger terminal, see chap. 7). Planning for a drastic expansion of the company's terminal properties at Jersey City began in 1910, and the first fruits were an addition of ten tracks to the freight yard in the Communipaw neighborhood and the construction of a new steel-framed concrete-floored pier for general cargo at the marine terminal that stood beside the passenger station. Both works were designed and built in 1911–12 under the direction of Joseph O. Osgood, the company's chief engineer. The expansion of terminal facilities for both freight and passenger traffic required a new engine house, which was added in 1913–14 to service 300 units per day at a summertime maximum. The next step in the C. N. J.'s program had to be delayed until the end of the war freed men, equipment, and materials for the most ambitious undertaking. In 1919–20 the company replaced its antique gravity-type coal piers with the largest and most completely mechanized marine terminal for the transshipment of coal in New York Harbor. The central features of this black-painted and dust-blackened monster, with a capacity to move 7,000,000 tons of coal per year from hopper cars to vessels and storage pockets, were a reinforced concrete pier 1,584 feet long, the steam-operated cradles for emptying cars by rotating them in the vertical plane through 180 degrees, the supporting framework, the thawing houses, and the boiler house, all of them served by a complex of yards comprising 23 miles of track. The future seemed unlimited to the officers of the Central of New Jersey, who saw its freight and passenger traffic expand respectively 23 and 43 percent between 1915 and

1920, and Chief Engineer Osgood must have felt that he directed imperial works; yet dwarf trees, shore vegetation, weeds, and grasses now grow where 450 freight cars a day were once turned bottom up to fill the holds of ships and supply the railroad's fleet of tugboats.

The Erie Railroad waited until the end of the war to renew its neglected harbor facilities. While the directors showed no interest whatsoever in improving its deteriorating passenger terminal, they were prepared to demonstrate a reasonably generous spirit in the construction of piers and freight houses. The first step came in 1921, when the company introduced the innovative practice of using motor trucks to deliver less-than-carload freight from shippers to car and from car to consignee (pick-up-and-delivery service, as it came to be called). For the implementation of this plan, which was initially adopted to escape from the excessive congestion of piers, the road built three inland truck terminals in downtown Manhattan, respectively located on Greenwich, Beach, and Watt streets. On the New Jersey shore the company launched into a ten-year program of large-scale replacements and expansions. Fire in 1921 destroyed all the existing timber piers at Weehawken, and in the following year they were replaced by a single pier built up of precast concrete block and carrying a two-story timber-framed shed. This work proved to be preparatory to the construction in 1926–27 of what may have been the largest combined rail, steamship, and lighterage pier in the harbor. Located close to the Jersey City ventilating shaft of Holland Tunnel, the huge steel-framed, concrete-floored structure measured 150 × 1,250 feet out-to-out in plan and rested on 845,000 lineal feet of piling.[32] The second installation for ocean vessels at Weehawken, built in 1930–31, was a steel-framed pier distinguished by a novel floor construction composed of light-weight interlocking steel panels. It proved to be the last work undertaken by the Erie Railroad in the harbor area. All the additions of the predepression decade were designed and constructed under the direction of F. A. Howard, the company's engineer of structures.

The Lehigh Valley, concentrating on its Manhattan facilities, was the second road to adopt the delivery of freight by motor truck, and it built stations on Beach Street and Washington Street in 1925 as necessary adjuncts to the service. The method of transferring shipments involved the movement of freight in trucks carried by ferries between the road's Jersey City railheads and the Manhattan piers, and thence to or from the stations by trucks operating on the city streets. The B. and O. inaugurated a similar program in 1927 to serve its recently opened freight terminal at the foot of West 26th Street (completed in 1915) and a newer station at South Ferry, close to the ships used by the ferries crossing to and from the Saint George terminal on Staten

Island. The last of the Lehigh's harbor improvements was a highly innovative work that advanced the structural arts as much as it did the techniques of urban circulation. The Pioneer Real Estate Company, a subsidiary of the railroad, and the Starrett Investing Company jointly sponsored the erection of the Starrett-Lehigh Building, constructed in 1929–31 over railroad trackage on Thirteenth Avenue between 26th and 27th Street. Designed by the architects R. G. and W. M. Cory and Yasuo Matsui, and by the celebrated engineering firm of Purdy and Henderson, the 19-story Starrett-Lehigh was at the time the largest multistory work in the United States of flat-slab concrete framing. The urbanistic importance of the building grew out of its special function and the internal features necessary to serve that end. It was constructed to provide rental manufacturing space, with the associated rail and truck facilities, for companies located in densely built urban areas that were too small or too handicapped by location to afford their own factories. In order to satisfy the needs of a variety of manufacturers in a multistory building the structure was erected around a central core embracing truck elevators, electrical conduits, and water, gas, steam, waste, and sewage pipes—in short, a vertical street. The original idea for such a building seems to have come, as we have seen, from the Harbor Development Commission's plan of 1920, but the first practical embodiment of the idea was the warehouse of the New York Dock Trade Facilities Company, constructed in Brooklyn in 1928.[33]

The Pennsylvania Railroad came late to the use of trucks for the local movement of freight, adopting the pick-up and delivery service in June, 1927, when the company completed the necessary Manhattan facilities. Two inland stations were opened, one at West and Laight streets for receiving freight, and the other at Watt and Washington streets for dispatching shipments to the West. A third was built at West and Cortlandt streets, near the Manhattan end of Holland Tunnel (opened to traffic in November of the same year) and equally accessible to the slips of the railroad's Desbrosses and Cortlandt Street ferries. By late fall the freight moving between the Manhattan stations and the Jersey City railheads was carried under contract by the United States Motor Trucking Company via the new vehicular tunnel. On 22 October the Pennsylvania placed in service an immense terminal for handling perishables, which took the place of the general freight terminal built in 1876 at piers 27, 28, and 29 on the Manhattan side of the Hudson River. With a total of 400,000 square feet of floor area and a capacity under roof of 700 carloads of fresh fruit and vegetables, it not only stood first of its kind in total size, but was also claimed to be the largest mechanically heated space so far built. The final step in the Pennsylvania Railroad's program for expanding and improving freight service in

New York was the electrification of that segment of the Long Island and the New York Connecting Railroad extending from Fresh Pond Junction to Bay Ridge Yard in Brooklyn, which was restricted to freight movements. The catenary system, an extension of the New Haven's installation, was completed in 1927 and the new service inaugurated in the following year, after the Public Service Commission of New York had advanced the deadline from 1 January 1927 to 1 July 1928. What remained to be done in the city itself was the implementation of the New York Central Railroad's program for the West Side line, but the interminable process of planning and revising, balancing legitimate municipal concerns with corporate needs, searching for the most appropriate technological solutions, and satisfying the manifold interests involved—these issues formed such a complex and tedious drama as to require a separate chronicle.

The West Side Program

The Hudson River Railroad completed its line between Albany and Chambers Street in New York City on 8 October 1851, having built its level track for the most part very nearly at the water's edge along the east bank of the river. In 1869 Cornelius Vanderbilt merged the property with the New York Central to form a new corporation under the combined names of the two roads, and in 1914 the enlarged company acquired and merged the Lake Shore and Michigan Southern Railroad, at the same time returning to the shorter title with which it began its corporate life. Much of the trackage of the Hudson River lay on the surface of streets in the lower west side of Manhattan, an area of high commercial and residential density that generated an equivalent density of traffic moving in unusually tangled patterns because of the presence of adjacent docks and industries.[34] The extension of urban development northward to 72d Street and the parallel expansion of the railroad's freight and passenger traffic soon guaranteed that what might have been a tolerable nuisance at mid-century became an intolerable obstruction to the proper use of streets and eventually a danger to life and limb. It was everywhere dirty and unsightly, but it seemed particularly offensive along Riverside Park, lying between 72d and 129th streets. An antique law requiring that every train be preceded by a flagman on horseback offered some protection to pedestrians, teams, and drivers, while the situation grew progressively worse. The railroad operated under a perpetual franchise, which it had no intention of surrendering, but the possibility of open conflict over the issue appeared as early as 1870, when the General Assembly passed a bill holding the city's waterfront to be inalienable. The question was to remain unanswered: what constitutes a waterfront, and how much may the city justly lay claim to? By the turn of the century it was clear to the farsighted that the mixture of rail, street, and dock traffic, as well as the legal conflict, would have to be disentangled, and each put in its proper place. Yet the dependence of the river shipping and the West Side industries on the rail line was such that it could not be moved very far from its original location.

The first plan in what was to become thirty years of planning, arguing, protesting, litigation, and eventual construction appeared in February, 1905, when the state legislature was preparing to consider a bill requiring the removal of the New York Central and Hudson River Railroad's tracks from Eleventh Avenue and other streets on the West Side. The act specifically authorized the company to place its right of way in a six-track tunnel, and to retain its franchise on two of the tracks while paying a rental to the city on the other four. The only technical problem for which there seemed to be no ready solution was that of carrying this oversized subway above or below the Pennsylvania tunnels. The railroad company, surprisingly enough, was in favor of this costly project, but that was insufficient to insure the passage of the bill. The Assembly, however, was determined to act, and on 26 March 1906 the legislators passed a law prohibiting the use of streets, avenues, or any public place by any railroad operating steam locomotives at grade level. This kind of legislation is always thought to produce results, but since it offers no means for solving the problem, it cannot guarantee the necessary realization. There were various individuals who came forward with proposals, and the first was William J. Wilgus, whose comprehensive plan of 1908 included the placing of the tracks in a subway to be used by passenger as well as freight trains. Two years later Calvin Tompkins, the city's commissioner of docks, proposed that the municipality construct an elevated freight line extending from 72d Street to Saint John's Park and a union freight terminal with float bridges at 30th Street, the latter to be operated by the participating railroads and presumably paid for by rental charges. One could predict with near certainty of being supported by events that any scheme involving a cooperative association of New Jersey railroads might get a hearing, but it would be promptly forgotten. Once again the state came to bat.

In 1911 the legislature passed two bills granting the municipal Board of Estimate the authority to enter into an agreement with the New York Central and Hudson River Railroad aimed at relocating the line in precisely the way that was adopted twenty years later. The tracks were to be placed in a roofed cut designed to carry a parkway from Spuyten Duyvil to 72d Street, and elevated on a steel-girder viaduct from 72d to Saint John's Park. Trains were to be drawn by electric motive power after 1915, and the whole project was to be completed by 1917. But such a program seemed to be too sensible, straightforward, and practical for ready acceptance. The officers of the railroad and other officials of the city held different ideas, which formed the basis of an agreement dated 15 January 1916. The various parties concerned proposed, in order from north to south, a tunnel under Spuyten Duyvil Creek, a roofed cut wide enough for six tracks extending from the waterway to 60th Street, a four-track elevated line from 60th to a point a little south of Saint John's Park, and a new extension to Cortlandt Street carried on a viaduct above the so-called marginal way between West Street and the bulkhead line. In addition to these expensive improvements, the road proposed the expansion of the existing freight yards and the provision of facilities for passenger trains, the latter introduced to remove some of the load from Grand Central Terminal and its approach and to offer much needed passenger service to the West Side. The total estimated cost, to be born entirely by the railroad company, was $65,000,000 at the price level of 1915, or about $1.3 billion in 1980.[35] The agreement between the municipality and the railroad on the relocation of the West Side line, an instrument that later came to be regarded by the company as a contract, was authorized by the state and supported by the Chamber of Commerce, the Merchants' Association of New York City, and obviously by the railroad, which would retain the operating rights it had held since 1851. But various citizens' groups mounted a vociferous and politically persuasive campaign of opposition based on the argument that the damage to Riverside Park would irreparably harm one of the city's aesthetic assets. The position was perfectly valid, but the citizens then went on to propose that the city recover the property and operating rights guaranteed to the railroad and refuse to grant any such rights of operation on public property unless the railroad paid the city a "fair compensation," the terms of which were to be renewed and readjusted every 25 years. The railroad's officers understandably held a dim view of this doctrine, and they threatened to take the issue to the courts.

At this juncture delays began to be compounded by confusion in the relations among the state, the city, and the railroad company, and the demands of war prevented the realization of such settlements as were achieved. Another agreement between the municipality and the railroad was reached on 14 February 1917, and although the terms were spelled out in detail, subsequent legislation and the continuing unresolved conflicts produced an impasse that extended well beyond the armistice. In June, 1917, the legislature at Albany passed a law which first nullified the existing contract between the railroad and the city, and second, required that all future plans be submitted for review to an impartial committee and for approval to the Public Service Commission of the state. A companion act then called for the immediate study of the February agreement by this external and impartial body. The issue appeared to be yielding to progress, and in December the Public Service Commission began the preparation of working plans. The earlier settlement, constituting the basis of these plans, rested on a complex exchange of property rights between the city and the railroad, certain features of which again aroused opposition from the citizens and the municipality. The railroad company was to release extensive areas of shore land to the city in return for the transfer of municipally held riparian rights to the company. The opposition centered chiefly on the loss of these rights, on the preclusion of competing rail service, and the damage to park land resulting from the expansion of the right of way. There were other gains to the city, notably electrification and the removal of trackage from streets, but some of the remainder were controversial in their value.[36] Such matters, however, marked only a beginning of the full ramifications: there were a number of fundamental questions having to do with good urban design, the city's responsibility therefor, the improvement of circulation, the necessity for and the extent of control over architectural and civic design by the municipal Fine Arts Commission. In short, the whole program raised old and never resolved arguments, as a correspondent of *American Architecture* acutely understood.

> We need to establish . . . general control at the outset, for the plan should have a direct bearing on the City's plan, the City's service and the City's appearance. We need a group of city planning experts and landscape architects, as well as engineers, to solve this problem. It is bound to be a great engineering feat, but its architectural and landscape and city planning aspects are not to be ignored. Thus far there has been considered only the City's side or the railroad's side of the scheme, not the harmonious and unified success to be obtained by collaboration. The bargain has thus far been no more than a proposed exchange of commodities; it would prosper all the better if the exchange were tempered by a spirit of cooperative effort.[37]

The burdens imposed by the war, the control of the railroads by the federal government, their financial difficulties in the immediate postwar years, the depression and the labor troubles that accompanied it—these delayed the implementation of the West Side program so many more years that few must have believed it would ever be realized. Yet the need for improvement in the system of freight distribution on Manhattan Island grew with every passing year. No one understood this better than Alfred H. Smith, who put the case very well in an address presented before the Merchants' Association of New York City in April, 1920. The essential point came only after he criticized the state and municipal governments for their legislative delays and the United States Railroad Administration for refusing to grant increases in freight rates comparable to those in wages.

> Manhattan Island lives a hand-to-mouth existence, because of the dearth of warehouses and storage facilities and of modern equipment for handling freight. The unnecessary costs and losses yearly are prodigious; none but a rich and growing city could have borne the burden. It has been estimated that $200,000 is the daily loss in New York because of inefficient methods of distribution. The daily newspapers have quite recently lost thousands of dollars because of a shortage of newsprint paper; they have paid for special trains and many extra bonuses for long hauls by truck, all this largely because of insufficient warehouse room. The New York Central's efforts to improve its freight facilities on the west side have for fifteen years been hampered by legislative and other obstructions. The upper part of Manhattan—Harlem—has a population of about 1,000,000 but has railroad facilities suitable for a town of twenty thousand; freight is hauled ten miles further downtown and then hauled back by wagon at 50 cents per ton mile. The citizens of New York, in 1847, when the New York Central's present freight railroad was built, appreciated its value; and [I have] called upon the members of the Merchants' Association to investigate and consider the problem of its usefulness, value and efficiency today; this in their own interest no less than that of the carrier.[38]

Another three years passed in this intolerably tedious controversy, and the legislation that constituted the next step in the action probably hindered still further the realization of the plans on which agreement might be expected. On 2 June 1923 the state government completed action on two laws together requiring the electrical operation of all trains within the city limits of New York by 1 January 1926. The four railroad companies affected by the acts immediately protested, one on technological and urbanistic grounds, the other three, as we might expect, on the ground of cost. The New York Central argued, most strenuously of all, that it could not operate the West Side line as it then existed by means of any available system of electric traction. The distribution of power by third rail was out of the question because much of the trackage below 60th Street lay in streets; the use of overhead trolley wires was forbidden by law in Manhattan, and battery power was insufficiently advanced for reliable use over long periods of time. The B. and O., which owned the Staten Island Rapid Transit and its associated freight-handling trackage, the Long Island, and the New Haven protested simply on the basis of what they considered prohibitive costs.[39]

Before the end of the year, however, events took a more encouraging turn: in December, 1923, the New York State Transit Commission made as accurate an estimate of costs as could then be drawn up and arrived at a total of $97,000,000, to be divided between $77,000,000 for the railroad, at the likely maximum, and $20,000,000 for the city (the total would come to about $875,000,000 at the 1980 building cost level). At least all concerned had a fairly reliable idea of how deeply they would have to dip into the coffer, although the actual sum that was eventually spent proved to be considerably below the commission's estimate.

While planning and calculating engaged the attention of the parties involved with the West Side program, the New York Central was investing large sums of money on a project that expedited the movement of freight over all the road's primary main lines east of Buffalo. The city of Albany, hemmed in by hills that left only narrow river terraces for rail trackage, yet a crucial junction point for lines radiating to Buffalo, Boston, New York, and the New Jersey ports, had become a troublesome bottleneck as early as 1910. In 1913 the Central organized the Hudson River Connecting Railroad to construct a suitable bypass that would allow the removal of all through freight from the junctions and bridges at Albany and Rensselaer. The selection and the planning of the route began in 1916, but years of further controversy with the War Department, the Congress, and the General Assembly over the location and the nature of the river crossing delayed the final authorization by the state and the federal government until 1920. Construction began in the spring of 1922, and the double-track line, joining the West Shore at Feura Bush, New York, with the Boston and Albany at Niverville, was opened to traffic on 20 November 1924. Since the chosen route passes close to the town of Castleton on the Hudson River, the entire line is known as Castleton Cut-Off, and the river crossing is designated the Alfred H. Smith Memorial Bridge in honor of the man who had served the nation as well as the railroad industry with distinction. The 4-mile link is carried directly and at a uniform grade over the Hudson valley at hilltop level, with the consequence that it passes through or over an unbroken succession of cuts, fills, steel-girder viaducts, and long-span truss bridges. This impressive piece of railroad construction was the creation of the company's engineering department, and it added $25,000,000 more to funds that the railroad had to pour into its New York enterprises and into stations it was then planning at Buffalo, Cleveland, South Bend, and Hamilton, Ontario.[40]

The prospect of spending money in princely style on monumental projects always seemed to arouse the enthusiasm of the New York Central's directors. A flurry of governmental and corporate activity affecting the West Side program at last began to yield results. The Public Service Commission and the Transit Commission of the state reviewed all the existing plans for improvement in November, 1923, and began to hold hearings on their implementation before the end of the year. The length of new line would be 11 miles, but the total estimated cost had fallen to $70,000,000. The railroad's plan called for a number of viaducts, the longest to extend almost continuously from the lower terminal to 72d Street, a roofed cut through Riverside Park, a new swing bridge over Spuyten Duyvil Creek, expansion and improvement of yards, and the abandonment of the freight terminal at Saint John's Park in favor of a facility to be located near Washington Street between Spring and Clarkson streets. The New York Transit Commission took what may be regarded as the initial step toward actual construction in 1924, when it ordered the railroad to begin the removal of all grade crossings between 60th Street and Spuyten Duyvil in the summer of 1925. The second step, taken by the state's Public Service Commission in November, was the authorization for the railroad to operate the West Side line by standard electric motive power north of 72d Street and by the newly developed diesel-electric locomotive to the south, the use of such power having been inaugurated by the railroad on an experimental basis in the spring of 1924. The commission decided to adopt this scarcely tried novelty with revolutionary implications because it allowed the railroad to continue operations during the period of construction prior to the elimination of the grade crossings below 60th Street. The chief engineer of the Public Service Commission, William C. Lancaster, regarded the new form of power as superior to both the steam and the electric locomotive for working in densely built urban areas.

> The Diesel electric locomotive . . . has none of the objectionable features of the steam locomotive; it is substantially noiseless and its movements are virtually the same as those of the electric locomotive of the same capacity. It has one other feature which . . . has an advantage over the overhead system of contact or the third rail. In the case of the latter there are frequent momentary discontinuances which draw arcs causing vivid flashes. These are a source of annoyance and . . . would be objectionable to those living along Riverside drive. This results where the contact shoe jumps from one conductor to another and such intervals would be frequent . . . in the third rail system.[41]

The railroad company undertook preliminary construction in December, 1925, while it continued the seemingly endless process of working out an agreement with the city. At the same time it ordered the initial lot of 650-volt direct-current electric locomotives from the General Electric Company, the first of which was delivered in 1926. The diesel-electric locomotive placed in operation in 1928 was a unique three-power variety in which the electric current was drawn either directly from the third rail or from a battery inside the cab, or generated by the diesel engine.

The completion of working drawings and the preparation of the final agreement with the municipality consumed another two years, so that the execution of the necessary documents did not come until 5 July 1929. The signatories were Mayor James J. Walker (all who had ever heard of him knew him as Jimmy), R. D. Starbuck, a vice-president of the railroad, and E. F. Stephenson, the company's secretary. The cost of building the new line and associated structures had risen by this date to $175,000,000, while the traffic on the overworked artery had reached an average of 1,688 loaded and empty cars per day. The plans on which construction was based were prepared by the engineering staff of the West Side Improvement Engineering Committee, an ad hoc organization that was dominated by those officers of the state and municipal bureaus concerned with the program.[42] The agreement between the company and the city specified a timetable of completion as well as a program of construction. The electrification above 72d Street and the diesel-electric motive power for operations to the south were to be installed by 1 June 1931, and all train movements on city streets were to be ended by 30 June 1934. The double-track line was to be relocated to a viaduct between Saint John's Park and 34th Street, the irregular alignment of which was dictated by the layout of streets in the area, and placed within walled cuts and a walled and roofed enclosure above 34th Street, although much of the intervening area between the viaduct and the park was occupied by the extensive 60th Street Yard (figs. 36, 37). The two major yards (30th and 60th Street) and three smaller yards (17th, 41st, and 145th Street) were to be expanded to a total capacity of 4,000 cars, and the freight terminal at Saint John's Park was to be replaced either on the original site or at Spring Street.

The railroad gave the city more than it asked for. Those lengths of the steel-girder viaduct standing over private right of way passed directly through the buildings along the route, and provisions were made for the loading and unloading of freight within their enclosures. Spurs and sidings serving adjacent warehouses and industries were also carried on elevated structures that entered such buildings at upper levels. The technique of tunneling through structures indicated that what was in effect overhead construction was feasible even at the elevated track level, and the first work in a new air-rights development on the West Side came with the opening of the Cudahy Packing Company's building on 14th Street in 1932. The five yards along the way were expanded to a capacity of 4,800 cars, nearly all of the increase divided among the three at 30th, 60th, and 145th Street (Manhattanville). Between 72d and 126th streets the two tracks were enclosed within concrete walls and roof supported by a

Fig. 36. New York Central Railroad. Map showing the elevated length of the West Side freight line, 1931–37.

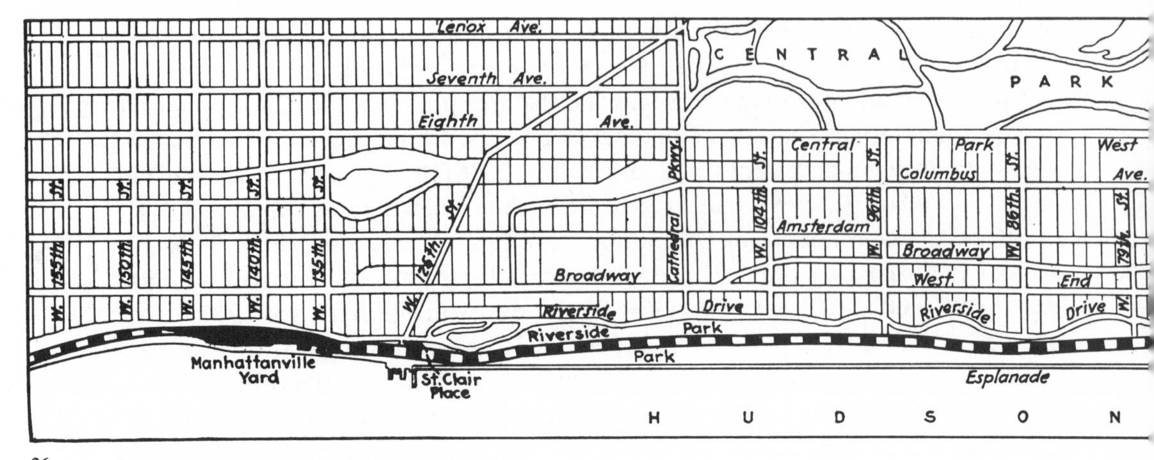

36

Fig. 37. Henry Hudson Parkway, 1933–36. The parkway and the adjacent extension of Riverside Park were built over the New York Central's West Side freight line.

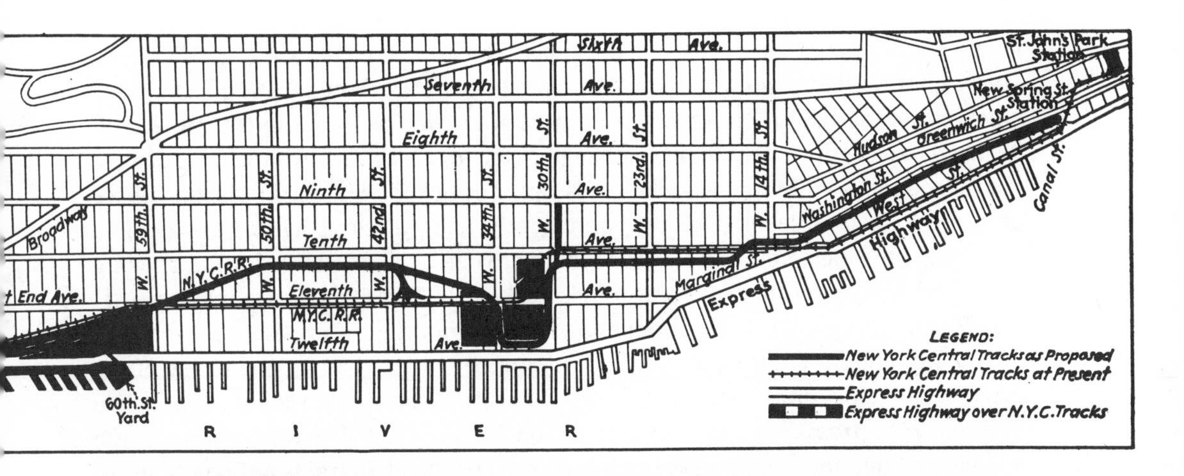

37

long, closely ranked file of steel rigid frames. This concrete box was buried under a landscaped fill that extended Riverside Park to the water's edge and considerably enlarged its total area. North of 126th Street the two tracks lie on a shelf-like fill beside the river, the narrow contour-hugging right of way scarcely noticeable against the rugged topography and wooded landscaping of Inwood Hill Park. The first phase of a program that seemed to be permanently fixed at the stage of documents, legalities, meetings, and controversies finally reached completion with the opening of the new freight terminal at Saint John's Park on 28 June 1934. Further compensation for the thirty-year delay undoubtedly came from the irrepressible presence of Mayor Fiorello La Guardia at the dedication ceremonies. The second phase of the project, the relocation of the tracks from Eleventh Avenue to a walled cut between 34th and 64th streets, was opened to traffic on 27 June 1937. The whole intricate job was carried out under an average uninterrupted traffic of 70 trains per day. Almost simultaneously with the rebuilding of the railroad's West Side line came the construction of the elevated West Side Express Highway, which together with its counterpart on the East Side, Franklin D. Roosevelt Drive, constituted the first step in the city's vast and thoroughly controversial expressway program.[43]

The New York Central's West Side project, with its consequent improvement in the quality of freight service, the movement of trains, urban circulation, and the quality of the air, was supplemented by two other additions to the system of freight distribution in Manhattan. The first was the establishment by the railroad in 1928–29 of a network of six truck routes centered at Yonkers by means of which freight could be expeditiously moved from stations on the Electric Division to others on the Harlem. The previous and cumbersome technique involved the movement of freight in yard cuts through the dense passenger traffic of the line along the Harlem River and through Mott Haven Junction. It was one of several pioneer steps in what might have been a symbiotic partnership of rail and highway carriers, a subject to which we will return in our concluding chapter. The second addition was a much greater undertaking bringing benefits to the whole urban economy. In 1931–32 the Port of New York Authority constructed the Union Inland Freight Station in the block bounded by Eighth and Ninth avenues and 15th and 16th streets, to provide the city with its first unified rail-truck terminal and its largest building for the time. Designed by the architectural and engineering firm of Abbott, Merkt and Company, the steel and concrete structure covers the entire block to a height of 16 stories and comprises a total of 2,550,000 square feet of gross floor area. The first two floors function as a terminal for all less-than-carload shipments carried by truck to and from the piers of the eight trunk-line railroads that originally participated in the construction and operating program (B. and O., C. N. J., Lackawanna, Erie, Lehigh, New York Central, New Haven, and Pennsylvania). The West Side line, however, continued to be the primary artery in the freight-handling system of the island. Its yards and spurs directly served manufactories, standard and refrigerated warehouses, freight houses, express terminals, piers, float bridges, team tracks, milk sheds, one hay market, produce and poultry markets, grain elevators, and coal yards. The engine terminals at the major yards constituted the essential support facilities for this extensive if narrowly funneled tide of commerce. The rebuilding and relocation of the trackage, together with the few terminals and piers constructed during the decade of the twenties by the New Jersey roads, were a decisive factor in enabling the unwieldy port, after the costly breathing-spell of the Depression, to cope with another world war.

5

Pennsylvania Station through the Second World War

If the freight-handling facilities of New York Harbor staggered to the brink of collapse under the burdens of war and winter, the meticulously designed electrified terminals of Manhattan repeatedly proved that they had no peers for the comfortable accommodation of passengers and the safe and efficient movement of trains. The Pennsylvania Railroad in particular, having survived the disasters of 1917–18, was prepared to demonstrate a seemingly unlimited capacity to transport people and goods. The United States Railroad Administration, now cordially hated by all right-thinking railroad officers, became a thing of the past on 1 March 1920; the accumulated deficits of the wartime years began to yield to profits; the post-war depression actually had little effect on the traffic of the big passenger carriers, among which the Pennsylvania stood at the top. Only the sometimes violent labor troubles of 1922 marred the cheerful prospects of the coming decade, but these misfortunes proved of short duration. The total number of rail passengers reached its high point in 1920, and even though the long decline unfortunately set in before another year had ended, it was more than offset for the New York carriers by a steady expansion in metropolitan suburban traffic. For the Pennsylvania the shrinkage in the general total of through passengers was further offset by a most gratifying and unexpected rise in the wintertime Pullman travel to the Florida resorts. The scene appeared full of promise, and the huge railroad system demonstrated its readiness to accept its share of the nation's business when it posted an enviable record for the year 1921: the company's entire fleet of passenger trains reached their destinations on time for 96.8 percent of all scheduled runs. It is possible, as the road claimed, that this performance had never been previously matched, and has not subsequently been improved. Fifty years after this unsurpassable standard was set, the American traveling public came to regard such claims as belonging to the realm of folk legend and fairy tale.

The Performance of the Station

The capacity of Pennsylvania Station in New York was calculated with an accuracy and a long-term foresight that may place it in a unique category among transportation facilities. Although there is no record that it ever reached its theoretical limit of 500,000 passengers per day, the daily average through the peak year rose close enough to the maximum to suggest that it was several times reached and possibly surpassed. In 1911, the first full year of operation, the total number of passengers was a little more than 12,500,000 for the year, yielding a weekday average of 39,200. Through the two decades of 1910 to 1930 the Jersey City terminal continued in active use, since the majority of Manhattan commuters headed to or from the great concentration of office space in the downtown triangle. After the war, however, the balance shifted steadily and at an accelerating rate toward the new midtown skyscrapers, with the consequence that in 1920 traffic at Pennsylvania Station rose to a level exactly three times that of a decade earlier, 37,800,000 passengers for the year, or 118,000 per weekday. The constant expansion continued up to the peacetime record of nearly 66,000,000 passengers for the year 1930, or 206,000 for the daily average. By this time the totals had risen to more than five times the level of the immediate postinaugural year. The depression of the 1930s exacted a staggering toll, but the attrition in the local New York traffic of the Long Island and the Pennsylvania was surprisingly modest. By 1933 the Pennsylvania system as a whole had suffered a loss of one half of its passenger business, but the volume at the New York terminal was only 28 percent below the pre-Depression peak. Recovery was agonizingly slow and intermittent through the thirties, and the brief spurt that came with the New York World's Fair of 1939/40 made the subsequent decline all the more discouraging. These vicissitudes were suddenly and explosively ended when the United States plunged with its full national resources into the Second World War.[1]

The successful operation of the Pennsylvania's Manhattan terminal required not only the accommodation of an extremely dense and steadily rising rail traffic, but the development as well of techniques for safely and expeditiously moving the greatest diversity of trains concentrated on a particular railway line. On the East River approaches the suburban trains of the Long Island Rail Road almost overwhelmed the smaller number of through-coach and parlor-car trains that the road dispatched to and from its eastern terminals at Greenport and Montauk. The homogeneity of this traffic guaranteed the extreme density of train movements through the morning and evening rush hours. In the Pennsylvania's Hudson River tunnels, by contrast, rush-hour pressures were less taxing, but the daily schedules ranged through multiple-unit suburban trains, accommodation locals, conventional coach and parlor car runs, heavy Pullman flyers, many frequently operated in extra sections, numerous special trains, mail and express trains, and, west of Newark, a comparable assortment of local and through freight trains, the intervals along the way often filled with moving service equipment. From the standpoint of passenger operations on the main and approach lines, on the station tracks, and in the coach yard, the movement of an immense fleet of sleeping and parlor cars proved to be the most exacting task. Only the New York Central approached the Pennsylvania in the number of such runs; other roads with a respectable and renumerative passenger service, like the B. and O., for example, could show only a small fraction of this total. Both of the big carriers served the same western terminals, chiefly Cleveland, Detroit, Chicago, Saint Louis, and Cincinnati, but the Pennsylvania's connections with southern roads at Washington and Cincinnati boosted its total of through sleeping-car routes well beyond that of its rival to the north. At the high point of Pullman service in 1929–30 the Pennsylvania timetable listed 229 daily Pullman runs, of which 57 served southern terminals, from the resorts of the Carolina, Georgia, and Florida coasts to New Orleans, Shreveport, Memphis, and Nashville in the west.[2] A sudden upsurge of traffic was handled as expeditiously as the daily tide, as a particularly impressive example serves to demonstrate. On 23 September 1926 the Pennsylvania Railroad transported 20,000 passengers in 25 special trains from New York to Philadelphia and return, on the occasion of the Jack Dempsey–Gene Tunney boxing match in the latter city's Sesquicentennial Exposition Stadium. Similar crowds were regularly transported during the appropriate season to and from the football games at Princeton University.

The magic ingredient in the railroad's capacity for moving great numbers of passengers was its unparalleled ability to operate a multitude of passenger trains on close headway and on extremely exacting schedules demanding not only high speeds on the open track, but also quick engine changes and the expeditious movement of trains through the huge terminal ganglia, like New York, Philadelphia, and Pittsburgh. Two sensational special runs of the mid-twenties served to advertise the railroad's prowess and to provide valuable lessons for the motive power and operating departments. Both occasions involved cooperative efforts with the still youthful but enormously popular art of the motion picture. The first train was operated from Washington to New York on 4 March 1925 under the sponsorship of the International News Reel Corporation. The intention was to carry newly exposed movie film showing the inauguration of President Calvin Coolidge, to develop the film en route, and to project the finished print in the New York theaters on the same day. The use of the train as a mobile photographic laboratory gave the International firm a clear advantage over competitive newsreel companies, which resorted to the equally novel technology of the airplane, but which delayed the process of developing the film until the arrival in New York. The special train covered the 226-mile run in 3 hours, 40 minutes, for an average speed of 61.6 miles per hour. Not many years later the Congressional Limited was to improve slightly on this performance simply in meeting the daily schedule (3 hours, 35 minutes, yielding an average speed of 63 miles per hour). The locomotive that hauled the 1925 special was one of the road's justly celebrated Class E Atlantics (4-4-2 type), which the motive power department had developed to a state as near perfection as the mechanical arts allowed.

The second of the high-speed special runs was more spectacular than the first by virtue of the performance itself and for its association with an event that attracted worldwide attention. On 4 May 1927 Charles A. Lindbergh successfully completed the first solo flight across the Atlantic Ocean. Following his reception in Washington on 11 June very nearly the same drama was re-enacted: the International News Reel Corporation again engaged a special train, aboard which films of the event were developed and printed en route to the New York theaters. By 1927, however, the competing airplanes were flying at higher speeds, and the train crew, accordingly, was called upon for heroic performances. The train, consisting of a coach and specially fitted baggage car, ran the 226 miles from terminal to terminal in 3 hours, 7 minutes, for an average speed of 72.54 miles per hour. There were two stops along the way: the first was made at Wilmington to fill the tender with water, because the attempt to scoop it from a track pan at high speed resulted in the loss of most of the water taken in; the second came at Manhattan Transfer to replace Atlantic-type locomotive Number 460 with electric power. The two stops added the 7 minutes to the three-hour mark; the average speed in motion, as a consequence, stood just above 75 miles per hour. The highest sustained speed was reached over the 66.6-mile segment between Holmesburg Junction, near Philadelphia, and South Street in Newark, where the elapsed time of 47 minutes yielded an average of 85 miles per hour and an estimated maximum of 115 miles per hour (in the lively days of the 1920s, locomotives were not yet equipped with speed recorders).[3] The chief lesson for the railroad was that with a single electric locomotive to eliminate the two stops, the distance could be covered in 3 hours, for a regularly scheduled average speed of 75 miles per hour. When electrification came eight years after the run of the Lindbergh special, the Congressional Limited was to maintain its daily average of 63 miles per hour with five regular stops en route. The spectacular shrieking and roaring though grossly inefficient steam locomotive provided the excitement, of course, but far more important was the fact that the quiet and undramatic electric power assigned to the Lindbergh run covered the 9 busy miles from Manhattan Transfer to the midtown terminal in 9 minutes. Another lesson that led to decisive action was the recognition of the need for improved signaling. In 1928–29, accordingly, the railroad supplemented the new position-light signals with the installation of continuous cab signals in all locomotives regularly assigned to the New York Division.

By the mid-twenties the operation of special trains and extra sections of regularly scheduled trains had reached the stage of a scientific technique requiring the coordinated efforts of a number of separate railroad departments. The need for extra or special trains, that is, trains running on what we might call nonrepeated ad hoc schedules, arose either because an outside organization commissioned an entire train for a specific event, such as the Lindbergh special, or because of a great surge of traffic occasioned by popular sporting events, national conventions, nationally prominent shows, and presidential inaugurations. The first category, from which ticket-holding passengers were barred, was ordinarily the concern only of certain operating and maintenance personnel, chiefly train crews, towermen, engine foremen, and others from the motive-power department. Passenger movements large enough to require two or more special trains, however, called for more extensive planning. The process began with the passenger-traffic department, which calculated the expected volume of traffic from the numbers of tickets sold, these data provided by the agents in the appropriate ticket offices. With cumulative totals available, representatives of the passenger and operating departments worked out schedules by coordinating and interbalancing a number of factors—namely, the route of the trains, the motive power available, the crews that could be assembled at terminal and division points, the necessary servicing en route, and the correlation with existing schedules. When the ad hoc schedule was decided on, the staff of the general passenger agent circulated notices containing the pertinent information to dispatchers, towermen, train masters, and road foremen of engines. Such information at the minimum included the route, the schedules, the requirements for rolling stock and motive power, and sometimes the stocking of dining cars. The dispatcher at the originating point issued orders giving schedules and number of trains to all operators at towers and stations along the selected route. The operation of extra sections of regularly scheduled trains was essentially the same except that the movement of additional sections was governed by the established schedule of the regular train. The practice on the Pennsylvania Railroad, which was universal up to the mid-thirties, was to designate sections by the number of the regular train prefixed by the ordinals *first, second, third,* and so on. If the eastbound Broadway Limited ran in three sections, for example, they would have been designated first, second, and third Number 28. In customary practice the first section, regarded as the regular train, was operated on the published schedule, while the trailing sections were each operated at intervals of five to ten minutes behind its predecessor, the time interval being re-established at each division point. As long as crews operated trains in accordance with the printed rules, timetable instructions, and signal indications, there was nothing to prevent them from running one or more of the advanced sections ahead of schedule, providing that departures from way stations adhered to the published times. Multiple sections, though an obvious delight to passenger agents, were a source of confusion to passengers and persons meeting them who could not remember Pullman car numbers.

No experiment in the transportation of human cargo seemed more promising and indeed more prophetic as the luxury-loving decade approached its climax and its debacle than the provision of transcontinental service between New York and Los Angeles by means of the coordinated schedules of trains and airplanes. This travel novelty was established on 8 July 1929 by the Pennsylvania and the Santa Fe railroads and the Transcontinental Air Transport Company. The equipment for the aerial segments of the journey consisted of trimotor planes manufactured by the Ford Motor Company and powered by Pratt and Whitney engines. The Pennsylvania went so far as to introduce a new train, marked by the unfortunate public-relations name of Airway Limited, as its contribution to the new service. The total elapsed time for the coast-to-coast trip, including time consumed in transfers, was 50 hours, 37 minutes, with the rail and air schedules almost equal. The one defect of the westbound arrangement was that more than 80 percent of the layover time occurred in Waynoka, Oklahoma, a community that offered the traveler little in the way of entertainment or lively urban scenes. By contrast with the train-air trip, the combination of the fastest, most closely integrated rail schedules between the terminals yielded a total time of 88 hours, including the layover in Chicago. The reason for the adoption of the unified rail-air service and for the optimism of railroad officers over its future possibilities was the hazard of nighttime flying during the early years of air transport. For a short time the new arrangement was successful: 30,000 passengers were carried through the first year of operations, and the total reached 5,688 for the peak month of June, 1930. The deepening Depression and the steady shortening of air schedules, however, soon led to the abandonment of this briefly useful partnership.[4]

In spite of the gathering momentum of the Depression and the beginning of the disastrous slide in rail traffic, all-rail travel continued to seem full of promise, at least for the coming prosperity that was always just around the corner. Perhaps nothing better underscored this cheerful view than the fact that the Broadway Limited posted an on-time record of 99.2 percent for 1931. Years of successful experience with high-speed running, accompanied by a steady reduction in the accident rate, made it seem perfectly feasible that the schedule of the premier train should be shortened. On 24 April 1932, shortly before economic troubles ended the rail-air plan, the

Pennsylvania returned the Broadway to the 18-hour schedule that it had followed from 1905 to 1912. The train had been operated at 20 hours through the intervening years, and the new time raised the average speed to 50.4 miles per hour. In one respect the melancholy year was the most auspicious of all for American railroads: no passenger lost his life in a railway accident, and the fatality rate of zero was never again to be reached by any mode of transportation.

The most important key to the Pennsylvania's daily movement of a vast fleet of trains at high speeds, with the near certainty of their reaching way stations and destinations at the times shown in the public tables, was the reliable, day-and-night, never resting operation of the huge New York terminal and its appurtenant facilities. In the ten years of 1920 through 1929 the number of passengers accommodated in the Manhattan station increased 73 percent, from a total of nearly 38 million in the earlier year to 65.5 million for the later. On a typical weekday of January, 1929, the four railroads using the station operated 712 trains, consisting of a total of 5,742 cars and carrying 204,400 passengers. The Long Island, as we might expect, accounted for nearly two-thirds of this traffic, on wheel and on foot, while the Lehigh Valley came in a very distant fourth. The chief burden on the facilities at the Sunnyside coach yard arose from the need to service an average of 400 Pullman cars per day.[5] The peak interval at the terminal complex came with the two hours of 7:30 to 9:30 A.M., when the Long Island operated 79 trains and the Pennsylvania 24 for a total of 103, or one train every 1.17 minutes. Even when everything ran smoothly on the normal day that never really occurred, the whole intricate system of men and machines had to work like the clocks that acted as the railroad's implacable gods.

The expeditious functioning of the terminal complex required the meticulously coordinated operations of the station head house and trackage with its numerous appurtenant yards and structures. The primary support facility has always been Sunnyside Yard in Queens, which originally embraced 87 tracks having a total capacity of 1,078 cars, sufficient to give it the status of being the largest railroad coach yard in the world (in 1929 the number of working tracks was given as 73). Its chief functions were the performance of all maintenance work and all repair work not requiring heavy shop equipment, and the daily cleaning and servicing of all coaches regularly assigned to through trains terminating or originating beyond Philadelphia, and all Pullman cars of whatever functional type. When air conditioning was introduced on the Pennsylvania Railroad rolling stock in 1933, followed by its rapid spread to most through-train equipment, the tasks of routine maintenance and repair suddenly increased in complexity, demanding skills necessary to the servicing of new kinds of electrical and mechanical apparatus. The five yards that flanked the inner approaches of the Manhattan station comprised a total of 33 tracks with a capacity of 222 cars. These minor facilities were reserved exclusively for the cleaning and light servicing of cars assigned to trains with a short layover period, which were ordinarily all Long Island and Pennsylvania suburban trains and the hourly express trains running to and from Philadelphia. All switches, movable frogs, locks, and signals in the station area, the station yards, and Sunnyside Yard were controlled by seven interlocking towers, of which the master facility remains Tower A, supported above the throat at the west end of the station yard. Four subsidiary towers control the balance of switches and signals within the station proper, and two control those at the east and west ends of Sunnyside Yard.

The overriding aim of those responsible for the conduct of station affairs has been to adopt the most expeditious procedures and to retain them in as unvarying a form as unforeseen exigencies allow. Incoming loaded trains of the Pennsylvania entering from the west, trains of the Long Island from the east, and empty trains moving into the station from the coach yard are ordinarily assigned to specific station tracks day after day. The setting up of the routes by the crews of the interlocking towers located within the station area is carried out following the receipt and acknowledgment of the appropriate signals from the towermen at Newark and Sunnyside. The flow of information on incoming empty trains through chains of communication uniting Sunnyside and the Manhattan station guaranteed that all operating personnel directly received within seconds the appropriate messages. The centers of intelligence in this system were the road dispatchers, from whose offices the notices of incoming trains were sent by the telautograph instruments to the train and locomotive dispatchers, the chief towerman of Tower A, the station master, the information desk, and the tender of the bulletin board that carried his handwritten announcements of incoming trains. The levermen of the controlling and the subsidiary towers set up the routes that carried the trains to the preassigned tracks. Much of the speed and efficiency of these intricate workings depended on the prompt unloading of trains, the final event of the rail journey, when passengers discovered that train and station crews meant business and no dawdling along the way. Incoming suburban trains of the Long Island and the Pennsylvania were unloaded in 2 minutes, then quickly sent to their respective yards. Outbound suburban trains of the two roads were loaded in 10 minutes, and the Pennsylvania's through trains, with their usual mixture of coaches and sleeping cars, were allowed 20 minutes for the process (the premier trains carried sleeping or parlor cars only). During the years of maximum traffic on the Long Island—over 100,000,000 passengers per annum in 1925–30 and 1945—boarding the rush-hour expresses could be a terrifying experience to the timid stranger, or even to the seasoned traveler, especially if he happened to be laden with suitcases. As many as 1,800 homebound commuters might converge on the doorways, to be funneled into the cars that delivered them to their fireside communities.

The most important arteries in the whole terminal system were the four East River tunnels that joined the station tracks to Sunnyside Yard and the west end of the Long Island's Jamaica trunk. On a typical weekday during the peak years of 1925–30 and 1941–45 as many as 730 loaded and empty trains passed over these subaqueous pathways, again according to the principle of preassigned routes that governed the placing of trains throughout the complex. The most heavily used of these tracks was Line Number 3, the right-hand of the two Sunnyside connectors, if one faced to the east. The maximum traffic density at the time of the survey conducted in January, 1929, was 230 train movements in 24 hours, or one train every 6.25 minutes through the single-track tunnel. During the late night hours, from 1:00 to 5:00 A.M., trains would run few and far between, while towermen yawned in boredom; through the rush hours of morning and evening, however, trains might run on 1-minute headway, and no man dared rest a hand. A motor failure in one of the East River tunnels was crucial: the action of dispatchers and towermen that brought the locomotive to the rescue from Sunnyside was measured in seconds, and no one was permitted the luxury of error. The electric power assigned to regular and emergency service between Manhattan Transfer and Sunnyside Yard was operated by crews that formed a special pool restricted to the electrified runs. Of the 45 locomotives with their associated enginemen and firemen ordinarily reserved for the terminal service, 26 were assigned to the first two shifts (7:00 A.M. to 11:00 P.M.), and 19 to the graveyard shift (11:00 P.M. to 7:00 A.M.). The station during the halcyon days was never quiet, but around four o'clock in the morning one might be likely to encounter only a scattering of lonely derelicts and late-hour drunks, with a few sober night workers keeping a respectful distance from them. The New Jersey ferries, in contrast, were as lively during these end-of-the-night hours as they were at midday, especially when the day's produce began to pour into the West Side terminals around 2:00 A.M.

Pennsylvania Station, like its fellow on 42d Street, was almost a microcosm of the unsleeping city that lived by unceasing movement. If one seemed rather far removed from the never dimmed glitter of Broadway and Times Square, he could not fail to sense, nevertheless, that the urban world concentrated in and around these ganglia perhaps found its fullest symbolic re-enactment in the musical revue of the 1920s. The substance and the action of the city reached a perfect artistic expression in the music of George Gershwin and, by the end of the decade, Cole Porter, in the

Ziegfeld Follies, where the world of Yiddish dialect comedy was ruled by Fannie Brice, Willie Howard, and Lou Holtz, in the special forms of a new Aristophanic madness offered by the Marx Brothers at the Palace, in the Central Park Casino, playhouse of the rich in a people's park, in a new kind of sophisticated music hall dancing exhibited by Bill Robinson, Jack Donahue, and Fred and Adèle Astaire, in every song-and-dance routine from the Cotton Club Revue to the Grand Street Follies, with Minsky's Burlesque along the way. At a higher level of musical creativity, jazz was in the full tide of its migration from New Orleans to Chicago and New York, at the same time reaching new levels of richness and complexity. What was more appropriate to this world than a charming playboy mayor known as *Jimmy* Walker, or a dedicated liberal, pure New York–Irish governor called *Al* Smith, who wore a brown derby? The great railroad terminal was a microcity, with shops, restaurants, lunch counters, bars, bookstores, communication centers, offices, first-aid stations, bootblacks, panhandlers, and pimps, the subway under one side of it, the hotels across the bounding streets, a special passageway to the huge department stores a block to the east, the roaring traffic's boom all around it, the never resting trains like giant moles in their hidden tunnels. Broadway in effect provided the artistic representation, but the station itself and all attached thereto constituted a vital mechanism, like a heart in a living creature.

The Depression that followed the debacle of October, 1929, was a national calamity and stupefying anticlimax, like an act that collapses on the stage at the end of an abortive run. Every city suffered, and New York was no exception; yet it possessed sources of strength that kept it in a state of relative economic health. Most obvious was the robust state of waterborne commerce: foreign tonnage declined by nearly 40 percent between 1930 and 1935, but the domestic cargo fell no more than 20 percent. Although recovery was slow at first, the port had very nearly regained the enviable traffic of 1929 by the time the Second World War ended the depression decade. Since the operation of the harbor terminal system was in good measure a handicraft art, the comparatively vigorous commerce of the 1930s guaranteed modest levels of employment among the stevedores and the pilots. The land economy of the city was distinguished by a unique manufacturing system. To an unparalleled degree the industrial plant of Manhattan, Brooklyn, and Queens was composed of a great multitude of very small businesses, the majority of them numbering fewer than a hundred employees. The central business district of Manhattan—everything up to 59th Street—was covered with every conceivable element of a service economy, from one-man lunch counters and fruit stands to legions of stores and hotels of a size matched only in Chicago. The wages of all who served, or who sewed ladies' garments in the lofts of lower Broadway, or rolled cigars, or sliced salami in the corner delicatessens might have been nickels and dimes, but they were money in the pocket, and enough to preserve the sense that men and women were at least earning their bread. A third factor in the local economy was the largesse that President Franklin Roosevelt's New Deal lavished on the city. Through the decade of the thirties only Rockefeller Center kept the skyscraper business alive, with the consequence that the great public-housing projects of Harlem and the lower East Side provided the chief source of income for the building industry. To sum it all up, one could fare much worse in other metropolitan areas, or perish of dietary deficiencies in rural areas from Appalachia to the Dust Bowl.

The slow revival of what is still called prosperity, abetted by massive programs of public works, would have brought some of the lost passengers back to the rails in any event. What brought them back in a flood reminiscent of the Jazz Age, however, was the World's Fair of 1939–40, the first to be held in New York since 1853. Even at the low point of the Depression, 1933, traffic at Pennsylvania Station maintained a level equal to nearly three-quarters of the 1929 volume. The intermittent recovery of the intervening years, slowed by the recession of 1938, gave way to the spectacular rise of 1939, when the total of somewhat more than 69,600,000 passengers came to 46 percent above the doldrums of 1933 and nearly six percent above the high point of 1930. The daily average during the first year of the fair stood at about 217,700, high enough to take some measure of the station's true capacity.[6] The year 1939, however, was filled with ironies for the United States and its foremost city; one experienced them directly at the international exposition but sensed similar ambiguities among the streams of humanity that again surged through the station. On a Sunday evening in the late summer, when no tide of rush-hour commuters swept everything before it, the crowd of weekend and vacation travelers was scattered in irregular masses under the softly illuminated glass vaults of the great concourse. The largest of these loosely defined throngs usually stood patiently around the gate leading to the workhorse of the railroad's Washington stable, train Number 137, the Arlington, a random mix of head-end cars, coaches, and sleeping cars, the Pullmans to be transferred to the Fast Flying Virginian of the C. and O., the Robert E. Lee of the Seaboard (one sleeper destined for so exotic a place as Memphis via Birmingham and the Frisco), and the Washington-Atlanta Express of the Southern. The general atmosphere was that characteristic of a vacation crowd—good-humored patience, random conversation, mostly of travel details, and expressions suggestive of pleasures shared; yet one could not escape the undercurrent of tension, expectations of the future combining hope and foreboding, since the guns had sounded once again in the waning summer, and the Second World War had begun on 1 September.

The performance of the rail and marine system of New York Harbor during the war years was such a paragon of expeditious port operations as to make the troubles of the First World War seem like a remote bad dream.[7] One may plausibly argue, as a matter of fact, that the decade of the 1940s marked the high tide of the city's functional power, its prosperity, its dedication to the discharge of its immense wartime tasks, the stability and balance, the civic responsibility, and essential decency of its human community. The passenger terminals were prepared for their role: the electrified Manhattan stations were still regarded as urban monuments of the first rank, clean and majestic in external appearance and in sound working order within; the intricate techniques of their operation, as we have seen in the case of the Pennsylvania's property, had reached the status of an exact science. The explosive rise in traffic that came in 1942 was little expected, but the great terminal on Seventh Avenue experienced no difficulties in coping with it. After the close of the World's Fair in 1940, traffic for a brief period sank discouragingly toward depression levels, but in the succeeding four years (1942–45) it climbed steadily upward to a gain of nearly 80 percent over the first year of the war.

The ultimate record for Pennsylvania Station came in 1945: very nearly 109,350,000 passengers surged through its gates and concourses, for an unparalleled average volume of 342,000 passengers per day. The station had forged ahead of Grand Central in total traffic more than twenty years earlier, and it was never to relinquish its lead. The immense tide of Long Island passengers, of course, was the primary factor in the establishment of this supremacy. Reliable historical data on the traffic at the largest railroad terminals is exceedingly difficult if not impossible to discover. On the basis of such fragmentary evidence as one can find, however, Pennsylania Station stood in the same rank as the leading terminals of Europe, such as Liverpool Street, Victoria, and Waterloo in London, and Saint Lazare in Paris. It is entirely plausible to suppose, therefore, that its peak traffic may have exceeded that of its European counterparts. No record of the maximum daily total at Pennsylvania Station appears to have been preserved, as it was in the case of Grand Central, but on the days when the greatest numbers of servicemen were passing through the city, especially if such swellings of the normal tides came at periods immediately preceding or following holidays, there can be little question that days of half a million passengers may have occurred with some frequency. The point is of fundamental importance, and we will return to it in our final chapter: when the equivalent of the entire populations of major cities can daily move safely and expeditiously through a primary transportation nexus with no disturbance to civic life and fabric, with no chemical, visual, or auditory pollution, the problem of circulation in the city has been given its only acceptable solution.

The Extension of Electrified Lines

By 1980 the railroads of the United States lagged far behind those of the western European nations and Japan with respect to the extent and the quality of electrified operations, but through the decades of the 1920s and the 1930s they were still well in the lead. Outside the metropolitan areas of New York, Chicago, and San Francisco, many long tunnels and mountain grades had been converted to electric power, among which the most impressive was the installation of the Milwaukee Road in Montana, Idaho, and Washington, encompassing at one time 663 miles of main track. On the high-density main lines of the eastern carriers there was every argument in favor of getting rid of the steam locomotives, but only the Pennsylvania Railroad was prepared to act on a scale commensurate with need and potentiality. The successful completion of the New York extension in 1910, with the economies and operating advantages it conferred, convinced the officers of the company that the great benefits of electric power under the traffic densities common in large metropolitan areas justified the heavy capital investment required by a major expansion of the existing mileage. The obvious target, accordingly, for the extension of electrified lines was the Philadelphia Terminal Division, where the focal point of Broad Street Station accommodated an average of 574 trains per week-day during the years 1908 to 1913.[8] If electrification could be recommended anywhere, the first consideration would be this overburdened stub-end terminal at the very center of Philadelphia's core area. Planning with such an end in view began shortly after the New York station was opened, and the first stage in the implementation of the program was the electrification of the suburban service on the divisional main line from Broad Street to Paoli in 1913–15. During the following thirteen years the suburban trains were brought under the wire, as the railroad argot puts it, on the branch lines to Chestnut Hill (1915–18), Whitemarsh (1924), and Westchester (1926), and on the main line to Wilmington (1926–28). Before the railroad could develop further plans, the municipal government of Baltimore urged the officers to electrify the main line through the city to eliminate the smoke in the long tunnels and to improve the appearance of the new Union Station that was opened in 1911. If the company had complied with this reasonable proposal, it would have meant the conversion of the main line to electricity over only the limited segments of the Baltimore tunnels and between Philadelphia and Wilmington, leaving a patchwork of steam and electrical operation that would have largely nullified the economic and technical advantages of conversion to the new form of power.

The railroad company, as a matter of fact, had already begun to develop grander and bolder plans. In 1925–28 the road carried out an exhaustive and detailed investigation of the industrial economy and the transportation needs of the regions centered at New York and Philadelphia and of rail operations conducted by means of alternating-current distribution in Sweden, Germany, and Switzerland, and on the New Haven, Norfolk and Western, and Virginian railroads in the United States. On the basis of this study, in view of the extremely heavy freight and passenger traffic on the regional lines (for the most part those composing the New York, Philadelphia, Philadelphia Terminal, and Maryland divisions), and of the expected economic advantages, the Pennsylvania Railroad's president, W. W. Atterbury, announced on 1 November 1928 the preliminary plans for the largest electrification program so far undertaken in the United States. The decision was thus reached in the spirit of a scientific technology and only after the most painstaking economic analysis. What was most attractive to the managerial mind, of course, was the well-established conclusion that drastically lowered operating costs would accompany the replacement of steam power by electric traction. Operating necessities as well as economies dictated increased speed for all classes of trains in the face of the steadily rising volume and density of both freight and passenger traffic on the lines east of Harrisburg. One persuasive factor was the rapid expansion of passenger business to and from Florida, which recovered quickly from the decline that followed the collapse of the Florida land boom in 1926. Moreover, electric traction was seen as a civic boon as well as an economic and operating benefit, especially in the case of the new stations that were being planned at Newark and Philadelphia. A final consideration was a demographic projection indicating that by 1950 the New York metropolitan area would extend from the mid-line of Long Island to New Brunswick, New Jersey, and embrace a population of 30,000,000 souls. If all who traveled and everything they consumed moved by rail according to the railroad share among the transportation modes of the mid-1920s, the horizon for the Pennsylvania would have, indeed, been unlimited.

The plan that was announced in November was somewhat less ambitious in scope than the program that was soon adopted. The electrical system was to differ radically from the original installation for the New York extension and was nearly identical with that of the New Haven Railroad: the 25-cycle alternating current was to be distributed at a potential of 11,000 volts by means of an overhead or catenary system, and the transmission potential was to be fixed at 132,000 volts. The trackage that was to be placed under wire comprised the following segments: the New York extension (Manhattan Transfer to Sunnyside Yard); the combined freight and passenger line extending from Jersey City and Manhattan Transfer to Wilmington, Delaware; the similar line between Philadelphia and Atglen, Pennsylvania, about midway between Philadelphia and Harrisburg; the freight line known as Trenton Cut-Off; and the low grade freight line extending from Atglen to Columbia on the Susquehanna River. The total length of electrified line would have been 325 miles, embracing an aggregate of 1,300 miles of track. Three types of road engines were proposed for all classes of through service, and they were to be operated either as single units or in multiple arrangement of two or more units, so that they could haul trains of any length, weight, or speed. All suburban trains in the metropolitan areas of New York and Philadelphia were to be composed of multiple-unit equipment. The estimated total cost of $100,000,000 was divided between $60,000,000 for transmission lines, substations, distributions lines, and ancillary elements, and $40,000,000 for motive power and rolling stock.

The original choice of terminals was somewhat arbitrary and showed little concern for the pleas of the municipal establishment at Baltimore. Shortly after the work of installation began in 1930, however, it was recognized that in order to realize the full economies and operating benefits inherent in electrification it would be necessary to extend the system to the chief transfer points for freight trains, with their associated classification yards, which meant in effect that passenger service would be operated in a similar manner to the closest terminals or way stations. As a consequence of these deliberations, the final plan called for the extension of electric power from Atglen and Columbia to Harrisburg and Enola Yard, on the west side of the Susquehanna River, and from Wilmington to Washington Union Terminal and Potomac Yard, midway between Washington and Alexandria. The citizens of Baltimore were at last to be satisfied. The new service to Philadelphia was inaugurated on 16 January 1933, when overhead wires and alternating current replaced the original third-rail, direct-current installation on the New York extension; operations to Washington and Potomac Yard came a little more than two years later, and the whole grand scheme was completed on 15 April 1938, when the electrical operation of freight trains to and from Enola Yard was initiated. The system by this date, including the recent additions to the Long Island's electrified lines, embraced 656 route miles and 2,677 miles of track, in extent of line and volume of traffic far beyond any other installation in the United States.

When service to and from Washington was established in 1935, the normal flow of traffic over the entire main line between Pennsylvania Station and Potomac Yard, and over any segment thereof—that is, the sum total of all classes of traffic moving from end to end of the line or anywhere between the terminals—included 830 passenger trains and 190 freight trains, for a total of 1,020 trains per weekday. The protection of this multitude of schedules required 118 passenger, 88 freight, and 65 switching locomotives, or 271 active units in toto. The ultimate cost in 1938 came to

$176,000,000, a sum which the railroad would have readily been able to raise in the financial markets had it not been for the economic collapse of the 1930s. The officers of the company were among the first tycoons to turn to Washington with hats in hand: two-thirds of the investment was born by two government loans, one of $45,000,000 from the Reconstruction Finance Corporation, provided in 1932 at an interest rate of 6 percent, and another of $77,000,000 from the Public Works Administration, made available in 1934 at a rate of 4 percent. The final negotiation in the vast enterprise came on 15 June 1938, when the Pennsylvania and the Long Island railroads contracted to purchase electric power from the Consolidated Edison Company of New York, the quantity estimated on the basis of traffic in 1937–38 to be 290,000,000 kilowatt-hours per year. This arrangement included the sale of the railroad company's generating station at Hunter's Point to the utility.[9]

Long before the Pennsylvania Railroad had begun to plan the extension of its electrified lines, it had embarked on an experimental program aimed at determining the optimum form of alternating-current motive power. Between 1917 and 1931 the company's Juniata Shops at Altoona, working in cooperation with the Westinghouse Electric and Manufacturing Company, produced four models, of which the first was designed exclusively for freight operations and used for switching and helper service on the main line of the Philadelphia Terminal Division between Zoo Junction and Paoli (the junction of the lines extending from Philadelphia to New York and Pittsburgh lies immediately adjacent to the city's zoological garden). The next two locomotives, manufactured in 1924 and 1930, were assigned to both passenger and freight service, but both proved to be steps along the way rather than the ideal for which the engineers were searching. The fourth of the prototypical machines, a 2-C-2 type produced in 1931, was retained for regular freight and passenger service as the railroad's Class P-5.[10] After prolonged testing on a specially built track at Claymont, Delaware, equipped with strain gauges to measure horizontal impact at the rail, the company's motive-power department introduced modifications that led to an apparently satisfactory performance. The railroad and the Westinghouse company manufactured an additional 90 units, which were placed in service in 1932–33. The P-5 locomotives performed well enough in hauling trains, but the modifications following the Claymont tests failed to improve the riding qualities to the point where the track was spared excessive horizontal thrust under normal operating conditions. The difficulties arose chiefly from the short, rigid driving-wheel base and the high unit load of 36,667 pounds per driving wheel, or 73,333 pounds per driving axle. The railroad, accordingly, embarked on another series of tests, using the special track at Claymont and a borrowed New Haven locomotive with a 2-C + C-2 wheel arrangement (double the number of driving wheels under the Pennsylvania's P-5). The articulated wheel base, the shorter rigid length, and the lower unit load of 22,667 pounds per driving wheel brought about so great an improvement in riding action as to reduce lateral horizontal thrust at the rail to easily manageable levels.

The motive-power engineers adopted the articulated base and the wheel arrangement of the New Haven locomotive as the foundation for a design that quickly proved to be the masterwork in the technology of electric traction. The prototype of the new class, designated GG-1, was jointly manufactured in 1933 by the General Electric Company and the Baldwin Locomotive Works and was first tested on the Claymont track in February of the following year (fig. 38).[11] The results of these grueling tests astounded the manufacturers as well as the railroad: the locomotive, drawing trains of various weights, was operated at speeds up to 115 miles per hour and repeatedly accelerated, with one car in tow, to 100 miles per hour in 64.5 seconds, for an acceleration rate of 1.55 miles per hour per second. To gain speed at this rate the locomotive had to deliver 9,300 horsepower, more than double the continuous rating, but substantially less than the 11,000 horsepower required of a diesel-electric locomotive because of the loss of power in the latter between the engine and the generator and between the generator and the motor. The extraordinary powers of the GG-1 grew from several carefully designed features. Each of the six driving axles was powered by two motors rated at 385 horsepower per unit, or a total of 4,620 continuous horsepower for the twelve. The motors, however, could be overloaded to the point of delivering 9,240 horsepower by drawing current for short periods of time up to 9,000 amperes, as opposed to the normal withdrawal of 2,000 amperes. The smooth and rapid acceleration was a consequence not only of the multiplicity of relatively small motors, but also of the quill-and-spider drive, which provided six driving cups for each driving wheel, or a total of 72 for the entire machine (fig. 11 shows the quill-and-spider assembly for a New Haven locomotive). Finally, the starting tractive force of 70,700 pounds was greater than that of steam locomotives designed for fast freight service. The high distribution potential of 11,000 volts was stepped down by means of transformers in the locomotive to 700 volts. The advantages of high transmission and distribution voltages could thus be combined with internal electrical equipment of modest dimensions, the combination guaranteeing speed, power, efficiency, quiet operation, and minimal maintenance of track and machine. In short, the GG-1 provided the lesson for the future. In a civilization infatuated with petroleum, however, the lesson went unheeded.

Over the ten years of 1934–43 the Pennsylvania added 139 locomotives of the new class to its stable of electric power. They were as distinguished in appearance as they were in operating prowess. Using the railroad's prototypical form as a base, the

Fig. 38. Pennsylvania Railroad. Electric locomotive, Class GG-1, 1934.

industrial designer Raymond Loewy created a simple but visually effective form of flowing, rounded surfaces and gently tapering silhouette between the center cab and the narrow ends. The practice under the exigencies of war was to restrict the older P-5 locomotives to freight service and to reserve the GG-1 class for passenger trains, which on the New York and the Philadelphia Terminal divisions greatly outnumbered the freight. When traffic rose to the floods of 1943 and 1944, however, the never resting GG-1s were frequently assigned to fast freight schedules and were nearly always double-headed for the heavier trains. In the summer of 1944, when the great Allied drive had begun in Europe, the Pennsylvania Railroad was operating an average of 293 trains per day through Trenton, the equivalent of one train every 4.9 minutes. A particularly impressive demonstration of exacting wartime operation was provided on one occasion during the year: GG-1 locomotive Number 4808, hauling a 15-car train weighing 1,150 tons, left Trenton 18 minutes late and arrived in Washington one-half minute behind schedule. The distance of 162.2 miles was covered in a running time of 138.25 minutes, to post an average running speed of 70.8 miles per hour. A particularly heady burst came on the Maryland Division, where the train sped through the 15.2 miles between Odenton and Landover at a steady rate of 93.5 miles per hour. This thundering tide of freight and passenger trains, frequently running side by side on multiple-track lines, traveled over a right of way that was a paragon of high-quality maintenance. Deep ballast, 152-pound rail, supported joints, and exactly superelevated curves guaranteed smooth operations, and the travelers' complaints were centered only on the antique rolling stock the road was compelled to press into service. The whole performance was a marvel of how well systems of mass transportation can move human beings and cargo, but the overloaded equipment and the ceaseless, sometimes desperate race with time in maintaining it would, soon or late, exact their toll. The price was paid in a freakish and disastrous accident at Philadelphia. On 6 September 1943 the first section of the Congressional Limited, its 16 cars carrying 541 people, was passing through Frankford Junction at 60 miles per hour when a journal on the leading truck of the seventh car burned off. The forward end of the suddenly immobilized car was thrown into the air and struck the heavy steel girder of a catenary frame, which in effect sheared the car from end to end just below the roof level. The consequences were appalling: 79 passengers were killed and 103 injured, for a casualty rate inside the train of 33.6 percent. There were others during the wartime years, but measured against billions of passenger-miles, the resulting fatality rates were numbered in microscopic fractions.

Two final constructions in the metropolitan area of New York rounded out or proved of supplementary value to the Pennsylvania's second electrification program. The earlier, although it was designed to serve the end of moving cargo rather than passengers, functioned as well to reduce the burdens on the New York station. The railroad's existing express terminal, which was located at Pier D on the Jersey City waterfront, was operating under increasingly severe handicaps by the end of the war. Outmoded in design, dependent on water transfer for the vast majority of shipments, overwhelmed by the rapidly expanding traffic that came in the decade of the twenties, it could no longer function by itself, with the consequence that the company was compelled to set aside tracks and platform areas in the Manhattan station to supplement the Jersey City space. A new terminal placed at a location obviating the need for water transshipment was a matter of necessity. The railroad's engineering staff selected a site adjacent to Sunnyside Yard and drew up detailed plans in 1924–25, and the contractors completed the new facility in the spring of 1927. With a floor area of 245,000 square feet and a capacity for the simultaneous loading and unloading of 84 cars on its six tracks (as opposed to 24 cars at Pier D), the steel-framed brick-walled enclosure was easily the largest such structure in the United States. It was immediately called upon to demonstrate its utility: during the first summer following its completion the terminal staff handled 55,000 shipments composed of 80,000 separate pieces per working day, or the equivalent of about 35 percent of the total express traffic for the metropolitan area. The division of the Pennsylvania's share into 75 percent for outbound shipments and 25 percent for inbound is another indicator of the city's importance as a manufacturing center of consumers' goods, as well as the nation's administrative capital. Since the new terminal was located at Sunnyside, the cars carrying express shipments were either incorporated into passenger trains or made up into solid mail and express trains, which meant that in either case, express, like mail, was moved through the river tunnels and the passenger station by electric locomotives.[12]

The extension of electrified lines beyond the original limits and the conversion of the terminal zone to alternating current required a revision of the company's facilities at Newark and simultaneously rendered the engine change at Manhattan Transfer obsolete. The officers of the road planned the total reconstruction of the Newark station and its associated trackage, together with the extension of the Hudson and Manhattan Railroad line into the new station, which together made possible the abandonment of all the facilities at the Transfer. The program at Newark was a cooperative undertaking of the Pennslvania Railroad (legally acting through its subsidiary, the United New Jersey Railroad and Canal Company), the Public Service Corporation of New Jersey, and the city of Newark, and it included extensive civic works as well as railroad construction. The Pennsylvania's share comprised the erection of a new station near the existing structure on Market Street, new express and freight-handling facilities, the elevation of the entire line within city limits, a new lift bridge over the Passaic River, new signals, and a new, much enlarged interlocking tower. The railroad company was also largely responsible for the construction of the Hudson and Manhattan line into the station on the new elevated right of way, and for the extension of the Hudson and Manhattan tubes to Parkhurst Street. The chief projects of the city and the state were filling the channel of the Morris Canal, laying a boulevard on the fill, and placing a street railway line in the median. The first contracts were awarded on 9 January 1929; the station was opened on 30 March 1935; the extension of the Hudson and Manhattan tracks was completed in the fall of 1937; and the entire complex of station and engine terminal at Manhattan Transfer was abandoned early in the following year. The station building was designed by the architectural firm of McKim, Mead and White, and the railroad engineering work was carried out under the direction of L. P. Struble, the engineer in charge of the Newark program, and A. C. Watson, chief engineer of the company's New York Zone. The total cost, at the depression price level, was $25,000,000.[13]

The steel-framed station embraces eight tracks, of which two are reserved for the trains of the Hudson and Manhattan. The head house and the long walls that enclose the track-platform area are sheathed in granite at the base of the building, limestone and brick over other areas. The formal treatment might be described as the Art Deco mode modified by classical detail on the exterior and as pure Art Deco on the interior. The elevated island platforms are unusually generous in length, ranging from 900 to 1,120 feet, to insure quick loading and unloading of the long trains of coaches that predominate on the always heavily used New York–Philadelphia–Washington axis. Two structural features distinguish the engineering work of the Newark station and its eastern approach. The skylighted concrete train sheds are carried on arched girders over the tracks and heart-shaped trusses above the platforms, the latter being a modification of the similar forms that carry the train sheds of Chicago Union Station (1916–25). The approach tracks from New York pass over the Passaic River lift bridge immediately east of the station. The rising, falling, and interweaving tracks of the Hudson and Manhattan, carried on separate steel-girder viaducts east and west of the station, required a double-level bridge over the river. The structure was further modified from conventional forms by the suspension of the center track from transverse trusses by means of I-section hangers. This device allowed the use of continuous floor beams extending across the full width of the deck in place of transverse series of the simple end-supported members. The chief advantage was a reduction in the depth of the beams in question. The bridge is carried between towers by massive Warren trusses with a uniform depth of 44 feet. The great terminal in New York was not permitted to survive, but the well-designed station complex at Newark stands as it was originally built, in sound working order and remarkably clean, thanks to electric power.

The final stages of the Pennsylvania's program of improvements were the work of its subsidiary, the Long Island, and they extended over a period of 17 years, beginning and ending well outside the ten-year plan of the parent road. The continuing rapid and seemingly irresistible expansion of the Long Island's immense passenger traffic prompted expenditures that the privately controlled corporation was never to make again. In the eleven years from 1920 through 1930 the number of passengers rose nearly 63 percent, to the ultimate peak in the latter year of 118,000,000 riders. The Depression took its toll, as we might expect, but the war years brought another steep rise, to a near-record total of 116,000,000 passengers in 1946. In the expansive decade of the twenties the road was prepared to spend money in keeping with the rising demands on its facilities, although its officers were already beginning to complain that a fixed schedule of fares made it impossible to meet increasing costs in spite of the growth in traffic. Electrical operations were extended in three stages—from Jamaica to Babylon in 1925, over the connecting line between Valley Stream and Mineola in 1926, and on the branches from Floral Park to Creedmoor and from Garden City to Salisbury Plains in 1929. These additions were somewhat offset by the abandonment of electric power on the Whitestone Landing Branch in 1932. Expanding traffic and extensions of electrified line required regular additions to the rolling stock, so that by 1930 the road was operating 1,000 multiple-unit cars in daily service.[14] The losses of the Depression were recouped to a gratifying degree by the traffic growing out of the New York World's Fair of 1939–40. Since the site of the fair lay immediately adjacent to the railroad's right of way beside Flushing Meadow, the company built a temporary station of radically modern design within an easy walk of the entrances. The designed capacity of 18,000 passengers per hour proved none too generous in view of the fact that the special shuttle trains operated to and from Pennsylvania Station and the regular trains running via Jamaica carried a total of 93,000 passengers on the opening day in 1939.[15] The final improvement in the Long Island properties was an extensive and long-delayed series of grade separations undertaken as part of the state's program of public works designed as much for the relief of unemployment as for the physical improvements. Over the years of 1940–42 the railroad and New York state together spent $37,646,000 on the construction of subways and elevated lines in Brooklyn, Queens, and the immediate vicinity of the Aqueduct Park racetrack. This ambitious project comprised the reconstruction of the double-track Atlantic Avenue subway between East New York and Dunton, the elevation of the double-track branches to Rockaway Beach and Far Rockaway on steel-girder viaducts, and the elevation of 7,500 feet of the four-track line at Aqueduct Park partly on an embankment and partly on short girder bridges over the streets. The subway extended 4.75 miles, and the viaduct to the south shore beaches 4.25, making a total with the alterations at the race track of 10.75 miles. The railroad could never have accomplished this task alone; the achievement offered a useful example of the fruitful partnership between private corporations and the government that the Depression brought. The Long Island performed admirably under the wartime burdens, repeatedly at the peak of its capacity, with rolling stock every wheel of which was built prior to 1930. But the burdens of one hundred million passengers per year again exacted a heavy toll: accumulating troubles and disaster struck together in the early postwar years, and the days of the railroad as a Pennsylvania property were drawing to a close.

6

Grand Central Terminal through the Second World War

The New York Central Railroad, born under that title in 1853, was recreated in 1914 by a merger of the New York Central and Hudson River and the Lake Shore and Michigan Southern railroads. The acquisition of the western road doubled the length of the primary main line and added extensive branches in Ohio, Michigan, and Pennsylvania. Leases had long before brought the West Shore and the Boston and Albany into the fold, while earlier mergers had pushed the Central's properties north to the Saint Lawrence River and south to the anthracite coal fields (fig. 39). The program of conquest inaugurated by Cornelius Vanderbilt in 1873 eventually brought major railroad systems of the Great Lakes region and the Middle West under control and extended the New York Central authority over an immense network that spread to the extreme outposts of Mackinac, Charleston, Peoria, and Saint Louis. The two largest fiefs, the Big Four and the Michigan Central, were extraordinarily prosperous companies, with the happy consequence that the Central's stock-holdings brought to the coffers many millions of dollars in nonoperating income.[1] The parent company, its leased properties, and its numerous affiliates served the major industrial centers of Massachusetts, the entire area of New York state, the Ontario peninsula, the basins of the Great Lakes, the Ohio Valley at strategic places from Pittsburgh to Cairo, and the broad belt bounded by the lakes and the Ohio River. As long as the nation's industry was concentrated in what we might call the northeastern quadrant of the United States, and as long as bituminous coal was the primary source of its power, the enviable prosperity of the New York Central Lines was guaranteed. With respect to passenger traffic the Central could everywhere compete favorably with its arch-rival, the Pennsylvania, except between New York and Saint Louis, where the latter enjoyed a 100-mile advantage in length of main line. Although the Central possessed no such traffic generator as the New York–Philadelphia–Washington axis, this defect was partly offset by direct main lines to Boston, Buffalo, Cleveland, Toledo, and Detroit. In short, the officers of the New York Central had no grounds for complaint and many reasons for rejoicing.

The railroad was far more deeply rooted in the New York ambience than the Pennsylvania could hope to claim. The latter was always regarded as something of an alien: its corporate headquarters were located in Philadelphia; the company's trains reached New York Harbor on leased lines; and its executive officers customarily came up through the ranks, often via the engineering and operating departments of the original Philadelphia-Pittsburgh line. The Central, by contrast, had established

Fig. 39. Map of the New York Central Railroad and its controlled lines, 1926.

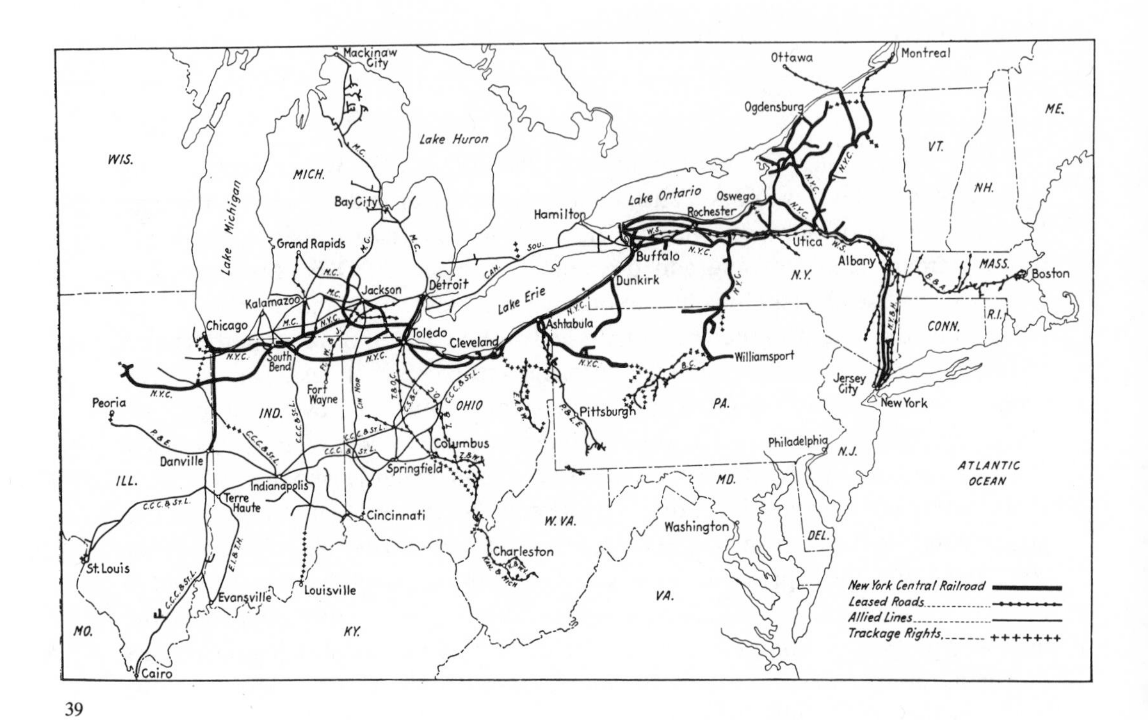

39

itself in New York in 1869, opened its first terminal in the city two years later, and drew much of its staff from the regional population. Although the New York and Harlem Railroad, which formed the main stem of the Manhattan lines, was a leased property, it had been so thoroughly absorbed into the Vanderbilt domain that little more than the title remained. Grand Central Depot and its successors were established institutions of the city, and they eventually played the major role in shaping a great commercial and residential precinct in the heart of the midtown area. The attractive power of this magnet has never waned, so that it has determined, as we have seen, much of the very form and circulatory pattern of Manhattan Island. Grand Central Terminal was finally spared in the wave of civic barbarism that reached ruinous proportions in 1960, because it was seen to be part of the city's living tissue, whereas its equally impressive though less well rooted fellow on Seventh Avenue was sacrificed. The heroic age of the terminal came in the thirty years of 1915 to 1945, when, like Pennsylvania Station, Grand Central demonstrated continuously how great urban transportation ganglia ought to work. At the midpoint of these decades the investment in the terminal properties was reported by the company to be $598,000,000, or well over $5 billion translated to the 1980 price level.

Traffic and Operations at the Station

In spite of the fact that the Grand Central passenger traffic was nearly double that of the Pennsylvania Railroad alone (entirely the consequence of the high tide of suburban travel on the New Haven as well as on the New York Central's three divisions in Westchester County), the volume could never match the flood of Long Island commuters, so that the terminal on 42d Street gradually fell behind Pennsylvania Station in the total of daily passengers. In 1914, the first full year of its operation, somewhat more than 22,500,000 passengers arrived at or departed from the New York Central's terminal, whereas Pennsylvania Station accommodated only 17,500,000. By 1920, however, the relative proportions of the two were reversed: traffic on the New York Central and the New Haven together increased nearly 64 percent above the level of 1914, to give Grand Central a total for the year of nearly 37,000,000 passengers, whereas traffic carried by the Pennsylvania and its tenants more than doubled, so that the total at Pennsylvania Station rose to somewhat below 38,000,000 travelers. From that time the Pennsylvania's terminal steadily increased its lead, and by the peak years of 1929–30 the ratio was nearly 66,000,000 passengers (1930) to slightly fewer than 46,600,000 at Grand Central (1929).[2]

Even though it stood in second place, the huge terminal on 42d Street produced some spectacular records in the years during the First World War and the decade that followed. On the basis of admittedly fragmentary evidence, the number of weekday trains appears to have risen rather slowly between 1915 and 1930, although the number of daily passengers increased irregularly from 97,800 to 141,100 during that time. Through the summer of 1919 the average was 466 trains and 96,370 passengers per day. By 1928 all the figures had increased: 475 daily trains, consisting of a total of about 4,000 cars, carried close to 140,000 passengers per weekday. The documented record showed that the high point came on 25 November 1916, the Saturday of the Yale-Harvard football game for that season, when the terminal accommodated 667 trains and 129,486 passengers in the 24-hour period. The strike of the New York subway motormen that began on 17 August 1919 led to still other records: on the following day 189,838 passengers filled 624 trains made up of a total of 4,905 cars. The peak in number of trains for the decade of the twenties came on an unspecified date in 1928, when it was claimed that 800 trains entered and departed from the terminal, the total made up of 6,200 cars carrying 166,075 passengers. (The figure on the number of trains is of doubtful reliability.) The Central's extensive and profitable Pullman traffic rose to spectacular volumes during major holidays and the times of special events that attracted large crowds. One of the ironies of the time is that the annual Automobile Show, which was usually held in New York or Chicago, generated extremely heavy rail travel. On 8 January 1923, the first day of the show at Grand Central Palace, 26 trains carrying 4,028 sleeping-car passengers arrived at the terminal before noon, the number of regular and extra sections being more than double the normal complement of 12 trains listed in the public timetables and consisting in whole or in part of Pullman cars. Included in the total for January were five sections of the Twentieth Century Limited from Chicago (Number 26) and another five of the Detroiter from the automobile capital (Number 48). Both trains carried Pullman cars only, except for the diner, which was one of the Central's practices designed to attract an upper-class clientele.

The Century, as all the traveling world knew, was the bellwether of the railroad's flock of sleeping-car flyers. Its patronage through the 1920s provided a reliable index to the railroad's fortunes in the highly profitable passenger business. The number of occupants in its berths, compartments, and drawing rooms steadily increased throughout the decade, and the number of separate trains necessary to carry them in Pullman luxury rose in corresponding proportion. In the mid-twenties the train carried an average of 218 daily passengers eastbound and 177 westbound; and since it made no intermediate stops for passengers except for Harmon, where steam and electric locomotives were interchanged, the great majority of its patrons traveled between Grand Central Terminal and the comparatively seedy La Salle Street Station in Chicago (fig. 40). In 1927 the average number of passengers, estimated from the number of sections operated, rose to about 350 per scheduled run (that is, for the number of sections operated per day), and in 1928 to about 400. During the earlier year the celebrated train ran in a total of 2,261 sections, for an average of 3.1 per scheduled run in each direction and in the later year it was operated in 2,151 sections, or an average of 2.95 in each direction. In 1928, however, the average length of train was about 20 percent greater than in the previous year because of the introduction of the high-capacity Hudson type or 4-6-4 locomotive as the standard motive power for the New York Central's fast through trains (see p. 189). A remarkable aspect of the Century's traffic volume in 1928, one that warmed the hearts of the company's passenger agents, was that the number of reservations increased every month over the previous month throughout the year. The record, accompanied by an impressive operating performance, came on 3 December 1928, when the westbound train (Number 25) ran in seven sections to carry 800 passengers, and the last of the seven arrived at La Salle Street Station on time, the first six having arrived at various intervals ahead of schedule. The record was to be broken in a little more than a month: on 7 January 1929 the eastbound train (Number 26) was operated in seven sections for 822 passengers, the occasion once again being the national Automobile Show at Grand Central Palace. The willingness of the railroad to divide the Century into a number of sections of intermediate length provides the key to the sybaritic comforts that the train offered to the traveler. The individual section through the years 1927–29 was usually dispatched with no more than 120 reservations, generally distributed at 12 to 17 passengers per sleeping car. The tycoons and the celebrities on board were thus comfortably removed from their fellows, they were virtually guaranteed seats in the dining car when they wanted them, and of course they were far removed from the common herd in the crowded day coaches, which on the Central were always relegated to secondary trains.[3]

The increasing density of high-speed coach and Pullman trains that came with the traffic surge after the First World War was pushing the New York Central's existing track and signaling system to its limits. The number of through schedules remained nearly constant during the decade that ended in 1930, the steady attrition of local and accommodation runs being more than offset by the expansion of long-distance sleeping-car service. Timetables selected at intervals over the quarter-century of 1920 to 1945 show a surprising constancy in the number of scheduled runs, but the practice of adding numerous extra sections was a particular phenomenon of the

Fig. 40. Five sections of the Twentieth Century Limited at La Salle Street Station, Chicago, Christmas-New Year holidays, 1928/29. Courtesy Chicago Historical Society.

40

twenties. In 1928 the Central operated 68 scheduled daily trains between New York and Albany over the Hudson Division (exclusive of the West Shore line or River Division), but this total must be increased by about 15 percent to account for extra passenger trains and mail and express trains. The count for 8 January 1923, however, revealed that 14 passenger-carrying trains were operated into New York during the morning hours beyond the regular schedules, which indicated that at times of special events and major holidays the total of extra trains on the Hudson Division might rise to twenty or more. In short, there were occasions throughout the year when the line was called upon to accommodate 85 to 90 first-class trains per day. On the basis of the number of freight cars dispatched over the West Side line, one may estimate a daily freight traffic of 30 to 40 trains, yielding a total for all classes other than suburban service of 100 to 130 trains per weekday. Although the line was at the time largely four-track, a multitude of sharp curves and several double-track bottlenecks tended to inhibit the flow of this heavy, diversified traffic. On the main lines between Albany, Buffalo, and Cleveland the squeeze was even tighter: a daily average of about 70 passenger and mail trains (of which 59 were shown in the public timetables) and a likely total of at least a hundred freight trains east of Buffalo, with an additional twenty between Buffalo and Ashtabula, Ohio, the junction point with the Youngstown Branch and the Lake Erie harbor spur, represented the saturation level for conventional right-hand operation with automatic block signals divided between the upper- and lower-quadrant varieties.

The magnitude of the coming tide was clearly discernible in the early twenties, and the New York Central's signal department began to adopt drastic remedies for coping with the situation. The engineers struck simultaneously on three fronts—namely, the replacement of existing signals between New York and Cleveland, the adoption of traffic segregation on the main lines of the Mohawk, Syracuse, and Buffalo divisions, and most impressive of all, the first steps in a program of introducing automatic train control that eventually put the Central in the first position among the world's railways. The last of the three strategies appears to have been planned first, but the chronology is exceedingly difficult, if not impossible, to determine. The initial bids for the installation of automatic stop were invited on 28 December 1923; the system that was then adopted was to cover 514 route-miles on the New York Central, the Boston and Albany, the Michigan Central, the Big Four, and the Pittsburgh and Lake Erie railroads. The first public announcement of the program, including the indication that bids would eventually be requested, had been made on 13 June 1922, but before a systematic procedure of design, preparing specifications, and inviting bids could be completed, the disaster struck that everyone must have secretly feared. Late on the night of 9 December 1923 at Forsyth, New York, the second of three sections of the westbound Century, having hit an automobile at a highway crossing, had stopped for the necessary investigation. The engineman of the third section reduced speed at the approach signal but passed the stop signal at a rate of speed too high for the emergency brake to halt the train after passing the flagman. A group of passengers enjoying midnight conviviality were helplessly exposed in the public section of the observation-lounge car. All of the eight passengers and the porter were killed when the locomotive burst through the rear wall of the car, but only five of the remaining complement of ticket-holders were injured, for the good reason that they, along with everyone else, were in bed. The investigation established the essential facts, but like all such facts, they only pointed to essential questions. What are the appropriate signals for high-speed, high-density, multitrack operation? What is the acceptable headway when one flyer chases another with still a third close behind it, over level tangent track where speed limits were often regarded as personal challenges? What is the optimum pattern of dispatching separate classes of trains while maintaining unobstructed traffic flow? What supplementary controls are necessary? The New York Central's engineering and operating staffs found the answers, but they were exceedingly costly.[4]

The first step in the new signaling plan seems to have been the adoption of automatic train control, the ultimate program for which was to embrace the primary main lines of both the parent road and all its major affiliates. The initial installation was begun in 1924 and further enlargements were completed in successive steps by January, 1928, over most of the main lines from Boston to Pittsburgh, Chicago, and Saint Louis. These lines together comprised a total of 1,664 route-miles, which included 4,697 miles of track, the ratio of nearly 3:1 indicating the high proportion of multiple-track right of way on the New York Central Lines. The number of locomotives equipped with the necessary electrical devices for automatic stop was 1,942. The eastern terminal of the system was Boston on the B. and A., but it was terminated at Poughkeepsie on the Central because the officers of the road planned as late as 1929 to extend the electrified zone northward from Harmon, the third-rail form of which is mechanically and electrically incompatible with automatic control.[5] At the same time that the control system was being installed, the railroad also began the replacement of semaphore signals with the color-light variety. When Grand Central Terminal was completed in 1913 the original lower-quadrant semaphores in the New York zone and on most of the main lines between New York and Chicago began to give way to the more efficient upper-quadrant forms, but within no more than ten years after the opening of the terminal, the company began to replace the newly installed semaphores with light signals of the three-color variety. By the mid-thirties the new system was in place everywhere on the main line between New York and Cleveland, except for varying segments on the Mohawk and Syracuse divisions, where the upper-quadrant semaphores were unaccountably retained until the removal of two of the four tracks and the introduction of centralized traffic control during the years following the Second World War. The installation of new signals during the twenties coincided with the adoption of a unique system of segregating freight and passenger trains on the four- and five-track main line between Albany and Buffalo. Under the new practice the two or three tracks reserved for freight trains were restricted to the north side of the right of way, while the two for passenger trains lay on the south side. Interconnecting tracks were located mainly at the numerous junctions along the route.[6]

The crucial length of New York Central track, however, and the one that eventually compelled the most extensive revision of signaling and operating procedures was the trunk of the metropolitan network, the four-track approach to Grand Central between the upper terminal throat and Mott Haven Junction at 138th Street. Although the terminal yard embraces more than three times the number of tracks in Pennsylvania Station, and its approach line includes double the number, the huge stub-end complex was subject to considerably more serious congestion because of the multitude of empty movements over the same tracks occupied by scheduled inbound and outbound trains. The need for improvements in signaling and track usage was recognized in 1922, and the first step aimed at expediting the flow of traffic on the approach line was taken in 1923–24. The conventional right-hand movements governed by semaphore signals were modified to the extent of introducing reverse-direction signaling with three-position color lights on Track 4, which was chosen because it provided the most nearly direct connection with the lead tracks serving the Mott Haven coach yard. The new system of signaling made it possible to move trains in either direction on the chosen track.[7] The revision expedited the movement of trains at the time, but by 1928 the congestion was worse than ever. Because of the highly unbalanced flow of traffic in the morning and evening rush hours, at least one track lay largely idle, and under certain circumstances two of them might be radically underused. It was obvious that the troublesome situation could be greatly improved by converting all four tracks to operation in both directions, but the safe and efficient working of such a technique required an extensive system of crossover tracks and closely spaced multiaspect signals.

The railroad company undertook a detailed investigation of the entire pattern of train movements on the terminal approach in 1929, with the immediate aim of developing a method for increasing the capacity of the four tracks by 25 percent. The results of this study showed that on an average weekday during the year the terminal and its approach line accommodated 540 scheduled trains and 140 empty movements, for a total of 680 train movements per day. The maximum volume, which was reached on days immediately preceding or following such holidays as Labor Day, Thanksgiving, Christmas, and Independence Day, was 850 train movements in 24 hours, divided between 650 scheduled and 200 empty trains. The rush-hour densities constituted the crucial factors: during the three hours between 7:00 and 10:00 A.M. or between 3:00 and 6:00 P.M., the average flow was 55.3 trains per hour, with the peak as high as 70 trains in a single hour (still well behind the maximum for all terminals in the United States of 90 trains per hour at South Station, Boston). The number of sleeping- and parlor-car runs fell substantially short of the total at Pennsylvania Station, even with the New Haven to swell the total, but the traffic was sufficient to tax the circumscribed area of Mott Haven Yard to its limits. The Central listed an average of 115 Pullman-car routes in the 1929–30 schedules, which may have required as many as 350 cars at times of peak traffic, while the New Haven timetables listed 52 in the same period, for a likely maximum of about 150 cars. The program that the signal department adopted on the basis of the investigation, with the aim of ending delays and the threat of accidents, comprised the replacement of all semaphore signals by the color-light form on all tracks extending from 56th Street to High Bridge on the Electric Division and to 162d Street on the Harlem Division, the arrangement of signals for reverse- or double-direction operation, the construction of new interlocking towers at 106th Street and Mott Haven Yard (the former a new addition, the latter to take the place of four existing towers), the installation of new crossover tracks at 56th and 106th streets, the realignment of the lead tracks for Mott Haven Yard, and the lengthening of the overpass at 144th Street to cross a greater number of tracks. The lines under reverse-direction signaling were divided into three segments for operating purposes: the north was to be placed under the control of the Mott Haven tower, the central under the tower at 106th Street, and the south under the existing 56th Street tower. Signals and crossover tracks were arranged to allow for a theoretically continuous movement of all trains north of the terminal throat at a speed of 35 miles per hour and under a headway of 1.5 minutes, which is equivalent to a distance of 4,620 feet.

The implementation of this program was initiated in 1929 and was completed two years later, when the depression had drastically reduced the volume of traffic and hence nullified the possibility of an immediate test. It was 1944 before the new system could demonstrate its full potentiality. The only unusual engineering feature in what is for the most part straightforward signaling work, however elaborate, is the support of Tower NK (106th Street) on a steel-truss-framed gantry extending over the four tracks. Since they lie on the Park Avenue viaduct above 97th Street, where it is tightly hemmed in by the two halves of the street, there is no space to allow for the construction of a tower at trackside. Extensions of the framework on the north and south sides of the brick-walled enclosure carry the signals at this location. The color-light signals grouped on an individual mast show five positive aspects, and they are spaced at an average distance of 936 feet, the minimum being 719 feet and the maximum 1,151. The average spacing indicates that the 1.5 minute headway comprehends nearly five blocks, theoretically sufficient to guarantee a clear or high-approach signal for any train immediately following another. When every train, loaded or empty, and every motor running light is moving, this intricate system of signaling, communications, and interlocking controls makes it possible to operate all rolling equipment in both directions on each track, at a uniform theoretical speed of 35 miles per hour outside the terminal yard limits, and under the minimum safe headway at the allowable speed. In short, the installation of 1929–31 guaranteed that within the limits of human error the hardworking Park Avenue trunk could safely and expeditiously accommodate at least one thousand train and engine movements and possibly 400,000 passengers per day. The written records that have been preserved indicate that the traffic at the terminal has never reached such a level. Twice—on the days preceding Christmas, 1942, and Thanksgiving, 1945—the number of passengers reached 240,000 and the number of loaded trains, according to a speculative estimate, about 700 for the 24 hours. The greatest total for a single month came in January, 1946, when 5,598,732 New York Central and New Haven passengers passed through the terminal. The record for a single day was 252,288 ticket-holders, who constituted the mixture of commuters, shoppers, and holiday travelers on 3 July 1947. It was the year in which the terminal reached its annual peak of slightly more than 65,000,000 passengers. The total number of scheduled trains through these last years of rail ascendancy, 1944–47, remained fairly constant at 520 per weekday, with a probable total of loaded, empty, and engine movements around 650.

The operation of Grand Central Terminal varied in detail from time to time over the years, some variations dictated by Depression-born economics, others by wartime exigencies and postwar changes, but in essence it has remained substantially unaltered since the new signaling installation was completed in 1931. Certain features were retained from the previous phases of the terminal's evolution. The station master ruled the whole domain of head house, tracks, and railroad equipment, but the chief dispatcher was the fountainhead and final authority on all train movements. He established the schedules and the routing of all trains running between the terminal and Harmon on the Hudson Division and White Plains on the Harlem. He issued the orders that governed the movements of all trains and locomotives, authorized the changes in routings that the long-term fluctuations of traffic demanded, and maintained a comprehensive record of movements day by day, compiled from the individual records of the clerks in the interlocking towers. Their written entries are still designated "OS" in the railroad argot, the initials of the phrase "on the sheet," which goes back to the origins of rail telegraphy in the mid-nineteenth century. It was the task of the towermen to translate the authority of the dispatcher into the alignment of switches and signals that guided the trains under the control of the motormen who must read the signals, interpret them correctly, and adjust their speed appropriately. The established fundamentals were the routing of trains according to preassigned approach, ladder, and station tracks, and the division of the approach line into three inbound and one outbound track in the morning rush hour, or the reverse in the evening. The successive actions of towermen and levermen within the new signaling limits determined how well the enormous, intricate complex worked, its mysteries incomprehensible to the passenger, who took it all for granted.

When an inbound train enters the interlocking limit at Mott Haven, the towerman calls his counterparts at Tower NK (106th Street), Tower U (56th Street), and Tower A (50th Street), where electronic technology guarantees that the messages are received simultaneously. The levermen at NK, working under the authority of the towerman, align the switches and set the appropriate signals for the movement of the train over the approach from 138th to 56th Street. The progress is ordinarily straight ahead on the assigned track, but there are many occasions when the crossover switches must be set in such a way that the train may pass from one track to another. Tower NK, roughly at the halfway point of the trunk, may be regarded as the valve that controls the flow of traffic into the terminal. The levermen at Tower U align the switches for the passage of the train through the outer throat, where the approach widens from four to ten tracks, and those at Tower A arrange the route over the ladder and other crossover tracks into the designated station berth. At the time the message from Mott Haven is received, the assistant towerman at A makes the OS entry that records the number of the train, the locomotive, and the track, the number of cars in the train, and the time of arrival; he then lays out the route which the levermen execute at the interlocking machine. The illuminated track diagram above the bank of levers shows the progress of the train from the point where it enters the interlocking limits to its final position at rest on the designated station track. The procedure for an outbound train begins when the towermen and levermen at Tower A, B, or C align the route and set the dwarf signals along the terminal tracks about two minutes before the scheduled departure time. After the gateman on the concourse admits the last passenger, staggering breathless with his luggage, he locks the gate, which automatically illuminates the departure signal at the outer end of the platform. The conductor then signals the motorman, at which point the men in the towers at 56th Street, 106th Street, and Mott Haven repeat the operations they follow in reverse order for an inbound train. All loop tracks within the terminal have continued in use for turning trains, except for the inner loop on the lower level, the curve of which has been almost from the beginning of station operations in 1913 too sharp for any equipment of the New York Central or the New Haven. The multiple-unit equipment of the suburban trains is not turned on the loop tracks since it can be easily reversed for movement in the opposite direction. With the completion of the signaling program initiated in 1929, the terminal and its approach tracks could safely accommodate 90 train and engine movements per hour, or an average of one movement every 40 seconds, and could allow the dispatching of three departing or entering trains at one time (under a 1.5-minute headway the theoretical capacity would be 120 train movements per hour; that is, 3 × 60/1.5).[8]

The constant expansion of traffic at Grand Central Terminal and on the West Side freight line compelled the railroad to enlarge its fleet of electric motive power. Seven switching and two road freight locomotives were manufactured and installed in 1925–26, and ten passenger units, designated Class T-3, were placed in service in 1926–27, the last group bringing the total number built for operations in the road's New York electrification to 92 units. The T-3 locomotives were conservative: the absence of guiding trucks in the wheel arrangement of B-B + B-B indicates that although the maximum safe speed was specified as 75 miles per hour, they were in fact intended for the rather modest ruling speeds on the Electric Division. The machines were primarily designed to start and accelerate heavy trains of sleeping cars in a zone where numerous changes of speed are necessitated by a tight succession of curves, junctions, crossover tracks, and yard restrictions, a characteristic which is borne out by the high starting tractive force of 69,450 pounds. The final extension of the New York Central's electrified mileage in metropolitan New York came at the same time. In February, 1926, the road began the electrical operation of the seven-mile Yonkers Branch, which unites the Putnam Division at Sedgewick Avenue with Getty Square in the city of its name, and a few months later the company established a similar operation on the Port Morris Branch in The Bronx, a short line that has always been restricted to freight service.

The New Haven, faced with a heavier and more diversified traffic throughout its electrified territory, inaugurated a much bolder program of motive power acquisitions shortly after Grand Central Terminal was opened. In 1916 the road launched into a forty-year period of acquiring electric locomotives which for their variety of form and their range of speed and power, had no counterpart on any other American railroad. Additions to the company's fleet came in 1916, 1919, 1923–27, 1931, 1938, 1942–43, and 1955, and the successive designs virtually recapitulated the evolution of electric traction over the years since the beginning of the First World War. Unfortunately, expensive locomotives combined with seemingly unmanageable troubles—Depression, bus and truck competition, short average haul, high terminal costs, extensive branch-line mileage, and questionable administrative practices—pushed the road to incurable financial sickness, with the consequence that it was compelled to file a petition for bankruptcy on 23 October 1935. Not even the flood of traffic that came with the Second World War was enough to restore the ailing property to economic health. A completely hopeless case, however, was the state of the New Haven's subsidiary, the New York, Westchester and Boston Railroad, which had little reason to exist in the first place. Shortly after the parent road's receivership, the Westchester came to be regarded as beyond salvation, and it was totally abandoned on 31 December 1937.

The New York Central and its motive-power department offered a considerably more cheerful picture, even through the Depression, but one had to look beyond the Electric Division to appreciate the full scope of its great contributions to the art of locomotive design. A high and growing density of heavy, fast passenger trains urged the motive power engineers to undertake an analysis of the performance requirements and the potentialities of the steam engine that resulted in an orthogenetic evolution of the high-speed, high-horsepower passenger locomotive without parallel among the railroads of the United States. Seven successive classes of Pacific type or 4-6-2 locomotives were introduced over the years from 1903 to 1926, all of them together representing a continuous and systematically designed progress in performance and efficiency. What was simultaneously the culmination and the greatest innovative step in this development followed from the accession of Paul W. Kiefer to the position of chief engineer of motive power and rolling stock in 1926. The immediate fruit of his talents proved to be the most celebrated of all steam power: on 14 February 1927 the railroad introduced the first 4-6-4 locomotive, assigned to Class J in the company's taxonomy and appropriately named the Hudson type, which became the standard designation for this wheel arrangement (fig. 40). In the succeeding eleven years the company installed 275 of these machines; they were immediately put to work hauling the through trains between New York, Chicago, and the chief cities along the way, and from 1930 on they spread progressively over the primary main lines of the major subsidiaries, the Boston and Albany, the Pittsburgh and Lake Erie, the Michigan Central, and the Big Four. They were the last word in motive power at the time, when the New York Central Lines operated the largest fleet of steam locomotives in the land, and no one foresaw that a quarter-century in the future (1954) steam power was to disappear from the railroad that had played the foremost role in bringing it to the highest stage of design and performance.

Air-Rights Developments

The full importance of Grand Central Terminal as a generator of intensive urban development at the highest levels of architectural design did not emerge until the construction boom of the twenties was well underway. The laying out of the track-platform system, occupying at its greatest breadth the full distance between Madison and Lexington avenues, and the expansion of the inner approach to ten tracks simultaneously opened a large area for commercial building and guaranteed the visual potentialities of the setting through the reconstruction of upper Park Avenue as a divided parkway. The transformation of the precinct into a civic space wholly without antecedent in the history of the city became apparent soon after the postwar depression ended in 1921. The property owned by the New York Central and the New York and Harlem railroads, which was available for air-rights development, forms a paddle-shaped area consisting of an irregular rectangle based at 42d Street, bounded by Lexington, Vanderbilt, and Madison avenues on the east and west, and sharply narrowing on the north into a long tongue that extends northward along the breadth of Park Avenue from 56th to 59th Street (fig. 47). The original horizontal or ground area of developable properties, exclusive of streets and sidewalks but including the area within the peripheral walls of the terminal head house, was 1,253,304 square feet, or 28.8 acres.[9] When the station was opened in February, 1913, only seven buildings, and those of rather modest size, covered the tracks and platforms that lay outside the confines of the head house. Four stood to the west along Vanderbilt Avenue (from south to north, as they were eventually designated, the Vanderbilt Avenue Building, the Biltmore Hotel, the Yale Club, and the Vanderbilt Concourse Building), and three to the east on Lexington Avenue (the Post Office, 466 Lexington Avenue, and Grand Central Palace). For one viewing the area from a position within it, especially if he stood at an upper-story window in the hotel or the office building, there was spread out below him a spectacle that had no counterpart in the world of railroad operations or civic functions: the mighty fan of tracks and the ceaseless drama of moving trains in the largest terminal ever built provided an awesome demonstration of creative urban power. Perhaps the sight should have been preserved for the ages, but that was not the intention of those who knitted together the vast fabric. There was incalculable wealth in this gold mine of civic space, and the renewed exploitation of its financial possibilities began soon after the terminal was completed (figs. 41, 42).

World War I inhibited private building, especially the prestige and luxury varieties we might expect in the terminal precinct, so that the construction program gathered momentum rather slowly. The city experienced a progressive shortage of every kind of commercial space through the years from 1914 to the boom that began in 1921, but the deficit was most crucial in the case of hotels. If the uniform rectangular spaces they defined were appropriately exploited by architects, Park Avenue and the intersecting streets over the electrified trackage promised a setting possessed of an incomparable urbanity that one could not find even in London and Paris, the only comparable cities. It is hardly surprising, then, that hotel buildings not only led the way in the air-rights program, but constituted a majority of all buildings when the phase of construction between wars was completed. The first was the Marguery, erected in 1916–17 on the west side of Park Avenue between 47th and 48th streets. The 12-story building surrounding an interior court, the whole composition marked by the restrained Renaissance decor that was a hallmark of the late Beaux-Arts projects, set the standard for the works to come. Its overall silhouette, its size, and its scale were exactly appropriate to its ambience, and these characteristics were adhered to with remarkable fidelity until the Art Deco mode finally took root on the neighboring avenues in 1927. The Marguery was the first to go in the tidal wave of destruction that accompanied the second postwar boom: it went down in 1957 to make way for the Union Carbide Building. It was a presage of the unspeakable losses to come.

Grander exercises were soon to follow, and they brought the talented villains of the Grand Central melodrama once again to the forefront. Warren and Wetmore received two enviable plums when they were awarded the commissions within two years for the Commodore and the Ambassador Hotel. The first was constructed in 1917–19 on the northwest corner of Lexington Avenue and 42d Street, a site more noted for an avalanche of wheeled and pedestrian traffic than for urban amenities, but the fact that its lobby was located within easy walking distance of the terminal

41

Fig. 41. Grand Central Terminal. Air-rights development in the vicinity of the terminal by 1920.

42

Fig. 42. Grand Central Terminal. Air-rights construction in the vicinity of the terminal in 1922.

concourse placed it in a competitive position with the Biltmore. And there was the additional advantage of close proximity to the subway station under 42d Street (indeed, the foundations of the hotel building are contiguous to the walled enclosure of the subway line that curves from Park into Lexington Avenue). With 2,000 guest rooms, the Commodore was one of the largest hotels in the world, if not the first in capacity at the time it was opened, and it was not exceeded in size until the completion in 1925 of the present Palmer House in Chicago. The lobby, at any rate, was claimed from the beginning to be the most spacious of any ever built, and no one seems to have arisen to dispute the assertion. The value of the hotel for all concerned was handsomely underscored by the annual income of $175,000 that the railroad derived from the air-rights rental. The prewar Biltmore, by comparison, earned the company only $100,000 per annum.

In the year when the Commodore was opened, the Ambassador Hotel, from the hands of the same architects, was placed under construction on Park Avenue between 51st and 52d streets, at the north limit of the air-rights enclave, and was completed in 1921. The architects followed the ruling motifs of the earlier buildings in the formal design of the Ambassador, but the disposition of interior spaces was predicated on different functional requirements, since the building was planned as a residential as well as a transients' hotel. An indication of the level of opulence that obtained on the new expanded and landscaped Park Avenue may be gained from the rentals at the time the hotel opened: a five-room apartment, for example, rented for $2,500 per month (one might expect an equivalent of about $20,000 in 1980). In spite of the emphasis on such princely luxury, the air-rights developers did not neglect the life of the spirit. Saint Bartholomew's Church, one of the many distinguished works from the hand of Bertram Goodhue, was erected on Park Avenue at 51st Street in 1917–23, the very years when the most aristocratic hotels were under construction.

In 1922 the track area still lay uncovered over several blocks north of the terminal group. Those extending west of Park Avenue to Madison between 45th and 46th streets were available for new construction, as were parts of three blocks on the east side of the avenue between 46th and 49th streets, although rising steel frames were already beginning to fill in the space. At this time the Grand Central precinct gave the impression of a special temenos rather than a series of blocks that formed an integral part of the surrounding urban fabric. A double row of scattered new buildings stood out as works of high design in the mode of the American Renaissance, their nearly uniform cornice line held around 12 stories and the elegance of their carefully unified formal treatment giving them the quality of an exclusive enclave among the low, unprepossessing, sometimes seedy commercial and residential *insulae* that covered much of the midtown area, especially in the corridors immediately to the east of the terminal trackage. Within eight years the holes in the fabric were to disappear, and a great area extending from around 40th Street to 53d between Fifth Avenue and Lexington, was to be radically transformed with an explosive force that eclipsed the grandest imperial schemes. The magnetic power of the terminal as civic architecture and transportation nexus, and of the narrow ribbon of Park Avenue stretched out to the north, must have astonished even William Wilgus, who was himself given to entertaining imperial urban visions.

The first break in the exclusive dominance of hotels and the primacy of the west side of the precinct came with the construction of the Park-Lexington Building in 1922–23, on the east side of Park Avenue between 46th and 47th streets. Designed by the architects Warren and Wetmore and the structural engineer H. G. Balcom, the builders of the office block were the first to face in all its ramifications the challenge of erecting a 20-story steel frame over a double-level track system at the locus of an irregular track layout near the terminal throat. The switches, the curving turnouts, and the columns supporting the upper track floor dictated many of the column locations and the lengths and sections of girders in the entirely independent frame of the office building, no part of which could be connected with the track-floor structure because of the damage to framing members that might arise from the vibrations induced by passing trains. The construction process must have taxed the ingenuity of everyone associated with the enterprise: all tools, materials, and workmen had to be lowered through openings in the streets to the base of the suburban track level 50 feet below the surrounding grade. Column footings were poured between tracks and the elements of the frame were delicately inched into place, while all train and engine movements were continued without interruption.

Similar difficulties faced the builders of the Roosevelt Hotel, which was erected during the same years (1922–24) over a closely matching site in the west half of the air-rights corridor. Standing in the block bounded by Vanderbilt and Lexington avenues between 45th and 46th streets, connected with the terminal concourse by a special passageway, this paragon of hotel design was the creation of the firm of George B. Post and Sons, whose founder was one of the great constructive architects of the New York renaissance. Erecting the framing system of the Roosevelt posed a more formidable challenge than the construction of the office block because of the great diversity of interior spaces as well as the irregularities of the double-level track layout. The numerous shops, restaurants, meeting rooms, public spaces, and service facilities characterizing this microcity in the form of a hotel dictated an expensive variety of girders, trusses, and bracing elements of uncommon size. The Roosevelt offers a good example of the value of such costly and luxurious accommodations to the railroad company: in 1929 the rentals and other charges brought the New York Central (through the New York and Harlem lease) a total of $370,390 for the year, divided among $280,000 for ground rent, $82,390 for steam supplied by the terminal's steam generating plant, and $8,000 for electric power provided by the generating station on the Harlem River. Only the rental income, of course, represented a clear gain to the railroad, although profits were naturally involved in the other two items. The last open space above the Grand Central tracks was closed over with the construction of the Park Lane Hotel along the west side of the avenue between 48th and 49th streets, again, in 1922–24. A residential hotel with penthouses for tenants, the Park Lane brought the architectural firm of Schultze and Weaver to prominence, and brought the railroad another $130,000 per year in air-rights rentals. In a few years they were to design the crown piece and final work in the original air-rights empire, and by mid-decade the vast track system was shut off from the daylight once and for all (fig. 43).

The office building that followed the Park-Lexington brought the Art Deco mode to the Grand Central precinct for the first time. The Graybar Building, erected in 1926–27 from the plans of Sloan and Robertson, is symmetrically disposed in a multiwing plan on Lexington Avenue between 43d and 44th streets, immediately north of the Commodore Hotel, where it enjoyed direct access to the broad passageway that extends from Lexington to the terminal concourse. The Graybar was not the city's earliest essay in the new style, but it was one of the first on the scale of the contemporary skyscraper. The third office tower in the enclave marked a return to the classical details of its predecessors. Although it was a product of railroad sponsorship, the intention was to lease most of the space to tenants, reserving only a few floors of the high-rent space for the overflow of company personnel from the building at 466 Lexington Avenue. The New York Central Building, as the new work was officially designated by its owner, was constructed in 1927–29 in the pocket that still remained immediately north of the terminal complex.[10] Its design proved to be the last commission that the railroad company offered to the prestigious though not always morally edifying firm of Warren and Wetmore (fig. 44). As a matter of fact, it stood among the last major commissions enjoyed by any architectural office in New York to the end of the Second World War except for the consortium preparing the plans of Rockefeller Center. The choice of site for the company's own investment in its air-rights bonanza was an obvious one for practical reasons, but it was nonetheless an inspired recognition of the aesthetic potentiality offered by its location. Since the lofty building is exactly centered on a prolongation of the terminal axis, it stands

Fig. 43. Grand Central Terminal. Top: the yards at Grand Central Station as they appeared in 1906. Bottom: the same scene in 1926 shows the air-rights construction along Park Avenue above 45th Street.

43

Fig. 44. Buildings in the vicinity of Grand Central Terminal in 1929. The prominent buildings, taken counter-clockwise, are the following: Daily News (left foreground); Commodore Hotel (central foreground); Chrysler (under construction, center foreground); Graybar (right foreground); New York Central (far right); Biltmore Hotel (center, slightly to the left of the Chrysler); Public Library (far left). Short segments of Park Avenue and 42d Street appear in the left foreground.

directly athwart the ribbon of Park Avenue and is thus not only visible from as far north as the high point of the avenue on Mount Prospect, but provides a handsome closure to this long and impressive vista. The location required that the two segments of Park Avenue flanking the terminal group be relocated again by carrying them through the mass of the central tower in vaulted tunnels entirely walled off from the main enclosure. The curving wings balanced on either side of the 35-story shaft, the colonnade on brackets and the rich ornamental detail at the topmost stories, and the profusion of decorative motifs on the little tower above the pyramidal roof make the New York Central Building a fittingly extravagant conclusion to the orgiastic decade. By 1930 Grand Central Terminal was buried in a forest of skyscrapers, and the measured elegance of the air-rights structures had given way to eclectic and Art Deco splendors (fig.44). In the quarter-century of 1904–30 property values in the Lexington-Madison corridor between 42d and 96th streets had increased from $267,500,000 to $1,268,000,000 or 374 percent, and by the latter year the Central and the Harlem together enjoyed an income of $4,000,000 in rentals derived from air-rights constructions.

The grand finale in this booming real estate drama was not completed until the depression of the thirties had brought nearly all other enterprises to a halt. The Waldorf-Astoria Hotel was the last building to be erected over the railroad properties before the twenty-year hiatus of depression and war either paralyzed or distorted the normal functioning of the economy. Designed by the architects Schultze and Weaver and the structural engineer H. G. Balcom, and constructed in 1930–32, the Art Deco skyscraper with its familiar twin towers covers the entire block bounded by Park and Lexington avenues between 49th and 50th streets (fig. 28). The site had been occupied by one of the essential subsidiary structures in the Grand Central complex: designated the 50th Street Substation, it housed equipment for steam generation and hot-water heating, pumping machinery, the terminal substation for electric traction and lighting, and emergency storage batteries. Since the company had built a second steam-generating plant on Lexington Avenue at 43d Street (noteworthy for being roofed by the street itself and extending at its low point 100 feet below the local grade level), the officers decided in March, 1929, to abandon the steam-generating facility, move all other equipment from 50th Street to 43d, and to purchase steam from the New York Steam Company. These various moves freed the extremely desirable site—far too good to be occupied by a steam and hot-water plant and a substation—for another high-priced addition to the air-rights family. The Waldorf is very likely the only urban hotel, and possibly the only hotel ever built in any environment, to include a separate track for private railway cars at its basement level within the envelope of the structure (actually Track 61 of the Grand Central storage system). Railroad engineering combined with civic and architectural design, all standing at the highest levels for the modern commercial city, gave the terminal precinct its unparalleled magnificence. What followed in subsequent years can only be described as official metropolitan barbarism.[11]

7

The New Jersey Terminals through the Second World War

The railroads that terminated at the New Jersey shore shared in the prosperity of the 1920s, but the Depression took an immediate and for the most part a drastic toll that carried two companies into bankruptcy before the melancholy decade ended. The damages, however, were not irreparable, and they were quickly erased by the immense upsurge of traffic that came with the Second World War. If we set aside the Pennsylvania Railroad, which by 1910 was conducting both freight and passenger operations by means of extensive terminal properties in New York City, the volume of traffic among the remaining New Jersey lines revealed no clearly marked pattern of gain or loss in the decade following the First World War. Every road experienced a loss of passenger business over the years between 1920 and 1930, but the extent of that loss represented in nearly every case an inverse function of the proportion of suburban to total passenger traffic. The reason, as we have previously noted, was that the continuing and rapid expansion of commutation business in metropolitan New York tended to offset the serious attrition in the number of through passengers, losses which began to appear immediately after the peak of 1920. Freight traffic was less vulnerable than passenger to the effects of boom and Depression and of highway competition, so that the collective loss of the New Jersey lines for the entire decade of the 1930s was only a little greater than what they had experienced during the previous ten years, and the war brought uniformly distributed peaks of tonnage that few had ever known before.

The quarter-century between 1920 and 1945 not only saw unprecedented vicissitudes of boom, Depression, and inflated wartime prosperity, but also the beginnings of a fundamental yet unforeseen shift in the patterns of industrial production throughout the United States. During this 25-year period the fortunes of the individual railroads terminating at the Jersey waterfront provided a reliable index to their geographical position, to the historical characteristics of their traffic, their relative size, and their operating capacity. The only respect in which they enjoyed an approximate equality lay in their access to New York Harbor and its traffic potential.[1] Rail passenger traffic entered into its long decline in 1921, and the various New York roads, taken as complete systems within their extreme limits, were not spared from this misfortune. The seven companies we are here considering suffered a loss of nearly one-third the total traffic of the peak year by 1930, and the overall decline to 1940 took away more than another third. In the first of the two decades it was highway competition that did the damage; in the second it was a combination of economic collapse, competition, and the exasperating lethargy with which the rail bureaucracies adjusted their tariffs and operations to economic reality. The exigencies of war, abetted by gasoline rationing, restored nearly half the twenty-year loss of passenger business through the five years ending in 1945, but the extent to which the individual roads shared in the gains and losses perfectly illustrated the chaotic and fragmentary character of the industry.

For the Ontario, serving no populous regions and possessing no useful connections, the years brought uninterrupted disaster to its fortunes as a passenger carrier: by the end of the halcyon decade of the twenties it had lost three-quarters of its traffic; at the end of the Depression another three-quarters, and not even war, that panacea for capitalist enterprises in the United States, could stem the ebbing tide. At the end of the conflict more than 90 percent of its peak-year traffic was gone for good. The returns of the B. and O. in the same period reflected the most extreme fluctuations: nearly three-quarters of its once enviable passenger traffic had been lost to competitors by 1930; another half had deserted its rails by 1940, but the war brought a bonanza, multiplying traffic nearly 3 1/3 times in the succeeding five years. Only the Lehigh Valley, which saw its passengers increase three times in the same period, enjoyed such lavish benefits from the wartime economy. The most stable pattern of changes characterized the big suburban carriers, the C. N. J., the Lackawanna, and the Erie: if their wartime gains were rather meagre (most disappointing in the case of the Erie), their Depression losses were substantially smaller than those suffered by the other carriers. The Pennsylvania, by comparison, showed very nearly the same range of losses over the first two decades as the three smaller roads, and it was second only to the B. and O. in the extent to which the war called upon its resources for moving traffic, especially in its overburdened New York-Washington corridor.[2]

The freight tonnage transported by the nine railroads serving the west side of the port revealed much greater stability over the 25-year period than the movement of passengers. The former was less vulnerable at the time to the growing highway competition than passenger traffic, of which the local or accommodation variety rapidly disappeared before the onslaught of the automobile and the bus. By 1930 the nine roads had lost 10 percent of the tonnage they had carried ten years earlier, and the economic collapse followed by partial recovery during the Depression decade cost them another 10 percent. The war, of course, brought a quick and powerful reversal of the tide, which resulted in a 50 percent gain over the five years ending with 1945. Among the trunk-line carriers, the Reading, the Pennsylvania, and the B. and O. were most successful in preserving their traffic at a stable level in good part because their heavy coal shipments helped to offset the decline in the movement of manufactured products. The least disturbance to the year-by-year flow of traffic characterized two of the little railroads, the Ontario and the Raritan River, which suffered minimal losses through the boom and Depression decades. The Ontario, as a matter of fact, confounded all the economic laws by reaching the peak of its entire history in 1934, when it transported 8,288,146 tons of freight, a puzzling phenomenon that was the consequence in part of a sudden, never-to-be-repeated expansion in the demand for anthracite coal. The flood of traffic that came with the war years, although it taxed every road to the limits of its capacity, was moved expeditiously in and out of the port terminals with few interruptions and none of the paralysis that accompanied the American entry into the First World War.[3]

Improvements on the Central of New Jersey

If the New York roads suffered twenty years of losses in their total passenger traffic (as distinct from that proportion of the total moving in and out of the metropolitan area), the robust state of the port economy guaranteed that in nearly every case the number of passengers and the number of trains accommodated in the Long Island, Manhattan, and New Jersey terminals continued to expand with only temporary interruptions up to the Depression of the 1930s. The New Jersey stations offered no exceptions, but unfortunately only two roads were prepared to make alterations and additions aimed at substantially improving the efficiency of operations and the well-being of passengers, employees, and local communities. According to the most generous data, which were compiled by the Port of New York Authority from railroad sources, its own surveys, and those conducted by various commissions and public bodies, the total number of passengers moving via the New Jersey sector into, through, and out of New York increased by 41.3 percent during the ten years from 1911 through 1920 (the peak year for the passenger traffic of the national railroad system), and increased by another 18.5 percent up to 1929, the record year since the origins of local railroad service for the total New York rail traffic. The volume for the New Jersey sector for 1929 declined by more than a third to the Depression low point of 1940, then recovered somewhat less than a third by the wartime peak of 1943.[4] Such figures as are available for the New York passenger traffic of the individual roads show numerous discrepancies, but evidence in general suggests that the returns of the various companies closely reflected the changes in the volume for the systems as a whole. The Lackawanna, the Erie, and the two Weehawken roads appear to have fared better than the Central of New Jersey, while the Pennsylvania's Jersey City terminal continued to enjoy a slow increase in the number of passengers to 1921, after which date the Manhattan station rapidly eroded away the New Jersey traffic. The Erie Railroad experienced the heaviest volume of terminal passenger business among the New Jersey family, with the Lackawanna and the C. N. J. trailing substantially behind in that order, but it was least disposed to make any improvements in its antiquated and unattractive facilities.

The much smaller C. N. J., however, began to lay plans for a drastic expansion of its huge terminal complex in Jersey City as early as 1910. The planning and design, indeed, constituted a model of scientific analysis applied to the endlessly ramifying problems of rebuilding and operating a major metropolitan terminal. The station served about 14,500,000 passengers in 1911, the number increasing to 18,137,000 in 1920 and to 21,000,000 at the maximum in 1929, yielding weekday averages ranging from around 46,000 at the beginning of our survey to 67,000 in the last year. The Depression reduced the peak-year total to 13,500,000 in 1940, but three years later the wartime flood carried the annual volume to somewhat more than 18,000,000 passengers. The overwhelming majority were the surburban or commutation variety, the proportion being 78.5 percent in 1911 and varying from 75 to 80 percent over the years in which through trains were operated. All the road's New York City traffic moved via the trans-Hudson ferries, so that the problems presented by steady year-by-year expansions and rush-hour concentrations were compounded to an unusual degree by the need to coordinate the scheduling of vessels with the movement of trains. A special difficulty arose from the fact that one ferry route extended upriver to 23d Street, a distance that required a longer time of passage and a more complex adjustment of schedules than the direct east-west crossings. In spite of the overwhelming predominance of suburban service, the C. N. J. was an intercity carrier serving a great number of communities scattered throughout the length of New Jersey and over eastern Pennsylvania, among them the important traffic generators of Atlantic City, Allentown, Bethlehem, and Harrisburg. The resulting diversity of traffic was increased during those years when the Lehigh Valley and the Baltimore and Ohio were tenants in the Jersey City terminal. The sleeping and parlor-car runs of the Lehigh came to somewhat fewer than those required by the once lively parlor-car business of the C. N. J., but the B. and O.'s similar operations were nearly double those of the proprietary road. In 1912 the number of scheduled trains reached 370 per weekday, a number that necessitated from 1,200 to 1,300 train and engine movements over the terminal yards, with the consequence that the 12-track station of 1888 was hard pressed to avoid delays and to maintain a reason-

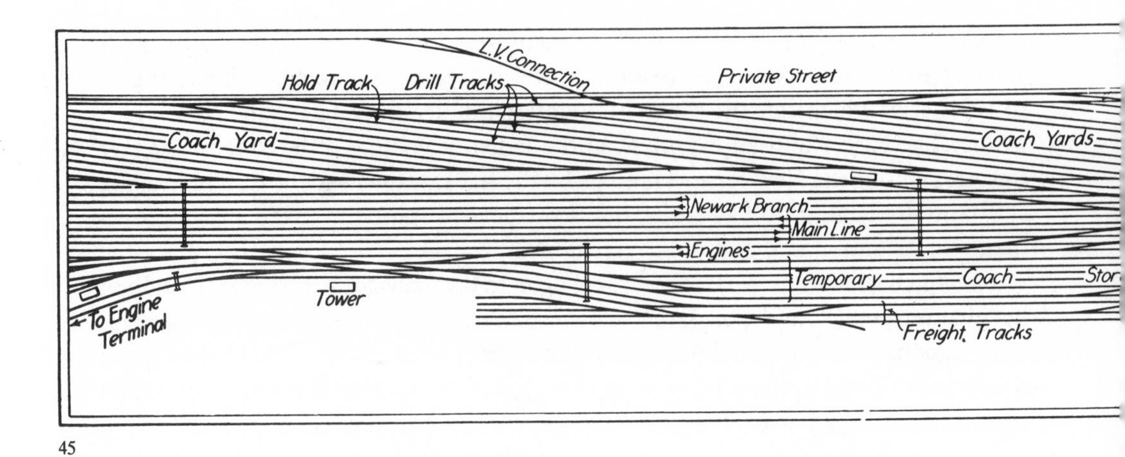

45

ably smooth flow of passengers between trains and boats. The company's operating and engineering staffs might have been able to squeeze the last ounce of capacity out of the station's facilities and appurtenant yards, but unlike those of the Erie, they were unwilling to put up with second-best, or worse. Operations over the four-track station approach, carried out under the guidance of automatic block signals, were hampered by the long bridge across Newark Bay, a double-track bottleneck with a drawbridge at the midpoint to add to the delays.

The plan adopted in 1912 included the replacement of the existing bridge as well as the expansion of the entire terminal complex, but it was 14 years before the full program was realized. The first step was the enlargement of the station yard from 12 to 20 tracks, the space for the additional berths to be taken from the freight yard and engine terminal immediately south of the existing station area. An analysis of train movements indicated that the chief source of delays was an inadequate inner approach system, which was called upon to serve not only as an access way for scheduled trains, but also for the utilitarian elements of the terminal complex and a diverging branch. The solution was a radical expansion of the approach system, from four to eleven tracks, and a complete segregation of the functions that the various lines were designed to serve.[5] The station throat, the ladder tracks, the location of the coach yard (on the north side of the approach) and of the engine terminal (on the south side) were planned for maximum flexibility and efficiency of operation, which were secured through nicely detailed arrangements that allowed the greatest number of simultaneous train and engine movements with a minimum of conflicting lines of

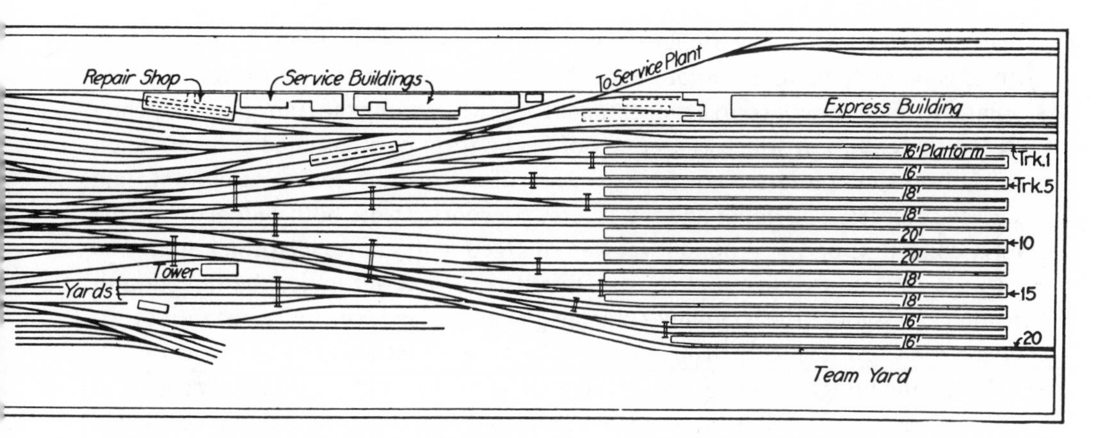

Fig. 45. Central Railroad of New Jersey. Reconstruction and enlargement of the Jersey City terminal, 1912–14. Plan of the station tracks, approach, and coach yard.

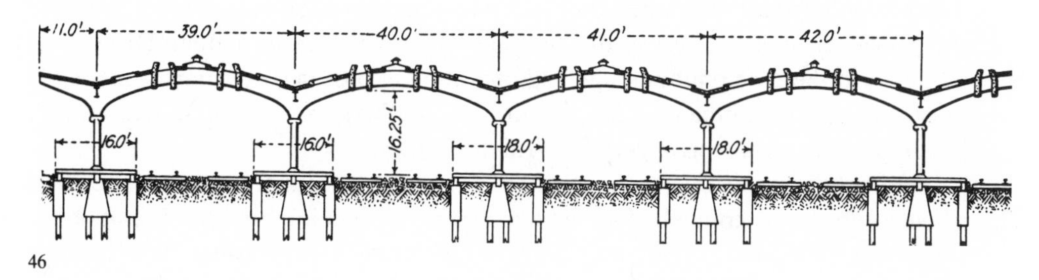

Fig. 46. Central Railroad of New Jersey. Reconstruction of the Jersey City terminal. Partial transverse section of the train shed.

46

movement. The broad approach required an equally generous system of signaling: a total of 16 signal gantries carried the signals that governed train and engine movements on the 11-track approach, of which the largest spanned 12 tracks. Many of the upper-quadrant semaphores that were installed for the program of 1912 were still in place when the station was abandoned in 1967.

Work on the C. N. J.'s terminal improvement was initiated in July, 1912, and completed two years later, in the midsummer of 1914, without interruption to a traffic of 370 scheduled trains per weekday (fig. 45). The old train shed was removed at very nearly the halfway point in the whole enterprise, during April, May, and June of 1913, after the driving of piles, excavations for new supports, and the pouring of concrete foundations, and prior to the erection of the Bush train shed that took the place of its gabled predecessor (fig. 46). The multivault shed was designed to cover 18 of the 20 tracks within an area measuring 390 × 815 feet overall. The roof is actually a series of concrete-slab gables with spans ranging from 39 to 43 feet, which are carried on steel arched girders supported in turn by columns set on the center lines of the platforms. The primary changes in the head house, originally designed by the Boston architectural firm of Peabody and Stearns, were the reconstruction and enlargement of the concourse that extends for 383 feet along the train gates, the chief structural feature of which is a new roof in the form of a flattened concrete vault carried on steel girders, and the expansion of the waiting room, restaurant, and service facilities. The upper and lower ferry concourses were both widened, and the ferry concourse on the ground level was enlarged to 4.5 times its former area. The entire program of design and construction was carried out under the direction of Joseph O. Osgood, the company's chief engineer, and his principal assistants, A. E. Owen and C. M. Tisworth. The structural design was for the most part the work of J. J. Yates, the bridge engineer, and his staff.[6] The total cost of the terminal project, at 1914 prices, was $4,000,000, or at least $80,000,000 at the 1980 building-cost level. There is no question that when the work was completed the railroad had provided the passenger with the best of the New Jersey accommodations. John Droege, an authority at the time on the design and operation of passenger terminals, made the most appropriate comment. "The layout . . . is nothing extravagant or exceedingly beautiful. It is, however, a very convenient station."[7]

In order to gain the full advantages from its enlarged terminal facilities the Central of New Jersey was compelled to remove the one remaining bottleneck in its four-track main stem, namely, the long double-track bridge over Newark Bay. The first structure, built in 1863–65 in the course of laying down the original line into Jersey City, was a timber trestle interrupted by a swing span that provided two 75-foot openings for the passage of vessels. It was the increase in the volume of shipping on the bay rather than the rise in rail traffic that prompted the company to make the first alteration, which consisted in the replacement of the swing span by a rolling lift span of steel in 1905. But with the number of daily trains passing the 300-mark and heading rapidly for 400, the structure impeded the flow of traffic not only because of its reduced trackage, but equally because of the slow orders demanded by the aging timberwork. The engineering staff of the C. N. J. recognized the necessity of building a new bridge at the time the reconstruction of the terminal was launched, but war and the unsettled state of economic affairs that followed it delayed the realization of the plan until 1922. And even then what looked like a straightforward work of railroad engineering turned out to be thoroughly controversial. When the company publicized the preliminary plans in 1922, the municipal officers of Newark asked that the location of the bridge be shifted northward a sufficient distance above the greatest concentration of docks along the shore of the bay to minimize interference with marine traffic. The newly established Port of New York Authority recognized the validity of the city's argument and backed its position to the extent of asking the state for jurisdiction over the design and location of the proposed bridge. The railroad took a very dim view of these demands, which would have required an extensive and costly realignment of a heavily used four-track rail line. The company brought suit against the two public bodies for the infringement of corporate rights and eventually carried it to the Supreme Court, and in a decision handed down in 1923 the court denied the jurisdiction over the planning of the bridge that the city and the Authority had sought.

With working plans completed, the contractors initiated construction in the summer of 1924, and the formal opening of the structure came on 27 November 1926. In a harbor area that was shortly to see some of the most spectacular bridges in the world, the monotonous series of steel girder spans in the Newark Bay bridge hardly qualified it for the front rank of the art. Yet the great length of the structure, 7,411 feet, the broad sweep of water on either side, the massive steel truss lift spans with their associated towers standing nearly at the midpoint, and the dense parade of trains during the rush hours, together gave it a kind of homely power appropriate to hardworking railroad usage. Perhaps the most impressive feature is entirely invisible: the soft marine sediments of the bay necessitated the driving of 17,000 piles to support the concrete piers. The design and construction of the long structure were carried out under the supervision of A. E. Owen, the company's chief engineer, and J. J. Yates, the bridge engineer. The consultant for the design of the lift spans was J. A. L. Waddell, an authoritative bridge engineer who had written a classic text on the subject. When the widely ramifying terminal complex at Communipaw was abandoned in 1967, traffic on the once impressive bridge rapidly fell away, and by 1980 it was an unwanted derelict.[8]

Both the freight and passenger traffic of the Central of New Jersey exhibited a high degree of stability through the decade of the 1920s, but the Depression losses of tonnage were severe. Competitive modes of transportation and the uneasy conditions that immediately followed the stock market crash of October, 1929, cost the road only 10 percent of its 1920 tonnage; by 1935, however, 40 percent of the 1925 volume was gone. The interest charges on the heavy investments in bridge and terminal facilities, combined with declining revenues and increasing New Jersey state taxes, left the road in a precarious situation. By the end of the Depression decade the company faced $7,229,614 in unpaid state taxes, along with fixed charges that it was increasingly unable to meet. The result was predictable: on 30 October 1939 the railroad filed a petition under the Federal Bankruptcy Act and became the third of the New York family to face receivership, following the New Haven in

October, 1935, and the Ontario in May, 1937.[9] The Second World War and the heady prosperity of its immediate aftermath brought a phenomenal restoration of health to the C. N. J. In 1950 the company's freight tonnage reached the high point of its entire history, nearly 51,000,000 tons for the year, a volume which was 2 ⅓ times the traffic of the mid-Depression level. This welcome flood, however, proved bitterly deceptive: 25 years later 85 percent of it was gone, and the once flourishing and innovative railroad faced the prospect of having little reason for continued existence.

New Electrifications and Related Projects

The passage of the Kaufman Electrification Act at Albany in June, 1923, and its amendment in May of the following year, required that all railroad lines lying within the limits of New York City or in areas contiguous thereto be operated by electric power as of 1 January 1926. The date of compliance was quickly seen to be unrealistic, since it proved impossible for the various companies to meet the requirement while maintaining full rail service, and the Public Service Commission, accordingly, extended the time limit to the end of 1931. With respect to passenger and freight operations in Manhattan, The Bronx, and the Long Island boroughs, the railroads had complied with the sense of the act embodied in its legislative predecessors by 1910, with the exception of the New York Central's West side line, which was in process of conversion when the Kaufman Act was originally passed. Among the remaining roads that were affected by the legislation, the B. and O. was faced with the heaviest investment because of its owned and subsidiary lines in Richmond Borough. In the case of the Central of New Jersey, the Lackawanna, and the Erie, electrification applied only to the switching operations in the yards supporting their respective carfloat and lighter terminals. The adoption of diesel-electric locomotives in lieu of straight electric power was regarded as acceptable, so that the C. N. J. and the Erie could choose the less expensive alternative. The New Jersey company once again demonstrated its pioneering spirit when it introduced in October, 1925, the first diesel-electric locomotive designed to be used for road service. The Lackawanna, however, had already embarked on grander plans, and it was prepared to maintain the tradition of lavish expenditures when it electrified its Brooklyn yard, which we will describe near the end of this section.

The largest installation to follow from the requirements of the Kaufman Act was the electrification of suburban service on the Staten Island Rapid Transit Railway, a subsidiary of the B. and O. which provided the larger road's entry to the harbor terminals. The officers of the road were pleased to meet the original deadline: the act was scarcely passed when the company made plans to electrify the 16-mile line extending from Saint George through Tottenville and Clifton Junction to South Beach, and the contractors completed the program on 1 July 1925. The system was a three-phase 60-cycle installation in which power was generated by the Staten Island Edison Company and transmitted at a potential of 33,000 volts to the five substations along the route, where it was reduced and converted to a 600-volt direct current for the overrunning third rail. The electrical equipment was manufactured by the Westinghouse company, and the 90 multiple-unit cars by the Standard Steel Car Company. The rolling stock was designed to match the cars of the Fourth Avenue subway in Brooklyn, since the city still clung to the plan of building a rapid transit tunnel under The Narrows between Staten Island and Bay Ridge. This valuable addition to the city's circulatory network was unfortunately never realized. Two features of the Staten Island electrical system placed it in the forefront of rail technology. The substations were fully automated, and the signaling constituted the first permanent adoption of the color-position light form following an experimental installation made by the parent company at Deshler, Ohio.[10] Switching service on Staten Island was provided by diesel-electric locomotives. Both modes of operation continued through the years, although the passenger rolling stock was progressively replaced by new cars when the New York City Transit Authority took over the suburban service following the lease of the Saint George–South Beach line to the city in April, 1956.

The Staten Island electrification came at the halfway point of a thirty-year program undertaken by the B. and O. and its subsidiary for the improvement of fixed property, equipment, and operations. The first and by far the most extensive phase was the complete renewal of many stations and the elimination of grade crossings on the Staten Island lines, an extensive project that was carried out over the years from 1913 to 1938 and from 1940 to 1942. The cost of much of the work accomplished in the period of 1935–42 was borne by grants from the federal Public Works Administration. The grade separations in the irregular topography and complex geology of the island involved a succession of cuts, fills, and viaducts which in places posed difficult problems of drainage and underpinning because of the excessive ground water that had collected in pockets of clay and peat formed by the filling of stream beds through glacial action. While the Staten Island company was improving its right of way, the B. and O. took several steps aimed at upgrading its passenger service. The road had acquired a fleet of motor buses in 1926 to transfer passengers between Grand Central Terminal and the Central of New Jersey station in Jersey City, over a route which included a long and visually unforgettable ferry passage between 23d Street and the New Jersey facility. To accommodate the buses at the C. N. J. station, the northernmost platform was converted to an asphalt-paved driveway lying on the axis of the upstream ferry slip, so that the buses could be driven off the boat, through an opening made in the brick front wall of the station, to points directly alongside the cars of the waiting train. The bus service was made more readily available to the passenger by the addition of two local stations in New York during the three years following its inauguration. The first, located on a subgrade level of the Chanin Building, at 42d Street and Lexington Avenue, was opened on 17 December 1928, while that Art Deco masterpiece was still under construction (1927–29). The new station was directly connected to the Grand Central bus drive by a special passageway constructed under 42d Street. The second facility, located on Columbus Circle, was opened on 26 August of the following year.

Of greatest importance for the future comfort of every railroad passenger was the B. and O.'s inauguration of the first completely air-conditioned train on 24 May 1931, exactly 101 years to the day after the road sold the first ticket for the transportation of a rail passenger in the United States. The train in question was the Columbian, operated between Jersey City and Washington with rolling stock restricted to coaches, parlor cars, and a dining car. Coaches with individual reclining seats were introduced in the same year, and air-conditioned sleeping cars appeared for the first time in April, 1932, when they were assigned to the road's National Limited for the Jersey City–Saint Louis run. The final improvement came with the introduction of diesel-electric locomotives in the spring and summer of 1938 to haul the National Limited, the Capitol Limited (Jersey City–Chicago), the Columbian, and the Royal Blue (another Jersey City–Washington flyer). The B. and O.'s decision marked an early step in what became a motive-power revolution after the Second World War. While the company was willing to invest money in these valuable innovations, the experience of the C. N. J. made the larger road wary enough of New Jersey's taxing policy to consider terminating direct operations in the state. As a result, on 31 December 1941 the B. and O. gave up the practice of operating trains by trackage rights over the Reading and the Central of New Jersey between Philadelphia and Jersey City and turned over the entire conduct of freight and passenger services to the two smaller roads, which thus enjoyed the revenues derived from the traffic and bore the expenses. The day was eventually to come when the B. and O. would cancel all passenger service east of its antique terminal at Baltimore.

No railroad among the New Jersey carriers approached the Lackawanna with respect to the construction of new terminal facilities, the leveling and rectification of the right of way, its elevation above city streets, and the improvement of passenger service. At the turn of the century the officers had embarked on a program aimed at making the property a showpiece of rail technology, and for nearly thirty years, until the Depression finally compelled a halt, they spent money as though they possessed an inexhaustible mine of gold. The most spectacular and innovative works were a series of reinforced concrete structures that began with a modest coal trestle in Hoboken (1906–07), quickly expanded to embrace coal piers and docks, stations, interlocking towers, grade separation projects in the New Jersey cities, the elevated approach to a new terminal in Buffalo, and arch bridges scattered through the Allegheny Mountains that reached a staggering culmination in the gigantic Tunkhannock Creek Viaduct at Nicholson, Pennsylvania (1911–15), still the largest concrete bridge in the world. The numerous and increasingly bolder projects in the north Jersey metropolitan area began modestly enough with a new station at Montclair (1912–13), designed by the architect F. J. Nies, who received a sizable proportion of the commissions for the numerous way stations the company erected between Hoboken and Buffalo. Most tended to fall into the pattern of the Roman Doric in a fabric of brick and limestone cladding over a steel frame. Undeterred by war and its attendant troubles in the Port of New York, the Lackawanna launched a program of track elevation and expansion of main-line trackage in 1916 that quickly eclipsed all the others. The first step, completed in 1916–18, involved the addition of a third main track and the elevation of the line through Orange, New Jersey, with a way station in the Byzantine mode thrown in along the way. The continuous viaduct over the suburban streets was an early work of flat-slab framing designed for railroad loadings. The second phase, carried out in 1919–20, was the construction of 782.5-foot flat-slab viaduct to carry three tracks over the Newark Turnpike in Newark. The last and largest, and the most valuable from the standpoint of civic aesthetics and the safety of local citizens, was the elevation of the double-track main line through East Orange and Brick Church, again on a flat-slab viaduct (1921–23). The three projects together eliminated 43 grade crossings by means of a form of bridge construction most appropriate to the suburban setting. All design and construction were carried out under a talented group of engineering performers—George J. Ray, chief engineer of the railroad company; A. B. Cohen and Meyer Hirschthal, concrete engineers; A. E. Deal, the bridge engineer, with F. J. Nies acting as associated architect.[11]

While these sophisticated works of concrete construction were in progress, the railroad's engineering staff were compelled to turn their attention to an increasingly serious problem at the Hoboken terminal. During the ten years following its completion in 1907 the train shed had settled irregularly to a depth ranging from 5¼ to 17¼ inches below its original level.[12] By the end of another year the problem had become acute, and in the spring and summer of 1919 maintenance of way forces were called upon to raise the entire structure by appropriate lifts without interruption to a daily traffic of 225 trains. The roof and the supporting framework, weighing 9,000 tons, were raised and leveled to their former position by means of a pair of jacks located at the sides of each column. While the roof was temporarily supported on the jacks, the old concrete footings were cut away and replaced by new bases the upper surfaces of which stood from 4 to 17 inches above their former elevation. There was no addition to the existing piling, but the roof appears not to have suffered any more troublesome settlement since the work was completed. Bridge engineer A. E. Deal again directed the operations, under the general supervision of L. L. Talyun, the acting chief engineer at the time.

On the completion of the viaduct at East Orange and Brick Church in 1923, the Lackawanna embarked on the initial step in the last and most beneficial improvement in its extensive suburban and freight-handling service. The passage of the Kaufman Act affected only the company's terminal facilities in New York City, which included the yard that served the float bridge terminal beside the Wallabout Canal in Brooklyn, but within a year after electrifying the yard trackage the road's officers decided to extend electrical operation to all suburban service radiating from the Hoboken terminal. The program at Wallabout Yard, carried out in 1925–27, included the first overhead or catenary distribution system wholly within the city. The supports for the 600-volt direct-current trolley lines proved to be the chief novelty of the installation. Because of an irregular pattern of tracks, platforms, and driveways in the yard and the poor bearing quality of the piling and fill on which these lay, the concrete supporting poles were restricted mainly to the periphery of the yard, so that the trolley wires had to be suspending from transverse and radiating hangers in which tension was maintained by means of springs fixed to the poles. The Westinghouse company manufactured the electrical equipment, and the railroad's construction forces put it in place. The widening use of diesel-electric power eventually led to the abandonment of the Wallabout electrification.

Events destined to leave a more profound and more nearly permanent legacy to the Lackawanna's patrons soon began to take shape among the north Jersey suburbs. On 27 March 1928 the chambers of commerce and other business organizations in Newark and the smaller communities served by the railroad submitted a petition to the road's president, J. M. Davis, urging the electrical operation of suburban trains. The petitioners believed that the Lackawanna's commuters, many possessed of comfortable incomes, would be willing to pay an additional 15 percent of the basic fares in return for the great benefits of electrification.[13] Since the commuters had in effect offered to pay the bill, the company's officers responded to the proposal with extraordinary alacrity and generosity: on 21 April they made the first public announcement of the plan to electrify the suburban service on the main line between Hoboken and Dover and on the Montclair and Gladstone branches, the three segments together having a total length of 66.8 route miles. The railroad carried 60,000 commuters per weekday in a minimum of 220 daily trains through the mid-twenties, a volume of traffic that would require an investment of $18,000,000 in fixed equipment, motor cars, and trailers. The investigation of alternative forms of equipment and rolling stock for the road's particular requirements, planning for the installation, design, and construction were carried out under the authority of a committee which included J. M. Davis and chief engineer George J. Ray.[14] Detailed planning for the program occupied the year from mid-1928 through the summer of 1929; construction began in September, and service was inaugurated on the various lines during the succeeding 15 months—to Montclair on 3 September 1930, South Orange on 22 September, Morristown on 18 December, and over the remainder of the trackage on 31 January 1931.

The Lackawanna's system, as welcome as it proved to be, was far less innovative than the grand work that the Pennsylvania Railroad had already initiated. The overhead wire of the Lackawanna supplied direct current at 3,000 volts for the operation of 141 motor cars and 141 trailers, an even division that allowed the exact pairing of power and trailing units in every train (the chief model for the Lackawanna's program was the electrification of suburban service on the Illinois Central Railroad in Chicago, (1923–26). The motor cars possessed two unique features for the time: the 235-horsepower motors were the first to operate at a potential as high as 3,000 volts, and the trucks were the first designed for suburban service to be equipped with roller bearings. The officers of the road entertained the idea of electrifying freight service throughout the New Jersey terminal area, but the cost and complexity of installing transmission and distribution lines over the numerous main and yard tracks, spurs, crossings, and junctions quickly discouraged the idea. In place of direct electrical operation the road adopted the diesel-electric power for the yard and transfer service embracing the Jersey City–Secaucus–Harrison triangle (an × would offer a more precise geometric representation). The locomotives were the so-called three-power variety, in which the motors could draw current directly from the overhead trolley, from a battery inside the cab, or from the generators driven by the diesel engine. The movement of both passenger and freight trains in the electrified territory was further expedited by the previous introduction of color-light signals of the multiaspect variety (1921–22), which allowed higher speeds and closer headway of trains than had previously been the rule with the old lower-quadrant semaphores. Everything was indeed up to date on the Lackawanna in 1930, and everything was in use fifty years later as it was originally built, although the rolling stock was clearly in need of replacement. No other strictly New Jersey road was prepared to follow the exemplary conduct offered by the C. N. J. and the Hoboken company: the Pennsylvania's Jersey City terminal was steadily approaching the end of its useful life; the Erie kept its smoke-blackened station in a semblance of working order by means of minor improvements in signaling; the Lehigh Valley was content to provide a new station in Newark (1912–13) designed by Kenneth W. Murchison; and the Ontario and the Susquehanna, as tenants of large proprietors, saw no point whatsoever in spending money on passengers.

This rather sorry record might suggest that there was no room for improvement, but however stoutly the railroad officers clung to this view, it was drastically at odds with the facts. There was nothing in the order of the universe that required the existence of five passenger terminals strung out from the south end of Jersey City to Weehawken, or their dependence wholly or in major part on costly and time-consuming ferry transfers, and nothing that compelled the continued operation of dirty, noisy, inefficient, and technologically obsolete steam locomotives—nothing, that is, except the heroic capacity for foot-dragging among railroad executives, combined with a pathological dislike for cooperative arrangements. There was a continuing need for unifying the terminal facilities of the north Jersey waterfront, and there were individuals prepared to submit plans describing in greater or less detail how this might be accomplished

No one who took the question seriously underestimated the magnitude of the problem. In 1925 the standard railroads and the Hudson and Manhattan carried slightly fewer than 169,000,000 passengers into and out of New York City through the New Jersey sector; four years later the total had increased 5 percent to the all-time record of nearly 178,000,000 passengers, or almost exactly half of the grand total for all railroads serving the metropolitan area. A conservative estimate suggests that roughly 80,000,000 passengers, or about 250,000 per weekday, used the five terminals spread out along the New Jersey waterfront (see table 6). Planners might reasonably set aside both the Weehawken station, because the Ontario and the West Shore (leased to the New York Central and operated as its River Division) were minor elements in the metropolitan transit, and the Pennsylvania's Jersey City station, because it must eventually become an anachronism. But this still left around

200,000 passengers traveling in some 700 weekday trains. Any solution approaching adequacy would have required cooperative efforts on a heroic scale, which in turn would have necessitated the entry of public bodies into the planning and the financing processes, even if the railroads had been willing to act together. The Erie was the only company other than the Pennsylvania whose officers at least entertained the idea of a New York terminal: they proposed such a station and an associated office building in 1902, and revived the idea in 1929, presumably with the backing of Mantis and Oris Van Sweringen, the big-money financiers of Cleveland who controlled the railroad. No one familiar with the road's resources and the condition of its Jersey City station would have expected action. Nothing suggesting it ever occurred.

A much more serious proposal, worked out in detail, was offered in April, 1924, by Daniel L. Turner, a consulting engineer to the New York Transit Commission. Turner wisely decided that a single union terminal was probably out of the question because of size, cost, and the difficulty of finding a suitable location in Manhattan. What he proposed in its place was a continuous subway loop uniting all the railroad terminals in New Jersey and in the Borough of Manhattan, and constructed with the clearance limits, signaling, track, electrical equipment, and station platforms necessary for the operation of the suburban trains of standard railroads. The existing terminals would thus have become way stations, or adjuncts thereto, and additional way stations were planned to serve midtown and downtown Manhattan. Two immediate and enormous benefits were conferred at one stroke—the entry of all suburban trains into the central business district of New York City, and the electrification of all suburban service in a major part of the metropolitan area. Turner worked out the costs and the financing in some detail: the investment in tunnel construction and fixed property he estimated to be $502,000,000, and in rolling stock an additional $185,000,000. The greater part of this admittedly staggering expenditure was to be born by a public corporation, leaving only $138,000,000 as the railroads' share. He calculated that a ten-cent fare added to the individual commutation ticket would be sufficient to amortize the investment in eight years, after which period the additional fare would be reduced to cover only operating expenses.[15] The Turner plan had everything to recommend it, and a cooperative agreement between the Port of New York Authority and the railroads could have led to the issuance of the necessary bonds and their retirement, if not in eight years, in something less than fifty. But the surrender to the automobile had already begun, and the Authority was planning highway bridges, not railroad tunnels.

Two more plans were to be formulated before the question of unified service became dormant until the postwar years, but the evidence suggests that they were never made public by means of the daily press, professional journals, or a separate printing. In 1930 Rockefeller Center had been placed under construction in the area bounded by Fifth and Sixth avenues and 48th and 52d streets. The time was not auspicious for the leasing of high-rent office space, and the Rockefeller interests, with their financial advisors, planners, and architects, were understandably concerned to make the midtown blocks as attractive as possible to potential tenants. One of the great defects of the site was and continues to be the absence of contiguous rapid transit lines, the Sixth Avenue elevated line having already been marked for demolition following the opening of the Eighth Avenue subway in 1932. In the following year the officers of the Center project engaged the consulting firm of Lockwood-Greene Engineers to draw up a plan for a third Manhattan railroad terminal, to be located between Sixth and Eighth avenues on the blocks centered along the axis of 50th Street. What companies were expected to be tenants in this facility is not clear, but given the existing arrangements, it seems obvious that the authors must have had the New Jersey roads in mind. If these were reluctant to join the enterprise, they were nevertheless to be connected with the terminal by means of a subway such as Turner had proposed six years earlier. An alternative was a crosstown subway under 50th Street, which would have proved to be an awkward location for the Grand Central nexus. This plan was placed on the shelf shortly after it was delivered to those who had commissioned it, and a second was put forth in 1934 which differed from its predecessor only in locating the terminal north of the Rockefeller site, between 51st and 53d streets, the working area again to extend west of Sixth Avenue. The Rockefeller family and their consultants placed the second plan in the file in 1936, when they abandoned all further study of the matter. The idea of terminal unification never wholly disappeared, but in the unrealities of the expressway world planners seem to "have now done with all such visionary schemes forever," as Lemuel Gulliver puts it.[16]

The Port during the Second World War

Those who expected a re-enactment of the melodramatic disasters that descended on the eastern railroads and the Atlantic coastal ports during the First World War were disappointed as the enterprise of mass killing rolled on with little hindrance throughout the years of the second world conflict. It is true that the weather mounted less ferocious onslaughts than it did in 1917/18, although the winter of 1944/45 struck hard at central New York; but the clemency of nature was more than offset by the devastating results of the German submarine campaign, which cost more than 500 vessels off the Atlantic seaboard during the first full year of American participation (1942). The chief questions for the historian, of course, are why the railroads were able to perform so effectively in the decade of the forties when they were so desperately crippled in 1917, and what lessons one might learn from this performance. The answers, as we might expect, involve a complex interweaving of national, local, economic, political, and technical events. There was plenty of control and direction imposed by the federal government, but the railroad companies were operated as privately owned corporations that were masters of their own destiny, subject only to the regulations of the Interstate Commerce Commission and the various ad hoc agencies created by the third Roosevelt administration for the prosecution of the war. The achievement of the railroads is all the more remarkable in view of the enormously greater military traffic of 1942–45 than that of 1917–18: 16,000,000 recruits as opposed to 5,000,000 in the earlier years; 200,000,000 tons of military freight against 11,200,000 in the previous conflict, for an annual average of 52,000,000 tons in the Second World War, as opposed to 7,100,000 in the First.

The general state of the railroad industry in 1940 differed in many essential respects from what it was in 1917, especially in the case of the major trunk lines, and the differences might be classified according to economic situation, mechanical and communications technology, and the operation of trains, the separation of which, particularly the last two, is an arbitrary convenience adopted by the historian. The overriding fact, the one that had drastically altered the economic position of the railroads over the 25 years between 1915 and 1940, was that whereas they enjoyed a virtual monopoly of intercity land transportation in 1915, substantial volumes of freight and passenger traffic had been eroded away during the intervening years by motor trucks, buses, private automobiles, and the barges moving on newly canalized rivers. Merchandise, furniture, automobiles, and packaged freight, less-than-carload shipments, much local freight of every description—traffic that generally moved under the highest tariffs in part because it was awkward and expensive to handle by rail—had passed in major proportion to highway competition by 1940. Bulk commodities such as coal and other mineral products moved in increasing quantities on the Ohio, Illinois, and Mississippi waterway systems. Local, accommodation, and suburban passenger traffic passed in such volume to buses and private cars that one was hard put to it to find a local train in the timetables of 1940. The economics compelled by the Depression and the growing threat of competition hastened an internal process that had begun with the formation of trunk lines after the Civil War. Mergers through absorption of independent or controlled lines reduced the number of separate companies and extended the mileage of large, unified, tightly organized systems.

Highway competition and Depression-born curtailments led to marked changes in the patterns of rail traffic, of which the most conspicuous was the drastic reduction in the total number of scheduled and extra passenger trains. The railroads experienced a slow but steady attrition of passenger traffic through the decade of the 1920s, but these losses were accelerated to such a degree during the Depression years that by 1940 local, accommodation, and branch-line schedules had virtually disappeared. This reduction was less noticeable among the New York carriers, with their high density of suburban and short-haul traffic, than was the case with railroads serving cities with little commutation business. For such communities the automobile and the bus simply swept the local train out of existence. And what may seem surprising, the war brought about no recovery of the local traffic. The experience of the railroads centered at Cincinnati, for example, was typical of those serving major transfer points with a limited suburban traffic. In 1928, when planning for the new union terminal was initiated, the seven roads of the Cincinnati family operated 224 trains per weekday; by 1934 this total had fallen to about 135 trains, of which 122 were regularly scheduled runs listed in the public timetables. The flood of wartime traffic necessitated the addition of only one scheduled train by 1944, for a total of 123 shown in the timetables, which probably swelled to 145 or 150 per day because of the numerous extra trains operated for military personnel. During the decade of 1925–35 the railroads lost half the passengers they transported in the earlier year; during the succeeding decade they more than regained their losses, but they were able to carry 910,000,000 passengers in 1944 and produce a record 95,000,000,000 passenger-miles (far beyond any previous levels) with very little increase in the number of scheduled and extra trains. The intensive use of rolling stock, to the point where through trains carrying 500 to 1,000 passengers were common in the heavily traveled corridors, not only brought a heady prosperity, but also an essential clearing of lines for the huge volume of wartime tonnage.

Technological innovations came rapidly during the prosperous years of the twenties, and together they greatly increased the efficiency as well as the capacity of trunk-line operations. The most visible of the mechanical improvements was the invention of the so-called superpower locomotive—that is, a machine equipped with a four-wheel trailing truck, which allowed a marked expansion of the grate area in the firebox with no increase in the weight on the driving wheels, for an attendant increase in the rate of steam generation, speed, and maximum horsepower. The New York Central Railroad was a pioneer in this development, having introduced two of the most common forms, the 4-6-4, or Hudson type, and the 2-8-4, or Berkshire type (the names indicate their parentage). The expensive new locomotives were confined to the major trunk lines, but many railroad systems found another advantage that was virtually an accidental by-product of the extreme changes occurring over the quarter century between 1920 and 1945. Not only did the big carriers possess a stable of new and powerful locomotives, they also found themselves with the greatest diversity of available power that they had ever known. Alert superintendents of motive power discovered that presumably worn-out little engines heading for the scrap yard, seemingly museum pieces for all practical purposes, could be repaired, modernized, and made to perform a host of useful tasks. Extensive lines with a great variety of tonnage trains and a remnant of light branch-line passenger trains found themselves operating every type of locomotive from the once universal and forgotten 4-4-0 to the latest behemoths produced by the manufacturers. Improved power, steadily lengthening engine runs that ultimately embraced entire main lines, the rational utilization of power, and the increasing mechanization of engine terminals made it possible to move immense volumes of freight and to dispatch it on short notice to the port cities where it was needed and could be most quickly reloaded into vessels.

Comparable improvements in signaling—the rapid spread of automatic block signals, the use of multiaspect and other special forms, and above all, the invention and spread of centralized traffic control—increased the capacity of lines and the safety of their operations, reduced delays, eliminated interlocking towers, and allowed a great reduction in the number of operators at a time of extreme manpower shortages.[17] Similar innovations in the operation of yards were perhaps more valuable in the face of wartime exigencies because of the necessity for the rapid assembling and classifying of freight cars for the transshipment of freight between car and vessel in the harbor cities. Car retarders, mechanical devices at the track level which serve the function of brakes on cars descending the grades of hump yards, automatic yard signals, and radio and telephone communications made it possible for a yardmaster and his staff in an elevated office to control the movement of cars in a yard that formerly required an army of switchmen and brakemen, of whom the latter were compelled to follow the hazardous practice of standing on the top running boards of moving cars. Increases in the capacity of main tracks and yards and in the power of locomotives were further enhanced by the steady, year-by-year expansion in the capacity of the average freight car, which grew more than 25 percent from 1918 to 1941, or from 40 to 51 tons.

The advantages provided by technological innovations, however, might have gone incompletely realized if they had not been accompanied by contemporaneous changes in the mental habits of operating, engineering, and administrative personnel. They learned the lessons taught by the United States Railroad Administration in 1918–20: hundreds of separate companies could no longer go their separate ways; the standardization of motive power, rolling stock, and operating procedures, and the unified operation of independent railroads were matters of necessity if rail transportation was to survive in the mid-twentieth century, whether at peace or at war. Under the happier conditions of the twenties the railroads learned, to their gratification, how to move more than a million loaded cars per week, a number which they first reached in 1923 and which proved to equal almost exactly the average volume of freight tonnage carried through the 52 weeks of 1929. The all-time peak came in the week ending 28 September of that year, when the railroads of the United States moved 1,202,111 loaded cars. Given the subsequent increase in freight-car capacity, loadings at this level in 1980 would have tripled the actual tonnage carried. The grand result of all these lessons learned and innovations put to practical use was the discovery of an enormous reserve capacity among the existing railroad lines and in the conduct of their operations. This realization was particularly impressive in the West, where single-track main lines were suddenly called upon to carry an extremely heavy westbound tonnage that had never previously existed. The consequence was that roads which formerly operated ten to twenty trains per day at the maximum found that they could move 60 to 70 trains in the same period without serious delays. On the multitrack main lines of the New York Central and the Pennsylvania traffic reached levels of 200 to 300 trains per day.

The endlessly ramifying machine worked very well, but as the military effort gathered momentum, special rules and procedures had to be adopted, especially with respect to freight destined for ports, among which New York still stood in the first position. During the American participation in overt military activities (December, 1941, to August, 1945) the steps taken by the federal government to maintain the flow of rail traffic were chiefly the allocation of materials, embargoes, priorities in shipments, and the integrated planning of the movement of freight and the use of port facilities. The quantities of steel and other necessary materials were allocated by the War Production Board and the Office of Production Management to the pertinent industries in order to provide for the manufacture of an adequate number of freight cars and locomotives. The production of passenger cars had been halted at the end of 1941, shortly after the delivery of 32 cars ordered by the New York Central Railroad to re-equip the Empire State Express close to its 50th anniversary. The device of local and commodity embargoes was used rather sparingly, and in the region immediately tributary to New York Harbor it was confined to freight moving to and from New England and to that destined for transshipment between cars and intercoastal vessels. The overall planning of the use of port facilities, the priority granted to direct military shipments and the transportation of military personnel, and quick changes in the routing of freight to those eastern and Gulf Coast ports that could most expeditiously handle it, together relieved much of the pressure on the Port of New York. Other provisions, mostly generated by the railroads themselves, were aimed at maintaining the flow of cars and their release with minimal delays, mainly through the device of graded priorities in the loading and moving of cars, which had been developed, though defectively used, during the earlier war. The only practices adopted by the railroads that specifically affected the operation of passenger trains were the lengthening of schedules, the curtailment of some local and suburban service, and the cancellation of sleeping car service in the early months of 1945 for all runs shorter than 400 miles.

The volume of freight moving into, through, and out of the Port of New York by rail and water during the early forties revealed unexpected anomalies that constituted one factor in minimizing congestion. The highest level for rail tonnage came in 1943, when the New York roads carried somewhat more than 139,000,000 tons of freight during the year, an increase of 72 percent over the total for 1940. Military activity reached its height in the European theater in mid-1944, but rail traffic fell about 3,000,000 tons below that of the previous year. The fluctuations in waterborne cargo, however, behaved in a different manner. Vessels docking at the port carried nearly 130,000,000 tons in 1940, but this total dropped year by year throughout the war entirely because of a steep decline in domestic tonnage, which accounted for 82 percent of the total volume in 1940. As a consequence, much berthing space was released, and the problems of loading and unloading export freight arose primarily from the growing shortage of manpower, which had become crucial by 1943. An intensive recruitment program carried on by the War Manpower Commission, the United States Employment Service, and the employment offices of the Railroad Retirement Board brought in enough hands, both male and female, to transfer cargo at a pace sufficient to avoid accumulation and the accompanying congestion that could back up over hundreds of miles of rail lines. Since 1943 proved to be the peak year, with rail tonnage at the port running 17 percent above that of 1942, the successful coping with the problem carried the harbor docks and yards over the hump, so to speak.

Continued meticulous planning by the Association of American Railroads and the Eastern Railroads' Operating Committee, working in collaboration with the wartime government agencies, guaranteed relatively smooth operations through 1944 and 1945, when the problem became that of rapid demobilization. A final factor, intangible but real and potent nonetheless, was what we might call the moral spirit of the city's population. It was no phony patriotic fervor, and no one would deny that jobs for all at high wages constituted a marvelous aid to good temper, especially after Depression privations; but whatever the hidden ingredient, the citizens demonstrated a social decency combined with unbounded practical energies that made the wartime decade in some ways the high point of the city's unparalleled development. The various ethnic and racial components of its population were relatively balanced among the definable neighborhoods of the urban area, lived in close proximity with one another but in harmonious association for all the dynamic intensity of urban life, and each contributed its share to the collective enterprise. The city's economy was as much distinguished by a multitude of little, close-knit businesses, most with fewer than a hundred employees, as it was by the institutions of high finance and the machinery of the largest and most complex transportation nexus in the history of mankind. Its celebrated skyscrapers were diversified in form, rich in detail and color, and built to a manageable scale for the dense urban milieu. Its achievements in the visual and performing arts continued to flourish at the high creative pace they had reached in the years following the end of the First World War. The troubles of later years sprang far less from internal weaknesses than from gross failures of the national economy.

8

The Terminal System after 1945

Changing Rail Traffic and the Port Terminals

When the Second World War ended in 1945 the economic health and the daily operations of the Port of New York were in a flourishing condition; and since the intricate rail and marine system had been thoroughly tested under wartime exigencies and only in minor details found wanting, it was assumed that the prosperity of the forties would continue indefinitely into the future. A few voices were raised in warning that its seemingly unassailable geo-economic position was not in fact impregnable, but for a decade at least the competition of distant ports, which New Yorkers may have had difficulty in locating on the map, and of associated industrial centers, could not be regarded as offering a serious threat. At this juncture, when everyone was reasonably confident about the local state of affairs, shifts in the patterns of manufacturing and transportation soon brought such drastic changes in the harbor economy and its terminal system as diametrically to reverse the processes of centuries. Several irresistible forces, nationwide in the scope of their effects, were chiefly responsible for these alterations. The first by virtue of its historical precedence was the steady westward movement of industry that had begun at the time of the Civil War, which manifested itself primarily in the relatively more rapid growth of industrial production and rail traffic in the Great Lakes region than in the Northeast and the Middle Atlantic states. Accompanying and following the Second World War was the far more rapid expansion of manufacturing in the South, the near Southwest, and the Pacific coastal states, most of which has been associated with the kind of growth industry that exaggerated by comparison the increasingly dinosaurian character of the traditional forms of steel, automotive, and machinery production.

Paralleling the rise and expansion of new industries was the rapid increase in the volume of cargo loaded and unloaded at the chief Gulf Coast ports, most notably Pensacola, Mobile, New Orleans, and Houston, where the rate of postwar expansion was in some cases five to seven times greater than it was at New York. Statistics assembled in the mid-fifties, as a matter of fact, revealed that even Philadelphia, Baltimore, and Norfolk were gaining traffic at a substantially higher rate than the more northerly city. Its latitude, however, was not an adverse factor, since the container port built by the Canadian National Railway at Halifax proved to be a potent magnet in drawing away a substantial share of North Atlantic shipping. The aging industrial facilities of New England and metropolitan New Jersey, coupled with steadily increasing property taxes and land prices—the latter often wholly at odds with its true value—exaggerated the effects of these broad historical and geographical processes. Finally, the decline of the railroads' share of the total freight tonnage, together with their extreme vulnerability to the heavily subsidized air and highway competition in the densely populated Eastern District, not only brought unprecedented financial troubles to the individual roads, but tended to exacerbate the economic difficulties of urban areas closely tied to rail fortunes. The grand result of all these causative factors was such an extreme alteration in the nationwide distribution of industrial capacity and such an unmitigated disaster for metropolitan New York as to indicate a political and economic failure on a national scale. But the historian is compelled to add that the city itself was far from an innocent victim: the reckless construction of office skyscrapers at the expense of housing and small business enterprises, the cruelly destructive building of expressways, at whatever cost to residential neighborhoods, the costly antediluvian character of many of the port facilities, even the gift of a depressingly unattractive bus terminal from the Port Authority (1948–50), all played their respective roles in making a dismal situation worse.

Measured in absolute terms, the traffic moving into and out of the port increased steadily if irregularly during the postwar years, reaching a total of 66,139,000 long tons in 1978, which was nearly double the level of 1950 and more than three times that of the Depression low point of 1935. If we set the comparative trends aside, there was thus no question that New York stood far above even its nearest competitor in volume of cargo moved. And for all the sufferings of the railroads, the movement of nearly 33,000,000 tons of freight into, through, and out of the port in 1974 would suggest that they were still fairly active in contributing to the local economy. The combined weight of all the shipments conveyed over the waters that constitute the harbor area, according to the Army Corps of Engineers, reached the staggering total of 220,099,319 tons in 1975.[1] As great as these totals are, however, a comparative analysis of trends over the years reveals a steady shrinkage of New York's share in the national total of foreign trade. In 1870 nearly 60 percent of all ocean-borne commerce passed through the Port of New York, but this proportion had shrunk to an estimated 12 percent a century later. In order to maintain such competitive position as it could still claim, the port was compelled to adopt containerized shipping in place of the traditional "break-bulk" technique, with its piecemeal unloading into lighters for transshipment to rail heads or other vessels. The new technique, of course, brought an enormous improvement in the efficient and expeditious handling of cargo, though at a considerable cost in jobs. The use of containers was introduced by terminal operators and the Port Authority for coastwise or domestic cargo in 1956, and for foreign trade in 1965. This necessitated the construction on the part of the Authority of entirely new container terminals at Port Newark in Newark Bay and at Howland Hook at the north end of Arthur Kill on Staten Island. The new practice was primarily responsible for the expansion in tonnage that came with the years following 1955, but the advantage was secured at a devastating loss of cargo-handling jobs, which declined from 25,033 in 1965 to 16,741 seven years later and an estimated 11,800 in 1978. By that date a total of 750 miles of docks, divided between 290 miles in New Jersey and 460 in New York, were still in use.[2]

If the port was holding its own with respect to water-borne cargo, the railroads which had served it so well during the war most emphatically were not. A direct quantitative representation of changes in the distribution of rail tonnage throughout the country as a whole immediately and forcefully reveals the absolute as well as the relative decline of the eastern carriers. A condensed 50-year recapitulation of freight traffic indicates a change of fortune of such depth and magnitude as to be without parallel in the history of the national economy. Between 1929 and 1978, a period marked by an immense though extremely irregular increase in the total body of industrial production, railroad tonnage rose by only 3.7 percent. One obvious factor that helped to determine this arrested growth was the steep decline in the railroads' share of all the freight moved, the losses being in considerable part reflected in the proportional gains of highway, waterway, and pipeline competitors. An equally decisive factor, particularly as far as the prosperity of the East was concerned, was the drastic shift in the geographical distribution of traffic that began to accelerate at the end of the war. By 1978 the Eastern District of the national rail network had lost 45 percent of its 1929 tonnage, whereas the Western District had gained 37 percent over the 1929 level, and the Southern District 111 percent. In short, the losses suffered by the eastern roads were almost exactly offset by the gains of those in the South and the West. Moreover, along the way the region had lost its first position to the West, and the South was very close behind it.[3]

The contraction in the total freight and passenger traffic of the roads that constitute the New York family almost exactly corresponded to the fate of all of those within the Eastern District, and the attainment of new traffic peaks during the war made the subsequent debacle seem all the more devastating. In the 30 years from 1945 to 1975 the New York roads lost a little more than half their tonnage and nearly two-thirds of their through and suburban passengers. The growth of freight traffic in the South and West is reflected in the loss of half their proportional share of the national total over the same years, but the relative stability of suburban traffic resulted in a small increase in the share of passengers carried. The total movement of passengers into and out of the metropolitan area reached its high point, as we have seen, in 1929 and very nearly regained the level in 1943, so that the long-term decline from 1929 to 1967 of slightly more than 56 percent was somewhat greater than the collapse that came after the wartime peak. The year-by-year stability of suburban traffic that followed the establishment of the Metropolitan Transit Authority suggested that there was not likely to be any further attrition in the unpromising future. Freight tonnage originating, terminating, and moving through the port was eroded away so rapidly that by the mid-seventies the traditional character of the rail-marine terminal system had ceased to exist, gone before newer and supposedly more efficient modes of transportation technology. The total volume of freight, however handled—interchange, lighterage, and local transfer—fell 76.5 percent between 1943 and 1974, which was not the end of the slide by any means. The most extreme feature of this complex body of changes was the virtual disappearance of cargo transfer by lighters in what was once the greatest lighterage harbor in the world. The prime cause of this attrition, of course, was that containerization had replaced nearly all the former break-bulk technology, with its associated lighterage movements. Under the new technique cargo is sorted according to type and destination, packed in steel containers, transferred by crane directly from ocean vessel to truck or rail car, and carried to the consignee or shipped without intermediate handling. One might regard it as a parcel post service on a gargantuan scale. Connection freight that was once carried across the harbor by carfloat was rerouted over circuitous rail lines between New England and the rest of the continent. Two highly visible consequences of all these mutations must always astonish those who were familiar with the port scene in other years: the unbroken phalanx of terminals and yards that lay along the Jersey waterfront from Weehawken to the Bayonne peninsula has given way to grass and weeds, and the broad waterways now flow unvexed to the sea, where they once looked like the aqueous equivalent of the streets at Herald Square.[4]

The postwar fate of the individual railroads varied in the extreme, ranging from a modest and recoupable decline in one case to such disastrous losses in others as to leave them unrecognizable cripples. In the 30 years of 1945 to 1975 the B. and O. managed to hold on to all but about 28 percent of its wartime traffic, and its merger with the healthy and expansive Chesapeake and Ohio Railway in 1960 brought advantages that the other New York roads could only envy—the refinancing of maturing obligations, the consolidation of departments and managerial functions, mutual aid in sharing and stimulating the revival of coal and merchandise traffic. It was the only cheerful plot in an otherwise unrelieved collection of gloomy stories.

The three roads that were to compose the Penn Central group—the Pennsylvania, the New York Central, and the New Haven—suffered a quickening erosion of traffic through the years, the New York Central the least, the New Haven the worst, and by 1975 nearly half their total wartime traffic was gone. A specific and very telling illustrations of how the gains of the South came at the expense of the East may be discovered in a comparison of the long-term fortunes of the Penn Central group with a representative southern carrier, the Louisville and Nashville. Over the 30 years in which the three eastern roads saw half their traffic disappear, the L. and N. added tonnage equal to three-quarters of its wartime peak, itself a record up to the time. The trends had actually been established long before Depression and war-induced boom: by the end of the 60-year period between 1915 and 1975 the Penn Central group had barely kept what it had in the earlier armageddon, whereas the southern road saw its tonnage reach a level 4.5 times greater, with no limit in sight (see table 10). The anthracite roads suffered devastation: the free-spending Lackawanna and the hard-working Erie together lost nearly 60 percent of their wartime traffic, while the Lehigh could congratulate itself on the ground that it lost only a little more than half. The Reading saw nearly two-thirds of its tonnage go with the end of anthracite mining, the flight of industry to the South, and the capture of short-haul merchandise traffic by the trucks. Two of the little railroads quickly lost such *raison d'être* as they possessed—with two-thirds of its tonnage gone during the first decade after the war, the hapless Ontario gave up the ghost on 29 March 1957, selling or abandoning everything it owned, and the Susquehanna survived by canceling passenger service on 30 June 1966, abandoning its Pennsylvania lines over the succeeding years, and filing a petition for bankruptcy in January, 1976. The Raritan River formed a conspicuous exception to the historical pattern of the dwarfs, losing only 30 percent of its wartime traffic by the mid-seventies. The C. N. J. suffered almost total disaster: its peak year, contrary to all the other trends, came in 1950, but during the succeeding 25 years it lost more than 85 percent of this tonnage. By the time of the road's third bankruptcy in 1967, the C. N. J. was totally insolvent, and the abandonment of more than half its mileage was the first step in the process of transforming itself into a north Jersey terminal company. The Long Island fell into a special category, since it functioned primarily as a suburban passenger carrier. It appears to have done fairly well in preserving its modest freight tonnage: after losing nearly half of the traffic in the 20 years up to 1965, estimates derived from revenues suggest that it regained about 25 percent of the loss during the following decade. The passenger losses of those companies that retained such service were for the most part greater than the decline of freight tonnage, ranging from 38 percent in the case of the Long Island to 93 percent for the B. and O. over the period of 1945 to 1970, the last full year before Amtrak took over most through passenger operations.[5]

The inexorable erosion of rail traffic was understandably accompanied by radical alterations in the structure and operations of the eastern railroad system, and these were most conspicuous in the New York Harbor area. The rate of loss gathered momentum during the postwar years, so that changes came slowly at first, but by 1960 it was clear to railroad officers that extensive mergers and abandonments of property, accompanied by corresponding curtailments of service, were necessary to the survival of most of the companies. The first steps were modest and were carried out on a piecemeal basis. Since the Pennsylvania's Jersey City terminal had become a redundant facility at the end of the war, it was abandoned in 1962 and demolished, along with its ferry slips and supporting utilities, immediately thereafter. In 1955 the Lackawanna and the Erie began the progressive cancellation of trans-Hudson ferry service in favor of the Hudson and Manhattan trains, and in the following year the respective presidents of the two roads, Perry M. Shoemaker and Paul W. Johnston, initiated the discussion of plans for unifying their terminal properties. The next step, unification on a systemwide basis, seemed obvious, but it required another four years of planning prior to practical implementation. The two companies were merged on 17 October 1960 to form the Erie-Lackawanna Railroad; within the next year the Erie gave up its antique station in Jersey City and moved its trains to the Lackawanna's Hoboken terminal. The move required no new construction, since the Erie trains could use an existing connecting track near the intersection of the two main lines immediately west of Bergen Hill. The two roads together once operated as many as 500 trains per weekday, but this total had shrunk to 240 by 1977, divided between 78 for the Erie and 162 for the Lackawanna.

The sudden upsurge of traffic on the Central of New Jersey over the years from 1945 through 1950 proved to be another example of the gods offering riches to those whom they intend to destroy. It was obvious as early as 1960 that the road would have to be placed under intensive care, and two years prior to that date the kind of disaster that was thought to be a thing of the past underscored the fact. On 15 September 1958 the engineman of an eastbound passenger train ran past the stop signal governing movements through the lift span in the Newark Bay bridge. The train left the rails at the automatic derail before the open draw, but the momentum of 42.5 miles per hour carried the diesel-electric locomotive and the first three cars into the water. It was not the worst such accident, but it clearly fell in the category of major wrecks: 48 people died and another 48 were injured. It helped to push the railroad to the brink, and in

September, 1960, the company entered into a contract with the state of New Jersey under which the state undertook to subsidize its declining but essential commutation service. Extensive revisions in the operation of trains and the abandonment of property soon followed, with the state unquestionably in control at last. Under the Aldene Transportation Plan, adopted by the legislature on 30 April 1967, the railroad gave up its handsome and, in former years, at least, well-maintained terminal in Jersey City and transferred its remaining trains to the Pennsylania station in Newark. The state invested $15,000,000 in the rehabilitation of the structure and the track-platform area, which emerged as a result an efficient and attractive joint facility for the Central of New Jersey and the two companies that were soon to become the Port Authority Trans-Hudson Corporation (formerly the Hudson and Manhattan), the National Railroad Passenger Corporation (Amtrak), and the Consolidated Rail Corporation (Con Rail), the last two the inheritors of the Pennsylvania properties in the Northeast Corridor. By 1976 the Newark station was serving 40,000 passengers and about 260 trains per weekday. Meanwhile, the enterprising state had begun to implement an ambitious plan that called for the rehabilitation of the Jersey City terminal, including the train shed of 1914, as the central museum, exhibition, and recreational space for an 850-acre historical park and wildlife refuge. The entire Communipaw terminal area outside the station building, once among the busiest in the nation, had by 1979 reverted to the vegetation that long ago covered it, with all trace of railroad usage gone.[6]

While the state of New Jersey was rescuing the C. N. J.'s suburban service and transforming its derelict station, the Port Authority at last began to lend its resources to the improvement of trans-Hudson rail service, but only after years of exclusive preoccupation with air and highway transportation. With all harbor spans but the Verrazano-Narrows Bridge (1959–64) in place over the port waterways, the Authority in 1946 undertook a program of acquisition and construction and greatly expanded its facilities serving truck and airplane operations. La Guardia and Kennedy airports were acquired through lease from the city in 1947; the Teterboro, New Jersey, airport was purchased outright from a private owner in the following year; construction of the New York truck terminal was completed in 1949, and of its Newark counterpart in 1950. The completion of the Union Bus Terminal in New York came at nearly the same time. This program of imperial conquest was rounded out with the lease of Newark Airport and the Port of Newark from that city in 1974. By the mid-fifties, however, a situation more crucial to the economy and well-being of the metropolitan area was approaching the crisis stage: The Hudson and Manhattan Railroad was nearing insolvency and collapse; yet with ferry service disappearing, its presence had become more than ever a matter of necessity. The concerned states were aware of the fact, and in 1957 the legislatures of New York and New Jersey appointed the Metropolitan Rapid Transit Commission to inquire into the problem of continuing adequate commutation service under the Hudson. In a report issued in January, 1958, the members proposed once more a loop or belt railway line uniting Manhattan and the Jersey communities by means of the existing Hudson and Manhattan lines and two new tunnels to be constructed to the north thereof. The cost was estimated at about $500,000,000. The first response was a thoroughgoing criticism offered by Herman T. Stichman, a trustee of the bankrupt H. and M., who argued that the company's existing trackage and tunnels offered the best and least expensive means of attaining the same ends. The property, however, would have to undergo wholesale rehabilitation at the cost of $100,000,000 or more. Only the Port Authority possessed the mandate and the financial position to issue the necessary revenue bonds, but it required several court decisions to allow the use of its funds for rapid-transit operations. The organization, in effect, adopted the Stichman plan when it established the Port Authority Trans-Hudson Corporation in 1962, through which is acquired the H. and M. and began to operate the lines before the end of the year. During the succeeding decade and a half (1963–76) the Authority invested $258,000,000 in the purchase of 256 units of new rolling stock and in the massive renovation of tracks, tunnels, drainage systems, transmission and distribution equipment, signals, and communications. The nearly prostrate H. and M. was transformed into a model service, perhaps the best in metropolitan New York, but it was being operated at a deficit of $40,000,000 per annum by 1976.

The Long Island Rail Road, serving the opposite side of the metropolitan area, shared with the Central of New Jersey the distinction of being a seemingly terminal case that managed to survive, but only because of a massive rescue operation by the state. During the first forty years of the century, while the road's traffic rose steadily to the level or more than a hundred million passengers per annum, its financial condition just as steadily deteriorated. Over the 41 years between 1900 and the entry of the United States into the war the company paid dividends only seven times, and in the last decade of that period, Depression years interrupted only by the World's Fair of 1939–40, it operated its property at a nearly unbroken succession of unmanageable deficits. These troubles, of course, were accompanied by an irreversible depreciation of fixed and rolling equipment. The chief consequence of these ills, other than the officers' regular and publicly voiced complaints, was that the Long Island became a guinea pig for investigative commissions, consultants, and assorted governmental bodies. The first of these diagnosticians was the J. G. White Engineering Corporation, which conducted a thoroughgoing inquiry into the railroad's physical and financial condition during the year following 16 June 1941 and issued a report in the summer of 1942. The primary conclusions were that whereas the fares were held by state commissions at the 1918 level, state and local property taxes rose beyond the company's operating income, 83 percent of its metropolitan traffic was lost in 1931–41 to competing rapid transit, and the resulting deficits for the eight years of 1933–40 reached a total of $20,000,000. In a supplementary report issued on 15 October 1948 the White firm recommended rather drastic therapy—a reduction in property taxes, an increase in fares, subsidy, purchase, and operation by the state. The state, as a matter of fact, had already entered the picture: the New York Public Service Commission made public a report dated 10 March 1947, the chief conclusion of which everyone knew, namely, that the road's passenger cars were in too poor a condition to provide adequate service. The parent Pennsylvania Railroad at the same time made the one useful gesture when it placed in operation ten double-deck multiple-unit cars during the spring of 1947. The long-expected announcement of bankruptcy came on 2 March 1949 with the filing of a petition for reorganization under the Federal Bankruptcy Law. The obligations due at the time amounted to $55,000,000, while the cash in the bank was a useless $60,000.

At this point death struck the Long Island with a fury that finally compelled the state government to recognize the appalling consequences that might flow from the breakdown of a vital public service. At 6:28 in the evening of 22 November 1950, a rear-end collision between a standing and a moving train at Kew Gardens caused the telescoping of two cars, the last and the first in the respective trains, with the predictable result: 78 passengers were killed and 203 were injured. The subsequent investigation indicated that it was a case of the motorman operating his train with something less than the requisite caution, but the general state of the equipment, the financial burdens of the railroad, and the deteriorating service made it at least politically expedient for Governor Thomas E. Dewey to appoint a commission charged with recommending a way out of the Long Island's sea of troubles.[7] The commissioners issued a report on 20 January 1951 that proposed the usual increase in fares, reduction in taxes, relief from other obligations to the state, and operation by a transit authority which would aim, of course, at a self-sustaining financial status. Legislation passed by the General Assembly in March, 1951, spelled out these proposals in detail, and the nonprofit Long Island Transit Authority then assumed the burden of administering the railroad. The end of receivership on 12 August 1954, accompanied by the inauguration of a rehabilitation program involving the expenditure of $60,300,000, began to produce results, of which the most tangible was the installation of 219 new cars. Another commission, appointed by Governor Nelson Rockefeller in 1964, led to the authorization by the legislature of the purchase of the road from the Pennsylvania Railroad in June, 1965. The final rescue came with the acquisition of the company by the newly established transit authority in 1966, when an extensive improvement program was set in motion: new multiple-unit cars, the expansion and improvement of the power supply, the extension of electrified operations, the rebuilding of track and stations, the installation of cab signals and automatic stop, new diesel-electric locomotives, earlier grand schemes for the future that had gone unrealized—these quickly absorbed the first $360,000,000 invested in the reborn Long Island.

The decline in the metropolitan passenger traffic, the uninterrupted rise in operating costs, and the deterioration of all fixed and moving equipment soon affected the other lines terminating in the city as well as on the New Jersey shore. The curtailment of ferry service, threats of abandonments or demands for state subsidies, and the complaints of long-suffering commuters helped to open the eyes of legislative bodies to the point where they saw the necessity for drastic remedies. The first step came in 1961, when the General Assembly at Albany inaugurated the direct purchase of new cars for the suburban carriers. During the next two years 53 cars were made available to the New York Central and 30 to the Long Island. It was a very modest beginning to the all-embracing program of renewal and reorganization that could not be long postponed. In an unusual reversal of the usual order, the money to take effective action was voted before the controlling institution was created. The Assembly then appointed committees to undertake the preliminary planning in 1966, authorized the New York State Bond Issue to be launched the following year, and established the New York Metropolitan Transit Authority as of 1 January 1968 to acquire, unify, and operate the rapid transit and surface lines of the city, the suburban rail lines directly serving the city, and various airports, bridges, tunnels, and parking facilities. It was without question the most comprehensive plan ever adopted by any American municipality. The new organization, with money in the bank and considerably more on the way, acted with admirable dispatch in taking possession of its properties: all subway and elevated lines were acquired on 1 March 1968, all bus lines on that date and on 3 June 1973, all railroads offering commutation service (including the Erie's trackage lying within New York state) at varying dates between 1 March 1968 and 1 June 1973, two airports, two tunnels, four parking facilities, and seven bridges, all on 1 March 1968. Through funds derived from the bond issue of 1967, from the Urban Mass Transportation Assistance Act of the federal government (1970), and from the surplus revenues of the Triborough Bridge and Tunnel Authority, the M. T. A.

could embark on the implementation of the greatest transit renewal program ever undertaken. In the fifth year of its existence (1972) it operated on a typical weekday 8,869 trains and 80,635 bus trips, the two modes, together with vehicular facilities, carrying 7,844,600 passengers. New rolling stock comprised 1,148 suburban railroad coaches and 1,845 subway cars. It considerably outdistanced its nearest competitors in volume of traffic and equipment, namely, the comprehensive transit systems of London and Paris. The two great works of new construction, the Second Avenue Subway and the East River–63d Street Tunnel, though placed under construction in 1970, were far from complete in 1980. The improved stations, the new track and signals, and the new rolling stock were distributed among all the rail and transit lines, on which the cars replaced all existing equipment except for a few New York Central veterans of the Grand Central opening.[8]

While the new transit authority was in the process of implementing its grand design, equally monumental changes were taking place on a systemwide basis among the standard railroad companies. The marriage of the Erie and Lackawanna in 1960 turned out to be the first step in the most extensive and most concentrated program of mergers in the history of the industry. Steadily declining freight revenues that began immediately after the war, staggering deficits in the operation of passenger trains, and uncontrollable increases in expenses soon impelled the Pennsylvania and the New York Central in the same direction. These accumulating troubles were also violently underscored by a series of accidents that reached a devasting climax early in 1951. On 6 February of that year a suburban train operated by the Pennsylvania and destined for Bay Head on the New York and Long Branch Railroad was derailed when a temporary timber trestle at Woodbridge collapsed under the moving load. The consequent pyramiding of cars took 83 lives and left another 330 injured. The official records were scarcely filed away when the Pennsylvania's Red Arrow plowed into the Philadelphia Night Express at Bryn Mawr, leaving 8 dead and 63 injured. The Central was spared these catastrophes, but physical and moral deterioration appeared to be spreading everywhere like a wasting disease, and the drastic pruning of affected parts was regarded as a necessity.

The respective presidents of the two roads, James M. Symes and Alfred E. Perlman, began to study the possibilities of merging the two giants in 1957 and made the first public announcement to that effect on 11 November. These discussions were canceled in January, 1959, chiefly because the Central's officers regarded the company as financially viable with suitable infusions of capital and curtailments of service, whereas they and other interested parties were beginning to see that the Pennsylvania was approaching desperate straits. Another complicating factor entered the Interstate Commerce Commission's view of the issue in July, 1961, when the mortally sick New Haven filed another petition of bankruptcy and became still another candidate for intensive therapy. Negotiations between the two larger companies were resumed in November and led to a specific commitment to merge in 1963, but the slow-moving Commerce Commission did not give its official sanction until 12 August 1966. More than a year of planning, objections from concerned roads (mainly the Delaware and Hudson, the Erie-Lackawanna, and the newly enlarged Norfolk and Western), the intervention of the Department of Justice, and court decisions had to pass before the final unification of the two behemoths could be effected in January, 1968. Exactly one year later the unwanted New Haven and the Central's lessor, the Boston and Albany, were included in the new corporation, officially designated as the Penn Central Railroad Company. With the passage of another year the original Pennsylvania Railroad filed a petition to reorganize under the federal bankruptcy laws and in the process gave the world an apppalling revelation of how a once great railroad system had collapsed into the state of a terminal disease. Gross managerial errors, based on the naive belief that the road still preserved the unassailable pre-eminence it enjoyed through the war years, motive power and rolling stock in need of major repairs if they were operable at all, track unable in many places to support a train, stations crumbling away, burned-out signal lights, most steel surfaces covered with rust, the surviving *esprit de corps* disappearing—it was a frightening picture of concentrated railroad pathology, and only the rescue by the federal government restored some useful life to this mutilated dinosaur.

That rescue came in two stages, national and regional. The accelerating erosion of passenger traffic, accompanied by proportionately rising deficits, finally persuaded the railroad officers that passenger service, in their view, had become a useless anachronism, and they openly proclaimed at least the hope, if not the intention, of wholesale abandonment. By the mid-sixties the question whether they would take such a step was becoming academic, since rolling stock was close to the point where it could no longer be used with safety. The prospect of the world's leading industrial power losing its through rail passenger service was not one that the government could take lightly, and the long overdue salvation came at the last minute before a progressive breakdown of operations. On 1 May 1971 the National Railroad Passenger Corporation, having been properly authorized by the Congress, acquired the locomotives, cars, and fixed equipment that composed the passenger-carrying plant of the nation's railroads.[9] After the pruning of more than half the existing passenger route mileage, the remaining system stood as a peculiar hybrid, in which the federal government in effect owned the appropriate moving equipment but operated it on privately owned rights of way and contracted with the owners for the maintenance of motive power and rolling stock. It was a makeshift of divided responsibility that was guaranteed to cause trouble, and the new corporation, given the public-relations name of Amtrak, was finally compelled to assume the burdens of repairing and maintaining as well as operating the trains.

Within a few years the new organization began to introduce extensive improvements in the primary lines serving New York, although the nucleus of this progress had actually taken shape under the Penn Central aegis. In January, 1969, the road placed in service between New York and Washington a number of high-speed multiple-unit trains known as Metroliners, which were designed for a maximum speed of 150 miles per hour. Initial operations at speeds up to 125 miles per hour made it clear that an overworked rail line carrying every conceivable form of traffic could not be called on to accommodate speeds 67 percent above the highest previous level. The Amtrak officers decided that the primary line of the Northeast Corridor, that lying between Boston and Washington, should be appropriately upgraded, and in 1972 they engaged the Pan-Technology Consulting Corporation to investigate the problems involved in such renovation and to recommend the necessary improvements. In a report issued in April of the following year the consulting firm spelled out in detail the extensive alterations to right of way, track, signals, stations, yards, shops, and electrical system essential to the safe and reliable operation of trains at the planned speeds. The estimated cost of this immense program was at the time $550,000,000. Amtrak depended on the federal Department of Transportation for the funds to implement the plan, and the first steps in the process did not come until 1976. On 11 February the national corporation acquired all of the Pennsylvania Railroad's terminal facilities at New York and Newark, and in the following summer it initiated the purchase of the property and physical plant of the entire Northeast Corridor, which includes the Philadelphia-Harrisburg line of the Pennsylvania as well as the primary trunk between Boston and Washington. The asking price was a modest $87,000,000, and William T. Coleman, the Secretary of Transportation, made immediately available $30,300,000 as a down payment. Before the end of the year Amtrak embarked on preparation of final plans for implementing the Pan-Technology report, but by this date the estimated cost had risen to $1,600,000,000. The modernization of the Corridor line involved the rebuilding of virtually all fixed equipment over the 456 miles between Boston and Washington, which comprised 1,075 track miles, during the years of 1977 to 1981, but by the end of 1979 this proposed timetable proved to be optimistic, and completion was not expected to be achieved until 1983. Meanwhile, uncontrolled inflation exacted its escalating toll, so that the most recent estimate of cost (1978) reached $1,820,000,000, of which $498,000,000 was reserved for track renewal alone.[10]

The presence of a national railroad passenger system and the mergers and abandonments of 1957–68, which left two railroad companies where once there had been six, failed to solve the problems that had called forth these developments in the first place. A far more pervasive restructuring of the eastern rail network was essential, and the major phase of the reorganization again required the intervention of the federal government on an unprecedented scale. The so-called anthracite carriers suffered in varying degrees from the same afflictions that marked the big trunk-line railroads, and the fate of the Pennsylvania made it clear by 1970 that none of the intermediate roads could count on continued solvency. One of them, the C. N. J., was a hopeless case, and the loss of tonnage among the rest, as we have seen, placed them in a marginal category at best. Their requirements for capital funds were so great and the possibility of raising them in the usual financial markets so unlikely, that the national government could be the only source. Accordingly, the Congress passed the Regional Rail Reorganization Act in 1973, under the authority of which it established the United States Railway Association as of 1 January 1974. This body was charged with the responsibility for creating an immense, unified, multiregional system consisting originally of the Penn Central, the Erie-Lackawanna, the C. N. J., the Lehigh Valley, the Reading, the Ann Arbor, and the Lehigh and Hudson River railroads, directing the rehabilitation of these properties, estimating the capital necessary to produce a viable and profitable system, and disbursing the funds made available by the Congress. The specific entity formed from the merger of the six companies was designated the Consolidated Rail Corporation; it acquired title to the constituent roads on 1 April 1976, and commenced the herculean task of trying to operate their badly deteriorated properties on the same date. Con Rail, as it conveniently called itself after the manner of a long-established railroad tradition, comprised rail systems with an aggregate length of 23,000 miles, but separations (mainly the Ann Arbor) and reckless abandonments quickly reduced it to 17,000 miles. Even in its truncated form the giant stood in first place among American carriers: route mileage equalled 8.9 percent of the national total; on the average during the first three calendar years of operation it carried 21.8 percent of the tonnage, and the region that it served included 45 percent of the country's population and 55 percent of its manufacturing plant.

The original plan of the Railway Association, had it been implemented, would have been more advantageous to the Port of New York than the final much weakened compromise. The establishment of Con Rail left the Eastern-Pocahontas district essentially dependent on three huge rail systems, the new company, the C. and O./B. and O. group (conveniently known by the public-relations name of Chessie System), and the Norfolk and Western.[11] The port was to be provided with competitive rail service, which it does not now enjoy, by the device of parceling pieces of the Reading and the Erie-Lackawanna to the two southern roads, thus enabling them to operate directly into the harbor area. The intransigence of railroad management and railroad labor, however, produced a perfect impasse: the N. and W. was unwilling to extend its lines north of its present upper limit of Hagerstown, Maryland, while the C. and O. and the rail unions could not reach the agreements mandated by the reorganization act. The latter failure, however, was in part offset by the presence of the B. and O.'s Staten Island branch. Genuine national control could have circumvented these obstacles, but the concerned parties rejected this alternative for two reasons: first, because it would not reduce costs (although no other approach has shown that it can achieve this end); and second, because it was likely to lead to public pressure for the retention of "unprofitable" service. An enlightened energy policy, however, would have placed such retention at the top of its priorities; we will pursue the question further in the final section of this chapter. Con Rail, of course, was required to satisfy the ruling dogma of economic theology by eventually earning a profit, even though no transportation mode in existence shows a net income from its operations without massive government subsidies.[12]

The question whether the establishment of Con Rail brought any benefits to the Port of New York, or whether it brought only losses, will very likely continue to be controversial until the adoption of an enlightened transportation policy by the federal government, but in 1979 this event seemed about as remote as the Second Coming. It is true that the creation of a workable railroad system in place of a heterogeneous collection of crippled insolvents might very well have saved the port from a paralysis worse than the one it had experienced during the First World War. And it is also true that the progressive loss of carfloat and lighterage service was a consequence of economic and technical changes partly beyond the control of the railroads and the city. The spread of containerization, the replacement of rail by highway transportation for short-haul shipments, and the abandonment of the increasingly cumbersome and costly water transfers for the movement of tonnage through the port—all these developments would have occurred no matter how well the revised rail network had been planned. Lighters and carfloats were operated exclusively by the Brooklyn Eastern District Terminal Railroad and the New York Dock Railway when Con Rail was established on 1 April 1976, at which date all free lighterage service was ended, and the water routes were restricted to those between Brooklyn, the B. and O.'s Saint George terminal on Staten Island, and Greenville Piers. Free carfloat service was retained by the Brooklyn terminal company, but its limits within the harbor were much reduced from the former widely ramified network—or tangle—of routes (figs. 32, 33). The all-rail routes for moving freight through or around the New York terminal district between New England and the regions to the west proved to be far from satisfactory substitutes even for the traditional water transfer. The chief alternative adopted by the railroads is the movement of through shipments over the circuitous route via the West Shore, Selkirk Yard, and Mechanicville, New York, but this solution has serious defects—namely, the rail isolation of New York Harbor and southern New England, and the concomitant surrender of both to the costly and inefficient truck transportation. The shorter rail route via Poughkeepsie Bridge, though it offers a certain geographical advantage, was a questionable alternative because of substandard trackage in secondary main lines and the absence of adequate yard facilities. Damage by fire and *de facto* abandonment have turned the great landmark into a derelict. Moreover, all existing rail routes through New York City (those of the former New York Central, New Haven, and Long Island railroads) are marked by antiquated clearance restrictions that prevent them from carrying trailers on flat cars, three-level automobile cars, and high-capacity box and hopper cars through the metropolitan area or over routes to the north thereof.

If the movement of rail freight through the harbor area is to be revived, it must be predicated on extensive alterations and new constructions. First and simplest is the removal of all obstructions to full clearance within the metropolitan area and between that area and Castleton Cut-Off (that is, over the former Hudson and River divisions of the New York Central). Second is a tunnel or a fleet of carfloats connecting an appropriate terminal on the New Jersey side of the harbor with its counterpart on Long Island. The plan that the Pennsylvania Railroad formulated at the turn of the century should have been adopted long ago, but if such an artery is to be placed in service, it obviously must be built to dimensions adequate for modern high-clearance traffic. Such a tunnel would offer several valuable advantages: the direct transportation by rail of containers moving between the Brooklyn docks and the New Jersey connections; the movement of all freight to and from western, New York Harbor, and New England terminals by rail rather than by the more expensive, less efficient, and more polluting trucks; the avoidance of a break in the transshipment process of ship-truck-rail if the container is moved locally by truck and over the long haul by rail; the reduction of the area given over to truck driveways, since the long existing rail lines will carry the traffic; the end of the rail isolation of lower New

England; and finally, a slower rate of wear in the vehicular tunnels. An alternative to the rail tunnel, which would substantially accomplish the same ends, is the less costly self-propelled carfloat, built to a size sufficient to convey an entire train across the harbor in a single crossing. Such a vessel is technologically feasible, but its adoption would require the construction of greatly enlarged float bridges and appurtenant facilities.

The program that was adopted by Con Rail, however, carried with it serious weaknesses that more than offset its few advantages. The existence of only one railroad company to serve the immense terminal system of the port not only meant the absence of competition that presumably might have stimulated improvements in service; it also carried a greater threat—namely, that no rail organization was left that had a stake in expanding the harbor traffic and maintaining its economic vitality. It was widely believed among officers of the Port Authority and various commissioners concerned with the port economy that Con Rail was chiefly designed to perform a rescue operation for the Penn Central Company, as that organization was designed in turn to salvage the Pennsylvania Railroad, which was oriented toward Philadelphia and felt no strong ties to New York. Moreover, the Authority claimed that this bias was reflected in the adoption by Con Rail of discriminating rates that favored the ports of Baltimore and Philadelphia over that of New York. Such controversies eventually reached the state of inconclusive judgments in the courts. Perhaps the greatest failure of the Con Rail program, on final assessment, was the reckless destruction of lightly used branches and secondary main lines (and in at least one case, a primary main line). The great multitude of manufacturing centers scattered throughout New England, New York state, and Pennsylvania formed the basis of a flourishing economy that was at once dependent on and tributary to the Port of New York. The grotesque distortions in the industrial pattern of the nation and the extreme inequalities in the distribution of federal largesse, coupled with the decline of rail service and the attendant escalating costs of transportation, guaranteed that the vicious cycle of flight and loss would perpetuate itself in the modest towns as well as the largest cities. The dilemma was expressed very well by Milton Shapp, the governor of Pennsylvania, at hearings conducted by the Department of Transportation in Chicago on 19 January 1978.

> Many of the major economic dislocations in Pennsylvania and throughout the Northeast-Midwest were worsened by the creation of Con Rail in 1976 with its emphasis upon contraction rather than improvement of service. . . .The merger of these so-called "duplicate" rail lines has cut competition and cut service to the point where transportation costs are actually driving industry out of our state and out of our region.[13]

The Port Authority, having long ago shown its enthusiasm for highway transportation, felt that its prejudice was abundantly confirmed by the endemic bad judgment and short-sightedness that survived through all the planning behind the Con Rail system. Viewed in an international perspective and in strictly quantitative terms, however, the Port of New York quickly reached pre-eminence in the shipment of containers, its total volume running 50 percent above that of Rotterdam, the first port in the world.

The Grand Central Air-Rights Development

The enormous alterations in the corporate and physical structures and in the operations of the New York railroads must inevitably have left their mark on the expensive, heavily taxed, and admittedly unremunerative New York terminals. They constituted a genuine gift to the city and to the people, but the officers of the floundering railroads soon found opportunities to treat their great accomplishments with a contempt worthy of the most hardened philistine. The civic and architectural values were revealed day after day, and the simple quantitative record underscored their importance. At the conclusion of military action in 1945 Grand Central accommodated 180,000 passengers per weekday, conveyed them into and out of the station in 600 trains, and as a microcity of major dimensions, played host to an additional 370,000 citizens who passed through the head house on their way to other destinations, many stopping at bars, restaurants, or shops along the way. This normal day's traffic of more than half a million customers and visitors was swelled by another hundred thousand or more on the day immediately preceding or following a major holiday. On the Wednesday before the Thanksgiving holiday of 1945, for example, the terminal reached a near-record when 240,078 passengers walked or ran through the gates, and possibly double that number came in to shop or to enjoy a cocktail. The total was second only to the historic high point of 252,288 passengers who used the terminal on 3 July 1947. But it did cost a shocking sum of money—about $24,000,000 per annum over and above the modest rentals by the mid-fifties—and the officers of the railroad initiated an increasingly desperate search for ways to stop the drain. The first plan emerged from the fertile and erratic mind of the Central's chairman, Robert R. Young, who in September, 1954, engaged the imperial real estate firm of Webb and Knapp to plan a gigantic tower to be erected over the terminal area.[14] These grandiose unmakers of cities proposed to demolish all the terminal facilities down to grade level and to erect a skyscraper with a floor area of

5,000,000 square feet (the largest in the world, Young was anxious to proclaim) over the entire area bounded by 42d and 45th streets, Vanderbilt Avenue, and Depew Place. As a concession to urban circulation, Park Avenue was to be extended through the building on a direct line. Two weeks after the first scheme was launched Patrick B. McGinnis, the president of the New Haven Railroad, and Fellheimer and Wagner, the leading architects of railroad stations during the last years of their construction, improved on Young's brainchild. They proposed restoring all cross-town streets as well as keeping Park Avenue on a straight line and putting up a 50-story building embracing a maximum of 6,000,000 square feet of floor area, including a 2,400-car parking garage. Hang the expense, they might have said: the cost was estimated at $100,000,000 (around $360,000,000 at the 1980 building-cost level), but it was expected to yield a rental high enough to cover the Grand Central's $24,000,000 deficit.

The reactions to the railroad's plan were a revelation of attitudes toward the city on the part of those who had some commitment to genuine civic values, spiritual or economic. A quickly assembled, informal group of 220 architects wrote an open letter to the editor of *Architectural Forum* presenting excellent arguments as to why the plan was destructive barbarism.

> The Grand Central Concourse is perhaps the finest big room in New York. It belongs in fact to the nation. People admire it as travel carries them through from all parts of the world. It is . . . . one of those very few building achievements that . . . . has come to stand for our country. This great room is noble in its proportions, alive in the way the various levels and its passages work in and out of it, sturdy and reassuring in its construction, splendid in its materials—but that is just the beginning. Its appeal recognizes no top limit of sophistication, no bottom limit. The most exacting architectural critic agrees in essentials with the newsboy at the door. . . . Masterpieces of architecture are no easier to replace than masterpieces of music. . . . To throw away a known masterpiece of architecture, tested and loved; to remove an important link between the city and its history; to grow careless with the evidence of past greatness, would be an adventure attended with great risk.[15]

A bitter and expanding controversy had begun, and Alfred Fellheimer, who as an associate of Reed and Stem had participated in the design of the terminal, added his comments, and most surprisingly, he sided with the railroad company in sacrificing his own handiwork. He and his partner Stewart Wagner, had already offered their own plan (September, 1954) for rebuilding the terminal and its associated street pattern, of which the latter seemed to them more important than the building.

> Congestion in and around the station, pedestrian as well as vehicular, is now as bad as anywhere in the city. And it is steadily getting worse. This is a matter of direct public interest, quite apart from the financial burden upon the railroads. . . . Our own studies were based . . . on the necessity of workable traffic patterns. These proposals include new street extensions, at different levels to minimize crossings; new facilities for rerouting bus and truck movements; removal of the major part of station-induced taxicab traffic from 42nd St. and Vanderbilt Ave.; restoration of the one-way street pattern; a major parking garage with multiple-ramp access from several streets; direct northward outlets for commuters to avoid backtracking toward 42nd St.; a roof plaza, restaurant and shopping center at the first setback level to keep tens of thousands of building occupants off the congested streets.
>
> We carefully weighed our pride in the present building, and its emotional and aesthetic significance to people all over the world. Our reluctant but firm conclusion is that neither pride nor reverence should be permitted to clot the vitality of a great metropolis.[16]

Fellheimer compelled attention, as his major creations demonstrated, but his plan missed the essential end, which was to improve the local circulation *and* preserve the terminal head house. The next plan for new construction on the terminal air rights was the first aimed at satisfying the owner's demand for rental property while keeping the terminal building intact. Offered by Richard Roth of the firm of Emery Roth and Sons in January, 1955, he proposed the construction of a 65-story office tower over that part of the station trackage lying entirely north of the head house, between 43d and 45th streets. All existing structures within the area were to be demolished above the grade level. The Roth skyscraper would thus have stood between the head house and the existing New York Central Building facing the northward length of Park Avenue. No architects attacked the Roth plan, in spite of the fact that it would have planted an extremely high tower directly behind an existing skyscraper in an area already overloaded with such structures and their associated traffic. As we shall note in the appropriate place, this is exactly what the developers and their architectural sycophants gave the city before another decade was to pass. One architectural office, however, was aware of the fact that there was railroad trackage threaded through Manhattan and The Bronx where large-scale construction could be introduced to improve rather than to destroy the immediate environment. In May, 1955, the architects Powers and Kessler proposed a complex of office buildings, shopping center, and parking space over the New York Central's coach yard at Mott Haven. The plan suffered the fate of most good ideas in the urban milieu: it quickly died. At the same time the railroad, suddenly confronted with the declaration from the city and the state of a fourfold increase in the taxable valuation of Grand Central Terminal because of potential air-rights construction, threatened to abandon the building in favor of a new station at 138th Street. But the barbarians were at the gates, and there was nothing that could stop them. It was time that the voice of philosophy at least spoke, whether anyone listened or not, and of course it was Lewis Mumford who was prepared once more to instruct the unteachable.

> By [1955] both [New York]stations need a thorough house cleaning, and Grand Central, with its tremendous litter of booths and advertisements, needs a visit from the junk man too. But they still retain some of the essentials of great architecture. . . . A scheme has been devised . . . to keep the concourse of the terminal and replace the rest of it with a sixty-story building. . . . Because of the heavy load of human beings that throngs the midtown area, which is itself the product of planned congestion, the Grand Central concourse has become, in addition to its proper function, a secondary traffic artery. . . . To pile twenty or thirty thousand more people in offices on top of the present facilities, to say nothing of the thousands of visitors to those offices, would make the station's daily pedestrian load what it is now only on certain frazzling national holidays. In addition, the secondary traffic needed to serve all those extra people . . . would so choke the streets around Grand Central that travelers reaching it by car or taxi would undergo more anxiety and miss far more trains than they do today. . . .
>
> Constructing facilities that can only partly relieve the congestion already created will cost the city many times the increase of tax revenue from the new skyscrapers that will augment that congestion. Not only that, but the delay and lost motion in street transportation is costing the community hundreds of millions of dollars a year and steadily driving business to the suburbs. (As far back as 1931 the Russell Sage Regional Plan calculated that this loss came to $500,000 a day in New York alone and to $1,000,000 a day in the metropolitan area. These figures would now have to be multiplied again and again.). . . . What [the railroads] propose as civic improvement is in fact a final debasement, and what they propose as profitable enterprise to make use of what they consider wasted air space will hasten the general metropolitan debacle whose symptoms are already obvious. . . .
>
> Even if midtown business building were to halt for a dozen years . . . that would hardly give time enough to relieve the congestion that already exists. As for most of the plans for improving the situation, they seem to be the product of sleepwalkers who have never observed the city by day. It would take a great mind indeed to decide which lot of planners is more irrational—the people who are piling up high structures in the overcrowded business districts of their cities, or the people who are creating cross-country expressways that dump more traffic into them. . . .

> Ever since the nineteen-twenties the municipal and state authorities have been plunging blindly from one grandiose traffic scheme to another without showing any striking understanding of the problems they were trying to solve. Traffic specialists take it for granted that the aim of good traffic planning is to give the maximum accessibility and the minimum facilities for movement by wheeled vehicles. But the aim of sound city planning is to achieve a healthy balance between the myriad activities of a community; it does not assume that private transportation has a prior claim on every resource of the community or that it is quite all right to make the city less and less habitable as long as enough roads are built to permit people to escape by car once a week—only to crawl back worn and defeated Sunday evening. . . .
>
> To cure our creeping paralysis, our community has committed its destiny to empiricists (alias specialists and experts) who have little insight into the needs of the modern city. Situations that were foreseen and correctly diagnosed a generation ago by a few perspicacious planners . . . have become too acute for any simple set of remedies and too complicated to be treated without first defining a sound common objective that will guide each operation from one critical step to the next and link them all together in a new urban pattern.[17]

The destructive rage had exploded, however, before Mumford's admirable diagnosis was published. The demolition of existing buildings within the bounds of the Grand Central air-rights precinct began in 1952, and in the succeeding years to 1979 a total of 15 hotels, apartment and office buildings went down, all of them architectural works standing at the highest levels of design and construction, all of them together, with the terminal, constituting one of the most urbane groups of commercial buildings in the world (fig. 47). The first of the upended glass boxes to take their place was the 53-story Union Carbide Building, designed by the office of Skidmore, Owings and Merrill and erected in 1957–60 over the double-track level in the block bounded by Madison and Park avenues and 47th and 48th streets. The elegant apartment building known as The Marguery went down to make way for the Union Carbide giant. On 11 May 1977 the directors of the company decided to move its headquarters to Danbury, Connecticut, where their architects planned office space for 4,000 employees. The first corporation to disfigure Park Avenue thus became the first of the new air-rights builders to desert the city, where the unlimited construction of office skyscrapers was believed to bring unlimited prosperity. There was no want of new tenants, however, and the planning of the Carbide building whetted the appetite of the railroad company for more of the same. Acting through a subsidiary, the New York State Realty and Terminal Company, the officers announced on 5 May 1958 their intention to erect a 50-story office building over that portion of the terminal complex immediately north of the head house. Designed by Emery Roth and Sons, with building to be carried out by the Diesel Construction Company, the tower was to embrace 3,000,000 square feet of floor area and was expected to yield an annual rental of $1,000,000 to the New York Central Railroad. The original name of this monstrosity was Grand Central City, but it was soon changed to the Pan American Building, when the airline signed the lease to become the largest tenant (fig. 48). Detailed planning in 1959–60 brought alterations: Walter Gropius and Pietro Belluschi were invited to act as consultants to the architects; the height was raised to 55 stories and the floor area reduced to 2,400,000 square feet. The building was opened to occupancy in the spring of 1963 to stand as one of the supreme acts of folly in the history of the city's real estate operations. The presence of Gropius as a consultant provided sufficient evidence that the wholesale application of Bauhaus dogmas to urban design would have turned New York into an architectural and circulatory nightmare.

At the same time that the Pan American Building was placed under construction, the railroad company proposed to vandalize the concourse of Grand Central Terminal still further by installing bowling alleys at some appropriate place in the enclosure, where presumably they would offer minimal obstruction to moving crowds. The owners had already turned the concourse into a billboard jungle, and the new desecrations without and within called forth the most penetrating comment from the architectural editor Douglas Haskell.

> No doubt the progressive cannibalization that has been going on in the great concourse ever since the . . . room was saved in 1954, filling its once magnificent space with signs, turntables, land-boom selling booths, oversized clocks, and other gimmicks to turn a quick buck, is all meant to offset declining "railroad" revenues because the owners are railroads.
>
> But the real fact would seem to be that the Grand Central Station from the beginning was far less of a railroading operation than a real estate operation. The New York Central system holds . . . a big chunk of land on which it and its close associates or subsidiaries own outright three major hotels and two office buildings, and are now erecting a tower of 2.4 million square feet for perhaps 15,000 occupants . . . which they proclaim the biggest office building in the world. They also have under ground lease four major hotels including the Waldorf-Astoria, and 11 existing office buildings including Union Carbide, and two projected office buildings to replace existing apartment buildings. From the very beginning the terminal was built "grand" as the real estate magnet, the focus, the drawing card, the lobby, so to speak, for all this highly profitable realty flanking it. . . .
>
> If the railroad people had better than pygmy imagination today about their real

Fig. 47. Street plan showing property owned by the New York Central and the New York and Harlem railroads and buildings constructed on railroad air rights along Madison, Vanderbilt, Park, and Lexington avenues from 42d to 59th Street, as of June, 1971.

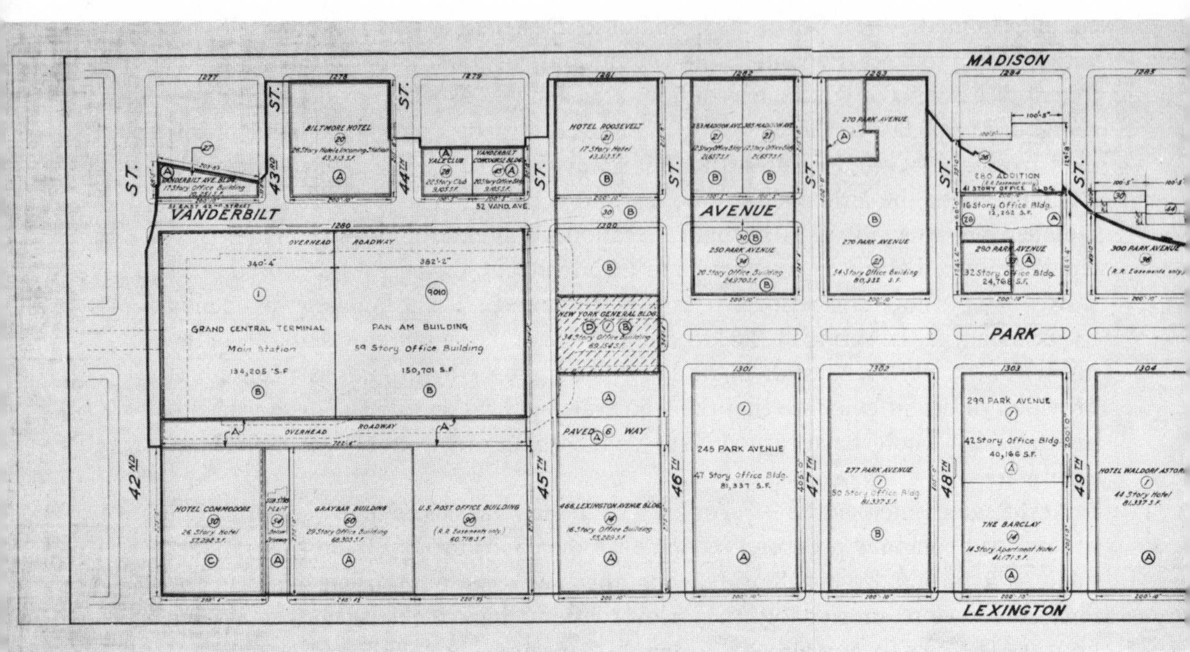

47

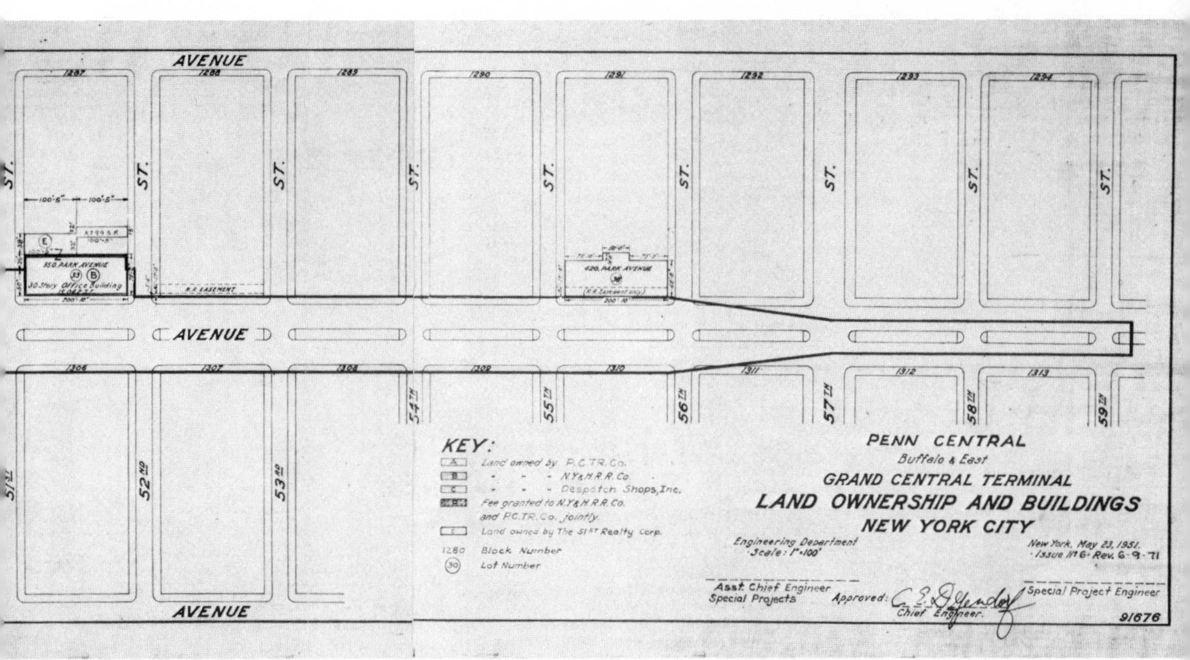
AVENUE
1287
1288
1289
1290
1291
1292
1293
1294
ST.
350 PARK AVENUE
30 Story Office Building
R.R. EASEMENT
420 PARK AVENUE
AVENUE
1306
1307
1308
1309
1310
1311
1312
1313
51ST
52ND
53RD
54TH
55TH
56TH
57TH
58TH
59TH
AVENUE
KEY:
Land owned by P.C.TR.Co.
" " " N.Y.&H.R.R.Co.
" " " Despatch Shops, Inc.
Fee granted to N.Y.&H.R.R.Co. and P.C.TR.Co. jointly.
Land owned by The 51ST Realty Corp.
1280 Block Number
30 Lot Number
PENN CENTRAL
Buffalo & East
GRAND CENTRAL TERMINAL
LAND OWNERSHIP AND BUILDINGS
NEW YORK CITY
Engineering Department
Scale: 1"=100'
New York, May 23, 1951.
Issue No 6 - Rev. 6-9-71
Asst. Chief Engineer
Special Projects
Approved:
Chief Engineer.
Special Project Engineer
91676

Fig. 48. Grand Central Terminal and the Pan American Building, 1964.

48

estate they would foresee that adding another 15,000 people plus those who do business with them will cause rocketing congestion and that the new . . . building will need every inch of breathing space that the terminal next door can provide. If the owners don't think of it that way, the city must; and the city should emphatically veto any added . . . clutter and congestion.

What so-called practical men such as these railroaders rarely grasp is the immense business value of great empty space as such. A wonderful environment . . . draws to it all healthy, normal, dignified people striving to spend their short time on earth as complete human beings. . . . If the railroads . . . got over their present attitude toward the public they might learn some things about getting more favorable attention for their very real railroading problems.[18]

When the Pan American skyscraper opened its doors in 1963 Douglas Haskell was again ready to enlighten the builders with a briefly sketched vision of what might have been done, but by this date he and Lewis Mumford seemed increasingly like Jeremiah crying out unheeded in his prison.

Under the older spirit of New York [the need for new air-rights construction] would have been the signal for a grand new push, which would have used the newest techniques to create an unprecedented kind of new urban precinct. . . . Conceivably the whole of Grand Central City would have been linked together along Park Avenue, above street level . . . . so as to become in effect an eight- or ten-block skyscraper laid on its side with the cross streets passing through it or under it, and with micro-transport available in a jiffy . . . to pull dozens of hotels, office buildings, clubs, theaters, and who knows what else into one swiftly, conveniently navigable micro-city. This could have been the first step beyond the Rockefeller Center concept, for here, in a crucially important area adequate land was already assembled. . . .

None of these, nor any other, possibilities for solving New York's congestion and its transportation together in the old-fashioned way, were realized, however; and instead of that the Central hired a real estate butcher to cut up its magnificent Grand Central City like a carcass. Piece by piece, individual lots were sold for individual office buildings, mostly cheap ones. In the end the choice piece of all . . . was let out to Erwin S. Wolfson, to see what he could do with it as a speculative builder. And Wolfson built Pan Am. . . .

What with New York's present leadership so nearly lost . . . . the call is for a younger generation. If these cannot swing it, New York will have proved itself too big for anything but herd and headless actions. And then things will be really tough for architecture, the art whose essential message is that man was not born to be defeated.

Great architecture rides on great ideas.[19]

Pleased by the rents that flowed into the treasury from the Pan American Building, the officers of the railroad saw no reason why a second skyscraper should not be built on the site of the head house, and they announced their intention to proceed with the plan in the fall of 1967. In the previous year, however, the New York Landmarks Commission declared the remaining terminal building an official landmark of the city, with the consequence that the head house, at least, would be spared if the courts upheld the declaration. Any further construction, then, would have to be carried out entirely above the existing station. The impossibility of creating a unified work out of this piggyback arrangement did not deter the developers and their architectural collaborators, and in the summer of 1968 Marcel Breuer proposed a 55-story tower to stand directly above the head house, of which only the facade and the concourse would remain. This deformed thing was widely and justly attacked, and the Landmarks Commission refused in 1969 to allow its construction. The commissioners' argument was simple but unassailable: "Grand Central is one of the great buildings of America. . . . a building overpowering in its grandeur, [which] has always been a symbol of the city itself.[20] The railroad then went to the courts to secure what it claimed to be its rights, starting what turned out to be nearly ten years of litigation. Irving H. Saypol, presiding judge in the State Supreme Court for New York County, ruled in February, 1975, that the designation of landmark status was invalid because it deprived the railroad company of the income it would rightfully earn from the proposed office building. The Appellate Division of the State Supreme Court, with Justice Francis Murphy writing the opinion of the majority, reversed Judge Saypol's decision on 16 December, holding that the terminal is legally and in fact a landmark, and enjoined the company from erecting the proposed skyscraper. Justice Murphy argued that such buildings as Grand Central "are important and irreplaceable components of the special uniqueness of New York City. Stripped of its remaining historically unique structures, New York City would be undistinguishable from any other large metropolis."[21] The railroad company exhibited what in other circumstances might be considered an admirable tenacity: it carried its case to the Court of Appeals of New York State, where it suffered another adverse decision, and finally to the United States Supreme Court, which settled the issue once and for all at the end of June, 1978. In upholding the city's position, the Court argued that "the preservation of landmarks benefits all New York citizens and all structures both economically and by improving the quality of life in the city as a whole."[22] But the protection of Grand Central offered no mandate to save a landmark train, and more than ten years before the final decision, in mid-December, 1967, the Twentieth Century Limited was discontinued after 65½ years of almost uninterrupted daily service. It was clear that an age of civilized travel was passing. Nor could the courts protect the hotels that flank the station head house. The last act of destruction within the air-rights precinct was the plan, launched in the spring of 1976, to transform the Commodore Hotel on Lexington Avenue into another box of mirror glass, its design (if that is the word) chiefly in the hands of the architectural office of Gruzen and Partners. This most recent example of replacing excellence with vacuity was well under way in 1980.

However great the decline in through rail travel, the importance of Grand Central Terminal as the focal element in an urban circulatory nexus of unparalleled size remains undiminished. Although the station is owned by Con Rail, it is operated under lease by the New York Metropolitan Transit Authority, the National Railroad Passenger Corporation, and the Connecticut Department of Transportation. Power for the station and the electrical operation of trains is generated by the Consolidated Edison Company, which uses the original generating plants of the New York Central at Yonkers and Port Morris and their associated substations for the conversion of the alternating transmission current to the 660-volt direct current in the third rail. Throughout 1976 the three rail companies together operated 447 weekday trains to transport 145,000 daily passengers, but the latter total is swelled by an estimated additional 355,000 people who use the station for one purpose or another in the course of their daily routines. The continuing role of the head house as a microcity may be gauged from the fact that in addition to the public services that it has always provided, the building houses a total of 95 definable shops, restaurants, and other facilities, if we may include in this census the bootblacks and the group of former ticket windows now used for the city's off-track betting service. The operation of trains within the terminal limits has changed during recent years in two respects. The New York Central's electric locomotives have been retired, and the through trains of Amtrak are hauled by diesel-electric machines equipped with contact shoes so that they can draw current for the traction motors directly from the third rail (the New Haven had introduced this technique in 1957). At the same time the New York Central's coach yard in Mott Haven was abandoned, and the rolling stock for the Amtrak trains is serviced in the station yard. In 1979 the immense subgrade track system comprised 188 numbered tracks, of which numbers 1 to 42 on the through-train or express level and numbers 101 to 117 on the suburban level are platform tracks for the accommodation of passengers. The remainder are reserved for the storage and servicing of motive power as well as rolling equipment. Although Con Rail has been criticized by commuters for its conduct of suburban rail service, the intricate signaling and interlocking system works to the same standards of excellence that obtained when when the terminal was opened in 1913. Except for the rescue of the building itself, every addition to the air-rights precinct has been a blunder, leaving permanent damage to the urban fabric and its architectural character. The only development by big-time real estate operators that shows a little promise for the city emerged in 1975, when the Trump Enterprises purchased 144 acres of unused yards in the largely derelict West Side line for a residential, office, maritime, and industrial complex. It might bring some life to a long neglected area.

The End of the Pennsylvania Station Building

Although the Pennsylvania Railroad experimented after the war with various innovations in steam and electric motive power, of which only the new electric locomotives equipped with mercury-arc rectifiers survived the diesel onslaught, the deterioration of the entire enterprise guaranteed that the road would explore every avenue for developing the air rights over its extensive New York properties.[23] The first step came in December, 1954, when James W. Symes and William Zeckendorf, respectively president of the railroad and the real estate development firm of Webb and Knapp, entered into preliminary negotiations aimed at replacing the Pennsylvania Station building with a complex of rental structures. As discussions continued, plans rapidly escalated into grandiose schemes. The two-block area occupied by the station was to be cleared and on its site the railroad company planned to erect the world's largest structure, a $100,000,000 building to house an international trade center and a permanent world's fair. For its better than a quarter-of-a-million daily passengers the road was willing to spend $13,000,000 on a subgrade station that would exhibit "the most modern decor" and offer the greatest "convenience, comfort and efficiency in the world. . . . The new terminal, with the structure of Mr. Zeckendorf's tremendous conception above it, will become, I am sure, the cornerstone for the whole development of the midtown west side area."[24] All this strongly implied fantasies of a pathological character and suggested that the worst fate was in store for the station and the innocent air above it. A few years had to pass before the firm outline was discernible: in 1960 the railroad and the Graham-Paige Corporation established the Madison Square Garden Center Company to construct a complex originally intended to include an office building, a sports arena, and a hotel, but the last was soon dropped. The company at first engaged the firm of Charles Luckman Associates (later to be replaced by the ubiquitous Emery Roth and Sons), who completed their plans in 1961–62, and it then revealed that it at least preserved the letter of democracy by announcing that public hearings would be held on the demolition of the station in December, 1962. The gesture struck some as disingenuous, in view of the fact that the Pennsylvania Railroad had awarded a contract to the Turner Construction Company in June, 1962, for the construction of the Madison Square complex.

The masterpiece from the hands of McKim, Mead and White did not fall without angry protests. An organization known as the Action Group for Better Architecture in New York was founded, chiefly under the leadership of the architect Norval White, to picket, to protest the demolition, and to gain public support for the preservation of the building. The group, which included such leaders of the new architectural currents as Victor Gruen, John Johansen, and Ulrich Franzen, offered the perfectly feasible proposal that the Port Authority clean and renovate the interior and operate the station in return for a rental to be paid by the Pennsylvania and the Long Island railroads. Since the Authority had already built a union bus terminal, which is an architectural atrocity, it would have had an opportunity not only to provide a similar public service, but to redeem itself by rescuing a great monumental work. The city and the owner, however, held different views, which they based on the arguments that are always presented in such cases as sacred dogma—namely, an increase in the city's tax revenue of $3,500,000 per annum, an annual rental of $2,100,000 to the sick railroad, swelled in effect by a $600,000 saving in annual maintenance costs. The New York City Planning Commission in January, 1963, granted a special permit to the Madison Square Garden Corporation to demolish the station, to construct a new interior with public spaces and service facilities reduced to a minimum, and to erect the building complex above the station area. It required three years to take apart this durable and resistant fabric while maintaining a traffic of nearly 600 trains and 200,000 passengers per day, but the ugly work was finally completed in 1966. The cylindrical arena, with a capacity for 20,000 seats, the 29-story office building, and the single-level station squeezed between the street grade and the platform area were constructed in 1966–68 at a total cost of $116,000,000 (fig. 49). They are prime candidates for the most poverty-stricken architecture in New York—indeed, it is questionable whether the structures and enclosures can be regarded as architecture at all—and the editorial page of the *New York Times* was the first voice to remind us of the corrosive implications of this fact.

> Until the first blow fell no one was convinced that Penn Station really would be demolished or that New York would permit this monumental act of vandalism against one of the largest and finest landmarks of its age of Roman elegance. . . . Monumental problems almost as big as the building itself stood in the way of

Fig. 49. Madison Square Garden Arena and the Pennsylvania Plaza Building, 1968.

49

> preservation; but it is the shame of New York, of its financial and cultural communities, its politicians, philanthropists and planners, and of the public as well, that no serious effort was made. A rich and powerful city, noted for its resources of brains, imagination and money, could not rise to the occasion. The final indictment is of the values of our own society.
>
> Any city gets what it admires, will pay for, and, ultimately, deserves. . . . We want and deserve tin-can architecture in a tin-horn culture.[25]

Douglas Haskell placed the loss of the station in the total urban perspective, where he could see the outlines of how the modern city, while preserving a tangible simulacrum of a presumably workable fabric, could destroy itself as a habitation of the human spirit.

> In every vigorous growing city there are buildings and building groups which although privately owned were developed as public institutions. The spot or the function demanded it. Outstanding in New York are four: the Stock Exchange, Rockefeller Center, and the two great railroad stations, the Pennsylvania . . . and the Grand Central. . . . The . . . degradation of [the latter] in different forms has hit the other groups that have been mentioned, for the wonderful Penn Station is being torn down to make way for fight promotion, and the Stock Exchange is being moved with no regard for its tradition, and Rockefeller Center as it spreads is being so unraveled as to destroy instead of build up the modern city fabric.
>
> Thus the decline of New York has been set in motion, not by communists or enemies, but by the city's unastute business leaders—its latest expatriates.[26]

Even in its dwarfed and misshapen state, however, Pennsylvania Station continues to function with some of its former efficiency, at least for trains if not for passengers. The interior space consists essentially of two parts, a large ticket lobby embracing a much greater area than is necessary for the moving traffic, and a combined waiting room and concourse that is an insult to the user: it is too small, too low, contains too few seats, and provides access to all train gates in such a way as to guarantee conflict and confusion. The decor might be described as men's room modern, and the food available in the restaurants ranges from unappetizing to unspeakable. The trains are provided with greatly superior arrangements, since the track, platform, signaling, and interlocking systems remain intact. The storage and service tracks that fill the trapezoidal corners of the station track area and the remaining 35 tracks of Sunnyside Yard continue to function as they were originally intended, although at a scale somewhat reduced below that of the great days of Pullman traffic. In 1971, when Amtrak took the place of the Pennsylvania and New Haven segments of the Penn Central in the operation of through trains, the weekday traffic comprised a total of

526 trains, of which 56.7 percent were Long Island schedules. The number has remained relatively stable under the aegis of the various public and subsidized authorities that operate the metropolitan and intercity passenger service. The average total for 1975, for example, was 552 trains per day serving about 205,000 passengers, with the Long Island again taking the lion's share. Although these figures fall well below the corresponding levels for the war years and their immediate aftermath (1943–47), the number of daily passengers is almost exactly what it was in 1929–30, indicating that the decline of through traffic has been offset by an increase in the suburban volume. This fact ought to make a greater impression on the minds of planning authorities than it appears to have done.[27]

What Was Left

All right-thinking economists believe as another divine revelation what we might call the axiom of inevitability, which can be most conveniently defined as the belief that whatever occurred would have occurred anyway. This rigid determinism denies any possibility of choice and thus leaves the city helpless before processes energized by those market forces that temporarily gain the ascendant regardless of long-term consequences; yet with respect to the urban economy, it is clear that much wiser decisions than those that were the rule in the interwar and postwar years could have been made. Any assessment of and any proposed restructuring of the circulatory and freight-handling systems of metropolitan New York can be most usefully made by placing local transit and shipping in the total context of national transportation. The old criterion of time elapsed or rate of vehicular speed is no longer valid in any society, whether economically developed to an advanced degree, or still in the developing phase, and it is against the new standards of energy efficiency, degree of pollution, and the consumption or urban space that transportation technology must now be measured.

Analyses repeatedly conducted by various individuals and organizations, some associated with the railroads, others serving no special interest or concern other than governmental policy, have accumulated massive evidence that freight can be transported by rail at a lower consumption of energy per unit of transportation than by any other mode with the possible exception of pipelines and waterways under certain circumstances. Three separate studies conducted between 1967 and 1973, for example, indicate that the energy efficiency of the railroad is decisively superior to that of trucks and airplanes, and of these one concludes that only the waterway is superior to the railroad. The average quantities given in the three studies show that trucks consume 3.57 times more energy per unit of transportation (Btu's per ton-mile) than railroads do, and airplanes 66.8 times more (a difference bordering on the criminal). A later investigation reveals, however, that because of the tortuous routes of many inland waterways, the advantage in efficiency actually lies with the railroad: the consumption of energy by diesel-powered barges on the Mississippi River, for example, is 60 percent greater than that of the freight train running between identical terminals.[28] The arguments in favor of the coal-slurry pipeline, the proponents of which claim it to be the technology of the future, were shown to be wholly without foundation. In 1978 the federal Office of Technology Assessment concluded from a comparative analysis that the energy consumption of the pipeline is nearly double that of the railroad, 610 Btu's per ton-mile as opposed to 310. Moreover, in regions of low rainfall the amount of water required to move the pulverized coal could only be regarded as another destructive looting of a precious resource. Measured in terms of the direct consumption of fuel in transporting freight, the railroad has been shown to be superior either to all other modes, or to all with the exception of waterways.[29] In the transportation of passengers the only competing mode that can give a better account of itself than the railroad is the bus, although such figures as are available vary considerably with the source. Again, however, it is the airplane that is shown to be responsible for the lowest levels of energy efficiency, its consumption of fuel per passenger-mile ranging from three to five times that of the railroad. In urban mass transit the automobile holds this unwanted distinction: its unit consumption is three times that of electrified mass transit.[30] David Freeman calculated that if 50,000,000,000 passenger-miles per annum were transferred from the highways and the airlines to the railroads, the result would be a saving of 2,800,000,000 gallons of fuel oil each year.

Rail transportation offers a range of other valuable advantages over its competitors. Perhaps the first is that its already enormous capacity can be expanded without further assaults on the environment and at a cost equal to a small fraction of that required for the extension of highways and navigable waterways. In view of the fact that the rail network repeatedly and successfully carried more than 1,000,000 loaded cars per week at intervals over the years of 1923 through 1929, and in view of the 40 percent expansion of freight-car capacity and the improvements in motive power and signaling since the Second World War, there is no question that the tonnage moved in 1979 can be doubled without any increase in the land area already occupied by tracks, yards, terminals, and appurtenant structures. The investment required to rebuild a double-track line to the standards necessary for high-speed, high-density freight and passenger service comes on the average to about $345,000 per mile as opposed to a range of $1,000,000 to $50,000,000 per mile for a freeway, and an estimated average of about $6,000,000 for a waterway, whether newly dug or enlarged from an existing stream. With respect to atmospheric pollution, the train is substantially superior to the truck: the average emission of pollutants from a diesel-electric locomotive has been calculated as 1.03 grams of pollutants per ton-mile, against 3.76 grams for the highway competitor. As for the airplane, the extent of its assault on the integrity of the environment is so great that its continued use must be regarded as a form of technological primitivism (that is, a belief in the unlimited magical power of technology). Its consumption of energy per passenger-mile ranges from three to four times that of the train, and the difference is so great in the movement of cargo as to justify an immediate prohibition of air-freight transportation. The operation of planes at the densities common to major airports results in auditory pollution at the physically and psychologically harmful level within a radius of 10 miles from the control tower, and at the thoroughly aggravating level within the range of another ten miles. In addition to direct chemical pollution of the atmosphere, the vapor trails of jet aircraft increase cloudiness to the extent that under certain circumstances clear skies may be turned to cloudy. As a consequence, meteorologists in northern Illinois have recorded a 20 percent increase in the number of cloudy days per year over the two decades of 1957–77, an increase substantially attributable to the expansion of airplane flights. The space necessary for the safe operation of planes is so great as to stand out of all proportion to the service they provide. O'Hare Field in Chicago, for example, covers a land area of 6,600 acres (far from the largest) and will probably reach the saturation point at about 200,000 daily passengers. By contrast, Grand Central Terminal, which embraces 78 acres as the largest in the world, can probably accommodate at least 500,000 passengers per day. North Western Station in Chicago, covering an area of 43 acres, was planned for a capacity of 250,000 passengers. Finally, the great distance of the airport from the central business district of the city requires secondary travel of such magnitude as to increase still further the already indefensible consumption of energy, the pollution of the atmosphere, the congestion of traffic, and the general disruption of urban life. In short, by every criterion that counts in the latter half of the twentieth century, air transport is a failure.

All the benefits inherent in rail transportation as it is presently conducted can be greatly increased by the adoption of electrical operation on a nationwide scale. The many short installations that existed at the end of the war, most them associated with long tunnels and mountain grades, have been progressively abandoned until only those in the metropolitan areas of New York, Philadelphia, and Chicago survive. Yet the evidence derived from investigations conducted around 1970 and succeeding years demonstrates convincingly that electrification offers immense economic and social benefits. An electric locomotive can produce as much as three times the total number of ton-miles or passenger-miles in high-speed, high-density service as a diesel-electric machine of similar horsepower rating over the same period of time. Even the overall efficiency of an electrified railroad, comprehending central generation, transmission, and distribution, as well as locomotive operation, is greater than that of the equivalent diesel-electric power because the central generating capacity available for rail use need equal no more than 25 percent of total locomotive horsepower, whereas the collective mobile generating capacity of the fleet of diesel engines must at least equal the total full-power requirement of the traction motors. The useful life of electric motive power may be two to three times longer than that of the diesel variety because of the greater number of rapidly wearing surfaces in the high-temperature ambience of internal combustion engines. Lubricating, maintenance, and repair costs, for the same reason, are only one-fourth to one-third those of diesel-electric locomotives. Progress in the technology of high-voltage transmission has steadily reduced the weight, the costs of installation, and the line losses of transmitting systems. The ultimate economic conclusion, as the railroad executive John W. Barriger wrote, is that "the United States can achieve a needed doubling of transportation output over the next 25 years without any increase in fuel consumption, largely through a shift to much greater dependence on [electrified] rail transportation."[31] And it is hardly necessary to add that electrified rail service generates no chemical or auditory pollution at the track and that it not only does not disrupt the urban fabric, it makes prime multiuse urban land available where none existed before. A hidden four-track subway line may safely and rapidly transport as many as 240,000 passengers per hour, while the life of the city's surface goes on undisturbed.

The necessary national and urban planning implied by these data is obvious, but a society addicted to its daily fix of petroleum distillates and power-consuming gadgets goes on innocently supposing that every technical problem carries its own solution. Four programs of national action ought to be initiated immediately, carried out simultaneously, and brought to a focus on all regions and metropolitan areas with equal force. The progressive electrification of the American rail network, confined at first and at the minimum to actual and potential passenger-carrying lines, accompanied by a steady expansion of passenger services uniting all major cities up to a distance between any pair of 500 miles, should be combined with a phasing-out of all airplane flights within the 500-mile limit. With respect to freight transportation, rail piggyback service ought to be expanded to the point where all tonnage carried by roadway truck beyond a distance of 300 miles is transferred to the railroad flatcar. The expansion of piggyback transit should be accompanied by an end to all construction or enlargement of inland waterways for navigational purposes on ecological as well as economic grounds and to contribute to a reduction in unnecessary governmental expenditure. The conservation of fuel through the shift to rail transport must be carried out in conjunction with the placing of the fossil fuel industry under national control and with the progressive replacement of such fuels by energy derived from renewable sources. The unification of urban terminal facilities and their location within or as close to the working core of the city as possible ought to be accompanied by an expansion of public transit ideally to the point where all daily movements essential to the urban economy, in those cities already served by a rapid transit system, can be made in public vehicles. Air-rights developments and new building stimulated by transit improvements might then offer the city the opportunity to regain control of land use and thus put an end to the exploitation of the urban fabric, municipal services, and the municipal authority by the corporations and the real estate operators for their own private gain, whatever the cost to the public welfare (a deeply ingrained American practice that the urban historian Sam Bass Warner called *privatism*). The ultimate aim in transportation ought to be not a revolution in how people travel and ship their goods, nor a constant multiplication of transit technologies, but the development of a balanced and hierarchical system of existing components, in which each mode is used in the manner to which it is best suited.

Over the entire period of state and federal appropriations for the subsidization of waterway, highway, and aerial transportation, up to 1975, the total of such expenditures came to $524,326,000,000, of which $427,762,000,000, or 81.6 percent, went to highways and associated structures. For the year 1975 the total of all appropriations reached $31,382,000,000, having risen 421.6 percent over the previous quarter-century, and the sum has continued to rise in subsequent years up to 1979. Loans and grants have been made by the federal government for the reconstruction of the Northeast Corridor and the rehabilitation of money-short railroads, among which Con Rail required by far the largest sum, but these expenditures represent only a modest fraction of the subsidies poured by the Congress without question or critical examination into highways, waterways, and airports. Had the total of some $30,000,000,000 been divided equally among the four transportation modes, and had this division been inaugurated at the time that Amtrak was established in 1971, we could now be well on the way to operating an electrified railroad system potentially capable of producing a hundred billion passenger-miles and one and a half trillion ton-miles per annum. Instead of this perfectly sound program of action, when Amtrak continued to operate at the deficits characteristic of all transportation systems in the world, the Department of Transportation in 1979 proposed the elimination of more than 40 percent of its mileage, a curtailment which the Congress subsequently reduced to about one quarter of the route miles. The venality that both the administrative and legislative branches of the federal government exhibit before the petroleum industry underlies this seeming lunacy, but by this date the voices of sanity began to be heard, at first directed to the question of continued passenger service. The clearest and most incisive statement came from Adriana Gianturco, the director of the California Department of Transportation.

> We believe that passenger trains are essential if we are to conserve petroleum and minimize the necessity for further costly freeway construction, but they can only be a decent alternative if we have enough of them to ride. . . .
>
> We realize that [the maintenance of service] would require additional funding, but even spending three-quarters of a billion dollars annually on passenger train service would be small potatoes, compared to subsidies of other modes. Amtrak now costs the taxpayer $500 million a year while highways cost the taxpayer over $23 billion a year.
>
> The current subsidy of the U.S. air traffic control system is $1.8 billion annually, and this represents only a small fraction of public subsidies of airlines. Former Transportation Secretary William Coleman estimated that air travelers pay only one-third the cost of their transportation. Amtrak passengers, by comparison, pay almost 40 percent. The subsidy of U.S. highways by non-highway revenue sources since 1920 totals well over $150 billion, and this does not take into account the social and environmental damages [from highway usage and construction] . . . .
>
> The fact that the U.S. D[epartment] of T[ransportation] has singled the passenger train out shows a complete lack of perspective on transportation costs. The money saved by the proposed cuts in Amtrak . . . would build two to three miles of urban freeway per year. For this we would have to give up 8,100 miles of rail service.[32]

A year later the cutting edge of Mike Royko's satirical wit effectively underscored the point.

> People in other industrialized nations must think we're crazy. After years of danger signals that energy is going to become scarce, we're the only country to have let our most energy-efficient mass-transportation system stagnate and shrink

> and to discourage people from riding trains. While other countries have improved their rail beds, designed modern equipment, and introduced faster and more comfortable trains, we've done precisely the opposite. . . .
>
> But it's not too late, and I have a suggestion to turn things around.
>
> The President should stop listening to his Department of Transportation. It's as full of fools as his Energy Department.
>
> Instead, we should swallow our pride and turn for help to our old enemies, the Germans and Japanese. Even the Italians, if they leave the salami out of the deal.
>
> We should hire them to come here and show us how to put together a modern passenger rail system that works. . . .
>
> We'd better do something, or we'll wind up as a nation of hitchhikers. With nobody out there to pick us up.[33]

The nation as a whole stands to gain more from the improvement in the transportation of freight by rail than the carrying of passengers, and an adequate program of the necessary subsidization, along with the rational coordination of the various modes, will require national planning rather than the customary parochialism of special interests and corporate greed, so often working in conflict that the gain of one usually nullifies the advancement of the other. Planners and economists began to recognize the need, as James Friedlander pointed out in an authoritative journal.

> It is likely that not only will public rail *planning* expand, but also the federal and state roles in *operations*. . . . Whether public ownership of rights of way comes to pass is problematical, but even some railroads see it as inevitable. Rail is energy efficient, and rights of way are already in place. Why discard them? Rail can be cheaper for transporting commodities which now move by truck. Good railroad service, therfore, is in the public interest, and can be optimized, even if railroad rationalization means railroad nationalization. . . .
>
> The costs of maintaining highways . . . may far exceed the costs of improving railroads. Thus, rail subsidy, or even nationalization, may be more economical than to let them die.[34]

The tentative programs inaugurated in 1976 focused to a major extent, as we have seen, on the fixed and rolling properties of Con Rail and the right of way of the Northeast Corridor, the full revitalization of which would prove highly beneficial to the New York economy. There is no question about the fact that the city's material, economic, social, and artistic life—all those characteristics that together have given it its world pre-eminence—reached the highest levels in the years between the ends of the two world wars, nor about the concomitant fact that the economic troubles which began to plague the port area around 1950 have taken a toll in every aspect of urban existence. The decades of confidence and great achievement were bound up with two particular manifestations of the New York spirit, the enormous, hardworking, and well-planned circulation system, and a sophisticated commercial architecture reflecting great creative talents and a profound understanding of the role of building in the urban milieu. The decades of trouble have resulted far less from internal weaknesses than they have from the failure of the national economy and the grotesque dislocations of its industrial patterns. The American system of monopolistic capitalism could not provide adequate income levels for minority peoples, who came to make up large, growing, and in some cases major proportions of the urban population. No governmental jurisdiction possessed the authority to control the wholesale migration of industry away from the northeastern states to the South and Southwest, leaving the cities of the North with intolerable burdens of welfare and public services, and no municipality possessed the planning resources and the legal instruments necessary to control the movement of industry and business headquarters away from the city, where they might have functioned in symbiotic interdependency with the urban environment, to the suburbs or the open country, where they can only disturb the environment. The national changes lay beyond the control of New York or any other city, but the damage left in their wake was magnified by unwise policies of the federal government and the municipal establishment. In New York the chief consequences of these policies took the form of the reckless building of expressways (the Robert Moses syndrome), the indiscriminate construction of more than 100,000,000 square feet of postwar office space in skyscrapers that ranged from the vacuous to the unspeakable, the progressive abandonment of rail facilities, and the irresponsible neglect of public transit. These collective enterprises led to the widespread destruction of the urban fabric, the impoverishment of neighborhoods and small businesses, a fourfold increase in the relief rolls, and the theft of the city from the individual human being in order to surrender it to automobiles and big-time real estate operators.

The question remains as to what elements of the circulation system could have been salvaged from this debacle, or what improvements might have been made in the relics that survived. A curious irony of American history is that the great age of rugged individualism, when all right-thinking people believed that the American form of business enterprise was divinely established, was also the age that gave us our most impressive commercial architecture and, in New York, the special gift of the huge metropolitan terminal designed as a people's palace at the highest levels of civic and building art. Such achievements became inconceivable in the years following the Second World War, so that we have had steadily to contract our expectations. Any question of the improvement of freight-handling facilities throughout New York Harbor eventually became academic when the Port Authority of New York and New Jersey concentrated its new container terminals on Newark Bay and Arthur Kill, but the Authority and other ad hoc agencies continued to advance plans, some parts of which held promise for the future, in the event that railroad service would ever be revived. In February, 1948, the Port Authority submitted a program of waterfront improvements to Mayor William O'Dwyer which involved an extensive unification and reconstruction of Manhattan piers. The 35 existing railroad-owned piers, with their associated stations, were to be replaced by four union carfloat terminals for nonperishable commodities and a single huge produce terminal, the five entities to lie along the Hudson River from a point a little south of Chambers Street northward to 23d Street. The twin aims were to locate all rail, truck, and marine traffic in a concentrated mile-long complex, and to remove all truck traffic from marginal streets. Massive changes in all forms of port traffic in a dozen years rendered this plan meaningless, but it contained the valuable idea of a balanced hierarchy of modes as well as the established concept of unification. If the plan had been enlarged to comprehend the east and west sides of the harbor area as well as Manhattan, then the long-forgotten rail-freight tunnel once proposed by the Pennsylvania Railroad and never built would have been an essential adjunct. Indeed, one may argue that the tunnel or the self-propelled carfloat has become an essential element, whatever plan is adopted.

A complementary plan for a union passenger terminal was prepared in 1947 by the New Jersey State Department of Economic Development in collaboration with the consulting engineer L. Alfred Jenny and submitted to the governor and the legislature in January, 1948. It proved to be the last of a series of proposals for ending the isolation of the New Jersey roads and drawing all of them into a Manhattan nexus. It had much to recommend it, but it need not have involved new construction on quite so grand a scale. The essential features were a new terminal to be built in the single block bounded by Sixth and Seventh avenues between 49th and 50th streets, a Hudson River tunnel extending east from North Bergen, New Jersey, on the midline of the 49th–50th Street block, a network of connecting tracks to bring the New Jersey roads into a junction with the tunnel line at North Bergen, and the electrification of the Erie Railroad's suburban routes and all newly constructed trackage. Since no action followed, and since the plan appears to have been lost in the filing cabinets of the state agencies, the New Jersey Regional Planning Commission in February, 1952, recommended the establishment of a bistate transit authority to begin all over again—that is, to find means of bringing New Jersey commuters into Manhattan by rail instead of highway. The total number of such commuters was estimated at 372,000 per weekday at the time. The plan of 1948 actually contained all the answers, but the state of rail traffic increasingly gave it the character of another academic exercise. Yet fundamental elements pointed in the right direction for the surviving roads.

There was enough life in the traditional system of rail and marine terminals to warrant still another study aimed at formulating a plan of unification. In 1961 the respective governors of New York, New Jersey, and Connecticut, Nelson A. Rockefeller, Richard J. Hughes, and John Dempsey, established the Tri-State Transportation Committee, which was given the more permanent-sounding designation of Commission in 1965. Its chairman was William J. Ronan, a protégé of Governor Rockefeller, his secretary at the time, and later the director of the Metropolitan Transit Authority. The ultimate aim of the Commission's inquiries was laudable enough, but it was predicated on the existence of a state of affairs that was changing so rapidly as to nullify many details of the proposed plan.

> The Committee proposed that marine and lighterage operations, equipment and facilities of all harbor railroads be consolidated. It was estimated that a saving to the railroads of almost $9 million per year would result. . . . One of the by-products of the proposed consolidation would be the release of land where marine operations of several railroads would be discontinued. There is an opportunity for redevelopment and marketing of these released railroad properties for other uses, resulting in financial benefits to the railroads and in general benefit to the public, who will have a better region in which to live.[35]

There was no harbor on earth where more redundant and conflicting movements needed to be unified through direct elimination and merger, but by the time the Commission issued its preliminary report in July, 1964, to say nothing of its final formulation in March, 1966, the eliminating process had gone so far that there was little left to unify (figs. 31—33 show the distribution of rail-marine facilities and the pattern of car-float routes as these existed up to 1960). For the land that was expected to be released through the removal of redundant facilities, the Commission suggested the development of residential projects and of recreational and industrial parks down the length of the Jersey waterfront from the Palisades above Fort Lee to the lower end of the Bayonne peninsula, the southward extension of Riverside Park to 42d Street in Manhattan, and a mixture of residential and commercial building down the North River shore, around the Battery, and up along the East River margin to Brooklyn Bridge. All this would have brought the greatest benefits to the citizens of New York and the New Jersey communities, but as of the end of 1979 only the

Liberty Park project was in process of realization. Many of the Commission's proposals for the improvement of suburban passenger service had been previously considered and were embodied in the programs of the New York Metropolitan Transit Authority and the New Jersey Aldene Plan. The most valuable and admittedly most expensive features, however, have never passed beyond the stage of theory. Chief of these are the extension of the Long Island Rail Road electrification eastward to the transverse median line of the island, the extension of such operation on the New York Central to Poughkeepsie (Hudson Division) and Brewster (Harlem Division), the revival of Austin Corbin's neglected plan to extend the Long Island's Atlantic Avenue line into Manhattan via the B. M. T. and Manhattan Bridge, the enlargement of the projected East River tunnel for use by the trains of both the rapid transit system and the Long Island, and the introduction of electrification to the suburban zones of the Erie and the Central of New Jersey, so that the trains of these isolated carriers could be brought into Pennsylvania Station.

These plans, together with such proposals for the future as they may suggest, must be measured against the inherent advantages of rail transport sketched at the beginning of this section and in the light of what parts of the New York circulatory system still exist. What we have called the Robert Moses syndrome left a legacy of enormous and often irreparable damage in the wake of the wreckers who cleared the way for its expressway network. There are obviously superior alternatives, and they do not require the abandonment of the automobile. In the first place, it is now impossible to discover any technical or financial reasons why the states of New York and New Jersey, aided by appropriations from the federal government, should not electrify all the lines of the former Erie, Central of New Jersey, and New York and Long Branch railroads used for suburban service, renovate the fixed electrical equipment and replace the rolling stock of the Lackawanna with new units, construct the necessary connecting tracks between the Lackawanna and the Pennsylvania lines at Kearny, and operate the trains of these roads to and from Pennsylvania Station. The completion of the Midtown tunnel for use by the Long Island as well as the subway transit, and the introduction of the company's trains into Grand Central Terminal, combined with incentives such as reduced fares and reasonably guaranteed all-weather operation on the lines of the New York Central and the New Haven, might then generate the volume of traffic that the immense and underused station can accommodate. If these changes were made, all New York rail traffic would be concentrated in three terminal stations, namely, the two in Manhattan and the Flatbush terminus of the Long Island, where a total of 86 platform tracks are now available (1980) for berthing passenger trains. Given the designed capacity of

Pennsylvania and Grand Central stations and the traffic once moving in and out of Flatbush, there is reasonable ground for asserting that the three could accommodate the peak traffic of 1,132,000 daily passengers that came in 1929, even though this number was divided among nine separate terminals. If the Long Island's Atlantic Avenue line were extended into Manhattan, a considerably greater number of passengers from the east could be moved directly into the appropriate subway stations.

The argument for the accommodation of a greatly expanded traffic is supported by the number of trains and daily passengers using the 15 operating terminals of the London rail network, which is the only urban circulation system comparable in its magnitude to that of New York. In 1976 the terminals of the London circuit accommodated an average of 6,989 trains per weekday, distributed over a total of 166 station tracks and carrying 1,157,038 daily passengers, for an average traffic density of 42.1 trains and 6,970 passengers per platform track. The density varied to an extreme among the different terminals, from nearly 110 trains per track per day at the small Charing Cross Station (restricted to multiple-unit suburban operations) to a little under 15 at King's Cross. Among the giants Victoria accommodated an average of 65 daily trains on each of its 17 tracks.[36] Such figures far exceed the maximum densities of train movements at the New York stations; and while there are differences in operating techniques between British and American practice, the chief distinction is the generally superior signaling and interlocking systems in the United States. Thus existing traffic volume and technology together indicate the presence of great reserve capacity in the New York stations. Pennsylvania Station in its original state and Grand Central Terminal prior to the uncontrolled air-rights development that began in 1957 could each have accommodated half a million daily passengers and something more than a thousand trains, but the total absence of foresight and the total disregard for future needs in their rebuilding and alterations—attitudes exactly contrary to the generous, forward-looking civic spirit that underlay their design and construction—has reduced their capacity for the accommodation of passengers. With minor enlargements and rearrangements, however, the Pennsylvania's facility could readily make room for the traffic that would come with the introduction of the Central of New Jersey and Erie-Lackawanna trains into the station. The adoption of either of the two proposals for the Long Island, the extension of the Atlantic Avenue line into downtown Manhattan or the operation of the road's trains in the 63d Street tunnel, would make available facilities which would swell the total capacity of the rail network to substantially more than a million daily passengers, exclusive of the P. A. T. H. service. There is every reason for aiming at this target, and the comfortable transportation of such numbers would require no more than half the nearly 7,000 trains of the sprawling London system. The possible attendant reduction in automotive traffic, associated with a massive upgrading of transit equipment, and the creation of new accessways between rail facilities and the chief foci of movement in the city, might at least begin the process of returning the urban fabric to the pedestrian.

The revival of freight transportation by rail presents larger and more refractory problems. The existing mixture of truck-rail-marine terminals can undoubtedly transship and store considerably more tonnage than they now handle, but expansion will without question require additions to the working elements. As of 1977 the Port Authority operated 15 general-cargo terminals in the harbor area and 20 terminals for the transshipment of petroleum and petroleum products, supplemented by an additional 17 owned by various oil companies. All of these facilities are served by rail lines, although it must be admitted that among them the former New York Central's West Side line is in a near-moribund state. If the potential of the remaining railroad network is to be realized, it will have to be enlarged by a full-clearance freight-carrying tunnel joining Brooklyn, Staten Island, and the vicinity of Greenville Piers, or any other suitable New Jersey point, where the necessary connections with the Port Authority's terminals in Newark Bay could be built at minimal cost. A possible and feasible alternative, as we have seen, is the high-capacity self-propelled car float. In this way the cumbersome, time-consuming, and expensive operations by means of lighters and tug-propelled carfloats might be forgotten once and for all, along with the circuitous transit of New England freight by way of Selkirk Yard and Mechanicville. If such steps were taken, there appears to be no reason why the port tonnage could not only be increased, possibly by as much as 100 percent, but the greatly enlarged volume could be removed more expeditiously, more efficiently, with less disturbance to the environment, and at smaller expense. Such a result, however, would require pervasive changes in the national way of doing business and in national policy with respect to transportation.

As for the architecture that might take shape in future air-rights developments over electrified rail yards, there is little ground for supposing that the new office and residential towers will reveal any improvement over the vacuities that disfigure other cities beside New York. The ephemeral, lifeless, and mechanistic character of this work is an inevitable consequence of the doctrine that a building is a disposable commodity the design of which at best represents a series of technological solutions to strictly technical problems. The ruling principle was nicely set forth by Richard Roth, one of the city's very active performers in the architectural profession. "These buildings are like Erector sets. All you have to do is unbolt them. I have seen a whole facade put up in a day. What goes up in a day can come down in a day."[37] Unlike Rome and Pennsylvania Station, we might add. Attempts by a few to recall that architecture is a visual art have usually produced alternatives in the form of capricious absurdities. Another useful and forgotten step that might readily be taken toward the revival of architecture is the re-establishment of the Municipal Art Commission with mandatory powers. One remembers almost with nostalgia the day when the Commission ordered Henry Hornbostel to return to the drawing board and prepare a new design for the abutment towers of Hell Gate Bridge. The conclusion seems inescapable that the circulation technology necessary for a livable city and the architecture essential to a great building and civic art existed at the beginning of the First World War; developments since the Second can hardly be regarded as progress.

Tables

TABLE 1 POPULATION OF GREATER NEW YORK AND NEW YORK CITY BY CONSTITUENT COUNTIES

Year	New York	Bronx	Kings	Queens	Richmond
1790	33,131		4,495	16,014	3,835
1800	60,515		5,740	16,916	4,564
1810	96,373		8,303	19,336	5,347
1820	123,706		11,187	21,519	6,135
1830	202,589		20,535	22,460	7,082
1840	312,710		47,613	30,324	10,965
1850	515,547		138,882	36,833	15,061
1860	813,669		279,122	57,391	25,492
1870	942,292		419,921	73,803	33,029
1880	1,206,209		599,495	90,574	38,991
1890	1,515,301		838,547	128,059	51,693
1900	2,050,600		1,125,830	152,999	61,153
1910	2,762,522		1,634,351	284,041	85,969
1920	2,284,103	732,016	2,018,356	469,042	116,531
1930	1,867,312	1,265,258	2,560,401	1,079,129	158,346
1940	1,889,924	1,394,711	2,698,285	1,297,634	174,441
1950	1,960,101	1,451,277	2,738,185	1,550,849	191,555
1960	1,698,281	1,424,815	2,627,319	1,809,578	221,991
1970	1,539,233	1,471,701	2,602,012	1,986,473	295,443

SOURCE: United States Census.

TABLE 2 TOTAL POPULATION OF GREATER NEW YORK, NEW YORK CITY, AND METROPOLITAN AREA, WITH PERCENTAGE INCREASES

Year	Population of City	Percent Increase	Population of Metropolitan Area	Percent Increase
1790	49,401			
1800	79,216	60.0		
1810	119,734	51.0		
1820	152,056	27.0		
1830	242,278	59.3		
1840	391,114	61.4		
1850	696,115	78.0		
1860	1,174,779	68.8		
1870	1,478,103	25.8		
1880	1,911,698	29.3		
1890	2,507,414	31.1		
1900	3,437,202	27.4		
1910	4,766,883	38.7		
1920	5,620,048	17.9		
1930	6,930,446	23.3		
1940	7,454,995	7.6	11,660,839	
1950	7,891,957	5.9	12,911,994	10.7
1960	7,781,984	−1.4	14,759,429	14.3
1970	7,894,862	1.5	16,178,700	9.6

SOURCE: United States Census.

TABLE 3 WATERBORNE FREIGHT HANDLED AT NEW YORK HARBOR, 1925–75 (U.S. TONS)

Year	Foreign	Domestic	Total
1925	27,872,100	87,849,928	115,722,028
1929	30,499,181	106,732,680	137,231,861
1930	26,622,168	93,773,297	120,395,465
1935	17,456,331	79,612,576	97,068,907
1940	23,248,287	106,463,899	129,712,186
1945	31,662,795	72,299,228	103,962,023
1950	32,482,493	112,461,065	144,943,558
1955	38,897,543	109,950,588	148,848,131
1960	45,039,689	108,158,931	153,198,620
1965	54,330,073	99,524,709	153,854,782
1970	57,932,094	116,076,014	174,008,108
1973	79,369,121	137,527,313	216,896,434
1975	55,691,050	122,123,568	177,814,618

SOURCE: United States Army, Corps of Engineers.

TABLE 4 FREIGHT AND PASSENGERS CARRIED BY CLASS I RAILROADS IN THE UNITED STATES, 1882–1975

Year	Tons of Freight	Number of Passengers
1870	72,500,000	
1882	360,490,000	289,031,000
1885	437,040,000	351,428,000
1890	636,541,617	492,431,000
1895	696,761,171	507,421,000
1900	732,000,000[a]	553,008,000
1905	784,920,188	711,498,000
1910	1,026,491,782	939,909,000
1915	925,697,000	957,683,000
1920	1,255,421,000	1,239,181,000
1925	1,247,242,000	888,267,000
1930	1,153,197,000	703,598,121
1935	789,627,000	445,872,300
1940	1,009,421,000	452,920,914
1945	1,424,913,000	891,127,614
1950	1,354,196,000	486,194,222
1955	1,396,339,000	431,998,922
1960	1,240,654,000	325,871,625
1965	1,387,423,048	298,690,604
1970	1,484,919,475	283,894,243
1975	1,401,002,155	269,393,808

SOURCES: Association of American Railroads; Interstate Commerce Commission; United States Department of Commerce.

[a]Figure for 1900 was calculated by extrapolation because of discrepancies among data given by the Interstate Commerce Commission for tons originated, tons received, and total tons.

TABLE 5 ANNUAL VOLUME OF FREIGHT MOVED BY RAIL IN AND OUT OF THE PORT OF NEW YORK, 1914–74 (1000S OF SHORT TONS)

Year	Interchange[a]	Lighterage[b]	Local[c]	Total
1914	12,928[d]		62,127	75,055
1938	5,944	6,632	52,001	64,577
1939	6,990	8,043	56,960	71,993
1940	7,622	10,964	62,334	80,920
1941	9,864	14,243	72,140	96,247
1942	11,656	14,972	92,716	119,344
1943	12,201	17,048	109,857	139,106
1944	12,173	17,191	107,033	136,397
1945	10,677	14,998	91,164	116,839
1946	10,966	13,350	85,397	109,713
1947	10,507	14,055	81,650	106,212
1948	10,672	12,044	76,332	99,048
1949	8,140	10.981	57,752	76,873
1950	8,624	9,425	62,716	80,765
1951	8,575	10,860	63,559	82,994
1952	8,457	10,621	59,509	78,587
1953	8,297	9,966	57,805	76,068
1954	7,213	8,339	54,476	70,028
1955	7,785	9,530	57,653	74,968
1956	7,529	9,798	59,456	76,783
1957	6,834	8,761	53,138	68,733
1958	5,999	7,172	46,104	59,275
1959	6,269	6,189	46,124	58,582
1960	5,701	6,547	45,717	57,965
1961	5,923	5,492	45,925	57,340
1962	6,328	5,175	44,794	56,297
1964	5,059[e]	4,389	42,264	51,712
1966	4,836	3,949	41,884	50,669
1968	3,727[f]	2,100	39,370	45,197
1970		1,732	38,704	40,436
1972		361	32,116	32,477
1974		129	32,569	32,698

SOURCE: Port of New York and New Jersey Authority, Central Research and Statistics Division.
[a]Interchange is rail-to-rail transfer.
[b]Lighterage is rail-to-ship transfer.
[c]Local is traffic moving in and out of the port without interchange.
[d]Interchange traffic for 1914 includes lighterage.
[e]Odd years are omitted in the Port Authority compilations after 1962.
[f]Railroad companies no longer provided data for interchange traffic after 1968.

TABLE 6 Annual Number of Railroad Passengers Carried in and out of New York, 1911–71 (1000s)

Year	New Jersey	Westchester and Connecticut	Long Island	Total	Weekday Average
1911	106,498	21,688	33,867	162,053	506
1912	104,499	23,429	37,320	165,248	516
1913	106,194	26,525	40,606	173,325	541
1914	104,140	27,530	41,634	173,394	541
1915	105,150	29,394	42,629	177,173	554
1916	112,961	34,813	45,803	193,577	605
1917	119,530	37,488	50,796	207,814	649
1918	125,060	35,649	55,004	215,713	674
1919	144,528	38,439	64,067	247,034	772
1920	150,519	45,329	72,744	268,592	840
1921	152,281	45,296	75,506	273,083	853
1922	156,663	46,191	79,657	282,511	884
1923	162,617	48,427	86,167	297,211	929
1924	165,757	50,810	92,991	309,558	967
1925	168,781	53,711	100,922	323,414	1,010
1926	170,883	56,943	104,794	332,620	1,039
1927	173,627	60,586	111,654	345,867	1,081
1928	173,271	63,098	112,547	348,916	1,090
1929	177,847	65,537	118,888	362,272	1,132
1930	170,661	63,610	118,190	352,461	1,101
1931	153,926	57,549	110,284	321,759	1,005
1932	135,107	47,743	91,714	274,564	858
1933	121,506	42,159	79,947	243,612	761
1934	120,990	43,081	79,135	243,206	760
1935	119,739	43,160	77,671	240,570	752
1936	124,629	46,631	82,279	253,539	792
1937	126,558	48,354	77,478	252,390	790
1938	117,017	41,332	70,395	228,744	715
1939	116,755	41,084	84,100	241,939	756
1940	114,925	40,086	77,548	232,559	727
1941	116,554	42,213	71,185	229,952	719
1942	132,912	53,923	85,423	272,258	851
1943	152,257	63,882	105,957	322,096	1,007
1944	148,442	67,643	108,707	324,792	1,015
1945	141,345	68,963	112,047	322,355	1,007
1946	131,814	67,560	115,839	315,213	985
1947	124,372	66,506	112,802	303,680	949
1948	117,533	61,492	109,451	288,476	901
1949	108,488	54,166	91,824	254,478	795
1950	98,028	50,160	83,589	231,774	724
1951	92,850	50,606	79,190	222,646	696
1952	84,510	51,126	76,392	212,028	663
1953	79,062	51,031	79,245	209,338	654
1954	75,314	51,221	78,022	204,557	639
1955	72,468	52,081	76,427	200,976	628
1956	72,736	54,010	75,277	202,023	631
1957	66,302	51,487	73,930	191,719	599

TABLE 6 (*continued*)

Year	New Jersey	Westchester and Connecticut	Long Island	Total	Weekday Average
1958	62,124	49,067	73,609	184,800	578
1959	57,292	46,403	73,935	177,630	555
1960	54,658	45,496	64,379	164,533	514
1961	53,813	42,028	69,102	164,943	515
1962	52,357	41,361	71,711	165,429	517
1963	49,997	39,857	71,513	161,367	504
1964	50,393	39,486	77,549	167,428	523
1965	46,311	38,763	73,995	159,069	497
1966	45,302	39,530	73,809	158,641	496
1967	44,289	39,452	74,283	159,024	494
1968	46,388	40,459	73,669	160,516	501
1969	51,076	41,725	72,356	165,157	516
1970	52,299	41,262	70,149	163,710	511
1971	51,188	39,202	69,515	159,905	500

SOURCE: Port of New York and New Jersey Authority; New Jersey Department of Planning and Development. Weekday average calculated by dividing annual total by a factor of 320.

TABLE 7 Annual Number of Passengers Using Pennsylvania and Grand Central Stations, 1902–76

Year	Grand Central	Weekday Average	Pennsylvania	Weekday Average
1902	15,557,421	48,600		
1903	16,135,667	50,400		
1904	16,383,320	51,200		
1905	18,213,897	57,000		
1906	19,268,104	60,200		
1907	18,791,984	58,700		
1908	17,957,209	56,100		
1909	19,705,302	61,600		
1910	20,177,999	63,000		
1911	20,082,815	62,800	12,549,164	39,200
1912	20,794,311	65,000	14,652,210	45,800
1913	21,983,014	68,700	17,073,024	53,400
1914	22,615,018	70,700	17,446,764	54,500
1915	23,962,280	74,900	18,391,789	57,500
1916	28,278,747	88,400	21,121,828	64,100
1917	30,653,045	95,800	22,987,288	71,840
1918	28,510,042	89,100	27,434,110	85,700
1919	31,301,004	97,800	34,444,216	107,600
1920	36,937,129	115,400	37,803,372	118,100
1921	36,157,012	113,000	38,673,178	120,900
1922	36,487,700	114,000	40,369,852	126,200
1923	38,360,362	119,900	43,949,932	137,300
1924	40,178,213	125,600	45,732,833	142,900
1925	40,369,538	126,200	51,654,100	161,400
1926	41,688,943	130,300	55,299,921	172,800
1927	43,855,185	137,000	59,893,038	187,200
1928	44,804,104	140,000	60,906,255	190,300
1929	46,597,975	145,600	65,409,772	204,400
1930	45,173,027	141,100	65,885,291	205,900
1931	41,057,196	128,300	62,458,905	195,200
1932	33,745,923	105,400	52,939,734	165,400
1933	29,513,297	92,200	47,741,058	149,200
1934	29,715,423	92,900	49,579,856	154,900
1935	30,159,763	94,200	49,994,098	156,200
1936	34,282,231	107,100	56,331,290	176,000
1937	37,454,398	117,000	57,578,089	179,900
1938	38,416,450	120,000	53,657,303	167,700
1939	38,260,143	119,500	69,662,810	217,700
1940	39,805,952	124,400	65,309,442	204,100
1941	41,386,229	129,300	61,188,803	191,200
1942	51,044,587	159,500	77,293,500	241,500
1943	59,929,493	187,300	98,855,676	308,900
1944	62,762,860	196,100	107,982,014	337,400
1945	64,719,574	202,200	109,349,114	341,700
1946	65,156,063	203,600	108,195,563	338,100
1947	63,471,983	198,300	100,533,590	314,200
1948	60,274,570	188,300	94,858,075	296,400

TABLE 7 (*continued*)

Year	Grand Central	Weekday Average	Pennsylvania	Weekday Average
1949	56,050,192	175,100	82,196,739	256,600
1950	53,222,016	166,300	74,764,582	233,600
1951	52,669,548	164,600	72,847,723	222,600
1952	53,704,759	167,800	70,094,598	219,000
1953	53,816,663	168,200	68,760,365	214,900
1954	53,916,435	168,500	67,639,148	211,400
1955	54,383,084	169,900	66,600,789	208,100
1956	55,832,676	174,500	66,257,877	207,100
1957	55,349,318	173,000	66,369,703	207,100
1958	52,976,391	164,000	64,748,774	202,300
1959	50,691,945	158,400	63,326,732	197,900
1960	49,607,221	155,000	55,923,516	174,800
1961	46,468,949	145,200	60,280,866	188,400
1962	45,377,049	141,800	61,853,545	193,300
1963	43,811,520	136,900	61,888,924	193,400
1964	43,408,570	135,700	67,360,453	210,500
1965	42,053,674	131,400	63,590,686	198,700
1966	42,818,841	133,800	62,207,867	194,400
1967	43,185,338	135,000		
1968	44,326,075	138,500		
1969				
1970				
1971				
1972				
1973				
1974				
1975			65,600,000	205,000
1976	46,400,000	145,000		

SOURCES: Office of the Station Master, Grand Central and Pennsylvania stations; *Railway Age*; Regional Plan Association of New York. Figures for 1975 and 1976 are approximations.

TABLE 8 FREIGHT AND PASSENGERS CARRIED BY LINE-HAUL RAILROAD COMPANIES SERVING THE PORT OF NEW YORK, 1860–1975

Year	Tons of Freight	Number of Passengers
1. Baltimore and Ohio		
1890	7,715,380	1,553,874
1895	32,048,371	11,089,283
1900	31,895,143	11,665,862
1905	47,285,183	15,518,372
1910	62,797,745	21,107,120
1915	64,375,595	20,581,992
1920	101,924,520	25,354,343
1925	104,637,773	14,745,684
1930	91,907,620	7,143,358
1935	65,945,938	3,442,031
1940	86,048,712	4,162,557
1945	137,455,955	13,705,733
1950	115,766,122	4,133,533
1955	115,289,980	3,635,661
1960	99,545,134	2,631,432
1965	113,181,000	1,781,720
1970	115,834,471	960,727
1975	98,258,432	864,132
2. Central Railroad of New Jersey		
1860	1,061,502	858,576
1864	1,491,455	1,397,616
1870	2,754,713	2,291,034
1875	3,527,529	4,456,944
1880	8,718,302	6,395,210
1885[a]		
1890	13,865,330	13,716,832
1895	10,906,307	12,933,677
1900	16,256,821	14,160,282
1905	22,843,429	18,517,577
1910	29,521,390	22,931,169
1915	31,515,349	23,322,502
1920	38,747,619	33,250,738
1925	38,106,483	27,265,076
1930	35,849,825	27,311,717
1935	22,868,995	16,272,637
1940	28,798,275	17,996,018
1945	44,101,503	23,838,651
1950	50,803,839	12,625,478
1955	33,732,323	10,299,405
1960	28,893,558	7,245,946
1965	31,660,548	6,069,777
1970	23,179,969	6,516,485
1974[b]	9,266,888	5,579,013

SOURCE: *Poor's Manual of the Railroads of the United States*.
[a]Figures included in annual report of the Philadelphia and Reading Railroad.
[b]Latest figures available.

TABLE 8 (*continued*)

Year	Tons of Freight	Number of Passengers
3. Delaware, Lackawanna and Western		
1870	2,461,956[a]	192,786[a]
1875	3,898,344[a]	596,445[a]
1880	6,721,790[b]	4,715,838[b]
1885	8,203,714	7,529,121
1890	11,097,152	10,890,168
1895	11,219,831	11,399,624
1900	12,481,875	14,428,880
1905	17,335,739	19,378,522
1910	20,679,986	26,246,749
1915	22,157,698	24,014,417
1920	28,315,359	30,612,516
1925	26,397,447	29,237,690
1930	25,512,937	26,665,498
1935	18,569,680	20,309,692
1940	22,488,768	20,321,053
1945	29,999,349	25,266,571
1950	24,452,086	19,461,143
1955	23,035,025	15,564,887
(See Erie-Lackawanna.)		
4. Erie		
1870		
1875	6,239,943	5,052,855
1880	8,715,892	5,491,431
1885	14,959,970	7,209,054
1890	24,127,160	13,256,671
1895	20,307,802	12,969,412
1900	26,947,892	16,527,876
1905	31,561,623	20,775,414
1910	38,763,600	25,277,283
1915	35,257,739	26,281,187
1920	46,467,928	33,215,357
1925	42,894,577	30,488,408
1930	44,242,999	26,247,945
1935	32,379,318	15,467,768
1940	35,847,581	13,762,280
1945	47,648,472	14,579,115
1950	43,339,984	11,038,075
1955	35,861,819	8,113,874
(See Erie-Lackawanna.)		

[a]Excludes traffic of Morris and Essex.
[b]Includes traffic of Morris and Essex, 1880–.

TABLE 8 (*continued*)

Year	Tons of Freight	Number of Passengers
5. Erie-Lackawanna		
1960	44,117,758[a]	17,174,208[a]
1965	45,969,122	13,833,342
1970	44,144,014	15,951,155
1975	31,798,870	16,696,154
6. Lehigh Valley		
1870	5,421,227	847,096
1875	4,946,354	1,068,664
1880	8,188,118	1,277,428
1885	9,428,190	2,273,710
1890	14,459,888	5,191,821
1895	14,712,546	4,748,037
1900	17,430,470	4,717,849
1905	23,774,287	4,535,233
1910	27,181,537	5,172,961
1915	30,268,701	5,206,972
1920	32,103,897	6,598,589
1925	28,090,749	4,040,013
1930	25,592,021	2,147,503
1935	17,881,789	878,409
1940	23,468,153	982,717
1945	34,698,835	2,939,429
1950	24,955,758	1,001,787
1955	25,324,213	880,365
1960	17,479,173	232,210
1965	16,371,695	nil
1970	14,644,018	nil
1974	19,440,732	nil

[a]Figures are combined totals for Erie Railroad and D. L. and W. Railroad to 17 October 1960; Erie-Lackawanna thereafter.

TABLE 8 (*continued*)

Year	Tons of Freight	Number of Passengers
7. Long Island		
1870	377,831	924,194
1875		
1880	320,837	6,228,292
1885	454,460	10,057,713
1890	686,940	13,139,691
1895	795,575	13,768,163
1900	1,513,387	12,387,649
1905	2,745,622	18,199,162
1910	3,814,209	30,998,615
1915	4,443,333	42,629,325
1920	5,886,969	72,743,820
1925	8,016,763	100,922,813
1930	7,890,423	118,189,901
1935	4,742,151	77,671,201
1940	5,466,511	77,548,416
1945	8,453,867	112,946,058
1950	5,919,256	83,585,949
1955	4,873,776	76,427,144
1960	3,791,902	64,378,591
1965	4,330,391	73,994,982
(Company acquired by New York Metropolitan Transit Authority, 1966.)		
8. New York Central and Hudson River		
1870	4,122,000	7,044,946
1875	6,001,954	9,422,629
1880	10,533,038	8,270,857
1885	10,802,957	12,747,801
1890	16,208,451	18,546,886
1895	19,741,495	23,809,465
1900	37,586,496	27,816,343
1905	42,861,974	45,507,047
1910	47,066,839	48,364,945
(See New York Central.)		
9. New York Central		
1915	87,828,429	48,397,627
1920	113,982,506	76,617,352
1925	111,223,698	69,169,940
1930	150,046,279	72,951,015
1935	104,482,468	44,381,459
1940	136,549,195	47,531,722
1945	180,822,800	78,877,809
1950	165,834,716	46,627,062
1955	161,070,694	43,432,503
1960	133,361,424	30,451,557
1965	142,649,000	24,790,153
(See Penn Central.)		

TABLE 8 (*continued*)

Year	Tons of Freight	Number of Passengers
10. New York, New Haven and Hartford		
1870	695,579	3,145,725
1875	827,832	4,034,239
1880	1,348,678	4,600,507
1885	2,148,463	7,765,575
1890	3,618,575	12,609,792
1895	9,665,236	43,838,676
1900	15,708,266	52,096,916
1905	18,321,327	63,323,475
1910	22,738,981	82,905,137
1915	23,842,023	78,172,698
1920	27,851,010	106,847,739
1925	28,294,849	70,169,708
1930	28,124,350	49,107,467
1935	18,054,889	30,920,975
1940	21,336,909	36,713,912
1945	32,659,875	68,909,978
1950	24,235,083	42,630,228
1955	22,723,284	44,797,373
1960	18,494,244	30,835,912
1965	19,328,948	24,374,788
(See Penn Central.)		
11. New York, Ontario and Western		
1880	255,410	273,778
1885	1,470,808	1,089,581
1890	955,558	647,841
1895	2,540,157	825,883
1900	3,416,606	1,213,291
1905	4,685,350	1,731,806
1910	5,680,781	2,148,972
1915	5,594,445	1,850,462
1920	5,279,972	1,925,897
1925	5,043,040	1,159,182
1930	5,578,920	534,049
1935	7,751,401	197,800
1940	4,943,723	156,736
1945	7,059,245	129,752
1950	3,687,685	55,523
1955	2,709,068	nil

TABLE 8 (*continued*)

Year	Tons of Freight	Number of Passengers
12. New York, Susquehanna and Western		
1885	849,315	790,559
1890	1,262,875	1,276,422
1895	1,815,729	1,753,495
1900	2,304,225	2,094,163
1905	3,060,502	2,754,176
1910	4,618,314	3,913,415
1915	7,449,544	3,056,202
1920	5,951,993	3,758,534
1925	5,528,699	3,155,387
1930	5,385,012	2,475,237
1935	4,617,703	1,379,007
1940	3,692,112	1,262,535
1945	4,833,867	2,019,125
1950	3,100,947	1,843,088
1955	2,884,369	1,513,777
1960	2,036,590	276,592
1965	1,364,036	75,719
1970	n.a.	nil
1975	n.a.	nil
13. Pennsylvania		
1870	5,427,401[a]	4,352,769[a]
1875	9,115,368	5,609,787
1880	15,364,788	7,757,940
1885	24,047,028	12,341,059
1890	66,648,730[b]	43,810,382[b]
1895	78,259,256	37,452,437
1900	109,471,266	41,922,569
1905	156,533,351	55,781,809
1910	129,858,353	69,979,457
1915	142,826,993	73,555,230
1920	196,046,777	164,766,666
1925	228,889,365	128,701,385
1930	191,315,758	99,019,359
1935	129,941,499	56,739,729
1940	174,303,212	64,243,942
1945	256,143,042	158,836,131
1950	207,102,828	75,191,753
1955	201,431,316	63,147,597
1960	161,314,785	46,271,208
1965	177,251,000	43,832,973
(See Penn Central.)		

[a]Figures do not include traffic of United Railroads of New Jersey (q.v.), 1870–85.
[b]Figures include traffic of all merged and leased properties, 1890–.

TABLE 8 (*continued*)

Year	Tons of Freight	Number of Passengers
14. Penn Central		
1970	281,724,167	86,922,466
1975	239,153,624	72,647,685
15. Philadelphia and Reading[a]		
1865	n.a.	1,444,257
1870	n.a.	5,766,934
1875	8,225,763	6,938,129
1880	12,323,453	9,822,422
1885	18,815,218	23,531,057
1890	20,798,741	18,103,893
1895	21,299,345	17,996,380
1900	29,404,294	21,910,349
1905	39,909,073	28,503,771
1910	47,431,262	31,333,231
1915	48,005,316	23,700,536
1920	69,713,564	31,556,953
1925	64,054,782	23,995,631
1930	61,136,296	14,224,192
1935	45,468,359	9,616,794
1940	59,163,819	10,857,652
1945	91,393,034	25,009,969
1950	73,378,274	13,968,946
1955	64,931,452	13,229,688
1960	55,046,361	10,468,700
1965	58,590,260	11,651,476
1970	48,763,025	13,699,373
1975	33,005,078	12,478,535

[a]Corporate title varies: also Reading Company.

TABLE 8 (*continued*)

Year	Tons of Freight	Number of Passengers
16. Raritan River		
1890		
1895	92,440	158,062
1900	198,540	157,935
1905	391,905	104,842
1910	576,366	122,674
1915	602,640	288,382
1920	774,466	556,815
1925	811,915	156,844
1930	740,411	59,432
1935	434,405	8,887
1940	734,814	nil
1945	1,157,179	nil
1950	938,412	nil
1955	1,400,969	nil
1960	957,176	nil
1965	887,532	nil
1970	790,480	nil
1975	n.a.	nil
17. United Railroads of New Jersey[a]		
1870		
1875		
1880	5,824,840	8,218,532
1885		
1890	14,953,268[b]	21,305,187
1895	16,498,034[b]	17,507,733
1900	22,199,048[b]	17,065,019
1905	28,084,756	20,887,726

[a]Corporate title varies: also United Companies of New Jersey and United New Jersey Railroad and Canal Company.
[b]Figures include tonnage of the Delaware and Raritan Canal.

TABLE 9 TOTAL TRAFFIC OF NEW YORK RAILROADS AND PROPORTION OF TOTAL TO THE NATIONAL RAILROAD TRAFFIC

Year	Tons of Freight (1000s)	Percent of U.S. Total	Number of Passengers (1000s)	Percent of U.S. Total
1890	181,445[a,b]	28.5	134,740[b,c]	27.3
1895	223,403	32.1	174,745	34.5
1900	304,614	41.6	199,190	36.1
1905	411,309	51.1	266,127	37.4
1910	440,729	42.9	339,168	36.1
1915	504,168	54.5	347,356	36.3
1920	673,048	53.6	556,250	44.9
1925	691,991	55.4	479,212	53.9
1930	673,022	58.4	431,851	61.4
1935	473,137	59.9	267,670	60.0
1940	602,843	59.9	284,683	62.9
1945	876,428	61.5	502,049	56.3
1950	743,015	54.9	298,194	61.3
1955	695,267	49.9	267,813	62.0
1960	565,038	45.5	199,498	61.2
1965	611,584	44.1	188,754	63.2
1970	534,362[d]	36.0	180,499	63.6
1975				

SOURCE: *Poor's Manual of the Railroads of the United States.*

[a]Includes tonnage of Philadelphia and Reading Railroad, 1890–; company inaugurated service to New York Harbor in 1892.

[b]Traffic of the Raritan River Railroad estimated for 1890.

[c]Excludes the passenger traffic of the Philadelphia and Reading Railroad, 1890–; company offered no independent passenger service to and from metropolitan New York.

[d]Tonnage of the New York, Susquehanna and Western Railroad estimated.

TABLE 10 COMPARISON OF LONG-TERM TRENDS IN FREIGHT TRAFFIC OF PENN CENTRAL GROUP AND LOUISVILLE AND NASHVILLE RAILROAD

Year	Penn Central Group (Tons)[a]	Annual Change (1915=100)	Louisville and Nashville (Tons)	Annual Change (1915=100)
1915	254,497,445	100.0	27,731,561	100.0
1920	337,880,293	132.8	47,098,325	169.8
1925	368,407,912	144.8	58,076,917	209.4
Peak	480,512,326[b]	188.8	63,898,695[c]	230.4
1930	369,486,387	145.2	51,735,263	186.6
1935	252,478,856	99.2	35,830,970	129.2
1940	332,189,316	130.5	49,429,151	178.2
1944[d]	500,861,943	196.9	73,374,452	264.6
1945	469,625,717	184.5	70,235,764	253.3
1950	397,172,627	156.1	68,283,021	246.2
1955	385,225,294	151.4	61,068,625	220.2
1960	313,170,454	123.1	73,793,737	266.1
1965	339,228,948	133.3	93,524,302	337.2
1970	281,724,000	110.7	109,321,000	394.2
1975	239,153,624	94.0	122,338,175	441.1

SOURCE: *Poor's Manual of the Railroads of the United States.*

[a]Total tonnage of New York Central, New York, New Haven and Hartford, and Pennsylvania railroads.

[b]Peak year prior to 1944 was 1926 for the Pennsylvania, 1929 for the New York Central and the New Haven.

[c]Peak year prior to 1944 was 1927 for the Louisville and Nashville.

[d]Peak year of World War II.

Notes

CHAPTER 1

1. The initial unit pressure in the compressed-air locomotive was 180 pounds per square inch. At the end of the 11-mile run, on which the maximum speed was only 25 miles per hour, the total pressure had fallen to 700 pounds and the unit pressure to 75 pounds per square inch. The locomotive could scarcely qualify even for industrial switching service.
2. Quoted in "Grand Jury on Fourth Avenue Tunnel," *Railroad Gazette* 33, no. 32 (9 August 1901): 565.
3. "The Park Avenue Tunnel in New York," *Railroad Gazette* 33, no. 33 (16 August 1901): 576.

   Among the alternative kinds of motive power that the railroad company considered, none seems more curious than a locomotive operated by means of superheated water. The boiling point of water is a function of pressure as well as temperature: the higher the circumambient air pressure is raised, the higher will be the boiling temperature. If the pressure within a boiler is elevated above normal air pressure, water can be heated above the normal boiling temperature while still remaining in the liquid phase. A slight reduction in pressure will then cause the water to be transformed rapidly into expanding steam capable of doing mechanical work. I have never heard of the successful operation of such an engine, and it would inevitably be exposed to the danger of a boiler explosion. The fireless locomotive was a form that was not equipped with a firebox and that operated by means of steam injected from an outside source into the cylindrical "boiler," which was no more than an insulated tank. The period of operation, of course, was limited to a few hours. Such locomotives were used wherever switching operations involved repeated or prolonged working inside a building, especially if it contained combustible materials.

   The idea of a loop track as part of a terminal yard originated in the United States with the plan for South Station, Boston (1896–99), which was originally designed to be built with a subgrade loop that was never installed. Terminal planners had to pay attention to South Station: from its opening to the time of the Second World War it was the busiest facility in the United States, both with respect to total numbers of trains (825 per day at the high point) and to density (90 trains during the peak hour, or one scheduled train every 40 seconds).
4. On the basis of the dynamometer car measurements, the calculation of horsepower, the conversion of horsepower to watts according to the factor 1/746, and the determination of average quantities for various units of time, Arnold obtained a figure of 1,800 kilowatts as the average daily input for all service. The total consumption for the year would thus be 1,800 × 24 × 365, or 15,768,000 kilowatt-hours. The total ton-mileage for the year, derived from the sum of all the products of locomotive and train weight multiplied by the distance each traveled, was 250,285,710. Dividing the latter into the former yielded the figure of 63 watt-hours per ton-mile. The characteristics that made this investigation a particularly excellent model of mathematical-empirical science were Arnold's techniques of separating what we might call the stable variables of weight, average speed, and tractive force from the unpredictable variables of velocity and direction of wind, condition of track, and relative skills of enginemen, and obtaining averages of measurements over long periods of time in plotting his curves of mean and average kilowatt input against time. All his calculations were based on the assumption that electric power was at least as efficient as steam, but there was already abundant evidence that the electric locomotive would outperform the older type at lower energy consumption.

5. The specific figures were as follows: operating, repair, maintenance, and cleaning expenses per locomotive-mile were $0.2305 for steam power and $0.1580 for electric; respective fixed charges per locomotive-mile were $0.0113 and $0.0783, yielding totals of $0.2418 for steam and $0.2363 for electricity.
6. Bion J. Arnold, "A Comparative Study of Steam and Electric Power for Heavy Railroad Service," *Railroad Gazette* 34, no. 26 (27 June 1902): 499.
7. The steam locomotive was a tank engine (that is, one in which the coal bunker and the water tanks are carried as fixed and integral parts of the locomotive proper) of the 2-6-6T wheel arrangement. The weight comparison would have to be made between the weight of the locomotive on driving wheels and the total weight of the two cars, since all axles of the latter were equipped with motors (the respective figures were 128,000 pounds and 140,000 pounds, or 9.4 percent higher for the two motor cars). The tractive force was about 18,000 pounds in each case.
8. The net energy consumed, in watt-hours per passenger, is given in the following table:

Number of Cars	Number of Passengers	Steam	Electricity
1	64	187.8	45.2
2	128	103.0	45.2
3	192	77.4	37.5
4	256	57.5	33.5
5	320	52.2	32.1
6	384	43.9	29.7

(Source: Arnold and Potter, *Street Railway Journal*.)
9. The automatic electric cab signal was invented by H. V. Miller, telegraph superintendent of the Chicago and Alton Railroad, and first installed on the Chicago and Eastern Illinois Railroad in the fall of 1900. The original form, used in conjunction with the automatic electric block signaling system, involved a special track circuit that transmitted current to the locomotive cab to illuminate one of two incandescent lights covered by white and red lenses, respectively indicating a clear and an occupied block. The Park Avenue signaling installation was the kind of automatic block known as an overlap system. Under such an arrangement the point in the track circuit where the passage of a train activated the relay that controlled the movement of any given signal was located 800 feet ahead of the signal succeeding it. In this way a signal would not clear from stop to approach until the train passed a point of 800 feet beyond the next signal.
10. "The Verdict on the Tunnel Accident," *Railroad Gazette,* 34, no. 5 (31 January 1902) 79.
11. E. H. McHenry, "Heavy Electric Traction on the New York, New Haven & Hartford Railroad," *Street Railway Journal* 30, no. 7 (17 August 1907): 242.
12. The four motors of the Class S locomotive provided a normal rated horsepower of 2,200, under a normal full-load current of 3,050 amperes; with an allowable maximum full-load current of 4,300 amperes, the horsepower could be raised to 3,000. Consumption at this level, however, was limited to short periods of time when starting a train. The normal running tractive force was a modest 20,400 pounds, and the maximum starting tractive force 32,000 pounds. A current of 4,300 amperes at 660 volts would require a power input of 2,838 kilowatts.
13. The alternatives to the gearless drive are the geared and the quill forms. Controversy as to the relative merits of the three types went on for years following the completion of the City and South London Railway in 1890 (see vol. 1, chap. 6).
14. All tests on the 5.5-mile track were designed to simulate the conditions of actual service, and they were to be carried out at speeds and rates of acceleration likely to be required by

the runs described in the final specifications: the 550-ton train was to complete a round trip from the terminal to Croton in 2 hours, 20 minutes, with a 20-minute layover and one stop in each direction; the 435-ton train was to complete the round trip in 1 hour, 28 minutes, with a one-hour layover; the 400-ton train was to complete it in two hours, with six stops en route and a one-hour layover. The two lighter trains were to maintain their schedules continuously over various predetermined periods of time.

The friction tests were particularly characteristic of scientific method because of the techniques developed to isolate, measure, and determine the effects of the variables involved, namely, bearing, journal, and motor friction, and the resistances offered by wind, curves, uneven track, and changes of grade.

The "accidental conditions" embraced the following: one and two motors rendered inoperable because of damage to the armature or field coils; controller defects arising from loss or damage of parts; failure of air brakes, with braking power obtained by operating the motors as generators (the fundamental principle of regenerative braking).

The special tests were concerned with a number of electrical and mechanical details—position of commutator brush holders, optimum size of fuses, effects of motor magnetism on metal objects near the track, consequences of short circuits arising from various causes, lateral thrust against rails when passing through curves, relative merits of third-rail and overhead distribution, and the results of minor wear of and damage to mechanical elements.

15. The essential comparative data in the acceleration tests are given in the following table:

Characteristic	Steam Power	Electric Power	Difference in Favor of Electric
Length overall (including tender of steam locomotive)	67′, 7¾″	36′, 11¼″	30′, 8½″
Total weight (including tender of steam locomotive)	342,000 pounds	200,500 pounds	141,500 pounds (1.7:1.0)
Weight per driving axle	47,000 pounds	35,500 pounds	11,500 pounds (1.3:1.0)
Tractive force	28,000 pounds	34,800 pounds	6,800 pounds (1.0:1.2)
Average acceleration rate, miles per hour per second, to 50 miles per hour	0.246	0.394	0.148 (1.0:1.6)
Time required to reach 50 miles per hour	203 seconds	127 seconds	76 seconds (1.0:1.6)

(Source: "Comparative Tests," *Street Railway Journal*.)

16. The precise forces involved in the 205th Street accident, for a speed of 60 miles per hour, were the following: maximum shear on outer spikes for electric locomotives, 5,820 pounds; for comparable steam locomotives, 4,890 pounds; shear strength of steel spikes, 17,060 pounds, or 4,625 pounds at a safety factor of four. The actual force for the electric locomotive was thus 1,195 pounds above the safe limit.
17. The two communities are contiguous and lie immediately north of the mouth of the Croton River, but the station and terminal facilities are located at Harmon.
18. The original installation at Port Morris consisted of 16 boilers rated at 625 horsepower,

and four turbo-generators rated at 5,000 kilowatts. The ultimate planned capacity was 24 boilers and six generators. The Yonkers plant was similar in essential respects. The chief contractors for construction and equipment were the following: steel and brick curtain wall, superstructure, Butler Brothers Construction Company (Yonkers) and Thompson-Starrett Company (Port Morris); electrical equipment, General Electric Company; boilers, Babcock and Wilcox Company; steel fabrication, American Bridge Company.

19. The locations of the eight substations, with their distances from Grand Central Terminal, were as follows: number 1, 50th Street and Lexington Avenue, 0.36 miles; number 2, Mott Haven Junction, 5.49 miles; number 3, King's Bridge, 9.44 miles; number 4, Yonkers, 15.44 miles; number 5, Irvington, 22.11 miles; number 6, Ossining, 30.31 miles (the first six were located on the New York Central line, usually called the Hudson Division, but officially the Electric Division); number 7, Bronx Park, 9.30 miles, number 8, Scarsdale, 19.02 miles (both on the New York and Harlem, or Harlem Division).
20. William J. Wilgus, quoted in William S. Root, "The First Electric Train into Grand Central Station," *Railroad Men* 20, no. 2 (November 1906): 41.
21. "Terminal Electrification of the New York Central," *Railroad Gazette* 36, no. 21 (20 May 1904): 384.
22. The complete installation at Harmon included the following constituents: for steam locomotives, a 30-stall engine house, coal dock, coal storage yard, special yard for empty coal and ash cars, ash-handling equipment, water lines, pumps, and water columns; for electric power, inbound and outbound yards for multiple-unit rolling stock, storage yard, loop tracks, buildings for the storage, inspection, maintenance, and repair of locomotives and multiple-unit cars, steam and electrical generating plant, machine shop, and storage building for parts and supplies.
23. The ratings of the 1913 locomotive, designated Class T, were increased in later models, as the weight was increased from 115 to 139 tons: the horsepower was raised to 240 for each motor, or a total of 1,920 for the locomotive, and the tractive force to 69,000 pounds.
24. The complete chronology for the electrification of the New York Central and Hudson River and the New York and Harlem lines is given in the following table:

From	To	Date
Grand Central Station	High Bridge	12 December 1906
Mott Haven Junction	Wakefield	29 January 1907
Wakefield	Mount Vernon	28 February 1907
High Bridge	Yonkers	6 April 1908
Wakefield	North White Plains	16 March 1910
Yonkers	Glenwood	December 1910
Glenwood	Hastings	1 February 1911
Hastings	Tarrytown	19 November 1911
Tarrytown	Harmon-Croton	22 February 1913
Grand Central Terminal	Harmon (through trains)	20 June 1913
Sedgewick Avenue	Yonkers (Getty Square)	1 February 1926

The total length of electrified line is 63.73 miles, comprising 360.23 miles of track.

The distribution of regularly scheduled weekday trains at Grand Central Terminal through 1912 was as follows:

New York Central and Hudson River	
Electric (Hudson) Division	112
Harlem Division	144
Total New York Central	256
New Haven	269
Total both roads	525

25. A summary of the results of investigations relating to maintenance costs and reliability of performance is given in the following tables:

Year	Cost per locomotive-mile
1910	$0.0320
1911	0.0308
1912	0.0334

Year	Cost per car-mile
1910	$0.0190
1911	0.0210
1912	0.0108

Mileage Operated per Minute of Train Time Lost
as the Result of Engine Failures, 1912

Electric Failures

Locomotives	8,691 miles
Multiple-unit cars	10,798 miles

Mechanical Failures

Locomotives	10,277 miles
Multiple-unit cars	12,374 miles

(Source: E. B. Katté, *Engineering News*.)

Mileage Operated per Detention of Two Minutes or Longer, Resulting
from Engine Failures, All Classes of Electric Locomotives, 1912–15

Year	Electrical Failure	Mechanical Failure
1912	103,967 miles	48,271 miles
1913	86,716 miles	27,873 miles
1914	57,395 miles	35,625 miles
1915	107,440 miles	53,720 miles

(Source: "Mechanical Design of Electric Locomotives," *Railway Age Gazette*.)

CHAPTER 2

1. The comparative totals of number of passengers are given in the following table:

	1900	1910
New York Central	27,816,343	48,364,945
New Haven	52,096,916	82,905,137
New Haven over New York Central	90%	71%

2. The New Haven's annual report for the year ended 30 June 1904 showed the following results:

Freight revenue	$24,413,541
Passenger, mail, and express revenues	23,425,173
Miscellaneous revenues	441,195
Total revenues	48,282,909
Operating expenses	$35,159,211
Net operating income	13,123,698
Proportion of passenger-train to total revenue	48.5%

3. For the details of the Harlem River program, see pp. 37–39.
4. "Test of New York Central Electric Locomotive," *Street Railway Journal* 24, no. 21 (19 November 1904): 898.
5. The interchange of motor operation between alternating and direct current presented no very great difficulty once the appropriate experiments were undertaken. In a series-wound motor equipped with a commutator, which was the type installed in the New Haven locomotives, the phase frequency of the current energizing the field coils is identical with that of the armature or rotor, and the torque delivered by the rotor is a linear function of its speed. The presence of the commutator not only guarantees the uniformity of frequencies between the two parts of the motor under alternating current, but also makes it possible to operate the motor equally well with direct current. The interchange between currents, however, was not automatic, and the motorman was required to operate changeover switches.
6. The letter to Newman was dated 27 October 1905. The relative costs per mile of installing the two systems for a four-track line, as cited by Westinghouse, are given in the following table:

	Single-Phase Alternating Current	Direct Current
Substations	$ 1,714	$16,150
Distribution lines	12,436	18,872
Transmission lines	1,815	2,181
Bonding	308	308
Total	16,273	37,511
Total cost for double-track line	10,261	25,611

The great difference between the two totals arises largely from the high cost of direct-current substations, which all concerned recognized as unavoidable. What the direct-current proponents found it difficult to concede was the greater cost of installing distribution and transmission lines. If the latter, however, had to be placed in underground conduits, as they were required to be in New York City, the cost would undoubtedly rise above the comparable figures for installing an overhead system.

7. Lamme's letter was also written under date of 27 October 1905. His tests indicated that the unit power consumption was nearly identical for the two types of motor, namely, 30.0 watt-hours per ton-mile for the alternating-current form, and 30.1 watt-hours for the direct-current type. In a little more than a year the controversy, for a while quiescent, exhibited another renewal of energy. At a meeting of the American Institute of Electrical Engineers held on 25 January 1907, Lewis B. Stillwell and Henry St. C. Putnam presented a paper summarizing the superior merits of electric traction over steam power. The high command of the electrical world was present (Arnold, Lamme, Lyford, Potter, and Sprague), joined by A. H. Armstrong of General Electric and C. S. Muralt, a New York consulting engineer. Sprague continued all the arguments set forth by means of extensive comparative analyses of direct-current and alternating-current systems at a meeting of the same society convened in New York on 21 May of the same year. Charles P. Steinmetz of General Electric appeared among the faithful communicants of both sects on this occasion.
8. E. H. McHenry, "Heavy Electric Traction of the New York, New Haven & Hartford Railroad," *Street Railway Journal* 30, no. 7 (17 August 1907): 243.
9. Among the minor questions that continued to be discussed through the years of construction, one issue looked to the future. The New Haven followed the Central and the Pennsylvania in adopting a transmission potential of 11,000 volts, but there were members of the railroad's and the manufacturer's engineering staffs who argued for the radically higher figure of 22,000 volts on the ground that the higher the voltage, the smaller the transmission losses; the reduction, however, to the operating potential of 450–560 volts in the locomotives would have required costly high-capacity transformers on the line and in the narrow confines of the locomotive cab, where space was at a premium (see note 16 of this chapter). With the lower transmission voltage it was possible to eliminate all line transformers and to reduce the capacity and hence the size of those in the locomotives.
10. Editorial, *Railroad Gazette* 37, no. 12 (2 September 1904): 290. The area that the New Haven hoped to develop comprises the easternmost portion of The Bronx (within the city limits) and the communities of Pelham Manor and New Rochelle beyond the boundary. Extending eastward from the city along the East River and the embayments of Long Island Sound, it offered a pleasing wooded and shore topography, some of which the city wisely preserved through the establishment of three parks (Sound View, Ferry Point, and Pelham Bay). It even attracted the favorable attention of so ill-disposed an observer as Henry James when he was writing *The American Scene* (see p. 52 and note 28 of this chapter). The subway mentioned in the editorial is the Bronx Park branch of the original Interborough line; the subway terminates at 149th Street and Third Avenue, whence it continues northward on a viaduct.
11. The geometric relation of the three cables and the connecting elements are shown below.

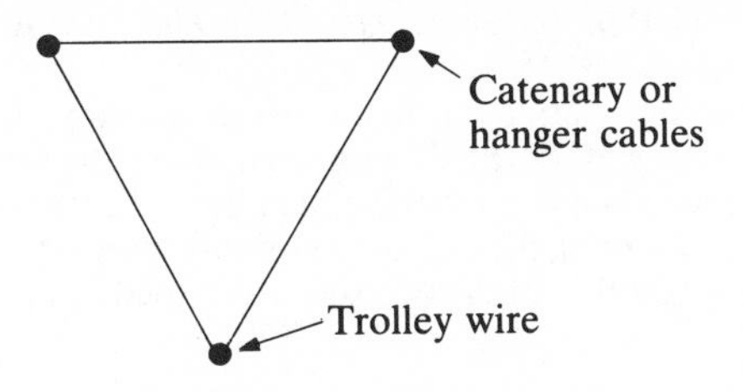

Operating experience soon revealed that this stable arrangement suffered from excessive rigidity for flexible pantograph action, a problem which the company solved by treating the original trolley or contact wire as another suspension element and hanging a new contact wire below it.

The term *catenary*, standard in electric railroad argot, is actually misleading in describing the geometry of the overhead distribution system. A catenary is the curve assumed by a perfectly flexible cord freely suspended from its ends, from which it follows that the suspended load is the weight of the cord and is hence distributed uniformly throughout its length. The hanger cables of an electric railroad, however, are ordinarily uniformly loaded along the horizontal line, since the suspenders that carry the conductor are spaced at uniform intervals. As a consequence, the hanger, like the cable of a suspension bridge, takes the form of a parabola. The respective shapes of the two curves are usually undistinguishable to the observer, but their corresponding algebraic functions are radically different.

12. "Overhead Construction on the New York, New Haven and Hartford," *Street Railway Journal* 30, no. 7 (17 August 1907): 241.

    A review of essential quantitative details of the New Haven system may serve to increase our admiration for the scientific thoroughness with which it was designed and installed. Loading factors for the gantries were the following: wind load on gantry frame, 25 pounds per square foot; wind load on conductor and hanger cables, 13.5 pounds per square foot of projected area of each; ice load at ½-inch thickness on 300-foot length of hanger cable, 75 pounds (my calculation); weight of 300-foot length of 9/16-inch steel cable, 216 pounds; total weight for 300-foot length of single iced cable, 291 pounds, or 582 pounds for two hanger cables; weight of 300-foot length of ½-inch copper conductor, 231 pounds; weight of 300-foot length of ice-covered conductor, 306 pounds; total weight of 300-foot length of two hangers and conductor, ice-covered, 888 pounds. The galvanized steel wire of the hanger cables has a tensile strength of 200,000 pounds per square inch, which is the customary unit strength of suspension-bridge wire. The triangular suspenders carrying the trolley wire are spaced 10 feet center to center. The wind load on the gantries, cables, and the Cos Cob drawbridge (27 pounds per square foot for the last) was calculated according to an empirical formula developed by the engineers who conducted the Marienfelde-Zossen tests in Germany (see vol. 1, chap. 6). Translated into English units, the formula was $P = 0.0027V^2$, where P is the wind pressure in pounds per square foot and V the wind velocity in miles per hour. A pressure of 27 pounds per square foot would thus correspond to a wind velocity of 100 miles per hour. (This formula was later modified in the United States to $P = 0.00256V^2$.)

    The contractors for the New Haven's installation were the Westinghouse Electric and Manufacturing Company for the turbo-generators and Westinghouse, Church, Kerr and Company for the power-house building and all equipment therein other than the turbo-generators. New Haven engineering and construction forces installed the catenary system.

13. "Along the 'Harlem River Branch,' "*Architectural Record* 24, no. 6 (December 1908): 422.

14. The series of illustrations in fig. 11 show the form and method of engagement of the various parts as well as the driving technique. The seven hollow pins which are integral elements of the plate fixed to the end of the quill are inserted into matching openings in a solid web surrounding the hub of the driving wheel. Spiders were fixed to both ends of the quill, and the rotation of the two sets was directly transmitted to the driving wheels at the

ends of the axle. It is interesting to note that the rotating force of the quill-and-spider assembly depended entirely on the shear strength of the steel pins.

15. The railroad and the engineering press seem to have been reluctant to publish these more spectacular data, possibly because of the adverse public reaction to the New York and Harlem's accident of 16 February 1907. The figures for the unusually high speeds appeared in a joint advertisement of the Baldwin and Westinghouse companies published in the issue of *Baldwin Locomotives* for April, 1924 (inside back cover). Advertisements are ordinarily blatantly dishonest, when they are not vacuous, but I doubt that such paragons of manufacturing rectitude would exaggerate the truth to this extent.
16. It is difficult to make a meaningful comparison between the forms and operating techniques of steam and electric locomotives, since the former are prime movers, while the latter are dependent on an outside source of power. In spite of this fundamental distinction, the whole intricate arrangement of power plant, transmission and distribution systems, substations, switching, controlling, and protective apparatus, and locomotives, taken as a unified working complex, was far more efficient than the individual steam engine. The various elements necessary to the satisfactory operation of electric motive power together formed a simpler functioning entity than the steam locomotive, with its heat-generating and thermodynamical equipment, but these constituents had grown in number and complexity during the astonishingly prolific decade following the completion of the B. and O.'s electrification at Baltimore. The New Haven's prototypical model included 120 essential, distinguishable operating and enclosing elements, distributed among braking system, circuits, current-collecting devices, locomotive structure and appurtenances, meters, motorman's control, motors and appurtenances, running gear, switches, and train-heating equipment.
17. Benjamin G. Lamme, "Alternating Current Electric Systems for Heavy Railway Service," *Street Railway Journal* 27, no. 12 (24 March 1906): 452–53.
18. This catalogue of potential horrors was not an exaggeration. Everyone familiar with the new technology had learned that a high-voltage conductor is surrounded by a potent dielectric field, so that the close proximity of a workman carrying any metal device is exposed to the danger of an arc forming between the wire and the conducting material. Maintenance crews on wire trains had to depend absolutely on the power dispatcher to cut off the flow of current in a section under repair, and to maintain a safe distance from the charged conductor. Derailments always posed a threat, but again the power dispatcher had to stand ready for an instantaneous cut-off. A number of devices were developed to shield the public at overpasses, but one bent on suicide could always find a means of access to the innocent-looking but lethal wire.
19. Letter dated 23 April 1906; quoted in *Street Railway Journal* 27, no. 17 (28 April 1906): 679.
20. "The New Haven Electrification," *Street Railway Journal* 27, no. 7 (17 February 1906): 267.
21. On the completion of the New Haven's program in 1914 the company operated 73 miles of electrified line, comprising 316 miles of main track and 184 miles of yard track and siding (the main stem between Woodlawn and New Haven is 61 miles of four-track line, but the six tracks of the Harlem River Branch were subsequently reduced to four as through freight and passenger traffic declined). The protection of the schedules as of November, 1914, required 100 locomotives and 69 multiple-unit cars, which together replaced 150 steam locomotives. The total investment in the electrical installation was $15,000,000 at the end of 1914, or about $315,000,000 at the 1980 price level. Power consumption and

operating costs for the various classes of service in November, 1914, are given in the following table:

Power Consumed in Passenger Service	
Kilowatt-hours per car-mile, through express	2.95
Kilowatt-hours per car-mile, through local	3.95
Kilowatt-hours per car-mile, multiple-unit	4.42
Operating Costs of Passenger Locomotives	
Cost of power per car-mile	$0.0276
Cost of repairs, wages, supplies per car-mile	0.0547
Total cost per car-mile	0.0823
Power Consumed in Freight Service	
Kilowatt-hours per 1,000 ton-miles, fast freight	28.0
Kilowatt-hours per 1,000 ton-miles, slow freight	29.7
Kilowatt-hours per 1,000 ton-miles, local freight	87.7
Operating Costs of Freight Locomotives	
Cost of power per 1,000 ton-miles	$0.1830
Cost of repairs, wages, supplies per 1,000 ton-miles	0.2890
Total cost per 1,000 ton-miles	0.4720
Operations of Cos Cob Power Plant	
Coal consumed per kilowatt-hour	2.78 pounds
Cost of generation per kilowatt-hour	$0.00764

(Source: W. S. Murray in *Railway Age Gazette.*)

In 1921 the New Haven passenger locomotives traveled an average of 33,000 miles per locomotive failure, and the average time lost per failure was 18 minutes. For freight power the average distance traveled per locomotive failure was 22,500 miles. The motive power department estimated that by 1921 the operation of electric locomotives had reduced coal consumption 65 percent below that in steam locomotives formerly operated over the electrified lines.

22. W. S. Murray, "The Success of Main Line Electrification" *Railway Age Gazette* 58, no. 18 (30 April 1915): 924, 928.
23. "The Scope of This Issue," *Street Railway Journal* 30, no. 15 (12 October 1907): 539. The allusion to the "single-phase leviathans" of the Pennsylvania is erroneous, since the locomotives were operated by direct current. See vol. 1, chaps. 6 and 8.
24. "The New York, Westchester and Boston Railway," *Engineering Record* 52, no. 23 (2 December 1905): 620.
25. The Westchester's track and electrical work was carried out under the direction of W. A. Pratt and H. S. Putnam, respectively chief engineer and electrical engineer of the railroad company. The contractor for trackwork, bridges, and stations was the City and County Contract Company of New York.
26. The Westchester freight locomotive was a somewhat smaller steeple-cab variation on the New Haven's original power: the wheel arrangement was the B-B form; the total weight was 79.75 tons; the four motors, each rated at 164.75 horsepower and equipped with a combination gear-and-quill drive, delivered a maximum tractive force of 39,800 pounds.
27. On the earlier history of Reed and Stem and the subsequent career of Alfred Fellheimer, see chap. 3.
28. Henry James, *The American Scene* (Bloomington: Indiana University Press, 1968), p. 143. The two eastern rapid transit lines in The Bronx eventually terminated at Dyre

Avenue (the Westchester terminal) and Pelham Bay Park. The other two reach 241st Street at White Plains Road and Woodlawn Road at the end of Jerome Avenue. These riches of public transportation (four rail lines and four rapid transit) powerfully stimulated the growth of population in The Bronx, but since it did not become a separate county until 1913, there are no reliable census figures until 1920. On the basis of such estimates as one can make, the population of the borough expanded nearly three times in the first 20 years of the new century, and grew another 73 percent between 1920 and 1930.

29. The precise volume of Westchester passenger traffic was 2,874,484 passengers in 1913 and 14,053,188 passengers in 1928; the maximum daily average was 44,000 passengers. The main line and the White Plains Branch could have comfortably accommodated 150,000 passengers per day.

CHAPTER 3

1. It is now impossible to make an accurate determination of the rate of increase of the New York Central's Pullman traffic in the early years of the century, but one can gauge it from the growth on the Pullman Company's total traffic. The number of Pullman passengers rose 161 percent during the decade of 1900–1910 (7,752,000 to 20,203,000 passengers) and more than five times (406 percent) between 1900 and 1920 (39,255,000 passengers in the later year). Since the New York Central and the Pennsylvania were by long odds the largest Pullman carriers, one may assume that their own sleeping- and parlor-car traffic was expanding at an even higher rate. The problems of coping with this traffic at Grand Central were compounded by the extremely high average speeds of the New York Central's premier trains just prior to the century year—for example, 40.4 miles per hour for the long run of the Southwestern Limited to and from Saint Louis, 41.0 miles per hour for the North Shore Limited to and from Detroit, and 46.7 miles per hour for the Empire State Express between New York and Buffalo.
2. For the annual and daily traffic at Grand Central Terminal, see table 7.
3. The total mileage of 3,774 was divided between 2,027 miles directly owned by the New York Central and Hudson River Railroad (53.7 percent of total) and 1,747 miles controlled and operated through leases (46.3 percent). Chief of the leased properties were the New York and Harlem, the New York, West Shore and Buffalo, the Boston and Albany, the Rome, Watertown and Ogdensburg, and the Fall Brook railroads. The last constituted the major part of the New York Central's Pennsylvania Division, which provided access to the anthracite coal fields and a connection with the Philadelphia and Reading Railroad. Many of the leased lines fell within the Adirondack, Saint Lawrence, and Ottawa divisions, which lay in thinly populated regions that generated little traffic beyond lumber and summertime tourists.
4. The first and most important plum in the Vanderbilts' western conquest was the Lake Shore and Michigan Southern Railroad, a direct and level double-track line between Chicago and Buffalo that had been established in the very year of the Central–Hudson River merger. Its grade-free straight-line route was effectively proclaimed by two notable works of railroad engineering: the cut-off known as Sandusky Air Line lies on a fill directly across the wide mouth of Sandusky Bay, and the great tangent of Butler Air Line, 62 miles in length between the west edge of Toledo and the town of Butler, Indiana, was drawn like a stretched cord over the face of the lake-country prairies. The chief acquisitions after the control of the Lake Shore were the Canada Southern and the Michigan Central to the

north, the little but valuable Pittsburgh and Lake Erie to the south, and the Cleveland, Cincinnati, Chicago and Saint Louis (the Big Four) to the west, a rail empire in itself that carried the Central's power to the Ohio and the Mississippi rivers. The previous acquisition of the Boston and Albany had given the larger road entry to the hub of New England commerce.

5. The inventory of the New York Central and Hudson River's motive power, rolling stock, and marine equipment as of 31 December 1900 was:

Locomotives	1,303
Passenger cars (including dining cars)	1,132
Baggage, mail, and express cars	349
Freight cars	58,651
Service cars	1,263
Barges, covered	71
Barges, hand-hoist	18
Barges, steam-hoist	7
Grain boats	32
Carfloats	28
Tugs	23
Ferries	7

6. The essential figures in the annual reports of 1900 and 1903 were:

	1900	1903
Gross revenues	$54,562,952	$77,605,778
Total expenses	34,051,586	53,459,314
Operating ratio	62.4%	65.0%
Net operating income	20,511,366	24,146,464
Nonoperating income	4,716,744	5,272,744
Gross income	25,228,110	29,419,208

7. The curious feature of the Lake Shore's test run was that the greater the distance the train moved from Chicago, the higher was its speed. The times and average speeds for the successive engine runs were as follows: Chicago-Elkhart, 101 miles in 92 minutes, 66.5 miles per hour; Elkhart-Toledo 133.4 miles in 114 minutes, 70.2 miles per hour; Toledo-Cleveland, 108 miles in 91 minutes, 71.2 miles per hour; Cleveland-Buffalo, 183 miles in 150 minutes, 73.2 miles per hour; overall, 525.4 miles in 7 hours 27 minutes, 70.5 miles per hour (Source: *Railroad Gazette*).
8. Untitled paragraph under "Editorial Announcements," *Railroad Gazette* 35, no. 10 (6 March 1903): 171. The biblical quotation is Nahum 2:4. It is not clear whether the *Gazette*'s editor, in his allusion to the Empire State Express, intended to say "dispensed with the gospel" or "dispensed the gospel." I suspect he meant the latter.
9. The formula for compensation to the city was worked out as follows: the railroad company was to pay the city an annual rental of $25,000 for the use of areas under viaducts; the railroad was further to pay all the costs of erecting transverse viaducts from 45th to 49th Street.
10. The precise land areas that would be appropriated by the railroad were the following: the equivalent of a three-block area bounded by Vanderbilt Avenue, Depew Place, 42d, and 45th Street for the head house and station tracks; six blocks bounded by Madison and Lexington avenues and 45th and 48th streets for the station approach and the adjoining

yards; the equivalent of two blocks in the Park-Lexington corridor from 48th to 50th Street for service tracks and a freight house with adjoining yard. I have made a rough estimate that this land was worth about $225,000,000 at the 1900 price level.

11. The idea of air-rights construction was nearly forty years old by 1903, but it is doubtful whether Wilgus or anyone else remembered the obscure source, if they had ever known it. The tracks of the Cincinnati and Indiana Railroad (later the east end of the Big Four's Indiana Division) were laid on the bed of the abandoned Whitewater Canal in Cincinnati and were thus depressed well below the surrounding street grade. The editor of the *Railroad Record*, which was published in the city, proposed in 1864 that the railroad company "erect buildings on the cross streets over their line. They could be used for manufacturing and other purposes, and their rental would make the valuable property . . . remunerative" ("Indianapolis and Cincinnati Railroad," *Railroad Record* 11 [7 January 1864]: 544). Nearly forty years after the 1903 plan Wilgus said that the idea of air-rights development came to him suddenly, like "a flash of light. . . . The most daring idea that ever occurred to me" (quoted in David Marshall, *Grand Central* [New York: McGraw-Hill Book Co., 1946], pp. 239–40).
12. The chief quantitative details in the plans of 23 December were the following: dimensions of the land area for the station complex, 680 feet on Vanderbilt, 300 feet on 42d, 260 feet on Depew, 275 feet on 43d, 460 feet on Lexington, 625 feet on 45th; the track system included 22 passenger, 8 express, 2 baggage, and 2 mail tracks on the upper level (total 34), and 9 suburban tracks on the lower. The track system was later greatly expanded as revisions came and went during the next four years.

    In most descriptions of the Grand Central project the term *express* is used to designate the trains and the trackage on the upper track level, but I have preferred the more cumbersome phrase *through train* because of the ambiguity associated with express in the United States. It is used to refer to packages and other kinds of light mixed freight carried in passenger trains (as in *express cars* or Railway Express Agency), fast through trains (Empire State Express, for example), through trains of any character, and fast, limited-stop suburban trains (White Plains Express, for example, as distinguished from White Plains Local).
13. "The New York Central's New Station in New York," *Street Railway Journal* 24, no. 27 (31 December 1904): 1160; editorial, *American Architect and Building News* 86, no. 1514 (31 December 1904): 105.
14. In the case of both the Marble Hill Cut-off and the Port Morris improvement, design, construction, and electrification were carried out under the direction of various members of the Grand Central team—William J. Wilgus, Edwin B. Katté, W. H. Knowlton, the principal assistant engineer, and A. B. Corthell, the terminal engineer. The contractor for the Marble Hill project was D. D. Streeter and Company, and for the Port Morris Branch the United Engineering and Contracting Company. Photographs of construction activity indicate that these two corners of The Bronx were then largely open land, wooded areas scattered among the grass-covered top surfaces of the rock.
15. The Giralda Tower, which stands above the older minaret once attached to a mosque, proved to be a particularly durable model for skyscraper designs. Twice used by Stanford White, it finally took lasting shape in two works designed by Graham, Anderson, Probst and White, namely, the Wrigley Building in Chicago (1919–21, 1923–24) and the Terminal Tower above Cleveland Union Terminal (1926–30). The original Madison Square Garden was demolished in 1925 as the first in an unending series of brutal acts of architectural vandalism in New York.

16. There are so many discrepancies between the two drawings respectively showing the initial plan and the revision that they strike me as entirely different works, the first showing an open track area, the second a court presumably lying over subgrade electrified trackage. The drawings are part of the manuscript collection of the New York Public Library; reproductions may be found in Middleton, *Grand Central*, pp. 65, 66.
17. The hotels of Warren and Wetmore include many of the most elegant and high-toned in the land, among them the Belmont, Ambassador, Ritz-Carlton, Vanderbilt, Commodore, and Biltmore in New York, and the Broadmoor in Colorado Springs.
18. "Stem v. Warren," *Miscellaneous Reports: Cases Decided in the Courts of Record of the State of New York* 96 (1917): 369–70. The buildings and structures the design of which fell within the responsibility of the Associated Architects, in order approximately from the terminal northward, were the following: head house of main station; Park Avenue bridge over 42d Street (at the conclusion of the First World War the street intersections and the area under the bridge were officially designated as Pershing Square); power house; the extension of Depew Place; the enlargement of Substation Number 1, ice storage plant; temporary facilities for passengers, scattered throughout the construction site; interlocking towers; various street viaducts; the battery house at 50th Street; buildings for the Adams Express Company, American Express Company, Merchants Loft, and the railroad Young Men's Christian Association; suburban stations at Fordham, Glenwood, Hartsdale, Ludlow, Mount Vernon, Ossining, and Scarsdale. The Associated Architects also drew up the plans for the Biltmore Hotel in 1910–11, for which the architectural office of D. H. Burnham and Company and its successor, Graham, Burnham and Company, acted as consultants, but the courts originally held that no compensation was due to Reed and Stem for this work.
19. The traffic and traffic density at leading metropolitan terminals built in the United States during the three decades preceding the opening of Grand Central Terminal, based on surveys carried out in 1908–13, are given below:

Station	Year Opened	Number of Tracks	Number of Trains Per Day	Number of Trains Per Track Per Day
Boston, North	1894	23	607	26.4
Boston, South	1899	28	786	28.1
Chicago, La Salle Street	1903	11	210	19.1
Chicago, North Western	1911	16	300	18.8
Chicago, Union	1880	9	270	30.0[a]
Cincinnati, Central Union[b]	1883	8	153	19.1
Hoboken, Lackawanna	1907	14	263	18.8
Jersey City, Pennsylvania	1892	12	334	27.8
Kansas City, Union	1913	16	313	19.6
New York, Grand Central	1913	67	479	7.2
New York, Pennsylvania	1910	21	392	18.7
Philadelphia, Broad Street	1893	16	574	35.9[c]
Saint Louis, Union	1894	32	322	10.1
Washington, Union	1907	26	244	9.4

(Sources: A. S. Baldwin, in *Railway Age*; Droege, *Passenger Terminals and Trains*.)

a. The figure for traffic density is misleading because the station was operated as though it were two stub-end terminals placed back-to-back, theoretically doubling its track capacity. A more accurate figure for number of trains per track per day would be about 20.

b. Central Union Depot in Cincinnati was the only station to be operated by means of switches hand-thrown at the track side.

c. Broad Street Station not only accommodated the highest traffic density, but also the highest peak-hour traffic (66 trains) for the number of tracks, or 4.1 trains per track per hour. The absolute maximum peak-hour traffic was the 90 trains of South Station, Boston, but this represented a density of only 3.2 trains per track per hour. Neither of these stations approached the total traffic volume and density of the major terminals of London, where densities at the most heavily used stations ranged from 50 to 60 trains per track per day.

20. The chief exterior dimensions of the head house and subsidiary structures in terms of the various street frontages were the following: 42d Street, 300 feet; Vanderbilt Avenue, 680 feet; 45th Street, 625 feet; Lexington Avenue, 460 feet; 43d Street, 275 feet; Depew Place, 260 feet. The head house was set back 40 feet on 42d Street and 70 feet on Vanderbilt Avenue. The entrance lobby with the ticket offices measured 90 × 300 feet; the grand concourse 160 × 470 feet in plan (72,500 square feet of floor area) × 150 feet in maximum height; the width of the main stairway was 25 feet; the platform width varied from 15 to 18 feet for through trains (rather parsimonious dimensions in view of the liberality of the head house spaces) and 17 to 29 feet for suburban. A loop track was planned for suburban trains. The cab stand on Vanderbilt Avenue measured 100 × 200 feet. A total of 250,000 square feet of floor area was reserved for offices.
21. "The New Grand Central Station," *Railroad Gazette* 37, no. 29 (30 December 1904): 678.
22. Frank Williams, "Grand Central City," *Architectural Forum* 128, no. 1 (January–February 1968): 54. The concourse is 16 feet below the street grade where Vanderbilt Avenue intersects 42d Street, but since the latter slopes downward toward the east, the broad pedestrian passage extending eastward to Lexington Avenue is level and at the same level as the concourse floor.
23. The dimensions of the chief interior spaces are: the building at grade level, out-to-out, 301 × 722.5 feet; the portion of the building above the elevated driveway, 301 × 649 feet; main through-train concourse, 120 × 271 feet in plan × 116 feet high to crown of vault; main waiting room, 59 × 207 feet in plan × 53 feet high; suburban concourse, 59 × 207 × 53 feet maximum; suburban waiting room, 59 × 260 feet; restaurant, 59 × 207 feet. The total enclosed area at grade is 217,472.5 square feet, and the total floor area devoted to station purposes is 1,188,000 square feet. The arched windows measure 33 feet wide × 60 feet high at the crown of the arch. The interior court is now covered by the Pan American Building.
24. The through-train tracks are numbered 1 to 42 from east to west, but tracks one to ten of the main system and an additional 33 tracks located in the triangular and trapezoidal interstices in the area of the terminal throat are reserved for storage and servicing. These tracks are numbered 50 through 93, with gaps at 66 through 71 and 85 through 89. The lead and ladder tracks in the throat are designated by letter, C through H and P, Q, and R. A total of 49 storage and service tracks, numbered 118 through 125 and 130 through 170, are disposed on either side of the throat on the lower or suburban level. The interlocking limits measure 810 × 3,850 feet, comprising an area of 3,118,500 square feet, or 71.6 acres. In the three blocks between 45th and 48th streets the walled precinct of the terminal extends from the inner sidewalk line along Lexington Avenue to the similar line on Madison, a distance of nearly 1,000 feet (fig. 23). The grades of the inner approach and

lead tracks are: upper level, 50th to 57th Street, 0.42 percent descending; lower level, 50th to 57th Street, 2.16 percent ascending.

25. The head of the engineering staff during the construction period was George W. Kittredge, chief engineer of the railroad company; under him was George A. Harwood, the chief engineer of electric zone improvements for the railraod. The structural engineers were Balcom and Darrow. Others responsible for various aspects of the project were the following: H. S. Balliett, engineer of signals; J. L. Holst, engineer of structures; W. F. Jordan, general engineer of construction; Edwin B. Katté, chief engineer of electric traction; W. L. Morse, terminal engineer; E. D. Sabine, resident engineer and assistant engineer of construction; W. J. Thornton, designing engineer.
26. The anchor ends of these cantilevers were designed to carry continuous column lines 23 stories in height for the projected overhead building. The individual girder is 9 feet deep, its section calculated for a maximum bending moment of 3,100,000 foot-pounds and an end shear of 288,000 pounds. The largest conventional girders in the head house are located in the frame at the third-floor level, where the depth ranges from 6 feet to 8 feet, 6 inches. The maximum interior span for a truss, 123 feet, 8 inches, characterizes those that support the elliptical vault of the concourse ceiling.
27. The live load was derived from the assumed presence of two 2-8-0 locomotives, each weighing 142 tons and coupled in tandem, which yielded the equivalent of 120,000 pounds divided between two driving axles set seven feet center to center, followed by a uniform train load of 4,500 pounds per lineal foot. The maximum allowable stress in tension was held to 10,000 pounds per square inch for the live load, the higher figure of 19,000 pounds applying only to dead loads. The equivalent compressive stress varied, since it was calculated by means of a formula involving length of span and the least radius of gyration for the member in question. For overhead construction the loading factors were a total floor load of 1,800 pounds per square foot for all stories and 20,000 pounds per lineal foot for building walls. The wind load of 30 pounds per square foot was fixed by the New York City building code.
28. Sections of columns supporting the ends of track-floor girders were calculated for loads varying from 1,275,000 pounds, divided between 446,000 pounds imposed by the track floor and 829,000 pounds from the overhead building, to 2,165,000 pounds, similarly divided between 685,000 pounds for the track floor and 1,480,000 pounds for the overhead column. For the long-span girders (length 44 feet, depth 7 feet, ¼ inch), the maximum bending moment, calculated on the basis of full live load and one-half dead load imposed by the track floor, is 3,850,000 foot-pounds. The corresponding end shear is 338,000 pounds. The highest calculated bending moment, under an assumed offset column delivering a load of 1,300,000 pounds, would have been 7,060,000 foot-pounds, and the shear 555,000 pounds. The weight of the box girder designed for these loads is 1,750 pounds per lineal foot. The largest of all girders in section, one designed to carry two offset columns over a span of 29 feet, 8 inches, is 10 feet, 5½ inches in depth.

    The problem of vibrations arising from passing trains was quickly seen to be crucial for high overhead frames. The solution consisted of the introduction of massive longitudinal concrete walls poured between adjacent pairs of appropriate columns, the walls acting as a kind of bracing with a mass sufficient to absorb floor and column vibrations.
29. This work was performed by two contractors: excavation and the laying of yard tracks was done by the O'Rourke Engineering and Construction Company, and building construction by the John Peirce Company.

30. The steel fabricators for the Grand Central project were the American Bridge Company, the McClintic-Marshall Construction Company, and the Phoenix Bridge Company. The construction contractors were the Terry and Tench Company. Leading pioneers of modern construction processes were among those who provided essential equipment: the concrete mixers were the type patented by Ernest Ransome; all rock drills and air compressors were manufactured by the Ingersoll-Rand Company.
31. The chief credit for the design of the Grand Central interlocking and signaling program belongs to H. S. Balliett, who is listed as engineer of signals for the railroad company at the time of construction, but this credit is apparently to be shared with his predecessor, W. H. Elliott, who directed the extensive signaling installation that accompanied the electrification of metropolitan lines. The contractor in both cases was the General Railway Signal Company, whose chief engineer, W. K. Howe, and manager of the electric railway department, S. Marsh Young, played a major role in the creation of the main-line signaling. Fitzhugh Townsend, a professor of electrical engineering at Columbia University, acted as an outside consultant.
32. The five towers comprise a total of 1,444 levers distributed according to size of machine as follows: B, 400 levers; A, 360; C, 160; U, 144; F, 80. The greater number of levers in Towers A and B arises from the fact that they control a high proportion of movements on the great array of passenger and storage tracks. Every tower operates under the authority of a towerman, whose assistants are levermen and a clerk or recorder.
33. The quantitative data for the signaling installation give some idea of its magnitude: total length of signaled track, 292 miles; 564 signal blocks (all four-track); 51 interlocking towers comprising 1,705 levers; 702 miles of wire on poles.
34. Indirectly supplementing the capacity of Grand Central was the expansion of most of the Hudson Division right of way (Harmon to Rensselaer) from two to four main tracks during the years 1910–13. This near-doubling of track miles necessitated the enlargement of the tunnels blasted through the spurs of pre-Cambrian crystalline rock in the Hudson Highlands. In places the rock is so dense and hard as to obviate the need for the concrete lining of tunnels. The daily traffic north of Peekskill at the time of the expansion amounted to 43 scheduled passenger trains, or about fifty actually operated, and an average of 30 freight trains. In 1913 the safe and expeditious movement of 80 trains per day on diversified schedules required four tracks, but with its highly developed system of automatic block signaling and interlocking controls, the line could easily have accommodated a much greater volume. After the Second World War this spacious artery, much of it twisting through sharp curves squeezed into narrow shelves between the water and the rocky cliffs, shrank to a mixture of double- and single-track.
35. The Steinway Tunnel, named after William Steinway, a member of the Board of Rapid Transit Commissioners and the founder of the famous piano manufacturing company, extends under 42d Street and the East River almost exactly on the line of the street to the Hunter's Point neighborhood in Long Island City. It was converted to rapid transit use in 1915, when the I. R. T. opened the first subway line into Queens Borough.
36. Douglas Haskell, "The Lost New York of the Pan American Airways Building," *Architectural Forum* 119, no. 5 (November 1963): 108.

    According to the architect Alfred Fellheimer, then a designer in the Reed and Stem office and hence one of the participants in the creation of Grand Central, even the architects' modest plans for circulation in and around the terminal were imperfectly realized.

In spite of my own pride in the station, I must say it has become an obstacle to attainment of important public objectives. . . .

Point one. When the present station was built, there were no cross streets between Madison Ave. and Lexington Ave. Traffic was mainly horse-drawn and light. The area was far north of the intense development of the day. Anticipating the growth of the city, the architects planned extension of all east-west streets across what was then an open-cut railroad yard, and continuation of Park Ave. in a straight line. East-west and north-south streets were to be at different levels, with ramp connections.

Result: through the insistence of the New Haven Railroad Park Ave. overpass at 42nd St. was restored—the one feature of the plan that was carried out.

Point two. For the growing number of commuters who would interfere with long-distance travelers the architects planned commuting facilities and exits along 46th St. (with express-train traffic oriented toward 42nd St.).

Result: zero.

Point three. To offset too great carrying charges the architects proposed a tall office building over the station (this won the competition for them). The railroad held that offices that far uptown would *never* rent but they reluctantly let foundation and column capacity over part of the property be designed to carry a 22-story building.

Result: additional capacity was incorporated . . . so the present station could support the limited amount of office space without structural change.

Point four. The architects proposed the then-unprecedented use of the air space over the yards for high-grade buildings. The railroads were doubtful, but permitted construction of one building. [This point, of course, contradicts Wilgus's claim.]

Result: the architects brought about organization of a group to finance Grand Central Palace, developed the first techniques of vibration control, and thus laid the groundwork for "air-rights" development of the Murray Hill–Park Ave. district. However, by then the station had been built. Realization of this potential came too late for redesign of urban traffic.

There were other disagreements on matters of future growth, such as the architects' recommendation that the right of way from the Mott Haven yards be eight tracks rather than four. [This was partly achieved by the signaling revisions of 1929–30; see pp. 183–88.]

(Alfred Fellheimer, quoted in "Can the Grand Central Concourse Be Saved?" *Architectural Forum* 101, no. 5 [November 1954]: 136–37.)

It is unfortunate that the Steinway and McAdoo subways were never built. They would have provided sorely needed links in the crosstown and East River transit lines. It should have been possible from the time the new Grand Central was opened, at the latest, to travel by subway without change from Brooklyn or Queens to the terminal, and from there to Pennsylvania Station.

37. The entrants in the competition for the Municipal Building were the following: J. Stewart Barney; Carrère and Hastings; Clinton and Russell; J. H. Freedlander; Cass Gilbert; Heins and La Farge; Hopkin and Koen; Howells and Stokes; H. H. Marshall; McKim, Mead and White; Trowbridge and Livingston; Warren and Wetmore. Gilbert, who had won the Customs House competition, withdrew and was succeeded by Helmle and Huberty. The design submitted by Howells and Stokes, with its strong vertical accent and its setbacks, was an anticipation of the Art Deco mode.
38. Gilbert's position in American architecture is secure (though he has yet to be the subject of the comprehensive monograph he deserves), but much of the credit for the Woolworth

must go to the structural engineers, the Gunvald Aus Company. They developed the intricate frame of K-truss, portal-arch, and knee bracing that gave the 760-foot tower its unique structural character.

39. Jean Paul Carlhian, "Beaux Arts or 'Bozarts'?" *Architectural Record* 159, no. 1 (January 1976): 133.
40. These umbilical attachments between the Biltmore and the terminal are no longer in functioning order. The railroad subsequently abandoned its generating system in favor of purchasing power from the Consolidated Edison Company, and the stairway rising from concourse to hotel lobby was eventually closed off because the derelicts of the city, wanted nowhere, found it less uncomfortable than streets and park benches. One detail of the building provided a mechanical counterpart to its architectural virtues: it was at the time the highest building in the world heated by hot water.
41. Douglas Haskell, "Futurism with Its Covers On," *Architectural Review* 157, no. 939 (May 1975): 301. Haskell is mistaken in his assertion that Park Avenue was the first parkway. The first in the United States was Elm Street in Manchester, New Hampshire (1840–41), but there were numerous European antecedents.
42. Rai Y. Okamoto and Frank E. Williams, *Urban Design Manhattan, Regional Plan Association* (New York: Viking Press, 1969), p. 38. The "access tree," a concept developed by the new Regional Plan Association, is essentially a metaphor referring to all forms of horizontal and vertical transportation conceived as the branches and roots of a multitrunk but unified system. For the Pan American Building and other air-rights constructions, see chaps. 5 and 8. I am unable to document the total of 60 acres of air-rights space. According to maps prepared by the Engineering Department of the New York Central Railroad, the total is 1,253,304 square feet, or 28.8 acres, including 134,205 square feet retained unleased but included in the Pan American Building envelope. The addition of the head house area would bring this to about 36 acres.

CHAPTER 4

1. The exact percentage increases in freight and passenger traffic for the New York roads are:

Freight Tonnage	
Increase 1900–1920	128%
Share of U.S. total 1900	41.6%
Share of U.S. total 1920	53.6%
Number of Passengers	
Increase 1900–1920	179.0%
Share of U.S. total 1900	36.1%
Share of U.S. total 1920	44.9%

(See table 9 for actual tonnage and number of passengers.)

2. The chief steps in this program of conquest began with the merger of the New York Central and Hudson River with the Lake Shore and Michigan Southern Railroad in 1914, when the older company adopted the shorter New York Central as its official title. By 1930 it had also merged the Cleveland, Cincinnati, Chicago and Saint Louis and the Michigan Central railroads. The equivalent acquisitions by the Pennsylvania were the Pittsburgh, Fort Wayne and Chicago and the Pittsburgh, Cincinnati, Chicago and Saint Louis railroads, both of which were in the fold by 1921. The B. and O. was a distant third with the

merger in 1917 of the Cincinnati, Hamilton and Dayton Railroad, a strategic Cincinnati-Toledo line considerably more important than its modest title suggested.

3. The outermost limits of the New York Metropolitan Switching District, taken in clockwise order, were as follows: Englewood station, Northern Railroad of New Jersey; Spuyten Duyvil Junction, New York Central Railroad; north end of Westchester Yard, New Haven Railroad; Fresh Pond Junction, Long Island–New York Connecting railroads; Fort Wadsworth and north end of Arthur Kill, B. and O.–Staten Island railroads; west end of Orange Street Yard, Newark, Lackawanna Railroad; west bank of Passaic River. The 95 freight stations in the district had a combined capacity of 4,000 cars. The daily movement of traffic through the system in 1919 required 640 eight-hour yard-engine shifts.

With the exception of the New Haven and the New York Central, all trunk-line railroads serving the Port of New York terminated at the New Jersey waterfront, where the various roads maintained a total of 70 open and covered piers, which included warehouse space with a total capacity of 20,000 carloads of freight. A special feature of port traffic at the time of the war underscores the magnitude of rail operations: in the fiscal year 1 July 1917–30 June 1918 the terminal district unloaded 90,000 carloads of perishable commodities, or an average of about 250 cars per day. Most of this traffic moved over the Pennsylvania Railroad and its affiliates via Washington, Saint Louis, and Chicago, and over the Erie Railroad via Chicago. All fruits and vegetables were unloaded, sorted, and auctioned on the premises of the company-owned produce terminals, and distributed to their destinations in the city by wagon and truck.

Railroad-owned marine equipment in 1919 comprised the following: 1,600 lighters with a combined capacity of 12,000 carloads of freight; 371 carfloats, combined capacity 5,300 cars; 134 tugs. A high proportion of grain was handled at floating elevators, and coal at special rail-water piers either gravity-operated or equipped with mechanical car dumpers.

The average number of regularly scheduled weekday passenger trains moving in and out of the various terminals through 1919 was:

Grand Central Terminal	392
Pennsylvania Station	608
Flatbush Avenue, Brooklyn	263
Central of New Jersey, Jersey City	248
Erie, Jersey City	248
Pennsylvania, Jersey City	147
Lackawanna, Hoboken	194
Ontario and West Shore, Weehawken	57
Total	2,157

At a time of numerous special trains, extra sections of scheduled trains, and mail and express trains, the total number of regularly scheduled trains shown in the public timetables should be augmented by a factor of about 15 percent, which would swell the total for metropolitan New York to about 2,480 trains. This number increased slowly and irregularly up to the Depression of 1930.

4. There are three classes of lighters: scows, or uncovered barges; barges, which are covered and sometimes heated or refrigerated; stickboats, which are scows equipped with a light crane consisting of no more than a boom, mast, and windlass. There were seven different transfer movements accomplished by lighters: from one rail line to another on a different shore; from railhead to vessel or reverse; from one vessel to another in a different berth;

from a rail line to a consignee on a different shore; from a shipper to a rail line on a different shore; from a vessel to a consignee; from a shipper to a vessel.

5. The limits of lighterage operations in New York Harbor, at their maximum extent, are given in the following table.

New York Boroughs
North
Hudson River at 135th Street
Harlem River at 161st Street
East River at Hell Gate
East
Harlem River at Bronx Kills and Hell Gate
Dutch Kills (tributary to Newtown Creek)
Whale Creek (tributary to Newtown Creek)
Newtown Creek at Metropolitan Avenue, Queens
South
Arthur Kill, north end
The Narrows at Pier 25, Richmond
The Narrows at 69th Street, Brooklyn

New Jersey Ports
North
Hudson River, 1,000 feet north of George Washington Bridge
East
Hudson River piers
South
Raritan Bay at the east city limit of Perth Amboy
West
Hackensack River at Newark Turnpike, Jersey City
Passaic River at Belleville Turnpike, Belleville
(Source: Maps of the Port Authority of New York and New Jersey.)

Quantities of marine equipment in operation at the time of the second World War (probably closely identical with the number of units in service from 1929 through the Second World War):

Barges, covered	919
Scows, deck	648
Barges, deck	581
Tugboats	561
Carfloats	295
Barges, coal	252
Barges, oil	226
Lighters, deck	207
Lighters, derrick (stickboats)	96
Barges, heated and refrigerated	87
Ferryboats	71
Tankers	54

Scows, dump	38
Barges, grain	37
Lighters, self-propelled	31
Miscellaneous	17
Total	4,120

(Source: Griffin, *The Port of New York*.)

Railroad-owned fixed equipment, 1929 through the Second World War:

Freight stations	196
Yards	109
Piers	56
Yard capacity, trunk lines	60,718 cars
Yard capacity, transfer lines	2,500 cars
Yard capacity, minor yards	6,322 cars
Total capacity	69,540 cars

Railroad-owned marine equipment, 1929 through the Second World War:

Covered barges	537
Carfloats	241
Scows	200
Lighters	103
Tugboats	101
Lighters, derrick	95
Barges, refrigerated	56
Barges and scows, special forms	24
Barges, derrick	6
Barges, oil-storage	3
Total	1,366

(Source: Port Authority of New York and New Jersey.)

6. The precise results of the 1914 analysis were:

Interchange freight	24,855,198 tons
Inbound rail	51,713,344 tons
Inbound shipping	22,000,000 tons
Outbound rail	10,413,797 tons
Outbound shipping	23,000,000 tons
Total	132,982,339 tons
Proportion shipped by rail	66.2%
Proportion shipped by vessel	33.8%
Quantity consumed in the port area	40,299,547 tons
Proportion of total tonnage	30.3%

(Source: *Regional Survey of New York, Transit and Transportation*.)

7. The construction of the various branch and connecting lines referred to in the foregoing paragraph is treated in the appropriate chapters of vol. 1.
8. "New York's Freight Terminal Problem," *Railway Age Gazette* 54, no. 15 (11 April 1913): 843.

9. The precise changes in freight tonnage between 1905 and 1915 were:

1905	784,920,000 tons
1910	1,026,492,000 tons (+ 30.8%)
1915	925,697,000 tons (− 9.8%)

10. The precise data pertaining to railroad construction and to freight car and locomotive orders were:

New railroad construction	
1905–7	15,223 miles
1915–17	3,010 miles
Decline	80.2%

Freight cars ordered	
1905–07	803,341
1915–17	354,483
Decline	55.8%

Locomotives ordered	
1905–07	15,389
1915–17	7,207
Decline	53.1%

(Source: *Railway Age.*)

11. The Pennsylvania Railroad in June, 1918, to cite a specific example, broke all previous records for the movement of tonnage over a particular route: on the low-grade freight line connecting the Philadelphia terminal area with Enola Yard, near Harrisburg, the company moved an average of 7,700 cars per day throughout the month, and reached the record for a single day of 9,531 cars. Since trains at the time seldom exceeded fifty cars in length, the peak movement represents about 200 trains for the day. The saving of fuel following the extensive cancellation of passenger trains made these operations possible.
12. William G. McAdoo, quoted in "Nation's Railroads Now under Government Control," *Railway Age* 64, no. 1 (4 January 1918): 2.
13. "Effects of Unwise Regulation Illustrated by 1917 Statistics," *Railway Age* 64, no. 1 (4 January 1918): 10.
14. The specific elements in the program of the Committee of Eastern Railroads indicate how many practical steps were involved in this massive unified effort. They comprised the following: the analysis of the railroad fuel supply (a particularly crucial factor) to determine the extent and locations of the most acute needs and the tonnage immediately available; the elimination wherever possible of circuitous routing; the cancellation of fast freight trains in favor of "full-tonnage" trains loaded to the locomotive capacity; the establishment of fifth-morning delivery for freight moving between Chicago and New York; special instructions for the operation of extra trains on emergency schedules; an embargo on all steel shipments to eastern ports except for those moving on government priority; an embargo on all freight shipped via Pittsburgh and its diversion to routes north or south thereof (the city posed a special problem because of labor shortages as well as congestion); the annulment of the Broadway Limited.
15. The Official Classification Territory covers all railroads within the area lying east of the Mississippi River and north of the Ohio River and the Mason-Dixon line, together with

the Chesapeake and Ohio, Norfolk and Western, and Virginian, as these companies existed in 1917.

16. Alfred H. Smith, instructions to eastern railroads, 31 December 1917; quoted in "Nation's Railroads Now under Government Control," *Railway Age* 64, no. 1 (4 January 1918): 4.
17. "The Pennsylvania's Fight with Jack Frost and the Snow Banks," *Railway Age* 64, no. 9 (1 March 1918): 449. It is questionable how cheerfully the employees endured their burdens.
18. I do not know precisely what lines were affected by the order of 26 January, but since the Erie main line east of Salamanca appeared close to breakdown, it was probably the primary target of this prohibition. The New York Central's four-track water-level route, with the parallel West Shore line available for a fifth track, gave the road advantages that not even the Pennsylvania enjoyed.
19. Smith's order of 29 January carries a historical meaning that urges a more detailed exposition. It can be divided into six parts, beginning with the location of freight-car concentrations and ending with the transloading operations at New York:

1. Freight is to be concentrated for shipment to New York or other eastern ports at the following cities: Chicago, for freight originating there or moving over routes tributary to the Chicago gateway; East Saint Louis, for freight originating in the Saint Louis Terminal District or moving through the Saint Louis gateway; Buffalo, for freight originating in Michigan, the Canadian provinces, and on the Niagara Frontier; Pittsburgh, for freight originating there and south of the Ohio River, or moving through the Pittsburgh gateway.

2. Freight is to be consolidated into full trains or groups of contiguous cars within trains for shipments as solid units to New York Harbor or other eastern ports.

3. The office of the assistant director is to be advised daily by telegram of the number of cars destined for each port and held at the appropriate concentration point, the route thereof, and the length of the longest delay to which a particular car has been subjected.

4. The departure time of every train leaving Chicago, East Saint Louis, Buffalo, or Pittsburgh is to be communicated by telegram at the moment of departure.

5. Each car is to be routed over the roads best equipped to move cars promptly. Smith did not leave the selection of routes to the railroad officers but specified the following lines as the first choices for the various New York carriers:

a. For the Baltimore and Ohio, shipments out of Chicago to be routed via the B. and O., out of East Saint Louis, via the Baltimore and Ohio Southwestern;

b. For the Central of New Jersey, shipments out of Chicago via the New York Central (this routing would require an intermediate link, since there was no physical connection between the two roads west of the New York Terminal District), out of East Saint Louis, via the Cleveland, Cincinnati, Chicago and Saint Louis (Big Four);

c. For the Delaware, Lackawanna and Western, shipments out of Chicago via the New York, Chicago and Saint Louis (Nickel Plate Road), out of East Saint Louis, via the Toledo, Saint Louis and Western;

d. For the Erie, shipments out of Chicago via the Erie, out of East Saint Louis, via the Toledo, Saint Louis and Western;

e. For the Lehigh Valley, shipments out of Chicago via the Michigan Central, out of East Saint Louis, via the Wabash;

f. For the New York Central, shipments out of Chicago via the New York Central, out of East Saint Louis, via the Big Four;

g. For the New York, Ontario and Western, shipments out of Chicago via the Grand Trunk Western, out of East Saint Louis, via the Wabash;

h. For the Pennsylvania, shipments out of Chicago via the Pennsylvania, out of East Saint Louis, via the Vandalia.

i. For the Philadelphia and Reading, shipments out of Chicago via the New York Central, out of East Saint Louis, via the Big Four. (The initial routings preserved as much as possible the existing affiliations and connection patterns among the railroad companies.)

6. Ships sailing to Great Britain, Belgium, France, and Italy were to be loaded at the following piers: for B. and O. freight, at Saint George, Staten Island; Central of New Jersey, at Communipaw terminals, Jersey City; Lackawanna, at Hoboken; Erie, at Weehawken (three of the Erie's four piers at this location were allocated to Belgian relief); Lehigh Valley, at Constable Hook; New York Central and West Shore, at Weehawken (the four West Shore piers provided the best accommodations, with a total capacity of nine or ten ocean vessels). The Pennsylvania Railroad owned no piers beside water with a depth sufficient for ocean vessels.

(Source: *Railway Age*.)

20. For the membership and other details pertaining to this commission, see vol. 1, chap. 7.
21. Wilgus presented his plan of 1908 directly to the Public Service Commission of the state in the form on a printed booklet. The foregoing version is taken from William J. Wilgus, "Transportation in the New York Region," in Harold M. Lewis, *Transit and Transportation; Regional Survey* 4 (New York: Regional Plan of New York and Its Environs, 1928): 172–73.
22. J. J. Mantell, "Operation of the New York Terminal District," *Railway Age* 67, no. 23 (5 December 1919): 1111.
23. My estimate of the probable investment required for the Lindenthal project can only be regarded as suggesting the order of magnitude. On the assumption that it would have cost at least three times as much as the Verrazano-Narrows Bridge (1959–64), the total cost at the 1921 building-cost level would have been about $350,000,000 or close to $3,000,000,000 at the 1980 level.
24. See table 9 for actual traffic volumes.
25. The following is a summary of the financial returns for 1920.

Railroad	Total Revenues	Total Expenses	Net Operating Deficit or Income	Operating Ratio Percent
B. and O.	$230,225,153	$233,340,170	-$ 3,115,017	101.4
C. N. J.	51,681,800	57,493,097	- 5,811,297	111.2
D. L. and W.	83,340,062	73,840,729	9,499,333	88.6
Erie	122,163,099	133,014,160	- 10,851,061	108.8
Lehigh Valley	75,229,584	80,503,974	- 5,274,390	107.0
Long Island	24,381,974	20,586,850	3,795,124	84.4
N. Y. Central	372,961,667	357,981,175	14,978,492	96.0
N. Y. N. H. and H.	123,512,310	126,346,384	- 2,834,074	102.3
N. Y. O. and W.	13,154,689	12,684,317	470,372	96.4
N. Y. S. and W.	4,920,489	5,955,692	- 1,035,203	121.0
Pennsylvania	566,860,758	609,121,731	- 42,260,973	107.5
Totals	1,668,431,585	1,710,868,279	- 42,436,694	102.5

(Source: *Poor's Manual*.)

26. Compact of April, 1921; quoted in John I. Griffin, *The Port of New York* (New York: Arco Publishing Co. for City College Press, 1959), p. 73.
27. The plans for port development formulated in 1920 by the Harbor Development Commission and apparently issued as a joint product of that body and the newly established Port of New York Authority included a considerably more innovative proposal for freight stations. Designated in the plan as "universal inland freight stations," they were to be combined with terminal buildings which were to contain facilities for warehousing, industry, and wholesale trade. The aim of this unified multiuse character was to consolidate facilities into a few strategically located centers and to simplify the patterns of freight movements between the railroads and the shippers or consignees. In order to realize this end the commissioners proposed that the metropolitan area be divided into zones of equal freight tonnage, with one universal freight station located in each zone. The freight moving between the rail terminals and the stations was to be carried by motor truck, while that moving from one station to another was to be conveyed in special 58-foot cars hauled by automatically controlled electric motive power over tracks laid in tunnels of standard rail dimensions. The description of the interstation system suggests the use of containers; this and the underground electrified rail line indicate a possible derivation from the Wilgus plan of 1908. I have not seen any technical details of the proposed automatic operation, which may have been more prophetic than anyone has realized.
28. Port of New York Authority, *Annual Report,* 1924 (Albany: J. B. Lyon Co., 1925), p. 23.
29. The chief structures built or acquired under the sponsorship of the Port Authority up to the Second World War, with dates of completion or acquisition, are the following:
Goethals Bridge, Arthur Kill, 1928
Outerbridge Bridge, Arthur Kill, 1928
Holland Tunnel, Hudson River, completed 1927, acquired 1930
George Washington Bridge, Hudson River, 1931
Bayonne Bridge, Kill van Kull, 1931
Inland Freight Terminal Number One, Eighth to Ninth Avenue, 15th to 16th Street, 1932 (p. 150).
Lincoln Tunnel, Hudson River, South Tube, 1937
Grain Terminal and Columbia Street Pier, Brooklyn, acquired 1944
Lincoln Tunnel, North Tube, 1945
30. All quotations in the foregoing summary are from William J. Wilgus, "Transportation in the New York Region," in Harold M. Lewis, *Transit and Transportation, Regional Plan* 4 (New York: Regional Plan of New York and Its Environs, 1928): 175–76. Wilgus first offered his proposal for an outer belt railway in a paper entitled "The Railroad Problem in Relation to the Metropolitan District," presented before the annual meeting of the New York Section, American Society of Civil Engineers, 12 May 1920.
31. For rail- and water-borne traffic in the harbor area, see tables 3, 6, and 9.
32. The piles for the Erie pier were driven in three superimposed tiers in a tight mass around and between the vehicular tunnels. The Jersey City ventilating shaft stood directly at the offshore end of the structure.
33. The Starrett-Lehigh Building, standing on the short diagonal connector between the lower ends of Eleventh and Twelfth avenues, was also close to the piers of the B. and O., Lackawanna, and Erie railroads and hence available for use by those companies. The contractor was Starrett Brothers and Eken, whose subsidiary was the cosponsor, the Starrett Investing Company.

34. The West Side line originally occupied the following strips of urban land from north to south: open ground at the river's edge from Spuyten Duyvil to the yard at 60th Street; the surface of Eleventh Avenue from 60th Street to 30th Street; the surface of Tenth Avenue from 30th Street to 12th Street; the surface of West Street from 12th Street to the terminal at Saint John's Park.
35. These plans were prepared under the direction and authority of the following officials of the city and the railroad: Ernest P. Goodrich, consulting engineer to the president of the Borough of Manhattan; Charles W. Staniford, chief engineer, New York Department of Docks and Ferries; John F. Sullivan, an engineer with the Bureau of Contract Supervision, Board of Estimate and Apportionment; George A. Harwood, chief engineer, Electric Zone Improvements, New York Central Railroad; H. D. Jewett, designing engineer, West Side Improvements, New York Central Railroad. A critique of this plan was formulated by R. A. C. Smith, a commissioner of the Department of Docks and Ferries, and a defense was prepared by William A. Prendergast, the city controller. Both documents were published in *Railway Age,* 7 April 1916.
36. The precise terms of the agreements and plans of February and December, 1917, were the following: the railroad to transfer to the city waterfront and subaqueous land owned by the company and valued at about $250,000,000, and to grant to the city the use, if not the ownership, of other marginal lands along the Hudson River to a distance of 200 feet from the shore; the transfer in return of municipal riparian rights to the railroad, contrary to the act of 1870. Municipal and public opposition to the agreement was concerned with the following issues: the loss of riparian rights; the absence of any provision for allowing the construction of tracks by any other railroad company seeking to enter Manhattan from New Jersey (the city had long wanted competing lines on the island); the absence of a provision for granting trackage rights to any other road; the closing of at least 12 streets providing access to the shore and to inner streets; the laying of two additional tracks for a total of six through Riverside Park, which the railroad agreed to place in a roofed cut with a cover of soil suitable for landscaping (the company agreed to set aside $300,000 for landscaping, but the city claimed the cost would be at least $500,000). The gains to the city included the following: the extension of Riverside Park northward from Dyckman Street to Spuyten Duyvil; the removal of tracks from the surface of Tenth and Eleventh avenues; the abandonment of the freight terminal at Saint John's Park and its replacement elsewhere; the removal of all trackage south of Canal Street; the elevation of the line from Canal to 60th Street over a private right of way lying between existing streets; the electrification of the entire West Side line within the city limits, to be completed within four years of the agreement, that is, by February, 1921. The questionable features were the loss of tracks below Canal Street, the extensive elevated trackage, and possible damage to Riverside Park. The civic groups that opposed the plan wanted the West Side line placed in a tunnel, but they do not seem to have considered the resulting difficult and costly problem of building dock and industrial spurs. The railroad company claimed to be prepared to spend $60,000,000 to $100,000,000, or about $860,000,000 to $1,400,000,000 at the 1980 price level.
37. Richard Franz Bach, "The City and the Railroad," *American Architect* 111, no. 2147 (14 February 1917): 99. The chief questions on the character of good urban design that went either unanswered or little considered in the discussions between the railroad and the municipality related to the following elements of the West Side plan: the 59th Street bridge over the south end of the railroad's 60th Street Yard; the establishment and the

nature of the long-discussed Henry Hudson and Robert Fulton memorial park at 14th Street; the equally long discussed crosstown rail tunnel for passenger, mail, and express trains, now shifted from 53d Street to the corridor between 42d and 45th streets; the covering of trackage at all existing or proposed parks; the control of architectural and urban design throughout the entire project by the city's Fine Arts Commission. The only concrete realization of all these discussions was the announcement by the railroad in January, 1915, of the construction of a new produce terminal in the block bounded by Eleventh and Twelfth avenues and 34th and 35th streets. The completion of the structure, however, was delayed until the end of the war.

38. Alfred H. Smith, summarized and quoted in "New York City and the Railroad Problem," *Railway Age* 68, no. 17 (23 April 1920): 1236.
39. The engineering officers of the New York Central apparently did not at the time consider the combination of electric motors and generators operated by internal combustion engines, although the successful development of this form of power for freight service lay little more than two years in the future. On the cost of electrification, the Long Island's officers felt that they would be most abused, being faced with an estimated expenditure of $30,000,000; the B. and O. anticipated a cost of $17,000,000, and the New Haven $5,000,000. The second company, however, quickly changed its corporate mind at least with respect to passenger service: the electrification of the Staten Island Rapid Transit was completed two years after the legislation of 1923 (pp. 208–9).
40. Castleton Cut-Off required the removal or emplacement of 6,000,000 cubic yards of earth and rock for cuts and fills with respective maximum depths of 70 feet and 80 feet. The Hudson River crossing consists of two through spans, 400 and 600 feet in length, in which the track is carried by massive subdivided Pratt trusses. The location of the cut-off allowed the railroad to unite four divisions (Mohawk, River, Hudson, and Albany, from west to east) with very nearly a straight-line connection. Part of the high cost of the project came from the laying out of Selkirk Yard at the New York town from which it takes its name. The replacement cost of the entire project would be well over $250,000,000 at the 1980 price level.
41. W. C. Lancaster, quoted in "N. Y. C. Authorized to Operate with Electric and Diesel Electric Locomotives in New York," *Railway Age* 79, no. 21 (21 November 1925): 963–64. Lancaster's argument rests chiefly on operating features objectionable to persons living or working near the line, considerations that have never arisen in the planning of expressways and airports, but he might have gone on to point out the vastly greater efficiency and flexibility of the diesel-electric locomotive compared to its steam counterpart. The manufacture of the new type of motive power was jointly introduced in 1924 by the American Locomotive Company, the General Electric Company, and the Ingersoll-Rand Company. The first units following the New York Central's experimental model were installed almost simultaneously during the succeeding year by the B. and O. and the Central of New Jersey railroads, in both cases for the switching of cars at the companies' float bridges in New York City.

A forgotten adjunct to the West Side plan was the proposal by Richard C. Sibley, put forth in 1925, to build a union freight terminal on the New York Central's line which was to be connected with the New Jersey railheads by a fleet of motorized carfloats large enough to bring in cuts of freight cars with the bulk shipments unbroken. Less-than-carload freight was to be delivered from the terminal to the consignee or from the shipper to the terminal by motor truck during the night hours to obviate the need for freight trackage on Manhattan Island.

42. The staggering cost of the plan, far above the actual final investment, was to be divided as follows: railroad company, $110,000,000; city, $50,000,000; state, $15,000,000. Indicative of the city's dependence on the railroad is the fact that the daily traffic over the West Side line included 328 cars of milk and 100 cars of express destined for the terminal of the Railway Express Agency at 33d Street and Eleventh Avenue, as well as the customary general freight. The great volume of express accounted for the number of mail and express trains operated by the New York Central that carried the designation West Side Mail in the operating timetables. The members of the West Side Improvement Engineering Committee were the following: William C. Lancaster, chairman of the committee, chief engineer, New York State Transit Commission; J. R. Slattery, acting chief engineer, New York City Board of Transportation; Arthur S. Tuttle, chief engineer, Board of Estimate and Apportionment; C. M. Pinckney, chief engineer to the president of the Borough of Manhattan; Billings Wilson, deputy manager, Port of New York Authority; R. E. Dougherty, engineering assistant to Patrick E. Crowley, president of the New York Central Railroad. Simultaneously with the signing of the final agreement between the company and the city, the Interstate Commerce Commission, on 2 July 1929, approved the lease of the Michigan Central and the Big Four to the New York Central, which set the stage for the merger of these extensive properties with the controlling railroad (the process was carried out in 1930–36).
43. All work on the West Side project was carried out under the direction of J. W. Pfau, the railroad company's chief engineer. For the first phase the general contractors were the James Turner Company and the George A. Fuller Company, while the steel contractors were the American Bridge Company, the McClintic-Marshall Company, and the Fort Pitt Bridge Works. The structural design of the Riveside Park enclosure, which fell within both phases, was the work of the Madigan-Hyland Company. The general contractor for the terminal at Saint John's Park was the James Stewart Company. For the second phase the contractors were the Thomas Crimmins Contracting Company, the George J. Atwell Foundation Corporation, the P. T. Cox Contracting Company, and the Corbetta Construction Company. All steel was fabricated by the American Bridge Company. The only deviations from straightforward engineering work in the construction of the West Side line were the use of bedrock caissons to carry the frames of air-rights structures and to support the track at the crossing of the Pennsylvania Railroad's tunnnels and the adoption of independent framing systems for the viaduct piers and flooring and for overhead buildings to insulate the latter from the vibrations of passing trains, or the impacts arising from switching cars. The total investment for the railroad came to about $30,000,000 at Depression prices, less than a third of the most recent estimates.

CHAPTER 5

1. See table 7 for precise data on the annual and daily traffic at Pennsylvania Station. A small part of the total traffic came from the transfer of the B. and O. and Lehigh Valley trains to the Pennsylvania terminal respectively on 28 April and 15 September 1918, following the specific orders of William G. McAdoo, director-general of the United States Railroad Administration. The aim for all the roads involved was the unification of facilities, but in the case of the B. and O. the Railroad Administration intended also to generate more traffic on the company's New York–Washington line in order to reduce the burdens on the overloaded Pennsylvania. To the best of my knowedge, no comparative studies were ever

made to determine the success of this plan. The B. and O. trains returned to the Central of New Jersey station on 29 August 1926 because of the high rental charges exacted by the Pennsylvania, which suggested that the larger company had ceased to share McAdoo's belief in the more equable distribution of traffic between the two roads.

2. Sleeping cars serving the east coast of Florida, Gulf Coast cities, New Orleans, Shreveport, and White Sulphur Springs, were operated by the Pennsylvania Railroad between New York and Washington; cars routed to and from Memphis, Nashville, and Louisville were operated via Cincinnati. One Memphis sleeper, however, followed an oddly circuitous route via Washington and Birmingham over the Seaboard Air Line and the Saint Louis–San Francisco Railway (Frisco). The number of cars necessary to protect these numerous schedules varied considerably over the year: at the minimum it would be one car per route, or a total of 229; at the maximum, during the Christmas–New Year holidays and the height of the Florida winter season, for example, the total might rise to three times the low figure, or around 650 cars. The average through the year was 400 cars per day. The Pullman Company's great mobile pool of sleeping, parlor, lounge, and club cars, varying portions of which could be shifted over the country as needed, made it possible for the road to meet these heavy and fluctuating demands.
3. The operation of locomotive Number 460 was entrusted to four men: three road foremen of engines, J. A. Warren, A. J. Sentman, and W. L. Anderson, took the throttle in turn, while fireman A. L. Hayden, with no mechanical stoker to help him, was kept extremely busy maintaining a hot enough fire to sustain the boiler pressure.
4. Coordinated rail-air service is now a historical curiosity, although any serious national program of energy conservation might have to include its revival. The schedule adopted in July, 1929, called for the following distribution of time: running time of train, 23 hours, 15 minutes; flying time, 21 hours, 51 minutes; transfer time, 5 hours, 31 minutes; total, 50 hours, 37 minutes. The transfer points were an airport near Columbus, Ohio, known as Port Columbus, and Waynoka, Oklahoma, where westbound passengers ate dinner in the Fred Harvey restaurant (all dining car and restaurant service offered by the Santa Fe was at the time provided by the Fred Harvey Company). The westbound connecting train on the Santa Fe was the Missionary, and the eastbound was the Scout, neither of which qualified as a high-speed luxury flyer.
5. The distribution of average daily traffic in January, 1929, was as follows:

Railroad	Number of Trains	Number of Cars
Long Island	466	3,588
Pennsylvania	213	1,853
New Haven	20	189
Lehigh Valley	13	112
Totals	712	5,742

A survey conducted by the staff of *Railway Age* for the same period yielded somewhat higher figures for number of trains, as follows: Long Island, 487; Pennsylvania, 223; New Haven, 21; Lehigh Valley, 14; total, 745. The number of daily passengers was calculated from the annual total divided by a factor of 320. The station traffic reached its peak during the halcyon days of 1928–29 on 3 September 1928, when 802 trains, consisting of 6,409 cars, carried 220,340 passengers in and out of the terminal. The average traffic density on the station trackage was thus 38.2 trains per track per day. The average density for January, 1929, based on the daily total of 745 trains, would have been 35.5 trains per track per day. The coach yard serviced sleeping cars moving over the Pennsylvania to and from connecting roads, which at the time were the Atlantic Coast Line, Seaboard Air Line, Richmond, Fredericksburg and Potomac, Southern, and Chesapeake and Ohio at Washington, and the Louisville and Nashville at Cincinnati.

6. The Long Island Rail Road offered a special ten-cent fare to the site of the World's Fair in Flushing Meadow, with the expected result that nearly 80 percent of the passengers who used the station in 1939 were carried by that road. The distribution of passengers for the year showed that, however unequal it was, the fair proved a boon to the owner and all the tenants. The total number of passengers by road in 1939 was:

Long Island	54,599,275
Pennsylvania	13,587,976
New Haven	931,185
Lehigh Valley	544,374
Total	69,662,810

The Lehigh Valley's share of the traffic represented an increase of about 75 percent above the average of the late twenties; for the New Haven, about 50 percent; but no more than 20 percent for the Pennsylvania, whose western lines had suffered an extreme attrition during the Depression.

7. For the operation of the freight terminals during World War II, and of the New Jersey passengers terminals from the first through the Second World War, see chap. 7.
8. Since Broad Street Station was a stub-end facility comprising 16 tracks, the average traffic density at 574 trains would have been 35.9 trains per track per day, somewhat above the 35.5 trains at Pennsylvania Station through the month of January, 1929. As a matter of routine operation, however, the Philadelphia terminal accommodated the greatest density of train movements in the United States, from its opening in 1893 to the completion of Thirtieth Street Station in 1934. The average over the forty years varied from 33 to 36 trains per track per day.
9. The original New York installation was not entirely replaced, in spite of the conversion to an alternating-current overhead system and the sale of the power plant. The Long Island clung to direct current, so that the 650-volt third rail had to be left in place in the East River tunnels, on the station tracks, and in all yards previously and likely to be used by the Long Island, and in the North River tunnels to provide power for trains used in the repair of wires, when the current had to be cut off in the segment under repair. For operations outside the New York metropolitan area, electric power was purchased from the Public Service Electric and Gas Company of New Jersey, the Philadelphia Electric Company, and the Safe Harbor Water Power Corporation. The total power required for operations between New York and Washington was estimated at 816,000,000 kilowatt-hours per year.
10. The designation of wheel arrangements for electric locomotives refers to the wheels visible on only one side or to the number of axles. The sequence of numbers and letters indicates, from end to end, the number of pilot-truck axles, driving axles, and trailing-truck axles (the equivalent arrangement for steam locomotives would be designated 4-6-4). Since the Pennsylvania's locomotives were designed to be operated with equal facility in either direction, the terms *pilot truck* and *trailing truck* are simply matters of convention.
11. The practice on the Pennsylvania was to classify electric power on a basis derived from the classes of steam locomotives. The wheel arrangement for steam engines that is equivalent

to a 2-C+C-2 electric unit would be 4-6-6-4, which may be regarded as the equivalent in turn of two ten-wheel locomotives placed back-to-back (4-6-0+0-6-4). Since all ten-wheelers on the Pennsylvania were placed in Class G, the new electric power would logically be designated Class GG-1.

12. The design and construction of the Pennsylvania's express terminal were carried out under the direction of Alexander C. Shand, chief engineer of the railroad, E. B. Temple, chief engineer of the Eastern Region, and D. M. Scheaffer, manager of mail and express traffic. The contractors were Henry Steers, Inc. (grading and concrete work), Shoemaker Bridge Company (steelwork), Turner Construction Company (erection of buildings), and Fishback and Moore (electrical installations).

    Total express traffic originating in or destined for terminals in metropolitan New York amounted to 46,660,000 shipments in 1926. All of this traffic was carried by the Railway Express Agency and a few small companies, whose only competitor at the time was the parcel-post service of the United States Post Office.
13. By the time the railroad awarded its second commission to McKim, Mead and White, all of the original partners in this magisterial firm of architects had died.

    The total cost of the Newark project was divided as follows: railroad share, $12,500,000; city's share for station appurtenances and streets, $7,000,000; city's share for boulevard and street railway line, $5,000,000. The state was involved in the vacating of the Morris Canal properties. The investment in the work at the 1980 building-cost level would have been about $275,000,000.
14. The Long Island Rail Road was also an early user of diesel-electric power, having installed a switching locomotive of Baldwin-Westinghouse manufacture in the spring of 1928.
15. The total Long Island traffic generated by the New York fair over the two-season period was 25,291,656 passengers, divided between 15,727,906 in 1939 and 9,563,750 in 1940.

CHAPTER 6

1. In 1926, for example, the Michigan Central Railroad earned $100 per share of stock and paid a dividend of $35, which was subsequently raised to $40. The corporate title of the Big Four is the Cleveland, Cincinnati, Chicago and Saint Louis Railway.
2. See table 7. This comparison of traffic volumes for different years arises from the fact that the peak for Pennsylvania Station prior to World War II came in 1930, whereas its equivalent for Grand Central was 1929. My intention is to compare the highest traffic levels. Pennsylvania Station's lead in traffic volume of 47 percent in 1929–30 was to expand to 68 percent in the record years of 1945–46.
3. When the Century was hauled by Pacific type locomotives the train usually consisted, in order from head end to rear, of a club car, three sleeping cars, a dining car, four more sleeping cars, and an observation-lounge car with a few compartments, for a total of ten cars. When the locomotives that the railroads called the Hudson type (4-6-4) were regularly assigned to the train, the customary length expanded to 12 cars through the addition of two sleepers. The seven sections of 3 December 1928 carried an average of 114.3 passengers per section, or a likely average of 12.7 passengers per car for the nine sleeping cars. On the record run of 7 January 1929, which was apparently never surpassed, the average would have been 117.4 passengers per train, or 13 per car. The earnings on such occasions drove other passengers agents rancorous with envy. On the basis of the standard fare of 3.6 cents per mile, an average berth–compartment–drawing room charge

of $10 (payable entirely to the Pullman Company), and an extra fare of $10, the total revenue for 822 passengers, exclusive of dining, club, and lounge car receipts, would have been about $44,850. Direct operating costs at the time were seldom more than $1.00 per train-mile, or $6,720 total for the seven trains. To this sum two items had to be added—namely, about $1,000 as the allocation for terminal and maintenance of way charges, and the $8,220 due the Pullman Company, yielding a total of about $15,940 for all disbursements, again exclusive of the net deficit incurred in the operation of the so-called nonrevenue cars. The net revenue for the operation of 7 January would thus have been around $29,000. The average revenue per train-mile in 1928 was $5.35, of which at least $3.00 was net income. On this basis the total revenue derived from the transportation of passengers for the seven-section run of 3 December would have been $35,952. There were other all-Pullman flyers that provided equally gratifying performances, with the consequence that the New York Central's passenger service was a highly profitable operation up to the Depression years.

One of the techniques adopted by the railroad for running extra sections ahead of schedule was to regard the last of the series as the regular train and to operate those in advance of it as trailing sections of the scheduled train immediately ahead of it. These confusing practices were simplified around 1936 by treating all extra sections simply as extra trains designated by the locomotive number.

A few isolated data may suggest something of the comparative passenger loads on different trains at various times. The Century during the thirties often ran with fewer than 100 reservations; the all-coach Pacemaker, on a day in September, 1940, when the New York Fair was still in progress, carried 208 passengers out of New York; the Empire State Express, on a typical wartime day of August, 1943, carried 1,036 passengers at the time the conductor collected all the New York tickets. On this occasion the two dining cars in the 19-car train served three meals between New York and Cleveland, and no one who had an appetite either went hungry or was forced to suffer the pangs of hunger beyond the customary hours of eating.

For illustrations of the Twentieth Century Limited over the years, see Arthur Dubin, *Some Classic Trains,* pp. 56–75.

4. A review of the facts in the Forsyth accident reveals the character of the right of way and the customary mode of operation. The town is near the New York–Pennsylvania state line and hence on the property of the former Lake Shore and Michigan Southern Railroad. The four main tracks were protected by two-arm lower-quadrant semaphore signals arranged for right-hand operation. Neither the Lake Shore nor the Central had adopted a comprehensive system of crossover tracks under interlocking control, and the only form of traffic segregation was that of placing slow-moving and local trains on the outer tracks, adjacent to station platforms, and fast through trains on the inner tracks (this conventional mode of operation remained in effect until the advent of centralized traffic control in the decade of the 1960s). On the night of the accident second Number 25 was running 6 minutes behind the first, and the third 8 minutes to the rear of the second. A veritable parade of trains was stretched out over whole divisions behind the Century. A premium was thus placed on the maintenance of continuous movement at the authorized speed limit, but this end was frustrated by the paucity of the crossover tracks that would have allowed a train to pass from one track to the adjacent track.
5. The lines equipped with automatic train control were the following: Boston to Albany; Poughkeepsie to Englewood (63d and State Street in Chicago); Indianapolis to Granite City, Illinois (Big Four); Detroit to Kensington (115th Street near Cottage Grove Avenue

in Chicago; Michigan Central); Pittsburgh to Youngstown (Pittsburgh and Lake Erie). The system adopted by the New York Central Lines consisted essentially of a transmitter close to the rail at trackside, a receiver on the forward truck of the locomotive tender, and the associated relays, switches, and circuitry. An adverse signal activated the transmitter, which induced a current in the receiver as it passed over the fixed element. The current operated the relays and switches that automatically set the brakes. The third rail of electric operations would clear neither the transmitter nor the receiver, and the field surrounding the electric current would render the apparatus inoperable in any event.

6. I have never found reliable documentary evidence to indicate the precise years in which the New York Central undertook its extensive resignaling program, except in the case of the Grand Central approach. My account is based on direct inspection in the field and on numerous photographs, many of which are undated or unreliably dated. The same state of affairs applies to the pattern of traffic segregation adopted for the Mohawk, Syracuse, and Buffalo divisions. This mode of operation can be best explained in terms of the accompanying drawing, which represents a segment of four-track line with the designations for track numbers that were standard on the New York Central (as in the case of train numbers, westward tracks bore odd numbers and eastward even numbers).

N ↑

Track 4: Eastward Freight→
←Track 3: Westward Freight
←Track 1: Westward Passenger
Track 2: Eastward Passenger→

Three purposes underlay this practice: to separate passenger from freight trains; to locate the freight tracks so that they could be turned outward to the north, away from the larger cities en route, in order to bypass passenger stations and densely built urban areas; to avoid the movement of freight and passenger trains in opposite directions on adjacent tracks. During the Second World War traffic over the Albany-Buffalo main line was so heavy that the railroad rearranged interconnecting tracks and signals in order to operate the parallel West Shore line as a fifth main track (a few segments of the primary main line had already been expanded to five tracks, making the West Shore a sixth main track).

7. Reverse-direction signaling was introduced on the Big Four Route in 1899 for operations on double-track line. The original technique involved special train orders granting a given train the right to cross over to the left-hand track, run against the normal current of traffic in order to pass a slower train moving in the same direction, then return to the right-hand track to clear both lines for continuing movements. The system was adapted to manual-block signals in 1926. Such an arrangement required double the regular number of home signals at the crossover points, since each track was governed by signals for movements in both directions. It was eventually adopted for all double-track lines on the Big Four. As a fief of the New York Central, the western road undoubtedly provided the basis for the Grand Central program.
8. An impressive example of the parallel running of trains was the near-simultaneous departure of the Pacemaker (inaugurated on 28 July 1939), the Century, and a New Haven suburban train, all of which left the terminal within one minute beginning at 6:00 P.M. The Century departed first and the other two trains left side by side close behind it. The schedules of the Century and the Broadway Limited were reduced to 16 hours in 1938; since the Pacemaker was scheduled at 17 hours, Number 25 steadily widened the

one-minute lead, but it was usually standing in the station at Harmon waiting for the steam locomotive when the coach train drew up on an adjacent track. The 16-hour schedule of the Century gave it an overall average speed of 60 miles per hour. Only a small handful of trains fell in this aristocratic mile-a-minute category.

9. I have calculated this area from the official site plan shown in fig. 47, using the following data: ground area leased for air-rights construction in 1972, 1,058,381 square feet; ground area of the terminal head house not leased for the construction of the Pan American Building (see chap. 8), 134,205 square feet (the total ground area of the terminal is 284,906 square feet); area sold for the construction of the United States Post Office, 60,718 square feet; total, 1,253,304 square feet. The track and street plans have not been altered, so that there is no reason why the areas available for development should not have remained substantially unchanged over the years. Since the lots on which the Post Office stands were sold outright to the postal service, the net developable area is the original total less 60,718 square feet, or 1,192,586 square feet. The division of ownership between the two railroads is roughly as follows: the Harlem owns the terminal area and the properties along the west side of Vanderbilt and Park avenues, whereas the Central owns those on the east side of Park Avenue; the two exceptions are the area under the Biltmore Hotel, which the Central acquired, and the block bounded by 47th and 48th streets between Park and Lexington avenues, to which the Harlem holds title.
10. The site of the New York Central Building was open in 1922, but by 1926 it had been covered by relocations of the inward curving segments of Park Avenue between the drives flanking the terminal and the parkway to the north.
11. My account of the air-rights developments in the vicinity of the terminal is not definitive. There are known as well as unknown omissions. I doubt that it will ever be possible to compile a complete inventory of structures erected over the track area, given the destruction of buildings and records during the years following the Second World War.

CHAPTER 7

1. The seven roads included in this general assessement are the B. and O., C. N. J., Lackawanna, Erie, Lehigh Valley, Ontario, and Susquehanna for the comparative analysis of passenger traffic, and the same seven plus the Raritan River and the Reading for the comparisons of freight tonnage.
2. The exact percentage changes in the passenger traffic of the New Jersey roads for the periods 1920–30, 1930–40, and 1940–45 are given in the following table:

	1920–30	1930–40	1940–45
B. and O.	−72	−42	+229
C. N. J.	−18	−34	+ 31
D. L. and W.	−13	−24	+ 20
Erie	−21	−48	+ 6
Lehigh Valley	−66	−54	+199
N. Y. O. and W.	−72	−71	− 17
N. Y. S. and W.	−34	−49	+ 60
Seven roads	−31	−37	+ 41
Pennsylvania	−40	−35	+147

(See table 8 for precise figures giving freight tonnage and number of passengers.)

3. Percentage changes in the freight traffic of the New Jersey roads for the periods 1920–30, 1930–40, and 1940–45 are given in the following table:

	1920–30	1930–40	1940–45
B. and O.	−10.0	− 6.4	+60
C. N. J.	− 7.5	−20.0	+53
D. L. and W.	−10.0	−12.0	+33
Erie	− 5.0	−19.0	+33
Lehigh Valley	−20.0	− 9.0	+52
N. Y. O. and W.	0.0	− 6.0	+43
N. Y. S. and W.	− 9.0	−31.0	+31
Raritan River	− 4.4	− 1.0	+57
Reading	−12.0	− 3.0	+54
Nine roads	−10.0	−10.0	+50
Pennsylvania	− 2.4	− 9.0	+46

(See table 8.)

4. The specific changes in passenger traffic for the New Jersey sector over the third of a century between 1911 and 1943 are as follows:

Year	Number of Passengers	Percentage Change
1911	106,498,000	
1920	150,519,000	+41.3
1929	177,847,000	+18.5
1940	114,925,000	−35.4
1943	152,257,000	+32.5

(See table 6 for complete data.)

It is instructive to note that the low points and peaks of New York rail traffic reflect local factors powerful enough to offset national trends and hence do not correspond to their national counterparts. The bottom year for total rail traffic in the nation as a whole was 1933, not 1940; the wartime peak was 1944, not 1943.

5. In the C. N. J. approach system the tracks were segregated from north to south according to the following plan: two coach yard leads, three tracks for the Newark Branch, four main tracks, and two engine terminal leads. To the best of my knowledge, this was the most spacious approach line serving any American terminal. The lead tracks for the Lehigh Valley's coach yard on the north side of the complex diverged from the similar C. N. J. leads. The only defect in the railroad's terminal plan was unavoidable: the connecting tracks for the main line of the Lehigh Valley passed through and over the coach yard.
6. The contractors for the C. N. J. project were the following: G. B. Spearin, foundation work and steel erection; C. T. Mills, Inc., ferry house and head house alterations; A. and F. Brown Company, ferry bridge machinery; Westinghouse, Church, Kerr and Company, electrical work.
7. John A. Droege, *Passenger Terminals and Trains* (New York: McGraw-Hill Book Co., 1916), p. 143. As a matter of fact, if Peabody and Stearn's head house is not "exceedingly beautiful," it is handsome enough to deserve a more generous comment. See chap. 8 for my account of its restoration.
8. The contractors for the Newark Bay bridge included the following: Henry Steers, Inc., and Arthur McMullen Company, piling and piers; American Bridge Company and

Bethlehem Steel Company, steel fabrication; Norwood Noonan Company, electrical equipment; Union Switch and Signal Company, signaling equipment; Atlantic, Gulf and Pacific Company and Great Lakes Dredge and Dock Company, dredging and channel work. The cost was $15,000,000 in 1926, or about $140,000,000 at the 1980 building-cost level.

9. The New Haven controlled the New York, Ontario and Western Railroad through the ownership of a majority of its capital stock. The arrangement brought benefit to neither company.
10. In the color-position light signal the indication is given both by the color and the position of paired lights: two green lights in the vertical row represent clear, two yellow in the diagonal row approach, and two red in the horizontal row stop. The positions correspond to those of the standard block indications given by the upper-quadrant semaphore.
11. The contractors for the various Lackawanna projects were the F. M. Talbot Company, the H. R. Curtis Company, and Hyde and McFarland. The railroad's innovations in concrete construction—trestles, special structures such as interlocking towers and shop buildings, flat-slab and arch viaducts of unprecedented size—were pioneer works of the greatest value to the advancement of the art. Ray, Cohen, and Hirschthal deserve the chief credit for ths achievement.
12. Precisely the same problem, revealing itself in almost exactly the same rate of settlement, has been a continuing plague at La Guardia Field, where it began a half century after the Lackawanna's difficulties and reached the crucial stage in 1979.
13. The commuters were apparently unimpressed by the Lackawanna's claim that female passengers, represented by the fictitious Phoebe Snow of company advertisements, could maintain white dresses in spotless condition on "the road on anthracite."
14. The other members of the Lackawanna's committee were E. M. Rine, general manager of the railroad; H. M. Warren, electrical engineer; E. B. Moffatt, general superintendent; C. J. Scudder, superintendent of motive power; and R. M. White, his assistant superintendent. The conduct of the work was the particular responsibility of Ray, Scudder, and J. S. Thorp, engineer of electric traction. Jackson and Moreland of Boston were engaged as consulting engineers. The General Electric Company manufactured all fixed and mobile electrical equipment, and the Pullman Company produced the motor cars and trailers.
15. The investment of $687,000,000 called for in the Turner plan, translated from the 1924 to the 1980 building-cost level, would expand to at least $6,185,000,000. Even the railroad's modest share would come to well over a billion dollars. I am unable to justify Turner's belief that this immense expenditure could be amortized in only eight years by means of a ten-cent increment added to basic fares. Even if the Long Island Rail Road were party to the scheme, the revenues from the additional fare in 1924 would have been only $31,000,000, and in 1929 somewhat more than $36,000,000, requiring from 19 to 22 years to retire the bonds without any decline in traffic. The model for Turner's proposal might have been the Circle Line of the London Underground, although this is restricted to light-weight rapid transit equipment. A proportionately larger loop or belt line, for the size of the city in question, was proposed in 1912 for the unification of interurban railway terminals in Cincinnati, and again in 1916 for the city's equally abortive rapid transit plan.
16. "A Letter from Captain Gulliver to His Cousin Sympson,"in Swift, *Travels into Several Remote Nations of the World* (New York: Oxford University Press, 1933), p. 7. There are, to the best of my knowledge, no public sources of the Rockefeller plans, which apparently remain as manuscript material in the family archives and business records. See Carol Krinsky, *Rockefeller Center* (New York: Oxford University Press, 1978), pp. 83–84.

17. Centralized traffic control is in effect the extension of the principle of interlocking controls to long segments of track, the length of the main lines of entire divisions in some cases. Under a C. T. C. system a single operator controls all switches for sidings and passing tracks and all associated signals over the length of line governed by the machine, so that he can set switches and signals for passing movements with minimal delays and no possibility of conflict, while relying on the associated automatic block signals to govern movements on unencumbered track. The question of the origin of this valuable innovation has not been settled, chiefly because the history of railroad signaling and communications has yet to be written. The weight of the evidence suggests that it was invented by B. H. Mann in 1927 and first used on the Missouri Pacific Railway.

CHAPTER 8

1. A comparison of cargo loaded and unloaded at the Port of New York in 1951 and 1978 indicates the continuing growth as well as the magnitude of operations (in long tons):

Cargo by Type, Destination, or Service	1951	1978	Percent Increase
General cargo, export-import	13,399,000	15,708,000	17.2
Bulk cargo, export-import	19,102,000	44,931,000	135.2
Total transoceanic	32,501,000	60,639,000	86.6
Coastwise shipments	2,493,000	5,500,000	120.6
Grand total	34,994,000	66,139,000	89.0

Increase 1935–78: 202 percent
(Source: Port Authority of New York and New Jersey.)

2. The changing share of New York's foreign trade in the total for the nation is given in the following table:

Year	Percent of U.S. total
1790	5.7
1830	37.0
1870	57.0
1910	46.0
1920	44.0
1955	32.5
1968	14.1
1970	12.0 (estimated)

The loss of both jobs and the New York share of marine tonnage was somewhat offset by the rapid increase in cargo handled at Port Newark and the Elizabeth Marine Terminal, as the following comparison of total traffic over a ten-year period shows:

Year	Cargo (tons)	Jobs	Payroll
1966	6,300,000	7,000	$40,000,000
1976	12,000,000	7,665	91,000,000

The small increase in the number of jobs for a near-doubling of tonnage reflects the growth of mechanization in the handling of cargo. Unfortunately for New York City, most of the workers lived in New Jersey. (Source: Port Authority of New York and New Jersey.)

3. These illuminating data are given in more complete detail in the following table:

Rail Freight Tonnage (1,000s of tons)

Year	United States	Eastern District	Southern District	Western District
1929	1,339,091	697,894	174,202	466,905
1978	1,389,084	384,413	366,880	637,791
Increase	49,993	−313,481	192,678	170,886
Percent	3.7	−45.0	111.0	37.0

The changes in ton-mileage have been even more marked because of the constant lengthening of the average haul of shipments, as the second table shows:

Rail Freight Ton-Miles (1,000,000s)

Year	United States	Eastern District	Southern District	Western District
1929	447,322	231,420	55,163	160,738
1978	858,105	197,633	162,417	498,056
Increase	410,783	−33,787	107,254	337,318
Percent	93	−15	194	210

In the same 50-year period the proportion of all intercity ton-miles produced by the railroads fell from 74.9 percent to 35.8 percent.
(Source: Association of American Railroads, *Yearbook of Railroad Facts.*)

4. The precise extent of the decline in rail traffic among the New York railroads and at the Port of New York between the wartime peak and the last year of available data is given in the following tables:

Freight Traffic of the New York Railroads (1,000s of tons)

1945	876,428 (61.5 percent of U.S. total)
1975	431,168 (30.8 percent of U.S. total)
Percent change	−50.8

Number of Passengers of the New York Railroads (1,000s)

1945	502,049 (56.3 percent of U.S. total)
1970	180,499 (63.6 percent of U.S. total)
Percent change	−64.1

(See table 9.)

Number of Standard Rail Passengers in Metropolitan New York (1,000s)

1929	362,272
1943	324,792
1967	158,024
Percent change 1929–67	−56.4
Percent change 1943–67	−50.4

(See table 6.)

Freight Passing into, through, and out of the Port of New York (1,000s of tons)

Year	Interchange	Lighterage	Local	Total
1943	12,201[a]		109,857[a]	139,249[b]
1944		17,191[a]		
1968	3,727[c]			
1974		129	32,569	32,698
Percent change	−69.5	−99.2	−70.4	−76.5

a. Peak year.
b. Total of 1943 and 1944 peaks.
c. Last year reported.
(See table 5.)

Under the "Final System Plan" adopted by the United States Railway Administration in 1975, carfloat and lighterage operations were to be eliminated by all the constituent companies of the Consolidated Rail Corporation. The only such service offered since 1976 has been provided by the New York Dock Railway and the Brooklyn Eastern District Terminal Railroad for the terminals of the C. and O./B. and O. System on Staten Island.

Carfloat transfers for New England freight, especially those formerly moving between Greenville Piers and Bay Ridge Terminal, have been replaced by the following all-rail routes: Pennsylvania–New Jersey Junction–New York Central River Division via Selkirk Yard (a few miles south of Albany) and the Boston and Albany or New Haven; Delaware and Hudson-Boston and Maine via Mechanicville, New York. The abandonment of carfloat routes virtually eliminated through freight traffic on the New York Connecting Railroad.

5. Comparative postwar losses in freight and passenger traffic of the various companies are given in the following table.

Freight Traffic by Railroad (1,000s of tons)

Railroad	1945	1950	1955	1975	Percent decline
B. and O.	137,456			98,258	28.5
C. N. J.		50,804		7,515	85.2
D. L. and W.[a] / Erie[a]	77,647			31,799	59.0
Lehigh Val.	34,699			15,537	55.2
Long Is.	8,454			5,300[b]	37.3
N. Y. C.[a] / New Haven[a] / Penn.[a]	469,626			239,154	48.1
N. Y. O. and W.	7,059		2,709		61.6
N. Y. S. and W.	4,834		1,364		71.8
Raritan River	1,157			773[c]	33.2
Reading	91,393			33,005	63.9

Number of Passengers by Railroad (1,000s)

Railroad	1945	1970	Percent decline
B. and O.	13,706	961	92.9
C. N. J.	23,839	6,516	72.7
D. L. and W.[a] / Erie[a]	39,846	15,951	60.0
Long Is.	112,946	70,149	37.9
N. Y. C.[a] / New Haven[a] / Penn.[a]	306,624	72,648	76.3
Reading	25,010	13,699	45.2

a. Separate companies merged.
b. Estimated from revenues; tonnage not available.
c. Latest year available.
(See table 8.)

6. The architects in charge of this admirable renovation program are Geddes, Brecher, Qualls and Cunningham of Philadelphia, with whom the John Milner Associates have acted as restoration consultants. The restored and reconstructed space, close behind the Statue of Liberty, is officially designated Liberty State Park.
The only renewal of functioning rail property in the area was the replacement by the B. and O. of the old swing bridge over Arthur Kill by a vertical lift span in 1955–57. The previous structure had been in existence since the line to Staten Island was opened in 1889.
7. The segment of tract on which the accident at Kew Gardens occurred is equipped with a particularly elaborate system of five-aspect automatic block signals, all of which were in working order at the time. The motorman of the second train passed a stop-and-proceed signal at the prescribed speed but accelerated his train at a rate such that he was unable to bring it to a stop when he saw the standing train. Weaknesses of equipment that could escape detection in the flood of needed repairs undoubtedly formed a contributory cause.
The members of Governor Dewey's commission—former Secretary of War Robert P. Patterson, the city's notoriuos park commissioner, Robert Moses, and a retired judge, Charles C. Lockwood—did not bring with them exactly the credentials the task called for. Their report tended to underscore the fact.
8. Among the various suburban lines acquired by the M. T. A., the Staten Island Rapid Transit was so close to final collapse within a decade following the war that it had to be rescued by the municipality as early as April, 1956, when the lease of the property and operation by the city became effective. The distribution of the Authority's traffic in 1972 is given in the following tables:

Number of Trains Operated per Weekday

New York City Transit Authority		7,544
Long Island Rail Road		663
New York Central Railroad		308
Harlem Division	179	
Electric and Hudson divisions	129	
New Haven Railroad		214
Staten Island Rapid Transit		134
Erie-Lackawanna		6
Total		8,869

Bus Trips per Weekday

New York City Transit Authority	48,400
Manhattan and Bronx Surface Operating Authority	31,816
Metropolitan Suburban Bus Authority	419
Total	80,635

Revenue Passengers

Service	Weekday Average	Total for Year
Long Island	245,000	59,821,000
New York Central	76,000	20,958,000
New Haven	59,000	16,755,000
Staten Island Rapid Transit	14,600	4,100,000
Erie-Lackawanna	600	135,000
Subway and elevated lines	3,922,400	1,145,129,000
Buses, N. Y. C. Transit Authority	1,276,500	379,109,000
Buses, Manhattan and Bronx Surface Op. Auth.	1,115,500	340,233,000
Buses, Metropolitan Suburban Bus Authority	60,000	19,984,000
Bridges, Tunnels, Parking	1,075,000	393,332,000
Totals	7,844,600	2,379,556,000

Number of Weekday Rail Passengers (1977)

New York (Metropolitan Transit Authority, Con Rail, and Amtrak)	
Long Island	225,000
New York Central	78,000
New Haven	61,000
Amtrak	32,000
Staten Island Rapid Transit	18,400
Total New York	414,400
New Jersey (New Jersey Department of Transportation and Con Rail)	
Port Authority Trans-Hudson	143,000
Pennsylvania	74,000
Erie-Lackawanna	70,000
Central of New Jersey	25,000
Total New Jersey	312,000
Grand Total	726,400

(Sources: New York Metropolitan Transit Authority, New Jersey Department of Transportation, *Modern Railroads*.)

The distribution of the Transit Authority's new rolling stock among the various services in 1972 was as follows:

Long Island	770
New York Central	178
New Haven	144
Staten Island Rapid Transit	52
Erie-Lackawanna	4
Total rail	1,148
Subway (to 1974)	1,845
Grand Total	2,993

This equipment was made up of multiple-unit cars, except for the coaches of the Erie-Lackawanna, which were the conventional form designed to be drawn by separate locomotives. (Source: New York Metropolitan Transit Authority.)

Two extensions of the Long Island Rail Road's electrified lines were made in 1968–70: Mineola to Hicksville (main line); Hicksville to Huntington (Port Jefferson Branch).

The Long Island, Staten Island, and New Haven lines (that portion of the last lying within the state of New York) were purchased; the New York Central lines and Grand Central Terminal were leased but operated initially by the Penn Central Railroad (1968–76), later by the Consolidated Rail Corporation (1976–).

9. Three routes that were continued in operation were omitted from the original settlement—namely, New York–New Orleans (Penn Central, Southern), Chicago-Peoria (Rock Island), and Denver–Salt Lake City (Rio Grande). Only the last survives as an independent service (1980).
10. The rebuilding of track in the Corridor program involved the first use in the United States of a comprehensive track-renewal machine, which in mechanical sequence takes up old ties and rail, lays, spreads, and compacts ballast, emplaces new ties, and lays the ribbon or welded rail (in place of the traditional jointed variety) on the rows of ties. The rail must then be aligned and spiked or bolted into place, the ballast given final compaction between ties, and the finished roadbed surfaced, that is, made level for tangent track and sloped to a conical surface for the superelevated curves. The individual track-renewal machine is 221 feet long and was priced at $1,900,000 in 1977. Like most such elaborate, all-purpose mechanical devices, its operation brought an intermittent stream of troubles.
11. The profitable Pocahontas roads began their relentless expansion northward and westward shortly after the war. The C. and O. merged the Pere Marquette in 1947, to make it the largest rail carrier in Michigan, and began the process of unification with the B. and O. and the Western Maryland in 1960. The N. and W. more than doubled its mileage at one stroke in 1964, when it acquired and merged the Nickel Plate Road (officially the New York, Chicago and Saint Louis Railroad), the Wabash, and the Pittsburgh and West Virginia. The lines outside the domain of the giants are the remaining New England roads, the Deleware and Hudson (the oldest transportation company in the United States), the much coveted Detroit, Toledo and Ironton (a plum for the connecting N. and W. because it would provide the latter with an entry from the east into Detroit), and various small roads in Ohio, Indiana, and Michigan, some created out of bits and pieces among the Con Rail leftovers.
12. After the first 39 months of its existence, a period ending on 30 June 1979, Con Rail had spent $2,545,000,000 to rebuild 3,200 miles of track, purchase 479 new locomotives and 6,000 new freight cars, and repair to sound running standards 2,771 locomotives and 59,000 cars. After this herculean labor the immense organization earned its first net income, $29,400,000, in the second quarter of 1979. The government's total investment, including the acquisition of the constituent lines, the cost of the Corridor renovation, loans and loan guarantees, special subsidies, planning for electrification and other improvements, and the loss of abandoned lines, came to $8,555,000,000.
13. Milton Shapp, quoted in "Warns Rail Mergers May Damage Economy," *Chicago Sun-Times,* 20 January 1978, p. 80.
14. Young's previous contribution to the improvement of railroad service was the exceedingly questionable proposal to operate through coast-to-coast sleeping cars from New York and Washington to San Francisco and Los Angeles. The practice was inaugurated by the

cooperating railroads (three eastern and four western companies) on 31 March 1946. It had virtually nothing to recommend it, involved full-day layovers for many connections in Chicago, required elaborate switching operations for all of them, and was quietly phased out of existence through May, June, and July of 1948.

15. Quoted in "Can the Grand Central Concourse Be Saved?" *Architectural Forum* 101, no. 5 (November 1954): 135.
16. Alfred Fellheimer, quoted in ibid., p. 137.
17. Lewis Mumford, "The Sky Line: The Roaring Traffic's Boom—I," *New Yorker* 31 (19 March 1955): 117–21.
18. Douglas Haskell, "Visionless Enterprise," *Architectural Forum* 113, no. 4 (October 1960): 87.
19. Douglas Haskell, "The Lost New York of the Pan American Airways Building," *Architectural Forum* 119, no. 5 (November 1963): 109–11. Erwin Wolfson was the owner of the Diesel Construction Company and another maker and unmaker of instant cities.
20. New York Landmarks Commission, quoted in "New York City's Landmarks Commission Gives Grand Central Station Reprieve," *Architectural Record* 146, no. 4 (October 1969): 37.
21. Justice Francis Murphy, quoted in "New York Court OKs Protecting Grand Central," *Chicago Sun-Times,* 17 December 1975, p. 50.
22. United States Supreme Court, quoted in "Court Decision Blocks Grand Central Project," *Traffic World* 175, no. 1 (3 July 1978): 89.
23. While the New York Central phased out the operation of electric locomotives, the Pennsylvania and the New Haven continued for a few years to advance the state of the art. The experimental rectifying locomotives for the Pennsylvania were manufactured by the Baldwin-Westinghouse team and the General Electric Company in 1950–51, and a permanent fleet of 66 such units, all produced by General Electric, was installed in 1963–66. The New Haven's first ten machines, again products of G.E., had been installed in 1954–55, and these were supplemented by an additional 12 purchased from the Virginian Railway in 1963. These modest efforts marked the end of the development of electric motive power in the United States until Amtrak began to acquire replacements for its corridor traffic in 1976.
24. James M. Symes, quoted in "New PRR Station Is Planned for New York," *Railway Age* 138, no. 24 (13 June 1955): 65.
25. Editorial on the demolition of Pennsylvania Station, *New York Times,* 30 October 1963, p. 38.
26. Douglas Haskell, "The Lost New York of the Pan American Airways Building," *Architectural Forum* 119, no. 5 (November 1963): 107.
27. The distribution of daily traffic at Pennsylvania Station in 1971 and 1975 is given in the following table:

Carrier	1971	1975
New Haven	20	
Pennsylvania	208	
Long Island	298	332
Amtrak		94
Penn Central		126
Totals	526	552

The distribution of daily passengers in 1975 was as follows: Amtrak and Penn Central, 60,000; Long Island, 145,000. The maximum number for a single day was 235,000. An estimated average of about 100,000 visitors use the station every day as an accessway to and from subways, shops, restaurants, and other foci of urban activities.

28. Various studies of the relative energy consumption of the transportation modes is given in the following tables:

Mode	RAND Corporation (1967) Btu's per Ton-Mile	Association of American Railroads (1970) Btu's per Ton-Mile	U.S. Department of Transportation (1970) Btu's per Ton-Mile
Waterway	500	680	540
Railroad	750	670	680
Pipeline	1,850	450	450
Highway	2,400	2,800	2,300
Airline	63,000	42,000	37,000

(Sources: Association of American Railroads, *Moody's Transportation Manual, Railway Age.*)

An investigation conducted in 1973 by Mark L. Smith, the manager of traffic research for the Missouri Pacific Railway, led to revisions of these conclusions that placed the railroads in the first position. Smith's data are as follows:

Mode	Btu's per Ton-Mile
Railroad	693
Waterway	1,105
Pipeline	1,850
Highway	2,400
Airline	63,000

(Source: *Trains.*)

29. Comparisons among transportation modes on the basis of ton-miles produced per unit of fuel consumed in 1979 are given in the following table:

	Ton-Miles per Gallon of Fuel	
Mode	U.S. Maritime Administration	Southern Railway
Waterway	250	200–250
Railroad	200	223.6
Highway	58	55.6
Airline		3.7

30. Various ways of revealing energy efficiency are given in the following tables:

	Btu's per Passenger-Mile	
Mode	Actual Load	Full Load
Intercity		
Bus	1,600	740
Train	2,900	1,100
Automobile	3,400	1,600
Airplane	8,400	4,100

Urban		
Mass Transit	3,800	760
Automobile	8,100	2,300

(Source: Association of American Railroads, 1970.)

Mode	Passenger-Miles per Gallon of Fuel
Jet plane	23
Automobile	33
Train	115

(Source: S. David Freeman, for Twentieth Century Fund, 1973.)

Mode	Consumption of Fuel per Passenger-Mile (Railroads = 100)
Bus	55.2
Railroad	100.0
Automobile	117.2
Airplane	289.7

(Source: Eric Hirst, for National Science Foundation, 1973.)

31. John W. Barriger, quoted in William D. Middleton, "Electrification: Is It Going to Happen?" *Railway Age* 176 (10 March 1975): 37.
32. Adriana Gianturco, letter to Secretary of Transportation Brock Adams, April, 1978; quoted in "Caltrans Answers the DOT," *Rail Travel News* 8, no. 8 (15 May 1978): 10, 15.
33. Mike Royko, "We're Missing the Train," *Chicago Sun-Times,* 15 May 1979, p. 2.
34. James M. Friedlander, "Rationalizing the Railroads: A New Planning Process," *Planning and Public Policy* 5, no. 1 (February 1979): 3–4.
35. Tri-State Transportation Commission, *The Changing Harborfront* (New York: Tri-State Transportation Commission, 1966), p. 1.
36. The distribution of daily trains and passengers at the London terminals for 1976 is given in the following table, in order of number of trains per weekday:

Station	Number of Tracks	Number of Trains	Number of Passengers
Waterloo	21	1,262	213,636
Victoria	17	1,106	178,126
Liverpool Street	18	1,005	154,307
Charing Cross	6	657	106,425
London Bridge	22	542	130,092
Euston	15	386	61,137
Paddington	11	378	46,380
Cannon Street	8	310	71,582
Moorgate	8	263	12,566
Fenchurch Street	4	262	63,187
Holborn Viaduct–Blackfriars	5	236	40,610
Saint Pancras	7	172	30,975
King's Cross	12	171	28,727
Broad Street	8	127	3,922
Marylebone	4	112	15,366
Totals	166	6,989	1,157,038

(Source: London Transport Board, Transportation Planning Department.)

37. Richard Roth, Jr., quoted in Suzannah Lessard, "The Towers of Light," *New Yorker* 54, no. 21 (10 July 1978): 58.

Bibliography

General Works on Urban and Railroad History

Balliett, Herbert S. "Development of Railway Signaling." *Railway and Locomotive Historical Society Bulletin,* no. 44 (October 1937), pp. 70–82.

Bruce, Alfred W. *The Steam Locomotive in America.* New York: W. W. Norton & Co., 1952.

Condit, Carl W. *American Building Art:The Twentieth Century.* New York: Oxford University Press, 1961.

Droege, John A. *Passenger Terminals and Trains.* New York: McGraw-Hill Book Co., 1916. Reprinted, Milwaukee: Kalmbach Publishing Co., 1969.

Dubin, Arthur D. *More Classic Trains.* Milwaukee: Kalmbach Publishing Co., 1974.

———. *Some Classic Trains.* Milwaukee: Kalmbach Publishing Co., 1964.

Interstate Commerce Commission. *Annual Report on the Statistics of Railways of the United States.* Washington, D.C.: Government Printing Office, 1889–.

———. *Statistics of Railways of the United States.* Washington, D.C.: Government Printing Office, 1891–.

Koester, Frank. "American City Planning—Part VIII: Traffic and Terminals." *American Architect* 104, no. 1975 (29 October 1913): 161–67.

Locomotive Cyclopedia. New York: Simmons-Boardman Publishing Co., 1906–.

Martin, A. *Enterprise Denied: Origins of the Decline of American Railroads.* New York: Columbia University Press, 1971.

Meeks, Carroll L. V. *The Railroad Station: An Architectural History.* New Haven: Yale University Press, 1956.

Muhlfeld, John E. "Scientific Development of the Steam Locomotive." *Railway Age* 67, no. 24 (12 December 1919): 1139–44; 67, no. 25 (19 December 1919): 1197–1202.

Official Guide of the Railway and Steam Navigation Lines in the United States, Mexico and Canada. New York: National Railway Publication Co., 1868—.

Poor's Manual of the Railroads of the United States, Street Railways and Traction Companies. New York: Poor's Railroad Manual Co., 1869—.

Railroad Research Bulletin: Development Issue. Washington, D.C.: United States Department of Transportation, Federal Railroad Administration, 1973.

Railroads in This Century: A Summary of the Facts and Figures with Charts. Washington D.C.: Association of American Railroads, 1944.

Railroad Transportation: A Statistical Record, 1921–1963. Washington, D.C.: Association of American Railroads, 1965.

Scott, Mel. *American City Planning since 1890*. Berkely and Los Angeles: University of California Press, 1969.

Stover, John F. *American Railroads*. Chicago: University of Chicago Press, 1961.

Tauarnac, John. *Essential New York: A Guide to the History and Architecture of Manhattan's Important Buildings, Parks and Bridges*. New York: Holt, Rinehart & Winston, 1979.

United States Department of Commerce. *Historical Statistics of the United States*. Washington, D.C.: Government Printing Office, 1960.

White, John H., Jr. *The American Railroad Passenger Car*. Baltimore: John Hopkins University Press, 1978.

Wood, Arthur Julius. *Principles of Locomotive Operation*. New York: McGraw-Hill Book Co., 1925.

Chapter 1. The Grand Central Electrification

"Accident on the Electrified Division of the New York Central." *Street Railway Journal* 29, no. 8 (23 February 1907): 344; 29, no. 9 (2 March 1907): 400; 29, no. 10 (9 March 1907): 438; 29, no. 11 (16 March 1907): 461–63; 29, no. 14 (6 April 1907): 621.

Arnold, Bion J. "A Comparative Study of Steam and Electric Power for Heavy Railroad Service." *Railroad Gazette* 34, no. 26 (27 June 1902): 498–99.

Arnold, Bion J., and Potter, W. B. "Comparative Acceleration Tests with Steam Locomotive and Electric Motor Cars." *Street Railway Journal* 20, no. 1 (5 July 1902): 46–50.

"Articulated Electric Locomotives for the New York Central." *Railway Age Gazette* 54, no. 15 (11 April 1913): 841–42.

Batchelder, Asa F. "Mechanical Design of Electric Locomotives." *Railway Age Gazette* 61, no. 22 (1 December 1916): 989–90.

———. "Types and Systems of Drives of Electric Locomotives." *General Electric Review* 17, no. 11 (November 1914): 1116–19.

"Block Signal System of the New York Central Electric Zone." *Street Railway Journal* 27, no. 23 (9 June 1906): 908–15.

"Comparative Locomotive Tests on the New York Central" *Engineering Record* 51, no. 20 (20 May 1905): 561.

"Comparative Speed Tests of Steam and Electric Locomotives." *Street Railway Journal* 25, no. 19 (13 May 1905): 865–67.

"Comparative Tests of Steam and Electric Locomotives." *Scientific American* 92, no. 20 (20 May 1905): 407.
"A Danger in Electric Traction." *Railroad Gazette* 34, no. 3 (17 January 1902): 42.
"Disastrous Rear Collision in Fourth Avenue Tunnel." *Railroad Gazette* 34, no. 2 (10 January 1902): 18.
"Discussion of New York Central's Plan." *Street Railway Journal* 20, no. 1 (5 July 1902): 56–57.
"Effect on Terminal Operation of the New York Central Electrification." *Street Railway Journal* 30, no. 15 (12 October 1907): 579–80.
"Effects of Sleet Storm on Different Types of Third Rail Protection." *Railroad Gazette* 40, no. 15 (13 April 1906): 384–85.
"Eight Motor Articulated Electric Locomotive." *Railway Age Gazette* 52, no. 26 (28 June 1912): 1608–12.
"The Electrical Maintenance Plants of the New York Central and Hudson River Railroad Company." *Street Railway Journal* 29, no. 23 (8 June 1907): 1014–27.
"Electric Equipment and Reconstruction of the New York Terminal Lines and Grand Central Station, New York Central and Hudson River Railroad." *Engineering News* 54, no. 20 (16 November 1905): 499–509.
"Electricity in the Park Avenue Tunnel." *Street Railway Journal* 18, no. 2 (20 July 1901): 75, 82; 18, no. 5 (3 August 1901): 133; 18, no. 6 (10 August 1901): 169; 18, no. 10 (7 September 1901): 267.
"Electric Locomotives for the New York Central." *Railroad Gazette* 36, no. 23 (3 June 1904): 418–19.
"Electric Power Preparations by New York Central." *Railway Age* 40, no. 9 (1 September 1905): 267.
"Electric Rolling Stock of the New York Central." *Street Railway Journal* 30, no. 15 (12 October 1907): 565–70.
"Electrification of the New York Central and Hudson River Railroad." *Electric Railway Journal* 34, no. 7 (14 August 1909): 268.
"The Electrification of the New York Central's Terminal Lines." *Scientific American* 93, no. 24 (9 December 1905): special supplement.
"Electrification of the New York Central Terminal in and near New York City." *Railway Age* 41, no. 4 (26 January 1906): 126–54.
Elliott, W. H. "Signal Arrangements for the New York Central Electrified Zone." *Railroad Gazette* 40, no. 2 (12 January 1906): 36–37, 40.
"Extension of the New York Central Electric Zone to North White Plains." *Electric Railway Journal* 34, nos. 19, 25 (13 November, 25 December 1909): 1024, 1277.

"First Electric Train into New York over New York Central Lines." *Street Railway Journal* 28, no. 14 (6 October 1906): 535.

"The First Electric Train over the New York Central." *Railway Age* 42, no. 14 (5 October 1906): 410.

"Four Improved Types of Electric Locomotives." *Railway Age* 64, no. 12 (22 March 1918): 717–22.

"The Fourth Avenue Tunnel Collision" (titles vary). *Railroad Gazette* 34, no. 3 (17 January 1902): 39, 42–44; 34, no. 4 (24 January 1902): 51–52, 61; 34, no. 5 (31 January 1902): 76–78; 34, no. 6 (7 February 1902): 92; 34, no. 7 (14 February 1902): 110–13, 119; 34, no. 10 (7 March 1902): 161–62.

"General Features of the New York Central Electrification." *Street Railway Journal* 30, no. 15 (12 October 1907): 540–43.

Gordon, Reginald. "New York Central Electric Locomotives." *Railroad Gazette* 40, no. 24 (15 June 1906): 648–52.

"Grand Central Terminal 100-Ton Electric Crane." *Railway Age Gazette* 56, no. 20 (15 May 1914): 1101–2.

Hanchett, George T. "The New York Central Electric Locomotive." *Street Railway Journal* 24, no. 3 (16 July 1904): 100–101.

"Heavy Electric Traction Projects in 1909." *Electric Railway Journal* 35, no. 1 (1 January 1910): 36–38.

"High-Speed Electric Locomotive for New York Central and Hudson River Railroad." *Street Railway Journal* 24, no. 21 (19 November 1904): 900–906.

"Indestructible Fiber Furnishings for New York Central Electric Cars." *Street Railway Journal* 28, no. 15 (13 October 1906): 584.

Katté, Edwin B. "Multiple Unit Train Service on the New York Central and Hudson River Railroad." *General Electric Review* 17, no. 11 (November 1914): 1025–32.

———. "Results Secured on the New York Central," under "Operating Results of Steam Railroad Electrification." *Railway Age Gazette* 58, no. 11*b* (17 March 1915): 548–49.

Lister, F. E. "Care and Handling of Electrical Equipment, New York Central and Hudson River." *Railway Age Gazette* 48, no. 22 (3 June 1910): 1367–74.

"Maintenance of Electrical Rolling Stock on the New York Central." *Street Railway Journal* 30, no. 15 (12 October 1907): 571–78.

"Mechanical Design of Electric Locomotives." *Railway Age Gazette* 62, no. 1 (5 January 1917): 13–14.

Middleton, William D. "Electrics into Grand Central." In *When the Steam Railroads Electrified*, pp. 36–71. Milwaukee: Kalmbach Publishing Co., 1974.

"Motor Trucks for the New York Central Electric Service." *Street Railway Journal* 27, no. 17 (28 April 1906): 680–82.
"Mr. Westinghouse on Electric Locomotives for the New York Central Terminal." *Railway Age* 40, no. 26 (29 December 1905): 834–35.
Neff, S. S. "The New York Central Accident—Electricity—Protection by Signals." *Railroad Gazette* 34, no. 4 (24 January 1902): 52–53.
"A New Design of Electric Locomotive for the New York Terminal Zone of the New York Central Railroad." *Engineering News* 69, no. 18 (1 May 1913): 900–902.
"New Steel Motor Cars for the New York Central and Hudson River Railroad." *Street Railway Journal* 26, no. 19 (4 November 1905): 837–38.
"A New Type of Electric Locomotive." *Electric Railway Journal* 41, no. 15 (12 April 1913): 684–85.
"New York Central All-Electric Signaling at New York." *Railroad Gazette* 40, no. 26 (29 June 1906): 705–11.
"New York Central and Hudson River Railroad to Electrify Harlem Division." *Electric Railway Journal* 32, no. 30 (26 December 1908): 1664.
"New York Central Electric Locomotive." *Railroad Age Gazette* 46, no. 26 (25 June 1909): 1527–32.
The New York Central Electrification. Schenectady, N.Y.: General Electric Company Bulletin GEA-902, January 1929.
"New York Central Engineering Commission." *Street Railway Journal* 21, no. 3 (17 January 1903): 125.
"The New York Central–New Haven Controversy on Electric Traction." *Railway Age* 40, no. 18 (3 November 1905): 550–51.
"New York Central Seeks Subway Line in New York." *Street Railway Journal* 28, no. 21 (24 November 1906): 1027.
"New York Central's Plans." *Street Railway Journal* 20, no. 6 (9 August 1902): 212; 20, no. 11 (13 September 1902): 357; 20, no. 24 (13 December 1902): 948, 961.
"The New York Central's Terminal Electrification at New York." *Railroad Gazette* 41, no. 14 (5 October 1906): 293–97.
"The New York Central Terminal." *Railroad Gazette* 34, no. 50 (12 December 1902): 944.
"New York Central to Extend Its Service." *Street Railway Journal* 29, no. 7 (16 February 1907): 303.
"New York Central Under-Contract Third Rail." *Railway Age* 40, no. 9 (1 September 1905): 260.

"No Legislation for the Grand Central Station." *Railroad Gazette* 34, no. 17 (25 April 1902): 311.

"Opening of Electrical Service on the New York Central and the New Haven Railroads." *Scientific American* 96, no. 3 (19 January 1907): 65, 72–73.

"Operation of Electric Locomotive during a Snow Storm." *Railroad Gazette* 40, no. 7 (16 February 1906): 152–54.

Park Avenue Tunnel (titles vary). *Railroad Gazette* 33, no. 8 (22 February 1901): 129–30; 33, no. 9 (1 March 1901): 137; 33, no. 32 (9 August 1901): 562–63, 565; 33, no. 33 (16 August 1901): 576; 33, no. 41 (11 October 1901): 699; 33, no. 49 (6 December 1901): 846.

"The Port Morris Power Station of the New York Central Railroad." *Street Railway Journal* 28, no. 13 (29 September 1906): 460–63.

Potter, W. B. "Developments in Electric Traction." *Street Railway Journal* 25, no. 4 (28 January 1905): 156–65.

Potter, W. B. "Electric Railway Equipment." *Street Railway Journal* 26, no. 14 (30 September 1905): 607–10.

"Power Distribution System of the New York Central." *Street Railway Journal* 30, no. 15 (12 October 1907): 552–59.

"Powerful Articulated Electric Locomotives." *Railway Age Gazette* 55, no. 19 (7 November 1913): 868–69.

"Powerful Electric Locomotives for the New York Central." *Electric Railway Journal* 42, no. 19 (8 November 1913): 1024.

"Power Station Practice of the New York Central." *Street Railway Journal* 30, no. 15 (12 October 1907): 544–51.

"The Power Stations for the Electric Zone of the New York Central R.R." *Engineering Record* 52, no. 20 (11 November 1905): 534–36.

"The Public and the Railroads." *Railroad Gazette* 33, no. 32 (9 August 1901): 562–63, 565.

"Results of Electric Traction on the New York Central Railroad at New York City." *Engineering News* 69, no. 19 (8 May 1913): 951.

Root, William S. "The First Electric Train into Grand Central Station." *Railroad Men* 20, no. 2 (November 1906): 41–45.

Shaw, J. A. "Electric Traction for Railroad Service." *Engineering Record* 52, no. 16 (14 October 1905): 423–26.

"Snow Test of the New York Central Motor Car Trains." *Railroad Gazette* 42, no. 7 (15 February 1907): 211.

Sprague, Frank J. Letter, New York Central and New Haven Electric Locomotives. *Street Railway Journal* 27, no. 17 (28 April 1906): 678–79.

———. "Some Facts and Problems Bearing on Electric Trunk-Line Operation." *Street Railway Journal* 29, no. 21 (25 May 1907): 907–18.

"Steam and Electric Railroads." *Scientific American* 93, no. 25 (16 December 1905): 474–75.

"Steel Cars for the New York Central's Electric Suburban Service." *Railroad Gazette* 39, no. 18 (3 November 1905): 424–25.

"The Storage Battery Equipment for the Electrified Divisions of the New York Central and Long Island Railroads." *Street Railway Journal* 25, no. 20 (20 May 1905): 929.

"Storage Battery Equipment of the New York Central and Hudson River Railroad." *Street Railway Journal* 29, no. 23 (8 June 1907): 1035.

"Sub-Station Practice of the New York Central." *Street Railway Journal* 30, no. 15 (12 October 1907): 560–64.

"Sub-Stations and Transmission of the New York Central and Hudson River Railroad." *Street Railway Journal* 28, no. 18 (3 November 1906): 875–77.

"Terminal Electrification of the New York Central" *Railroad Gazette* 36, no. 21 (20 May 1904): 384.

"Test of the New York Central Electric Locomotive." *Railroad Gazette* 37, no. 23 (18 November 1904): 549, 552–54.

"Test of the New York Central Electric Locomotive." *Street Railway Journal* 24, no. 21 (19 November 1904): 897–98.

"Tests of the Effect of Snow on Third Rail." *Street Railway Journal* 27, no. 7 (17 February 1906): 288–89.

"Tests of the New York Central Electric Locomotive." *Street Railway Journal* 25, no. 3 (21 January 1905): 112–16.

"Tests on the New York Central Locomotives." *Street Railway Journal* 28, no. 4 (28 July 1906): 154.

"Tractive Effort of New York Central Electric Locomotives." *Railroad Gazette* 44, no. 7 (14 February 1908): 229.

"Trial of New York Central Locomotive." *Street Railway Journal* 24, no. 19 (5 November 1904): 858.

"Under-Contact Third Rail for the New York Central." *Street Railway Journal* 26, no. 10 (2 September 1905): 336–37.

"Under-Running Third Rail for the New York Central." *Railroad Gazette* 39, no. 9 (1 September 1905): 198–200.

Wadsworth, G. R. "Terminal Improvements of the New York Central and Hudson River in New York" (titles vary). *Railroad Gazette* 39, no. 16 (20 October 1905): 366–69; 39, no. 19 (10 November 1905): 435–39; 39, no. 20 (17 November 1905): 462–66; 39, no. 21 (24 November 1905): 486–89.

Westinghouse, George. "Concerning Some Dangers from Electric Traction." *Railroad Gazette* 34, no. 2 (17 January 1902): 33.

Wilgus, William J. "The Electrification of the Suburban Zone of the New York Central and Hudson River Railroad in the Vicinity of New York City." *Proceedings of the American Society of Civil Engineers* 34, no. 2 (February 1908): 68–98.

———. "The Electrification of the Suburban Zone of the New York Central and Hudson River Railroad in the Vicinity of New York City." *Transactions of the American Society of Civil Engineers* 61 (December 1908): 73–155.

W-S Standard Under-Running Third Rail. New York: Standard Third Rail Co., 1911.

Chapter 2. The New Haven Electrification

"Along the 'Harlem River Branch.' " *Architectural Record* 24, no. 6 (December 1908): 417–29.

"Alternating Current Electric Locomotives." *Railroad Gazette* 39, no. 13 (29 September 1905): 301.

Arcara, Roger. *Westchester's Forgotten Railway*. New York: Quadrant Press, 1962. (Includes reprints of articles on the New York, Westchester and Boston Railroad in *Electric Railway Journal* 39 and 40 [1912], and *Railway Age Gazette* 52 [1912].)

Batchelder, Asa F. "Types and System of Drives of Electric Locomotives." *General Electric Review* 17, no. 11 (November 1914): 1116–19.

"Center-Cab Control Electric Switching Locomotive." *Railway Age Gazette* 53, no. 5 (2 August 1912): 210–11.

"Construction and Maintenance Costs of Overhead Contact Systems." *Railway Electrical Engineer* 7, no. 2 (July 1915): 39–40.

"The Effect of the Recent Blizzard on the New Haven's Electrifiied Zone." *Railway Electrical Engineer* 7, no. 8 (January 1916): 227–28.

"Eight-Motor Articulated Electric Locomotive . . . for the New Haven." *Railway Age Gazette* 52, no. 26 (28 June 1912): 1608–12.

"The Electric Locomotive Question." *Street Railway Journal* 27, no. 17 (28 April 1906): 661.

"Electric Locomotives of the New York, New Haven and Hartford Railroad." *Street Railway Journal* 30, no. 8 (24 August 1907): 278–85.

"Electric Railway Practice of the New Haven Railroad." *Street Railway Journal* 30, no. 15 (12 October 1907): 608–14.

"Electrification of the New York, New Haven and Hartford Railroad." *Street Railway Journal* 27, no. 7 (17 February 1906): 276–77.

"Four Improved Types of Electric Locomotives." *Railway Age* 64, no. 12 (22 March 1918): 717–22.

"Four-Track Columbus Avenue Viaduct." *Engineering Record* 66, no. 17 (26 October 1912): 462–64.

"Harlem River Branch Improvements; New York, New Haven and Hartford Railroad."*Railway Age Gazette* 48, no. 4 (28 January 1910): 186–90; 48, no. 5 (4 February 1910): 257–60.

"A Heavy Concrete Skew Arch." *Engineering Record* 66, no. 2 (13 July 1912): 53.

"Heavy Electric Traction Projects in 1909." *Electric Railway Journal* 35, no. 1 (1 January 1910): 36–38.

"The Installation of Electric Traction on the New York Terminal Section of the New Haven Railroad." *Engineering News* 58, no. 10 (5 September 1907): 239–47.

Lamme, Benjamin G. "Alternating-Current Electric Systems for Heavy Railway Service."*Street Railway Journal* 27, no. 12 (24 March 1906): 450–62.

Lamme, Benjamin G., and Westinghouse, George. "Arguments for Single-Phase Traction on the New Haven." *Railroad Gazette* 39, no. 25 (22 December 1905): 579–81.

"Locomotives of the New York, New Haven and Hartford Railroad" (titles vary). *Electric Railway Journal* 39, no. 7 (17 February 1912): 267, 268–75; 39, no. 25 (22 June 1912): 1085–86; 39, no. 26 (29 June 1912): 1136.

"The Maintenance of Electric Locomotives." *Railway Age Gazette* 62, no. 4 (26 January 1917): 129–34.

"A Matter of Standardization." *Railroad Gazette* 39, no. 16 (20 October 1905): 358–59.

McHenry, E. H. "Electrification of the New York, New Haven and Hartford Railroad." *Railroad Gazette* 43, no. 7 (16 August 1907): 177–84.

———. "Heavy Electric Traction on the New York, New Haven and Hartford Railroad." *Street Railway Journal* 30, no. 7 (17 August 1907): 242–45.

Middleton, William D. "New Haven's Bold Venture," In *When the Steam Railroads Electrified*, pp. 72–111. (Milwaukee: Kalmbach Publishing Company, 1974.

"Motor Cars for the New Haven Suburban Service." *Railroad Age Gazette* 47, no. 16 (15 October 1909): 707.

Murray, W. S. "The Advance of Electrification." *Railway Age Gazette* 58, no. 11*b* (17 March 1915): 549–50.

———. "Lecture on Single Phase Traction." *Street Railway Journal* 29, no. 13 (30 March 1907): 546–48.

———. "The Log of the New Haven Electrification." *Railroad Age Gazette,* 46, no. 1 (1 January 1909): 19–26.

———. "The New Haven Road and the New York Terminal Electrification." *Railroad Gazette* 39, no. 20 (17 November 1905): 458.

———. "The Success of Main Line Electrification." *Railway Age Gazette* 58, no. 18 (30 April 1915): 923–28.

"New Haven Locomotives." *Electric Railway Journal* 35, no. 19 (7 May 1910): 811, 829–31.

"The New Haven Electrification Plans in the Bronx." *Railroad Gazette* 37, no. 12 (2 September 1904): 290, 309–10.

"New Haven Shops For Electrical Equipment." *Railway Age Gazette* 62, no. 11 (16 March 1917): 445–48.

"New York and Westchester Trains 99.2% On Time." *Railway Electrical Engineer* 7, no. 3 (August 1915): 78.

"The New York Central–New Haven Controversy on Electric Traction." *Railway Age* 40, no. 18 (3 November 1905): 550–51.

"New York, New Haven and Hartford Improvements—Electricity out of New York." *Street Railway Journal* 24, no. 10 (3 September 1904): 354.

"The New York, New Haven and Hartford Locomotive." *Street Railway Journal* 27, no. 15 (14 April 1906): 587.

"New York, New Haven and Hartford Overhead Construction." *Railroad Gazette* 42, no. 7 (15 February 1907): 220.

New York, New Haven and Hartford Railroad Electrification. East Pittsburgh: Westinghouse Electric and Manufacturing Company, Special Publication 1698, June 1924.

"The New York, New Haven and Hartford Single-Phase System." *Street Railway Journal* 27, no. 12 (24 March 1906): 445.

"The New York, Westchester and Boston Railway." *Engineering Record* 52, no. 23 (2 December 1905): 620–22.

"Opening of Electric Service on the New York Central and the New Haven Railroads." *Scientific American* 96, no. 3 (19 January 1907): 65, 72–73.

"Operation of Electric Locomotives by the New Haven Railroad." *Street Railway Journal* 30, no. 15 (12 October 1907): 604–7.

"Overhead Catenary Construction for the New York, New Haven and Hartford Railroad." *Street Railway Journal* 27, no. 14 (7 April 1906): 558–59.

"The Overhead Construction of the New Haven Railroad." *Street Railway Journal* 30, no. 7 (17 August 1907): 245–54.

"Proposed High-Speed Line Near New York." *Street Railway Journal* 18, no. 3 (20 July 1901): 81–82.

Scott, Charles F. "The Single-Phase Railway System" *Street Railway Journal* 26, no. 14 (30 September 1905): 604–7.

"Single-Phase Direct-Current Locomotive for the New York, New Haven and Hartford Railroad." *Street Railway Journal* 27, no. 15 (14 April 1906): 588–95.

Sprague, Frank J. Letter on New York Central and New Haven Locomotives. *Street Railway Journal* 27, no. 17 (28 April 1906): 678–79.

———. "Some Facts and Problems Bearing on Electric Trunk-Line Operation." *Street Railway Journal* 29, no. 21 (25 May 1907): 907–18.

Stead, A. L. "Railway Electrification in the United States." *Railway Gazette* 43, no. 7 (14 August 1925): 228–31.

"Steam and Electric Railroads." *Scientific American* 93, no. 25 (16 December 1905): 74–75.

"To Prevent Trouble at the Grand Central Terminal." *Railroad Gazette* 39, no. 20 (17 November 1905): 453–54.

"Trunk Line Electrification." *Electric Railway Journal* 37, no. 15 (15 April 1911): 658, 667–70.

"The Westchester Railway Electric Traction." *Engineering News* 69, no. 24 (12 June 1913): 1208–17.

"The Westchester Railway Lines and Structures." *Engineering News* 69, no. 23 (5 June 1913): 1153–57.

Westinghouse, George. "The Single-Phase Alternating and the Direct Current System." *Railroad Gazette* 39, no. 25 (22 December 1905): 578.

"The Westinghouse Single-Phase Locomotives Adopted by the New York, New Haven and Hartford Railroad Company." *Street Railway Journal* 26, no. 14 (30 September 1905): 638.

Chapter 3. The New Grand Central Terminal

"Architect Wins His $500,000 Appeal." *New York Times,* 10 February 1920, p. 7.

"Automatic 'Light' Signals in Park Avenue Tunnel." *Railroad Age Gazette* 45, no. 19 (9 October 1908): 1090–93.

Bernard, Walter. "The World's Greatest Railway Terminal" *Scientific American* 104, no. 25 (17 June 1911): 594–95, 609–10.

"The Biltmore Hotel, New York." *American Architect* 105, no. 1990 (11 February 1914): 53–57.

"Columns in the New Grand Central Terminal, New York City." *Engineering Record* 67, no. 5 (1 February 1913): 125–26.

"Concourse Roof, Grand Central Terminal, New York City." *Engineering Record* 67, no. 8 (22 February 1913): 210–11

"Congestion of Traffic at the Grand Central Station and Its Remedy." *Scientific American* 83, no. 22 (1 December 1900): 338.

D'Esposito, Joshua. "Some of the Fundamental Principles of Air Rights." *Railway Age* 83, no. 17 (22 October 1927): 757–59.

"Eighteen-Hour New York–Chicago Service Inaugurated." *Railway Age* 39, no. 24 (16 June 1905): 921.

Elliott, W. H. "Signal Arrangements for the New York Central Electrified Zone." *Railroad Gazette* 40, no. 2 (12 January 1906): 36–37, 40.

"Erecting the Grand Central Terminal." *Engineering Record* 66, no. 8 (24 August 1912): 222–23.

"The Explosion . . . at the Grand Central Terminal." *Railway Age Gazette* 50, no. 6 (10 February 1911): 291.

Fellheimer, Alfred. "Design of Railway Terminal Stations." *Contract Record and Engineering Review* 37, no. 35 (29 August 1923): 844–46.

———. "Modern Railway Passenger Terminals." *Architectural Forum* 53, no. 6, pt. 1 (December 1930): 655–94.

———. "Principles of Terminal Station Design." *Railway Age* 75, no. 3 (21 July 1923): 109–11.

"Four-Tracking at Two Tunnels While Maintaining Heavy Traffic." *Engineering Record* 66, no. 14 (5 October 1912): 386–87.

"A Gateway to the Heart of New York." *Scientific American Supplement*, 74 (7 December 1912): 364–66.

"Girders in the Grand Central Terminal, New York City." *Engineering Record* 67, no. 3 (18 January 1913): 78–80.

"Grand Central Development Seen as Great Civic Center." *Engineering News-Record* 85, no. 11 (9 September 1920): 496–504.

"Grand Central Interlocking Machine." *Railway Age Gazette* 50, no. 19 (12 May 1911): 1115–16.

"The Grand Central Railway Station, New York." *Engineering* 95 (30 May 1913): 725–27, pls. 41–44.

"Grand Central's Outdoor Concourse." *Architectural Forum* 102, no. 2 (February 1955): 116–19.

"The Grand Central Station Improvements." *Scientific American* 93, no. 12 (16 September 1905): 213, 222–23.

"Grand Central Station Improvements and Connection with Rapid Transit Subway." *Scientific American* 88, no. 3 (17 January 1903): 39–40.

"The Grand Central Station, New York." *Architects' and Builders' Magazine* 2, no. 3 (March 1901): 201–8.

"The Grand Central Terminal—A Great Civic Development." *Engineering News-Record* 85, no. 11 (9 September 1920): 484–85.

"The Grand Central Terminal Building." *Architecture and Building* 45, no. 4 (April 1913): 140–54.

"The Grand Central Terminal, New York." *Railroad Gazette* 42, no. 8 (22 February 1907): 252.

"The Grand Central Terminal, New York." *Railway Age Gazette*, 54, no. 7 (14 February 1913): 279–84.

"A Great Subterranean Railway Junction." *Scientific American*, 103, no. 21 (19 November 1910): 393, 398.

Haskell, Douglas. "Futurism with Its Covers On." *Architectural Review* 157, no. 939 (May 1975): 301–4.

———. "Lost New York of the Pan American Airways Building." *Architectural Forum* 119, no. 5 (November 1963): 106–11.

"A History of Grand Central Terminals in New York." *Architecture and Building* 45, no. 4 (April 1913): 137–40.

Inception and Creation of the Grand Central Terminal. New York: privately printed for Allen H. Stem and Alfred Fellheimer, 1913.

Israels, Charles H. "New York Apartment Houses." *Architectural Record* 11, no. 1 (July 1901): 476–508.

Lubchez, B. J. "The Two Great Railway Stations of New York." *Journal of the Royal Institute of British Architects* 27 (12 June 1920): 369–78.

"The Marble Hill Cut-Off and Port Morris Branch, New York Central Terminal Improvements." *Engineering Record* 52, no. 19 (4 November 1905): 512–15.

Marshall, David. *Grand Central.* New York: McGraw-Hill Book Co., 1946.

Middleton, William D. *Grand Central, the World's Greatest Railway Terminal.* San Marino, Calif.: Golden West Books, 1977.

"The Miller Locomotive Cab Signal." *Railroad Gazette* 34, no. 8 (21 February 1902): 128–29.

"Monumental Gateway to a City." *Scientific American* 107, no. 23 (7 December 1912): 473, 484–87, 499–501.

"New Block and Interlocking Signals." *Railroad Gazette* 34, no. 28 (11 July 1902): 558.

"New Buildings at the Grand Central." *Railroad Age Gazette* 47, no. 2 (9 July 1909): 71–72.

"The New Grand Central Station." *Railroad Gazette* 37, no. 29 (30 December 1904): 677–78.

"The New Grand Central Station in New York." *Architects' and Builders' Magazine* 6, no. 6 (March 1905): 267–71.

"The New Grand Central Station in New York." *House and Garden* 7, no. 2 (February 1905): 63–65.

"The New Grand Central Station, New York." *Scientific American* 92, no. 3 (21 January 1905): 40, 46.

"New Grand Central Terminal Station." *Scientific American* 99, no. 23 (5 December 1908): 410–12, 417–18.

"The New Grand Central Terminal Station in New York City: An Underground Double-deck Terminal." *Engineering News* 69, no. 18 (1 May 1913): 883–95.

"New Terminal for New York Central Lines." *Electrical World* 60, no. 25 (21 December 1912): 1309–18.

"New York Central Improvements in The Bronx." *Railroad Gazette* 35, no. 6 (6 February 1903): 95.

"New York Central Office Building." *Railway Age* 43, no. 6 (8 February 1907): 182.

"New York Central's Interest Free Terminal." *Railway Age Gazette* 52, no. 11 (15 March 1912): 462.

"The New York Central's New Station in New York." *Street Railway Journal* 24, no. 27 (31 December 1904):1160.

"The New York Central's Plan for the Improvement of the Park Avenue Tunnel." *Engineering News* 47, no. 4 (23 January 1902): 67.

"The New York Central's Terminal Proposition." *Railway Age* 34, no. 25 (19 December 1902): 674–75.

"The New York Central Terminal" (titles vary). *Railway Gazette* 34, no. 50 (12 December 1902): 944; 35, no. 1 (2 January 1903): 2–3; 35, no. 6 (6 February 1903): 102; 35, no. 8 (20 February 1903): 135; 35, no. 17 (24 April 1903): 298; 35, no. 23 (5 June 1903): 392; 35, no. 33 (14 August 1903): 587.

"The New York Central Tunnel Improvement." *Railroad Gazette* 34, no. 40 (3 October 1902): 753.

"The New York Central Underground Passenger Loop." *Railway Age* 33, no. 5 (31 January 1902): 138–39.

"The Opening of a Great Railroad Terminal." *Engineering Record* 67, no. 6 (8 February 1913): 142.

"Opening of the New Grand Central Terminal, New York City." *Engineering Record* 67, no. 6 (8 February 1913): 144–48; 67, no. 8 (22 February 1913): 218.

"Opening of the New Grand Central Terminal, New York." *Railway Age Gazette* 54, no. 6 (7 February 1913): 235, 258–59.

"Plans . . . . New York Central and Hudson River Railroad," under "Notes and News." *Railway Age* 31, no. 2 (11 January 1901): 34.

"Progress at the Grand Central Terminal." *Railway Age Gazette* 49, no. 12 (16 September 1910): 503–7.

"Progress of the New York Central and Hudson River R.R. Terminal Improvements in New York City." *Engineering Record* 54, no. 10 (8 September 1906): 272–73.

"Progress on the Grand Central Terminal." *Railway Age Gazette* 53, no. 21 (22 November 1912): 981–86.

"The Proposed Tunnel Loop at the Grand Central Station." *Railroad Gazette* 34, no. 5 (31 January 1902): 71.

"Recent Work on the New York Terminal of the New York Central Railroad." *Engineering Record* 58, no. 25 (19 December 1908): 701–3.

"Removing the Grand Central Train Shed." *Railroad Age Gazette* 45, no. 9 (31 July 1908): 632–34.

Schneider, Walter S. "The Hotel Biltmore." *Architectural Record* 35, no. 3 (March 1914): 222–45.

"Signaling at the New Grand Central Terminal." *Railway Age Gazette* 49, no. 15 (7 October 1910): 620–24.

"The Signals in the Fourth Avenue Tunnel." *Railroad Gazette* 34, no. 12 (21 March 1902): 206.

Starrett, Theodore. "The Grand Central Terminal Station." *Architecture and Building* 45, no. 4 (April 1913): 129–32.

"Steel Coaches for the New York Central." *Railway Age Gazette* 54, no. 8 (21 February 1913): 326–28.

"Steel Construction in the New York Terminal of the New York Central and Hudson River Railroad." *Engineering Record* 59, no. 15 (10 April 1909): 485–87.

"Stem v. Warren." *Miscellaneous Reports: Cases Decided in the Courts of Record of the State of New York* 96 (1917): 362–76.

"Stem v. Warren." *Northeastern Reporter* 125 (30 December 1919–2 March 1920): 811–14.

"Stem v. Warren." *Reports of Cases . . . in the Appellate Division of the Supreme Court of the State of New York* 185 (1919): 823–35.

"Structural Details in the New Grand Central Station, New York." *Engineering Record* 59, no. 4 (23 January 1909): 99–101.

"Sub-Stations and Transmission System of the New York Central & Hudson River Railroad." *Street Railway Journal* 28, no. 18 (3 November 1906): 877.

"Terminal Yard Improvements of the New York Central and Hudson River R. R." *Engineering Record* 52, no. 21 (18 November 1905): 562–66.

"Third and Fourth Track Construction." *Railway Age Gazette* 54, no. 11 (14 March 1913): 505–7.

Twentieth Century Limited, under "Editorial Announcements." *Railroad Gazette* 34, no. 23 (6 June 1902): 414.

Wadsworth, G. R. "Terminal Improvements of the New York Central and Hudson River in New York" (titles vary). *Railroad Gazette* 39, no. 16 (20 October 1905): 366–69; 39, no. 19 (10 November 1905): 435–39; 39, no. 20 (17 November 1905): 462–66; 39, no. 21 (24 November 1905): 486–89.

Wilgus, William J. "The Grand Central Terminal in Perspective." *Transactions of the American Society of Civil Engineers* 106 (1941): 992–1051.

———. Miscellaneous Wilgus Papers. New York: New York Public Library, Manuscript Collection.

"Wind-Bracing in the Grand Central Passenger Terminal, New York." *Engineering Record* 66, No. 6 (10 August 1912): 165–67.

Chapter 4. The Freight Terminal System

"The Activities of the Railroad Administration." *Railway Age* 64, no. 5 (1 February 1918): 255–57.

Bach, Richard Franz. "The City and the Railroad." *American Architect* 111, no. 2147 (14 February 1917): 95–99.

"The Baltimore and Ohio Railroad Company's Freight Terminal in New York." *American Architect* 107, no. 2044 (24 February 1915): 116–18.

Bard, Edwin W. *The Port of New York Authority*. New York: Columbia University Press, 1942.

"Bars Unlicensed Freight." *New York Times,* 14 July 1917, p. 6.

"Battery-Oil-Electric Locomotive." *Railway Age* 84, no. 9 (3 March 1928): 525–27.

"The Bay Ridge Electric Traction Installation." *Railway Age* 85, no. 22 (1 December 1928): 1099–1102.

Brehof, F. H. "Oil-Electric-Battery Locomotives for the New York Central." *Railway Age* 89, no. 7 (16 August 1930): 326–29.

"Car Shortages Increasing. Speculators Using Rolling Stock for Storage Purposes Here." *New York Times,* 18 February 1917, sec. 1, p. 6.

Castleton Cut-Off: Hudson River Connecting Railroad. New York: New York Central Railroad Co., 1924.

"Comprehensive Terminal Plan Suggested Solution for Manhattan Freight Congestion." *New York Times,* 25 February 1917, sec. 8, p. 4.

"Cost of N. Y. C. Electrification and Grade Crossing Elimination in New York." *Railway Age* 76, no. 3 (19 January 1924): 258.

Craton, F. H., and Walker, J. F. "Performance of New York Central Freight Locomotives." *Railway Age* 93, no. 16 (15 October 1932): 930–32.

"Diesel-Electric Locomotive . . . Used in New York Switching Service by the New York Central." *Railway Age* 76, no. 33 (16 June 1924): 1599.

Dodd, S. T. "Oil-Electric Freight Locomotive." *Railway Age* 85, no. 3 (21 July 1928): 98–100.

"Eastern Operating Committee Issues Its First Orders." *Railway Age Gazette* 63, no. 23 (7 December 1917): 1023–24.

"Economic Control to Be Continued." *New York Times,* 12 November 1918, p. 20.

"Effects of Unwise Regulation Illustrated by 1917 Statistics." *Railway Age* 64, no. 1 (4 January 1918): 10–11.

"Electric Operation Inaugurated on N. Y. C. West Side Lines." *Railway Age* 90, no. 23 (6 June 1931): 1127.

"Erie R. R. Will Discontinue Many Suburban Passenger Trains." *New York Times,* 6 May 1917, sec. 1, p. 19.

"Export Freight in Trainloads." *Railway Age* 64, no. 6 (8 February 1918): 318.

"Factory of 19 Stories over Railroad Yard." *Engineering News-Record* 109, no. 1 (7 July 1932): 1–4.

"A Fifty-Million Dollar Improvement by the New York Central in New York City." *Railway Age Gazette* 60, no. 3 (21 January 1916): 135.

"Five Men Chosen to Run Railroads." *New York Times,* 12 April 1917, p. 4.

Freight congestion, embargoes, and terminals (titles vary). *New York Times,* 28 November 1917, p. 24; 21 January 1918, p. 3; 10 February 1918, sec. 2, p. 9; 4 March 1918, p. 13; 11 December 1918, p. 16. *Railway Age* 64, no. 5 (1 February 1918): 255; 64, no. 7 (15 February 1918): 381; 64, no. 8 (22 February 1918): 428–29. *Railway Age Gazette* 62, no. 3 (19 January 1917): 114–15; 62, no. 8 (23 February 1917): 332; 62, no. 21 (25 May 1917): 1116; 62, no. 25 (22 June 1917): 1420–22; 63, no. 4 (27 July 1917): 134, 153–54; 63, no. 6 (10 August 1917): 223–24; 63, no. 20 (16 November 1917): 910; 63, no. 24 (14 December 1917): 1084–85; 63, no. 25 (21 December 1917): 1136.

"Freight Facilities in Manhattan." *Railway Age Gazette* 60, no. 14 (7 April 1916): 809–10.

"Freight for Export Shows Falling Off." *New York Times,* 22 February 1917, p. 13.

"Freight Piles up as Ships Are Held . . . Since Germany Resumes U-Boat Activities." *New York Times,* 11 February 1917, sec. 1, p. 1.

Griffin, John I. *The Port of New York.* New York: Arco Publishing Co. for City College Press, 1959.

Guynes, W. M., and Hassett, J. C. "Design of New Electric Locomotives Substantiated by Performance." *Railway Age* 92, no. 24 (11 June 1932): 982–85.

Hamilton. W. S. H. "Performance of Three-Power Locomotives." *Railway Age* 92 no. 10 (5 March 1932): 411–14.

Harvey, J. H. "A 660-Hp., 87-Ton, Oil-Electric Switching Locomotive." *Railway Age* 84 no. 25 (23 June 1928): 1451–54.

Hines, Walker D. *War History of American Railroads.* New Haven: Yale University Press, 1928.

"How New York Central Transfers Freight by Truck." *Railway Age* 88, no. 4 (25 January 1930): 286–88.

Imlay, Robert. "Proposed Victory Bridge over the Hudson between New York and Weehawken." *Architectural Record.* 48, no. 3 (September 1920): 218–23.

"The Jersey Central Is Building a Modern Coal Pier." *Railway Age* 67, no. 9 (29 August 1919): 388–92.

Katté, Edwin B. "New York Central Electric Freight Locomotives." *Railway Age* 81, no. 18 (30 October 1926): 845–48.

"Lackawanna Cuts Service." *New York Times,* 25 December 1917, p. 8.

"Lackawanna Reduces Its Suburban Service." *New York Times,* 22 June 1917, p. 13.

"Large Freight Station to Be Opened in New York." *Railway Age* 96, no. 26 (30 June 1934): 944–48.

"Lease of 25 Years in West Side Plan." *New York Times,* 7 October 1917, p. 22.
Lewis, Harold M. *Transit and Transportation: Regional Survey of New York,* vol. 4. New York: Regional Plan of New York and Its Environs, 1928.
Mantell, J. J. "Operation of the New York Terminal District." *Railway Age* 67, no. 23 (5 December 1919): 1109–12.
McAdoo, William G. *Crowded Years: The Reminiscenses of William G. McAdoo.* London: Jonathan Cape, 1931.
"Nation's Gigantic Resources Mobilized." *New York Times,* 6 April 1917, pp. 1, 4.
"Nation's Railroads Now under Government Control." *Railway Age* 64, no. 1 (4 January 1918): 1–6.
"New B. & O. Freight House at Twenty-sixth Street, New York." *Railway Age Gazette,* 56, no. 4 (23 January 1914): 198–99.
"New Freight Pier at Communipaw, N.J." *Railway Age Gazette* 54, no. 19 (9 May 1913): 1023–25.
"The New Government Control of Railroad Management." *Railway Age* 64, no. 1 (4 January 1918): 7–10.
"New Haven Issues Embargo." *New York Times,* 13 July 1917, p. 11.
"New Haven Road Cancels 199 Trains." *New York Times,* 30 May 1917, p. 9.
"New Reading Coal Pier Has Interesting Features." *Railway Age* 64, no. 12 (22 March 1918): 709–13.
"New Union Inland Freight Station Opened in New York." *Railway Age* 94, no. 12 (25 March 1933): 440–43.
"New York Central Completes Elevation of 2.3 Miles of Busy Freight Line in New York City." *Railway Age* 96, no. 25 (23 June 1934): 908–14.
"New York Central Depresses Freight Line through New York City." *Railway Age* 103, no. 1 (3 July 1937): 6–12.
"New York Central Electric Freight Locomotive Tested." *Railway Age* 81, no. 13 (25 September 1926): 546.
"New York Central Freight Terminals in New York City." *Railway Age Gazette* 62, no. 23 (8 June 1917): 1205.
"New York Central Offers to Elevate Freight Line . . . in New York." *Railway Age* 78, no. 6 (7 February 1925): 392.
"New York Central Opens Unusual Building on West Side." *Railway Age* 93, no. 13 (24 September 1932): 449.
"New York Central Plans Extensive Improvements on West Side in New York." *Railway Age* 87, no. 4 (27 July 1929): 234–40.

"New York Central's West Side Improvements in New York City." *Railway Age Gazette* 51, no. 14 (6 October 1911): 636–37.

"New York Central," under "Railway Construction." *Railway Age* 79, no. 1 (4 July 1925): 57; 79, no. 13 (26 September 1925): 591–92.

"New York City and the Railroad Problem." *Railway Age* 68, no. 17 (23 April 1920): 1236.

"New York City," under "Railway Construction." *Railway Age* 70, no. 20 (20 May 1921): 1192.

"New York Law Calls for Electrification throughout N.Y. City." *Railway Age* 74, no. 27 (9 June 1923): 1364.

"New York's Freight Terminal Problem." *Railway Age Gazette* 54, no. 15 (11 April 1913): 843–45.

"N. Y. C. Authorized to Operate with Electric and Diesel Electric Locomotives in New York." *Railway Age* 79, no. 21 (21 November 1925): 963–64.

"N. Y. C. Electric Freight Locomotives." *Railway Age* 78, No. 3 (17 January 1925): 223–24.

"N. Y. Central Drops Observation Cars." *New York Times,* 1 December 1917, p. 11.

"N. Y. Central to Cut Service up the State." *New York Times,* 30 June 1917, p. 20; 10 January 1918, p. 3.

"N. Y. C. Freight Tracks in New York City." *Railway Age Gazette* 63, no. 23 (7 December 1917): 1049.

"Oil Electric Locomotive Makes Record Run." *Railway Age* 79, no. 26 (26 December 1925): 1190–92.

"Penn. R. R. Breaks Freight Records." *New York Times,* 15 July 1918, p. 15.

"Pennsylvania Adds to New York Freight Facilities." *Railway Age* 83, no. 4 (23 July 1927): 193–94.

"Pennsylvania Opens New Perishable Freight Terminal." *Railway Age* 83, no. 17 (22 October 1927): 793.

Pennsylvania Railroad passenger service reductions (titles vary). *New York Times,* 29 June 1917, p. 11; 28 November 1917, p. 24; 30 November 1917, p. 20; 5 December 1917, p. 5; 11 December 1917, p. 1; 13 December 1917, p. 15; 17 December 1917, p. 20. *Railway Age* 64, no. 1 (4 January 1918): 91–92; 64, no. 5 (1 February 1918): 286. *Railway Age Gazette* 63, no. 1 (6 July 1917): 39; 63, no. 3 (20 July 1917): 123; 63, no. 23 (7 December 1917): 1052; 63, no. 24 (14 December 1917): 1102.

"The Pennsylvania's Fight with Jack Frost and the Snow Banks." *Railway Age* 64, no. 9 (1 March 1918): 447–49.

"Plans for New York Central Freight Tracks in Manhattan." *Railway Age* 75, no. 22 (1 December 1923): 1031–32.

"Port Authority Orders New York Connecting Open to New York Central." *Railway Age* 78, no. 8 (21 February 1925): 483.

Port of New York Authority. *Annual Report.* Albany: J. B. Lyon Co., 1923–28. New York: Port of New York Authority, 1929–.

———. *Report with Plan for the Comprehensive Development of the Port of New York.* Albany: J. B. Lyon, 1921.

Railroad Operations: A Series of Lectures by Officers of the New York Central Railroad. New York: New York Central Railroad Co., 1927.

"The Railroad's Blind Spot." *American Architect* 111, no. 2153 (28 March 1917): 201–2.

"Railroads Extend Freight Embargo . . . Jam Less than Last Year." *New York Times,* 15 February 1917, p. 7.

"Railroads Save Coal." *New York Times,* 21 July 1917, p. 13.

"The Railways and the National Defense Council." *Railway Age Gazette* 62, no. 10 (9 March 1917): 409–10.

"Reclaiming a Waterfront." *Engineering News-Record* 118, no. 23 (10 June 1937): 863–69.

"Serious Results of Storms in New York, Pennsylvania, West Virginia, and Elsewhere." *Railway Age* 64, no. 1 (4 January 1918): 93; 64, no. 5 (1 February 1918): 283, 286.

"Shay Locomotives in Special Transfer Service." *Railway Age* 77, no. 3 (19 July 1924): 108–9.

"Starrett-Lehigh Building, New York." *Architectural Record* 71, no. 1 (January 1932): 30–35.

"A Suggestion to the Committee on Defense." *Railway Age Gazette* 62, no. 19 (11 May 1917): 982–84.

"Transportation Report in New York Regional Plan." *Railway Age* 84, no. 19 (12 May 1928): 1122.

United States Army, Corps of Engineers, Board of Engineers for Rivers and Harbors. *The Port of New York, N.Y. and N.J.* Washington, D.C.: Government Printing Office, 1966.

"Urge Full Freight Cars; Congestion Attributed Largely to Partial Loading." *New York Times,* 19 February 1917, p. 4.

Wilgus, William J. *Proposed New Railway System for the Transportation and Distribution of Freight by Improved Methods in the City and Port of New York.*

Submitted to the Public Service Commission of New York State, 25 September 1908. New York: Amsterdam Corp., 1908.
Wilgus, William J. *The Railroad Problem in Relation to the Metropolitan District.* New York: American Society of Civil Engineers, New York Section, 1920.
"Work Begins on N. Y. C. New York Improvements." *Railway Age* 79, no. 24 (12 December 1925): 1123.
"Would Electrify All Railroads." *New York Times,* 13 August 1918, p. 20.

Chapter 5. Pennsylvania Station through the Second World War

"Air-Rail Service Sets New Record." *Railway Age* 89, no. 3 (19 July 1930): 129.
Barriger, John. "Handling the Football Traffic at Princeton." *Railway Age* 75, no. 22 (1 December 1923): 1009–11.
"Beam-Light Signals on the Pennsylvania." *Railway Age Gazette* 58, no. 2 (8 January 1915): 61; 58, no. 9 (26 February 1915): 366; 58, no. 10 (5 March 1915): 404.
Bearce, W. D. "Initial Operation of Pennsylvania Railroad Electrification." *General Electric Review* 36, no. 6 (June 1933): 258–61.
Bezilla, Michael. *Electric Traction on the Pennsylvania Railroad, 1895–1968.* University Park, Pa.: Pennsylvania State University Press, 1980.
Condit, Carl W. "Railroad Electrification in the United States." *Proceedings of the Institute of Electrical and Electronics Engineers,* 64, no. 9 (September 1976): 1350–60.
Dahl, H. A. "Development of Electric Traction on the Pennsylvania." *Railway Age* 87, no. 1 (6 July 1929): 4–8.
"Difficult Building Column Changes Made Successfully." *Railway Age* 93, no. 5 (30 July 1932): 147–49.
Duer, J. V. B. "Pennsylvania Develops Three Types of Electric Locomotives." *Railway Age* 92, no. 21 (21 May 1932): 869–73.
———. "The Pennsylvania Electrification." *Railway Age* 89, no. 15 (11 October 1930): 734–37, 762.
———. "The Pennsylvania Railroad Electrification." *Journal of the American Institute of Electrical Engineers* 49, no. 9 (September 1930): 787–91.
———. "Scope and Character of the Pennsylvania A.C. Electrification." *Railway Age* 92, no. 18 (30 April 1932): 727–28.
"Electric Locomotives for the Long Island." *Railway Age* 82, no. 4 (22 January 1927): 285.

"Electric Locomotives for the Pennsylvania." *Railway Age* 89, no. 7 (16 August 1930): 338.

"Electric Passenger Locomotives." *Railway Age* 100, no. 7 (15 February 1936): 278–82.

Eunson, W. H. "Pennsylvania Exhibits New Electric Locomotive." *Railway Age* 76, no. 29 (12 June 1924): 1433–35.

"Evolution from Steam to Electric Traction." *Railway Age* 107, no. 13 (23 September 1939): 440–43, 446.

"First Washington-Philadelphia Electric Train on Pennsylvania." *Railway Age* 98, no. 5 (2 February 1935): 196.

Griffith, H. C. "Electric Locomotive Operation." *Railway Age* 111, no. 6 (9 August 1941): 230–35.

———. "Extension of the Pennsylvania's Electrified System." *Electrical Engineering* 57, no. 1 (January 1938): 10–15.

———. "Extension of the Pennsylvania's Electrified System." *Railway Age* 104, no. 8 (19 February 1938): 332–38.

———. "Extension of the Pennsylvania's Electric System." Ibid. *Railway Electrical Engineer* 29, no. 1 (January 1938): 1–7, 22.

Kerr, Charles, Jr., and Stoberg, R. H. "Motor Cars and Trailers for the Pennsylvania Electrification." *Railway Age* 96, no. 7 (17 February 1934): 259–62.

"Lehigh Valley to Use Pennsylvania Terminals." *Railway Age* 65, no. 11 (13 January 1918): 524.

"L.I. Tells Patrons about Its Problems." *Railway Age* 113, no. 20 (14 November 1942): 796.

"Long Island Gets Modernistic Station at the World's Fair." *Railway Age* 106, no. 19 (13 May 1939): 823–26.

"Long Island Railroad Centenary." *Railway Age* 96, no. 17 (28 April 1934): 609–10.

"Long Island to Improve and Extend Electric Service." *Railway Age* 73, no. 14 (30 September 1922): 602.

"Market Street Station, Newark, N.J.; McKim, Mead and White, Architects." *Architectural Record* 79, no. 3 (March 1936): 199–205.

"Master Model by a Master Model Maker: New Newark Station of the Pennsylvania Railroad." *Pencil Points* 13, no. 2 (February 1932): 118–21.

Middleton, William D. "The Great Pennsy Electrification," In *When the Steam Railroads Electrified,* pp. 312–63. (Milwaukee: Kalmbach Publishing Co., 1974).

"Moving Tonnage in Large Units." *Railway Age* 66, no. 25*b* (21 June 1919): 1648.

"New Pennsylvania Electric Locomotive Hauls Its First Train." *Railway Age Gazette* 63, no. 14 (5 October 1917): 606–7.

"New Westinghouse Electric Locomotives for the Pennsylvania Railroad." *Baldwin Locomotives* 11, no. 4 (April 1933): 37–39.

"Notable Progress in Heavy Electric Traction." *Electric Railway Journal* 73, no. 2 (12 January 1929): 67–70.

Oehler, A. G. "Electric Traction Takes a Big Step." *Railway Age* 86, no. 1 (5 January 1929): 41–42.

"Pennsylvania Completes Station at Newark, N.J." *Railway Age* 102, no. 26 (26 June 1937): 1044–50.

"Pennsylvania Electric Freight Locomotive." *Railway Age Gazette* 63, no. 21 (23 November 1917): 934–36.

"Pennsylvania Extends Electrification to Harrisburg." *Railway Age* 104, no. 8 (19 February 1938): 332–38.

"Pennsylvania Opens New Passenger Station at Newark, N.J." *Railway Age* 98, no. 13 (30 March 1935): 485–92.

"Pennsylvania Railroad Electrification Links Philadelphia and New York City." *Railway Age* 94, no. 8 (25 February 1933): 268–302.

"Pennsylvania Railroad Speeds Electrification Program." *Electric Railway Journal* 75, no. 3 (March 1931): 125–27.

"Pennsylvania Railroad to Electrify 1300 Miles of Track." *Electric Railway Journal* 72, no. 18 (3 November 1928): 806–8.

"Pennsylvania Railroad to Electrify 1300 Miles of Track." *Electric Traction* 24, no. 11 (November 1928): 574.

"Pennsylvania Railroad to Electrify 1300 Miles of Track." *Electric World* 92, no. 23 (8 December 1928): 1136–37.

"Pennsylvania R.R. Suburban Electrification." *Railway Electrical Engineer* 21, no. 1 (July 1929): 211–14.

"The Pennsylvania's New Electric Locomotive." *Railway Age Gazette* 62, no. 23 (8 June 1917): 1199–1201.

"Pennsylvania to Build Eight Electric Locomotives." *Railway Age* 80, no. 10 (6 March 1926): 591–92.

"Pennsylvania to Electrify 1,300 Miles of Track." *Railway Age* 85, no. 18 (3 November 1928): 870; 85, no. 19 (10 November 1928): 940.

Perry, A. M. "Significance of Pennsylvania Electrification." *Electric World* 92, no. 23 (8 December 1928): 1133–35.

"Plan New Long Island Terminal." *Railway Age* 84, no. 5 (4 February 1928): 321–23.

"Plans of Pennsylvania for Use of P. W. A. Funds." *Railway Age* 96, no. 5 (3 February 1934): 200.

"P. R. R. Builds Country's Largest Express Terminal." *Railway Age* 83, no. 7 (13 August 1927): 285–90.
"P. R. R. New York–Washington Electric Service Inaugurated." *Railway Age* 98, no. 7 (16 February 1935): 278; 98, no. 15 (13 April 1935): 584.
"P. R. R. Opens Newark Passenger Station." *Railway Electrical Engineer* 26, no. 4 (April 1935): 75–79.
"P. R. R. Sells Power Plant; Will Buy 'Juice' from Utility." *Railway Age* 105, no. 2 (9 July 1938): 89.
"Railroad's Carry 30,000 from New York to Philadelphia for Dempsey-Tunney Fight." *Railway Age* 81, no. 14 (2 October 1926): 646.
"Record Run Washington to New York." *Railway Age* 82, no. 29 (18 June 1927): 1974.
"Samuel Rea Retires as P. R. R. Head." *Railway Age* 79, no. 13 (26 September 1925): 563–66.
Say, M. G., and Smith, S. P. "Suburban Railway Electrification." *World Power* 9, no. 54 (June 1928): 619–22.
Sayers, H. M. "Pennsylvania Railroad Electrification." *Electric Times* 84, no. 2179 (27 July 1933): 112.
Schenck, B. S. "New Electric Motor Cars for the Long Island." *Railway Age* 68, no. 26 (25 June 1920): 1964–66.
"Taking Care of 700 Trains a Day." *Railway Age* 87, no. 12 (21 September 1929): 671–74.
"The T. A. T. Air-Rail Service." *Railway Age* 87, no. 1 (6 July 1929): 12–16.
"These Three Grade Separations Will Cost $37,646,000." *Railway Age* 108, no. 17 (27 April 1940): 737–40, 743.
"Three-Track Vertical Life Bridge Has Unusual Features." *Railway Age* 98, no. 14 (6 April 1935): 525–28.
Warner, Paul T. "Baldwin-Westinghouse Electric Locomotives for Trunk Line Service." *Baldwin Locomotives* 2, no. 2 (October 1923): 28–39.
———. "Improvements on the Pennsylvania Railroad." *Baldwin Locomotives* 9, no. 1 (July 1930): 3–18.
———. "Riding Baldwin-Westinghouse Electric Locomotives on the Pennsylvania." *Baldwin Locomotives* 12, no. 3 (January 1934): 17–20.
"Washington-New York Fast Run of June 11." *Railway Age* 83, no. 4 (23 July 1927): 146.
"Washington to New York in 220½ Minutes." *Railway Age* 78, no. 10 (7 March 1925): 573.

Westing, Frederick. "GG1: Story of the Most Famous Electric Locomotive in the Western Hemisphere." *Trains* 24, no. 5 (March 1964): 20–36.

White Engineering Corporation. *The Long Island Rail Road—Its Problems and Future.* New York: White Engineering Corp. and Long Island Rail Road, 1942.

Wurts, T. C. "Pennsylvania Railroad Builds Three Electric Locomotives." *Railway Age* 76 no. 4 (26 January 1924): 295–96.

Chapter 6. Grand Central Terminal through the Second World War

"The Ambassador Hotel." *American Architect* 119, no. 2370 (22 June 1921): 644–47.

Andrews, Wayne. *Architecture in New York.* New York: Harper & Row, 1969.

Armstrong, A. H. "A Comparison of Electric and Steam Motive Power." *Railway Age* 68, no. 8 (20 February 1920): 521–27.

"Big New York Stations Have a Good Year." *Railway Age* 110, no. 7 (15 February 1941): 328.

Brown, H. F. "Electrification of Railroads." *Electric Railway Journal* 70, no. 12 (17 September 1927); 499–503.

Burnham Alan, ed. *New York Landmarks.* Middletown, Connecticut: Wesleyan University Press, 1963.

Carter, F. W. "180 Ton New Haven Electric Locomotives." *Railway Age* 68, no. 23 (4 June 1920): 1563-65.

"The 'Century' in 1928." *Railway Age* 86, no. 7 (16 February 1929): 428–29.

"Civic Development at the Grand Central Passenger Terminal in New York." *Railway Review* 68, no. 6 (5 February 1921): 197–204.

"The Commodore—A New Hotel on Pershing Square, New York." *American Architect* 115, no. 2254 (5 March 1919): 337–38.

Crane, Jacob L., Jr. "Street Development in Relation to Railroad Terminals." *Transactions of the American Society of Civil Engineers*, 87 (1924) 795–801.

Duer, J. V. B. "What Electric Operation Is Doing." *Railway Age,* 116 no. 15 (8 April 1944): 685–87.

Elsworth, R. B. "Multiple-Block Signaling." *Railway Age* 99, no. 5 (3 August 1935): 154–56.

"Erecting Office Building over Complicated Track Layout." *Engineering News-Record* 90, no. 12 (22 March 1923): 532–33.

Farrell, Morgan G. "The Roosevelt." *American Architect* 126, no. 2458 (5 November 1924): 427–34.

Feininger, Andreas, and Von Hartz, John. *New York in the Forties.* New York: Dover Publications, 1978.

"First Hudson Type Locomotive." *Railway Age* 82, no. 8 (19 February 1927): 523–26.

"Five More Electric Locomotives Added to New Haven Fleet." *Railway Age* 115, no. 17 (23 October 1943): 654–56.

Gibbs, George. "Railroad Electrification." *Railway Age* 86, no. 24 (15 June 1929): 1364–68.

"Grand Central Busiest New York Station." *Railway Age* 71, no. 2 (9 July 1921): 63.

"The Grand Central Terminal." *Fortune* 3, no. 2 (February 1931): 97–99.

"The Grand Central Terminal—A Great Civic Development." *Engineering News-Record* 85, no. 11 (9 September 1920): 484–85.

"Grand Central Terminal Handled 189,838 Passengers." *Railway Age* 67, no. 8 (22 August 1919): 366–67.

"Graybar Building." *Architectural Forum* 48, no. 2 (February 1928): 158–62.

Kerr, Charles, Jr. "Electric Locomotives for Freight or Passengers Service." *Railway Age* 113, no. 11 (12 September 1942): 402–7.

Kiefer, Paul W. "High-Capacity Steam Passenger Locomotives." *Railway Age* 111, no. 7 (16 August 1941): 273–76, 283; 111, no. 10 (6 September 1941): 376–80.

"Motor-Generator Locomotives for the New Haven." *Railway Age* 77, no. 16 (18 October 1924): 697–98.

"Motor-Generator Type Electric Locomotive for the New Haven." *Railway Age* 80, no. 31 (12 June 1926): 1682.

Murchison, Kenneth M. "The Drawings for the New Waldorf-Astoria." *American Architect* 139, no. 2591 (January 1931): 28–35.

Murray, W. S. "The Success of Main Line Electrification." *Railway Age Gazette* 58, no. 18 (30 April 1915): 923–28.

"New Haven Files under Bankruptcy Act." *Railway Age* 99, no. 17 (26 October 1935): 542, 549.

"New Haven Football Traffic." *Railway Age* 83, no. 23 (3 December 1927): 1135.

"New Haven Receives Ten Electric Locomotives." *Railway Age* 91, no. 12 (19 September 1931): 443–44.

"New York Central," under "Construction." *Railway Age* 83, no. 3 (16 July 1927): 125.

"New York–Chicago Coach Trains Start." *Railway Age* 107, no. 6 (5 August 1939): 224.

"New York Passenger Traffic." *Railway Age* 100, no. 18 (2 May 1936): 738.

"New York's Big Passenger Stations Take Inventory." *Railway Age* 108, no. 9 (2 March 1940): 423.
"N. Y. C. Electrifies Yonkers Branch." *Railway Age* 80, no. 7 (13 February 1926): 448.
"N. Y. C. Plans 1704 Miles Automatic Train Control." *Railway Age* 83, no. 1 (2 July 1927): 32.
"N. Y. C. Re-Signals Tracks Entering Grand Central Terminal." *Railway Age* 90, no. 18 (2 May 1931): 856–58.
"N. Y. C.'s New Building in New York City." *Railway Age* 83, no. 15 (8 October 1927): 683.
Oehler, A. G. "What Railroads Are Doing with Electric Traction." *Railway Age* 74, no. 1 (6 January 1923): 45–48.
"Passenger Travel on the N. Y. C." *Railway Age* 69, no. 24 (10 December 1920): 1041.
"Power and Heat for the Grand Central Terminal Area." *Railway Age* 88, no. 11 (15 March 1930): 632–34.
"A Quarter-Billion of Passengers." *Railway Age* 69, no. 25 (17 December 1920): 1083.
"Railroad Passenger Traffic to and from New York." *Railway Age* 78, no. 21 (25 April 1925): 1054.
"Railway Station Design Data." *Architectural Forum* 53, no. 6 (December 1930): 767–68.
"Relation of Railroad Terminals to City Plan." *Railway Age* 68, no. 18 (30 April 1920): 1285–88.
"Reverse Signaling to Increase Capacity of Grand Central." *Railway Age* 87, no. 22 (30 November 1929): 1310.
Schultze, L. "Waldorf-Astoria Hotel." *Architecture* 64, no. 5 (November 1931): 250–308.
"Serious Delays in New York City by Flood." *Railway Age* 81, no. 8 (21 August 1926): 343–44.
Shepard, F. H. *The Development of the Electric Motor*. Chicago: American Railway Association Circular no. D.V.-358, 12 May 1924.
———. "Railroad Electrification at High Voltage." *Railway Age* 70, no. 25 (24 June 1921): 1441–44.
Smith, Homer K. "Some Service Records of Electric Equipment." *Railway Age* 73, no. 22 (22 November 1922): 1013–14.

Smith, Walter H. "New Single Phase Equipment for the New Haven." *Railway Age* 72, no. 24 (17 June 1922): 1477–79.
"The Sprague System of Auxiliary Train Control." *Railway Age* 72, no. 16 (22 April 1922): 963–67.
"Subways for Suburban Trains Proposed for New York." *Railway Age* 76, no. 22 (3 May 1924): 1084.
"A Thirty-Story Office Building at the Grand Central Terminal." *Railway Age* 79, no. 7 (15 August 1925): 325.
"Waldorf-Astoria." *Architecture and Building* 63, no. 6 (December 1931): 147–53.
Withington, Sidney. "Thirty Five Years' Experience with Heavy Electric Traction." *Railway Age* 90, no. 12 (21 March 1931): 577–79.

Chapter 7. The New Jersey Terminals through the Second World War

"Baltimore and Ohio Opens New Motor Coach Terminal." *Railway Age* 86, no. 4 (26 January 1929): 280–84.
Brehof, F. H. "Oil-Electric 600 Hp. Switchers for the Lackawanna." *Railway Age* 97, no. 7 (18 August 1934): 208–10.
"Catenary System for the Lackawanna Electrification." *Railway Age* 88, no. 24 (14 June 1930): 1408–11.
"Central of New Jersey Builds Remarkable Bridge." *Railway Age* 80, no. 3 (16 January 1926): 217–22.
"Contact System Mounted on Springs; Electrified Lackawanna Yard." *Railway Age* 83, no. 7 (13 August 1927): 297–300.
"Defends Operation of New York Port." *New York Times,* 8 October 1943, p. 27.
"Delays in Port Cut to Minimum Here." *New York Times*, 10 May 1943, p. 25.
"Developing the Track Layout of a Large and Busy Passenger Terminal." *Engineering Record* 70, no. 12 (19 September 1914): 316–18.
"D. L. and W. to Electrify Its Suburban Lines." *Railway Age* 84, no. 17 (28 April 1928): 958.
"An Economical Traveler for Dismantling a Long Train Shed." *Railway Age Gazette* 55, no. 3 (18 July 1913): 115–16.
"Economic Survey of Port Started: Study of War-Induced Changes to be Basis of Long-Range Commerce Program" *New York Times,* 5 October 1943, p. 40.

"Electric Locomotives for the Lackawanna." *Railway Age* (18 October 1930): 794.

"Erie Builds New Type Pier at Weehawken, N.J." *Railway Age* 74, no. 17 (31 March 1923): 852–55.

"Events of Interest in the Shipping World: Maritime Association Group Opposes the Proposal for a Lighter Pool Here." *New York Times*, 3 January 1943, sec. 3, p. 10.

"Events of Interest in the Shipping World: Role of This Port Stressed." *New York Times*, 7 June 1942, sec. 3, p. 7.

"Export Freight Increase." *New York Times*, 11 February 1942, p. 36.

"Grading Troubles Featured This Crossing Elimination Job." *Railway Age* 110, no. 6 (8 February 1941): 280–84.

Hirschthal, Meyer. "Development of Concrete in Railway Construction." *Railway Age* 73, no. 16 (14 October 1922): 705–9; 73, no. 18 (28 October 1922): 791–97; 73, no. 19 (4 November 1922): 843–46.

"An Interesting Type of Flat-Slab Construction." *Railway Age* 68, no. 17 (23 April 1920): 1233–35.

"Jersey Central Engine Terminal at Communipaw." *Railway Age Gazette* 56, no. 26 (26 June 1914): 1585–87.

"The Jersey City Passenger Station Improvements." *Railway Age Gazette* 57, no. 19 (6 November 1914): 860–64.

"Lackawanna Electrification Plans Completed." *Electric Railway Journal* 73, no. 7 (17 August 1929): 769–71.

"Lackawanna Elevates Tracks through East Orange." *Railway Age* 71, no. 7 (13 August 1921): 281–84.

"Lackawanna Improvements in Orange, N.J." *Railway Age* 65, no. 20 (15 November 1918): 845–50.

"Lackawanna Railroad." (by various authors.) *Proceedings of the New York Railroad Club* 41, no. 7 (May 1931): 9625–60.

"Latest Passenger Terminal Train Shed." *Engineering Record* 67, no. 1 (4 January 1913): 6–9.

"Lehigh Valley." *Railway Age* 89, no. 2 (12 July 1930): 88, 90.

Middleton, William D. "The Delaware, Lackawanna and Western." In *When the Steam Railroads Electrified*, pp. 301–7. Milwaukee: Kalmbach Publishing Co., 1974.

"Modern Signals Expedite Heavy Suburban Traffic." *Railway Age* 73, no. 18 (28 October 1922): 785–88.

"Motor Truck-Inland Station Plan Speeds Erie Service at New York." *Railway Age* 97, no. 21 (24 November 1934): 651–52.

"New England Tries to Police Rail Use." *New York Times*, 13 February 1942, p. 33.

"New Freight Embargo: Roads Not to Accept Goods for Intercoastal Ships." *New York Times*, 24 January 1942, p. 23.

"No Congestion in Port of New York." *Railway Age* 115, no. 10 (4 September 1943): 385–86.

"Novel Floor Construction Feature of New Pier." *Railway Age* 90, no. 7 (14 February 1931): 358–61.

"ODT Order to Halt 68 Jersey Trains." *New York Times*, 25 February 1944, p. 19.

"Operation of Three-Power Locomotives." *Railway Age* 94, no. 10 (11 March 1933): 363–66.

"Pelley Discusses Traffic: Reports at Special Meeting of Railway Association." *New York Times*, 28 February 1942, p. 21.

"Rail Problems in Bronx: Board of Trade to Discuss Plan to Eliminate Delays." *New York Times*, 10 June 1942, p. 33.

"Railroads Allowed Ground Storage Now." *New York Times*, 4 February 1942, p. 27.

"Railroads Study Labor Loss in War." *New York Times*, 28 February 1942, p. 21.

"Raising Large Train Shed under Traffic." *Railway Age* 67, no. 13 (26 September 1919): 609–12.

"Reconstruction of Jersey City Passenger Terminal Train Shed While in Service." *Engineering Record* 69, no. 22 (30 May 1914): 622–24.

"Reconstruction of a Jersey City Railway Passenger Terminal." *Engineering News* 72, no. 5 (30 July 1914): 238–43.

"Reconstruction of the Jersey City Terminal Yards." *Railway Age Gazette* 58, no. 15 (9 April 1915): 787–91.

"Remodeling Jersey City Passenger Station." *Engineering Record* 69, no. 26 (27 June 1914): 733–34.

"Skylights in Jersey City Train Shed." *Engineering Record* 69, no. 5 (31 January 1914): 146–47.

"Staten Island Electrification." *Railway Age* 79, no. 1 (4 July 1925): 31–35; 79, no. 21 (21 November 1925): 951–55.

"Suburban Cars for the D.L. and W." *Railway Age* 78, no. 17 (28 March 1925): 843–45.

"Traffic Direction by Signal Indication on D.L. and W." *Railway Age* 73, no. 26 (23 December 1922): 1185–88.

"Train Operation Improved by Grade Separation." *Railway Age* 75, no. 10 (8 September 1923): 420–25.
"Two-Car Units for Lackawanna Electrification." *Railway Age* 89, no. 11 (13 September 1930): 522–26, 544.
"Use Novel Methods in Building Bridge Substructure." *Railway Age* 80, no. 15 (13 March 1926): 795–99.
"Warning Is Given That Port of New York Faces Stiff Competition after the War." *New York Times*, 8 December 1944, p. 34.

Chapter 8. The Terminal System after 1945

"Additional New York Railroad Link under Study in New Jersey." *Railway Age* 124, no. 16 (17 April 1948): 755–56.
"AGBANY vs. Apathy at Penn Station" (titles vary). *Architectural Forum* 117, no. 3 (September 1962): 5; 118, no. 2 (February 1963): 11.
"Air-Rights Boom Picks up Speed." *Railway Age* 155 (11 November 1963): 14–18.
Ames, E. W., Hutchison, W. M., and Moore, V. A., Jr. "New Haven Installs Ignitron M. U. Cars." *Railway Age* 136 (15 March 1954): 66–68.
"Amtrak Gets the Show on the Road—and On Time." *Railway Age* 170 (10 May 1971): 22–23.
Association of American Railroads. *Basic Provisions of the Railroad Revitalization and Reform Act of 1976*. Washington, D.C.: Association of American Railroads, 1976.
Berman, Marshall. "Buildings Are Judgment." *Ramparts* 13, no. 6 (March 1975): 33–39, 50–58.
"Big PATH Order Goes to GSI." *Railway Age* 160 (17 January 1966): 11.
Bird, Frederick L. *A Study of the Port of New York Authority*. New York: Dunn & Bradstreet, 1949.
Burks, Edward C. "Authority Asserts Port Is Injured by Conrail's Monopoly on Freight." *New York Times*, 28 September 1976, pp. 55, 57.
———. "Europe Pushing Fast Rail Lines." *New York Times*, 19 May 1975, p. 12.
Burns, J. T., Jr. "The Pan Am Building." *Progressive Architecture* 44, no. 4 (April 1963): 61–62.
"C and O–B and O Showing Strength as Partners." *Railway Age* 158 (29 March 1965): 93.
"Can the Grand Central Concourse Be Saved?" (titles vary). *Architectural Forum*

101, no. 5 (November 1954): 134–39; 102, no. 2 (February 1955): 62, 116–19; 102, no. 6 (June 1955): 76.

"Carfloat and Lighterage Service in New York Harbor Available by the New York Dock Railway." *Port of New York Transportation Information*, no. 19, 14 May 1976.

"Carfloat Service in New York Harbor Available by the Brooklyn Eastern District Terminal Railroad." *Port of New York Transportation Information*, no. 20, 19 November 1976.

The Case for Competitive Equity: Rails, Highways, and Public Policy. Washington, D.C.: Association of American Railroads, 1979.

Chase, Edward T. "How to Rescue New York from Its Port Authority." *Harper's Magazine* 220, no. 1321 (June 1960): 67–74.

"Commuters Benefit Most from P.R.R. Ownership of L.I." *Railway Age* 113, no. 22 (28 November 1942): 901–2.

Condit, Carl W. "Railroad Electrification in the United States." *Proceedings of the Institute of Electrical and Electronics Engineers* 64, no. 9 (September 1976): 1350–60.

Creighton, Thomas H. "Defense of Grand Central Terminal." *Progressive Architecture* 41, no. 9 (September 1960): 242.

"Design of Grand Central City Accepted." *Progressive Architecture* 40, no. 3 (March 1959): 157; 40, no. 5 (May 1959): 59; 40, no. 8 (August 1959): 49.

"$85-million Rehab Job Ready to Go." *Engineering News-Record* 199, no., 25 (22 December 1977): 46.

Ellis, J. B., and Pearson, P. M. "Transportation Planning in Megalopolis." *High Speed Ground Transportation Journal* 3, no. 2 (May 1969): 230–37.

Epstein, Jason. "The Last Days of New York." *New York Review of Books* 23, no. 2 (19 February 1976): 17–27.

"Erie to Use D L and W Hoboken Terminal." *Railway Age* 139 (14 November 1955): 8.

Findley, Roger W., and Hannon, Bruce M. *Railroading the Army Engineers: A Proposal for a National Transportation Engineering Agency*. Urbana: Center for Advanced Computation, University of Illinois, 1976.

"Giant on the Tracks; Union Carbide Builds." *Architectural Forum* 107, no. 2 (August 1957): 142–45; 113, no. 3 (September 1960): 92–93.

Goble, Emerson. "Pan Am Makes a Point; a Plea for the Vertical City." *Architectural Record* 131, no. 5 (May 1962): 195–200.

Gowans, F. D., Widell, B. A., and Bredenberg, A. "Pennsylvania Tests New Type of Series A.C. Electric Locomotives." *Railway Age* 132 (28 January 1952): 36–40.
"Grand Central City." *Architectural Forum* 128, no. 1 (January–February 1968): 48–55; 129, no. 1 (July–August 1968): 72–73; 129, no. 3 (October 1968): 12.
"Grand Central Loses Landmark Status." *Architectural Record* 157, no. 4 (April 1975): 35.
"Grand Central Site for Largest Building." *Architectural Forum* 108, no. 6 (June 1958): 13.
"Gropius-Belluschi-Roth Design for Grand Central City." *Architectural Record* 125, no. 3 (March 1959): 10.
Haskell, Douglas. "The Lost New York of the Pan American Airways Building." *Architectural Forum* 119, no. 5 (November 1963): 106–11.
Hatch, P. H. "Electrification vs. Diesel-Electrification." *Railway Age* 125, no. 1 (3 July 1948): 21–22.
Hillman, Jordan Jay. "The Making of Con Rail." Orginally published in *I C C Practitioners Journal*, November–December 1977; reprinted in *Northwestern University Law School Reporter*, no. 58 (Spring 1978), pp. 27–31.
"How Much Moves Where on Penn Central." *Trains* 33, no. 12 (October 1973): 16–17.
Huxtable, Ada Louise. "The Bigger They Are." *New York Times*, 19 November 1972, sec. 2, p. 22.
———. "The Stakes Are High for All in Grand Central Battle." *New York Times*, 11 April 1969, p. 28.
Interstate Commerce Commission. *Report to the President and the Congress on the Effectiveness of the Rail Passenger Service Act of 1970; March 15, 1978.* Washington D.C.: Government Printing Office, 1978.
"Is Grand Central Terminal Outmoded?" *Architectural Record* 116, no. 5 (November 1954): 20.
[Kean, Olga.] *Longshore Labor Statistics, Port of New York.* New York: Tri-State Regional Planning Commission, Analysis Notes Number 2602, January 1974.
"The Lackawanna Looks Back on 100 Years." *Railway Age* 131 (15 October 1951): 70–77.
"Lease of Air Rights over P R R's Pennsylvania Station." *Railway Age*, 152 (21 May 1962): 55.
Lessard, Suzannah. "The Towers of Light." *New Yorker* 54, no. 21 (10 July 1978): 32–58.
"Lever House, New York: Glass and Steel Walls." *Architectural Record* 111, no. 6 (June 1952): 130–35.

Long Island Rail Road accidents (titles vary). *New York Times*, 18 February 1950, p. 1; 23 November 1950, p. 1. *Railway Age* 129, no. 22 (2 December 1950): 45, 72.
"Long Island Rail Road Bills Passed in New York." *Railway Age* 130 (26 March 1951): 53.
Maritime Association of the Port of New York. *New York Port Handbook 1977*. New York: Maritime Association of the Port of New York and Port Resources Information Committee, 1977.
"Metroliner Diary." *Railway Age* 166 (24 February 1969): 19.
Metropolitan Transportation Authority. *1968–1973: The Ten-Year Program at the Halfway Mark*. New York: Metropolitan Transportation Authority, [1974].
Middleton, William D. "Electrification: Is It Going to Happen?" *Railway Age* 176 (10 March 1975): 28–34, 37.
———. "Our 'First Major Publicly Owned Railroad.' " *Trains* 31, no. 3 (January 1971): 20–26; 31, no. 4 (February 1971): 40–46.
Minutes of Public Meeting on New York City Railroad Freight Program, New York Chamber of Commerce and Industry, 24 September 1979. New York: New York State Department of Transportation; New York City Department of City Planning; Port Authority of New York and New Jersey, 1979.
"The Modern Erie." *Railway Age* 130 (14 May 1951): 76–81.
Monteith, A. C. "Rectifier-Type Locomotives Now Being Built for the Pennsylvania." *Railway Age* 128, no. 12 (25 March 1950): 589–91.
Moody's Manual of Investments: American and Foreign Railroads. New York: Moody's Investors Service, 1940–.
Mumford, Lewis. "The Disappearance of Pennsylvania Station," *New Yorker* 34, no. 16 (17 June 1958): 106–13. Reprinted under the title "The Pennsylvania Station Nightmare," in *The Highway and the City* (New York: Mentor Books, 1964), pp. 152–60.
———. "The Sky Line: The Roading Traffic's Boom—I." *New Yorker* 31, no. 11 (19 March 1955): 115–21.
"NE Corridor to Use Latest Tie, Rail Repair Machine." *Engineering News-Record* 199, no. 21 (24 November 1977): 11.
Nelligan, Tom. "How P C Plus NH Equals Penn Central." *Trains* 30, no. 3 (January 1970): 20–24.
"The New Authorization." *National Association of Railroad Passengers News* 13, no. 7 (September 1979): 1–3.
"New PRR Station Is Planned for New York." *Railway Age* 138 (13 June 1955): 65.
New York City Planning Commission. *Plan for New York City, 1969: A Proposal*. 6 vols. Cambridge: M.I.T. Press, 1969.

"New York City's Landmarks Commission Gives Grand Central Station a Reprieve." *Architectural Record* 146, no. 4 (October 1969): 37.

"New Haven Receives Ten GE Rectifier-Type Locomotives." *Railway Age* 138 (11 April 1955): 47–49.

"NH Buying 12 Used Virginian Electrics." *Railway Age* 154 (10 June 1963): 45.

"NH 2-in-1 Locomotives in Action." *Railway Age* 144 (24 February 1958): 11–12.

"N.J–N.Y. Rapid Transit Authority Proposed." *Railway Age* 132 (18 February 1952): 53.

"NYC Seeks Air Rights Development." *Railway Age* 137 (13 September 1954): 9.

"NY Puts Up $65 Million for L. I. R. R." *Railway Age* 159 (5 July 1965): 33, 36.

"NY Transit Plan Cost: $500 Million." *Railway Age* 144 (13 January 1958): 13.

Okamoto, Rai Y., and Williams, Frank E. *Urban Design Manhattan*. New York: Regional Plan Association and Viking Press, 1969.

Olcott, Edward S. "Air, Land and Sea Transportation: A Decade of Progress." In Stanley B. Winters, ed., *Newark: An Assessment, 1967–1977*, pp. 184–91. Newark: New Jersey Institute of Technology, 1978.

"Old, New Skills Tapped to Rebuild Terminal." *Engineering News-Record* 201, no. 1 (6 July 1978): 28.

"$100-Million Hotel Project Proposed." *Engineering News-Record*, 196, no. 11 (11 March 1976): 15.

"One Hundred Years of Erie." *Railway Age* 130 (14 May 1951): 61–69.

"PATH Lifts Its Face—and the Skyline." *Railway Age* 166 (3 February 1969): 18–19.

"Penn Central: Racing the 'Unthinkable.' " *Railway Age* 168 (29 June 1970): 11–12.

"Penn Station Goes Down—and Up." *Railway Age* 159 (29 November 1965): 48–49.

"Penn Station: Site for New Madison Square Garden." *Architectural Record* 130, no. 3 (September 1961): 14; 132, no. 3 (September 1962): 23.

"Penn Station to Give Way to Madison Square Garden" (titles vary). *Progressive Architecture* 41, no. 12 (December 1960): 56; 42, no. 9 (September 1961): 65, 78; 42, no. 11 (November 1961): 182–83; 43, no. 9 (September 1962): 63; 44, no. 1 (January 1963): 48; 44, no. 12 (December 1963): 54–55.

Pennsylvania–New York Central–New Haven merger (titles vary). *New York Times*, 16 January 1968, pp. 1, 54; 19 January 1968, p. 43; 20 January 1968, p. 28; 21 January 1968, sec. 4, p. 6; 31 January 1968, p. 51; 2 February 1968, p. 47; 13 August 1968, p. 49; 8 October 1968, p. 61; 31 December 1968, pp. 26, 37.

Pennsylvania Railroad accidents (titles vary). *New York Times*, 7 February 1951, pp. 1, 24–25; 19 May 1951, pp. 1, 32.

Pennsylvania station, Jersey City. Letter from August Lockwood, dated 7 December 1979.

Pinkepank, Jerry A. "Central's Second Look at Commuters." *Trains* 25, no. 9 (July 1965): 20–27; 25, no. 10 (August 1965): 48–55.

"Plan to Update Grand Central Station." *Architectural Forum* 101, no. 4 (October 1954): 41.

Port of New York Authority. *New York Harbor Terminals* (map). New York: Port of New York Authority, 1956.

———. Trade Promotion and Protection Division. *The Port of New York: History of Railroad and Shipping Development.* New York: Port of New York Authority, 1955.

Port Resources Information Committee. *New York Port Handbook.* New York: Port Resources Information Committee, 1958.

Preisch, William W. "Peacetime Performance of a Wartime Facility." *Railway Age* 126, no. 14 (2 April 1949): 687–89.

"P R R Gets First New Electrics." *Railway Age* 149 (7 November 1960): 18.

"P R R To Sell Air Rights over New York Station." *Railway Age* 137 (6 December 1954): 11.

"Public Authority Demanded for L.I." *Railway Age* 130 (29 January 1951): 36–37.

Railroad Electrification: The Issues. Transportation Research Board, National Research Council, Special Report 180. Washington D.C.: National Academy of Sciences, 1977.

Rickershauser, Peter. "Jersey Central Had a Great Fall." *Trains* 32, no. 5 (March 1972): 20–28.

Rossi, Louis. "New York State's Rail Program." *AASHTO,* (April 1980): 6–8.

Schmertz, Mildred F. "Problem of Pan Am." *Architectural Record* 133, no. 5 (May 1963): 151–58.

"Staten Island—Laboratory Experiment in Socialized Transportation." *Railway Age* 133 (11 August 1952): 58–63.

"Tax Relief, Higher Fares, Seen as only 'Out' for Long Island." *Railway Age* 127, no. 6 (6 August 1949): 265–66.

"These Shippers Want Rail Service." *Railway Age* 130 (2 April 1951): 49–52.

"Today's Lackawanna." *Railway Age* 130 (15 October 1951): 78–81.

"Tower for Grand Central Station." *Railway Age* 163 (25 September 1967): 60.

"Transportation and Energy: Who Does What with How Much?" *Railway Age* 174 (25 June 1973): 40–41.

"Transportation's Place in the Energy Picture." Unbound monograph. Washington, D.C.: Association of American Railroads, 1979.

Tri-State Transportation Committee. *The Changing Harborfront.* New York: Tri-State Transportation Commission, 1966.

———. *Study of Consolidated Railroad Marine and Lighterage for New York Harbor.* New York: Tri-State Transportation Committee, 1964.

———. *Tri-State Transportation, 1985: An Interim Plan.* New York: Tri-State Transportation Commission, 1966.

"U.S. Proposes $1.2-billion Northeast Rail Plan." *Engineering News-Record* 195, no. 18 (30 October 1975): 10.

"Visionless Enterprise: Grand Central City." *Architectural Forum* 132, no. 4 (October 1960): 87.

Wagner, Walter F., Jr. "Wrong Criticism, in the Wrong Place, at the Wrong Time: Proposed 55-Story Tower above Grand Central Station." *Architectural Record* 144, no. 2 (August 1968): 9–10; 144, no. 4 (October 1968): 46.

"Warning Is Given That Port of New York Faces Stiff Competition after the War." *New York Times*, 8 December 1944, p. 34.

"Wasteland behind Statue of Liberty Being Turned into $200-million Park." *Engineering News-Record* 197, no. 1 (1 July 1976): 18.

"What a Century Did to Erie Locomotives and Cars." *Railway Age* 130 (14 May 1951): 70–75.

"What Are Odds on Big Merger?" *Railway Age* 143 (11 November 1957): 9–10, 13.

Whittaker, A. C., and Hutchison, W. M. "The Pennsylvania Receives Two Ignitron Rectifier Locomotives." *Railway Age* 132 (11 February 1952): 63–67.

"Why Is There Renewed Interest in U.S. Electrification?" *Railway Age* 174 (25 June 1973): 28–29, 32–33, 36.

"Will the DL and W–Erie Coordination Set a Pattern for the Industry?" *Railway Age* 140 (16 April 1956): 36–39.

Williams, Winston. "Energy, Coal and the Renaissance of the Railroad." *New York Times*, 6 April 1980, sec. 3, pp. 1, 5.

Wisby, Gary. "Jets' Vapor Trails Making Our Skies Cloudier?" *Chicago Sun-Times*, 12 February 1978, p. 3.

Yearbook of Railroad Facts. Washington, D.C.: Association of American Railroads, 1979.

Credits for Illustrations

1. Smithsonian Institution, Chaney Collection.
2. *Street Railway Journal*
3. Collection of Ed Nowak.
4. *Street Railway Journal.*
5. *Street Railway Journal.*
6. Smithsonian Institution, Chaney Collection.
7. Smithsonian Institution, Chaney Collection.
8. *Baldwin Locomotives.*
9. Smithsonian Institution, Chaney Collection.
10. *Street Railway Journal.*
11. *Street Railway Journal.*
12. New-York Historical Society; courtesy Leland M. Roth.
13. New-York Historical Society; courtesy Leland M. Roth.
14. *Railroad Gazette.*
15. Cooper-Hewitt Museum of Design, Smithsonian Institution.
16. *Railway Age Gazette.*
17. *Railway Age Gazette.*
18. *Railway Age Gazette.*
19. *Engineering News.*
20. New York Central Railroad Company (Consolidated Rail Corporation).
21. *Engineering News.*
22. Collection of Ed Nowak.
23. Collection of Ed Nowak.
24. *Engineering Record.*
25. Collection of Ed Nowak.
26. Collection of Ed Nowak.
27. New York Central Railroad Company (Consolidated Rail Corporation).
28. New York Central Railroad Company (Consolidated Rail Corporation).
29. Regional Plan of New York, *Transit and Transportation* (*Regional Survey*, vol. 4). New York: Regional Plan of New York and Its Environs, 1928; Arno Press, 1974.
30. Regional Plan of New York, *Transit and Transportation.*
31. Tri-State Transportation Committee, *Study of Consolidated Marine and Lighterage for New York Harbor.* New York: Tri-State Transportation Committee, 1964.
32. Tri-State Transportation Committee, *Study of Consolidated Marine and Lighterage for New York Harbor.*
33. Tri-State Transportation Committee, *Study of Consolidated Marine and Lighterage for New York Harbor.*
34. Regional Plan of New York, *Transit and Transportation.*
35. Regional Plan of New York, *Transit and Transportation.*
36. *Railway Age.*
37. New York Department of Parks.
38. Smithsonian Institution.
39. *Railway Age.*
40. Chicago Historical Society.
41. Collection of Ed Nowak.
42. Photo by Fairchild Aerial Survey; *Architectural Record.*
43. Collection of Ed Nowak.
44. Photo by Fairchild Aerial Survey; *Architectural Record.*
45. *Engineering Record.*
46. *Engineering Record.*
47. Penn Central Transportation Company (Consolidated Rail Corporation).
48. Collection of Ed Nowak.
49. Madison Square Garden Center, Inc.

Index

All bridges, buildings, cities (including boroughs, suburbs, towns, and urban neighborhoods), locomotives and rolling stock, railroad companies (including interurban and rapid transit), railroad construction and operation, railroad electrification, railroad lines, railroad stations (including junctions, terminals, and yards), railroad traffic and trains, and streets (including avenues, boulevards, expressways, and parkways) are indexed by name or type under those general entries.